The Hounds of Actaeon:
The Magical Origins of
Public Relations and Modern Media

Mauricio Loza

The Hounds of Actaeon:
The Magical Origins of
Public Relations and Modern Media

Mauricio Loza

Academica Press
Washington – London

Library of Congress Cataloging-in-Publication Data

Names: Loza, Mauricio, 1977- author.
Title: The hounds of Actaeon: the magical origins of public relations and modern media / Mauricio Loza.
Description: Washington : Academica Press, [2020] | Includes bibliographical references and index. | Summary: "In this innovative study, Colombian technology writer Mauricio Loza pursues an intriguing thesis on the origin of psychology and modern media, namely that they arise from the magical arts of the Renaissance, and it is there that we must seek what Ioan Culianu called "the prototype of the impersonal systems of the media, of indirect censorship, of global manipulation and of the trusts that exercise their occult control over the Western masses." The Hounds of Actaeon takes up Culianu's thesis to trace a history that unites such Renaissance luminaries as Marsilio Ficino and Giordano Bruno with modern thinkers, including Sigmund Freud, Wilhelm Reich, and Guy Debord. It covers a broad historical and intellectual terrain ranging from the Renaissance magic, through eighteenth-century medicine and nineteenth-century psychology, to the propaganda and media warfare of the twentieth century, proving that the modern era, secular in appearance, continues to be profoundly influenced by pre-modern ways of thinking. The importance of this study is twofold: on the one hand it elaborates a fresh perspective on certain themes of Renaissance erotic magic and its relation to mass psychology and psychoanalysis, while, on the other, it offers an alternative for the study of the media strategies that determine Western worldviews and behaviors"-- Provided by publisher.
Identifiers: LCCN 2020000575 | ISBN 9781680531206 (hardcover) | ISBN 9781680531275 (paperback)
Subjects: LCSH: Mass media--Psychological aspects. | Public relations--Psychological aspects. | Social psychology. | Manipulative behavior. | Psychology and philosophy. | Philosophy, Renaissance--Influence.
Classification: LCC P96.P75 L69 2020 | DDC 302.2301/9--dc23
LC record available at https://lccn.loc.gov/2020000575

Contents

Acknowledgements vii
Introduction 1
Prelude 11
Part I. The Bond of Bonds 21
1. Eroticism and Magic from the Ancient World to the Renaissance 23
2. High Tide in the Sea of Pneuma 67
3. Eros in the Era of the Multitudes 99
Intermezzo 139
Part II. The Magical Bonds in the Modern World 159
4. From the Land of Oz to the Banana Republic 161
5. Wilhelm Reich's Modern Heresy 207
6. Economy, Neurosis and Spectacle 249
Part III The Gaping Jaws of Unreality 293
7. Communalism, Cybernetics and the Digital Economy 295
8. Marketing, War and Demiurgy 319
9. The Digital Tide. From real to virtual pneuma 339
10. The Polymorphous Demon. *Magic in the post-soviet era* 365
Epilogue 399
Bibliography 405
Index 411

To my parents Ana and Victor,
with love

Acknowledgements

This book would not have been possible without the help and guidance of my "head librarians," Edgar Blanco and David Roa, whose careful selection of books over the years led me to Ioan Culianu's ideas on gnosticism, magic, and history. Likewise I would like to thank Juan Mejía who kindly introduced me to Ernesto Priani at the National Autonomous University of Mexico (UNAM). Professor Priani's generous correspondence and his careful reading of my manuscript greatly improved this book. René Segura, one of my oldest friends and literary partner, had a key role both as an interlocutor and a reader, his on-point parallels between European sympathetic magic and some ideas and practices present in the magical traditions of South America enriched my overall view of the themes of this book and offered a broader perspective to the project. Lastly, no acknowledgement of my work would ever be complete without mentioning Jessica, who put up with my endless and often merciless rambling about demiurgy, magic, and politics that would have certainly thrown a less generous soul into despair, my gratitude to you is eternal.

For a reality to seduce, it must evoke a phantasm.
Nicolás Gómez Dávila

A painful thought: that beyond a certain precise moment in time, history is no longer real. Without realizing it, the whole human race suddenly left reality behind. Nothing that has happened since then has been true, but we are unable to realize it. Our task and our duty now is to discover this point or, so long as we fail to grasp it, we are condemned to continue on our present destructive course.
Elias Canetti

Whoever seizes the greatest unreality will shape the greatest reality.
Robert Musil

Introduction

In what is nowadays called a totalitarian state, or a military state [manipulating the population] is easy. You just hold a bludgeon over their heads, and if they get out of line you smash them over the head. But as society has become more free and democratic, you lose that capacity. Therefore you have to turn to the techniques of propaganda. The logic is clear. Propaganda is to democracy what the bludgeon is to a totalitarian state.
Noam Chomsky, *Media Control*

This study expands upon a topic outlined by the philosopher and historian of religion Ioan Petru Culianu in his work *Eros and Magic in the Renaissance*. In this book, the late Culianu—who was murdered in obscure circumstances at the University of Chicago in the spring of 1991[1] — suggests an intriguing origin for psychology and modern media: namely that both emerge from the magical arts of the Renaissance, and that it is therefore there that we should look for "the prototype of the impersonal systems of mass media, indirect censorship, global manipulation, and the brain trusts that exercise their occult control over the Western masses."[2] In Culianu's vision, which proposes a continuity between the occult arts of the Middle Ages and Renaissance and the social sciences of the modern era, the magician takes his place as the "the distant ancestor of the psychoanalyst and the advertising and publicity agent."[3]

Culianu's thesis revolves around a brief work by Giordano Bruno, —best known as an astronomer condemned to death by the Roman Inquisition—entitled *De Vinculis in Genere*, or *A General Account of Bonding*. This work only quite recently began to be recognized as a veiled model for modern media establishments, an omission that puts us in a particularly hazardous situation in regards to the seeming omnipotence of today's corporate "masters."

All mankind, says Culianu:

> has heard of Machiavelli's *The Prince*, and many politicians have hastened to emulate his example. But only today can we appreciate how much *De vinculis* outstrips *The Prince* in depth, in timeliness, and in importance—today, when no head of state

of the Western world would any longer dream of acting like the Prince but would use, on the other hand, methods of persuasion and manipulation as subtle as those the brain trusts are able to place at his or her disposal. In order to understand and show to advantage the timeliness of *De vinculis*, we ought to know about the activities of those trusts, those ministries of propaganda; we should be able to glance at the manuals of schools of espionage, from which we may glean something of what happens outside the corridors of those organization whose *ideal* goal is to guarantee order and the common welfare, where it exists.[4]

In a startling premonition about the origin of a modern world, Bruno offered a coherent model not only for the manipulation of individual motivations but also for the control and indoctrination of the masses which, after the emergence of modern democracies, claimed a more participatory role. Ironically, as soon as these multitudes began to acquire a voice and political representation they were once again subjugated by old masters in new disguises, regimes that to this day continue to exercise some of the subtlest forms of manipulation ever devised by the human mind.

The core of *De Vinculis in Genere* is an erotic understanding of nature and human relations that, having been eclipsed by the rationalism of the Scientific Revolution, lay dormant for almost three centuries before reappearing in our culture with Freud's theory of libido and, in a more radical version, in the work of Wilhelm Reich. This eclipse is heavily mythologized: the West has become accustomed to thinking of modernity as a secular age produced by a revolution in the natural sciences and the establishment of reason as the *sine qua non* of human thought. In actuality, the "reappearance" of magical and religious ideas in many modern political movements, such as Nazism, and in modern disciplines such as psychology, can be explained as follows: these premodern ideas were never banished by the Enlightenment and the progress of reason and science. Rather, scientific and technological "progress" is a continuation of the monotheistic goal of salvation: a salvation within history.

British philosopher John Gray notes the persistence of this post-Enlightenment myth when he argues that "the belief that we live in a secular age is an illusion. If it means only that the power of the Christian churches has declined in many Western countries, it is a description of fact. But secular thought is mostly composed of repressed religion."[5] In this study I will put forward a recapitulation and renegotiation of one of these eclipses: the nature of those magical/erotic operations that underlie modern media, and their transformation into the basic substrata of modern disciplines such as psychoanalysis, public relations, advertising, and even sciences as dissimilar as ecology and cybernetics. This book's main purpose will be to outline a field of influence for certain magical ideas that have "resurfaced" in our current world under a modern appearance.

I should emphasize that the magical character of modern media may not be apparent to someone used to being "submerged" in it; all of us who were born in the West in the last century must admit that, like fish in the water, we have not breathed anything else. However, for Culianu, who managed to escape Romania's brutal communist regime, the contrast was pronounced, and it is perhaps in this personal circumstance, in the novelty and strength of the advertising spells he found upon his arrival in the West, where we find the origin of his idea of Renaissance magic as the predecessor of modern media.[6]

A similar position towards the Western media establishment figures in the thought of another immigrant from Eastern Europe, new-media theorist Lev Manovich. Manovich argues that Westerners see "the Internet as a perfect tool to break down all hierarchies and bring art to the people. In contrast, as a post-communist subject, I cannot but see the Internet as a communal apartment of the Stalin era: no privacy, everybody spies on everybody else, always present are lines for common areas such as the toilet or the kitchen."[7] Advertising, marketing and the new media can be used in the better direction described by Manovich, but both the West and post-Soviet Russia, knowing the harmful potential of these tools, have opted to exploit their totalitarian bent in subtler and more sophisticated ways than any other known form of manipulation. We are living in a *Digital Panopticon.*

Outlining an adequate context of our situation requires that we understand the historical circumstances that gave rise to what I will call the "modern manipulative impulse." This drive to control large sectors of the population emerged as a reaction to the sudden "explosion of interiority" that took place between 1100 and 1300 A.D. in what is known as the Renaissance of the Twelfth Century.[8] Prior to this period, European literature had mainly focused on the relationship of a knight with his feudal lord and on the former's achievements, which were recorded in the *Chansons de geste*. However, by the mid-twelfth century, a new literary tradition had emerged which, instead of emphasizing in the relationship between a vassal and his liege, focused on the knight's infatuation with a distant and inaccessible lady, who was usually married to the King — a forbidden relationship that could never be consummated. The focus had shifted from an external relationship determined hierarchically, the vassal-liege relationship, to an intimate relationship that denoted a rich inner and spiritual life, the knight's love for his lady.[9]

For historians such as Denis de Rougemont and René Nelli, this erotic dialectic was deeply influenced by the philosophical and mystical currents present in the south of France, and both argue that it was one of the social expressions of the Cathar heresy that flourished in Occitane at the time. According to this argument, first put forward in the early nineteenth century by Eugène Aroux, many troubadours were actually crypto-Cathars who spread their religious message through a new type of poetry, which sang to a form of love that covertly reproduced the mystical experience of the Cathar heresy. Aroux's line of thought was taken up a few years later by Gabriele Rossetti, who argued that the troubadours were Cathars or members of an anti-Catholic sect to which Dante, Petrarch and Boccaccio had belonged, and who had used the vernacular to perpetuate the ideas of the heresy after it was annihilated by the Inquisition. All speculation aside, the Holy Inquisition was indeed created with the express purpose of eradicating the Cathar movement, which, through its emphasis on personal mystical experience instead of adherence to ecclesiastical dogma (that is, of an inner life determined in a personal way against a dogmatically determined external relationship), posed a considerable threat to the hegemony of the Catholic Church in Southern France. According to Morris Berman, the purpose of the church's efforts was, from the outset, the colonization of the nascent inner world of medieval man.[10]

The two great manipulation systems of our time can be traced to this historical moment. The first of these is an "officialist" system rooted in the Inquisition, which gave rise to modern police states. In fact, the incipient "modernity" of the Inquisition's techniques is astounding. From the beginning, this institution kept continuous records of the depositions they heard and in time developed "handbook for heretic-hunters" summarizing the knowledge gained over years of activity. With these data and an organization that reached all over Europe, they had resources roughly comparable with those of a modern police organization; they could track suspects wherever they went and could threaten even the descendants of accused persons (who risked losing their inherited property). Any suspect could be be put under oath to testify to his or her beliefs, participation in forbidden rites, and knowledge of other suspects.[11]

The prescience of the Inquisition's methods prompted historian Joseph Strayer to declare: "Modern totalitarian governments have made few innovations; they have simply been more efficient."[12] Technological advance has spelled a considerable advance in repressive techniques.

Culianu argues, however, that as a manipulation system a police state is doomed to failure for "it always remains what it is: [...] the defender to the death of out-of-date values, of a political oligarchy useless and pernicious to the life of nations. The system of restraints is bound to perish, for what it defends is merely an accumulation of slogans without any vitality."[13] What officialist manipulation lacks in subtleness and flexibility abounds, however, in the other great form of manipulation that emerged in the twelfth century. This is a "magical-heretical" system influenced by the romantic love cult that resulted from the encounter of the Cathar heresy with the troubadours and which, when combined with the Hermetic, Neoplatonic and Islamic influences present in Southern Europe, consolidated itself as a robust set of practices of erotic magic during the early Renaissance. It is from this cultural milieu that Bruno's *De Vinculis in Genere* arises.

Here I should clarify an essential matter: these two manipulation systems are not exclusive and have continued to function in parallel since their introduction in the twelfth century. Not only do manipulation and torture techniques derived from the officialist system continue to this day, but they also may never cease to exist in a hierarchical society. However, the collapse of modern totalitarianisms such as Nazi Germany and the Soviet Union revealed the exceptional advantages of the magical-heretical approach to mass manipulation and control; a paradoxical victory in a supposedly secular world.

This magical system of manipulation occupies the center of this study. The prelude and the first part outline a picture of the history and nature of erotic magic and its relation to medicine and mass psychology. The second and third parts then reveal the impact of these practices on contemporary masses. As will become apparent by the end of this study, the present outcome of these magical operations has been the creation of a variety of media unrealities—*demiurgic bubbles* from a gnostic point of view—that enshroud our reality and threaten to sever our already faltering relation to the real world.[14] As in the case of the officialist system, modern technology has proved increasingly efficient at amplifying these magic spells and, as I write, our so-called "social" networks are at the helm of this trend.

This study is far from an exhaustive or final account of its subject matter, but I trust it will be a good introduction, a sufficient starting point for others to delve deeper into a subject of paramount importance to understanding the underlying currents of our present cultural context. My objective is to offer a fuller historical template for the development of alternative approaches to the study of those media strategies that to a great extent determine Western worldviews and behaviors.

A brief note on methodology. This study follows the scheme proposed by Culianu in his book *The Tree of Gnosis*. The historical journey presented here should not be taken as a linear and uninterrupted process that takes us from the Renaissance to the twenty-first century, but as the expression of a "system of magic" that reappears in various "transformations" throughout time. By "system" I mean those features common to the different branches of the hermetic magical tradition (one of them being the erotic nature of its operations), which can be identified independently of its place or time and which form a general and recognizable structure. "Transformations" here refers to the various forms of manifestation—practically unlimited, but restricted by the circumstances of a society and a time—that this system assumes in the world. One such transformation is the idea of *anima mundi*, or "world soul," from its origins in Platonism to its most recent incarnations in cybernetics and ecology; in this study, I will endeavor to determine its role and importance for magical operations.

A metaphor to facilitate the understanding of this scheme: imagine a pond in which water is time—a non-linear type of time. Pebbles with certain shapes and weights fall into the water, propagating in a series of ripples with specific patterns. Let us say that one of these ripples is Plato's influence and another that of Christianity, at the intersection of these two sets of waves happens what we know as Western culture. Another pebble that falls between these two ripples would correspond to the set of habits that became the magical practices of our tradition, which would propagate radially from its center, transforming itself when coming into contact with the waves of the other pebbles. This expanding set of circumferences corresponds to a specific transformation at a given time and place. The combinations resulting from this system are unlimited and, to a great extent, pluricausal.

Similarily, this study does not claim a direct, linear transmission of magical influences in modern media —although at times it exists and can be clearly identified— but rather a medium, or better yet, a *field of influence* manifested in this or other transformation, if the social, political and economic circumstances are adequate for its appearance and development. Seen in this light, the journey proposed here is not an uninterrupted chronology, a sequence that takes us from point A to point B, but the expression of a latent "system of magic" that resurfaces in certain historical moments. The fact that this journey takes the form of an apparently linear narrative responds entirely to the literary aspirations of this study. Of course, this methodology does not tell us why the system in question reappears at these significant intervals, but it provides the opportunity to observe its manifestation from a broader and more coherent point of view; to see it as a *dynamic event* and not as a simple occurrence, a *static configuration* of circumstances, "fixed" and isolated in its place within the chronology to which it has been assigned. The purpose of this methodology is to give the study of history a synchronic approach that exceeds the current, diachronic and linear conceptualizations of this discipline.

The field of influence or magic system I will examine is the so-called Alexandrian *mentalité*, a set of religious, philosophical and scientific ideas that flourished in this city during the first three centuries of the Christian era, and which covered movements as diverse as Gnosticism, Neoplatonism and Hermeticism. The fundamental argument of this study, elaborated by scholars such as Frances Yates and Ioan Culianu, is as follows: the magic system that arose with this mentality has not been really "overcome," such that, four centuries after the Scientific Revolution of the seventeenth century we still live under its influence. For Leon Marvell, understanding this matter depends on not seeing hermetic philosophy and magic as a bridge between the premodern and modern worlds that was dismantled with the arrival of modern science. Instead we must appreciate that diverse hermetic ideas and modes of understanding—the *anima mundi* among them—were never really expelled from the modern scientific project. Rather, they became its backbone.

"Figurations from the Renaissance phantasmic imaginary," Marvell argues, "would pass through the barrier of the emerging scientific culture of modernity, becoming in their passage distorted into the figures of the technological dream of a 'new world order.'"[15] This technological dream of a global social and economic order shares the same impulse to exert total control of the population through the techniques derived from the manipulation systems I have outlined in this introduction, spanning and resurfacing within a range of Western social contexts.

---

[1] *Eros, Magic and the Death of Professor Culianu* by Ted Anton, documents the evidence of the murder and gives a fairly complete biography of Culianu.

[2] Ioan P. Culianu, *Eros and Magic in the Renaissance* (Chicago: The University of Chicago Press, 1987), 90. A more current name for "brain trust" is the expression "think thank."

[3] Back cover copy, *Eros and Magic in the Renaissance.*

[4] Culianu, *Eros and Magic in the Renaissance*, 90.

[5] John Gray, *Seven Types of Atheism* (London: Allen Lane, 2018), 72.

[6] The idea that the operations of modern media are akin to a form of magic has a very interesting history in anthropology via the concept of *mana*, of which professor William Mazzarella makes a genealogy in *The Mana of Mass Society* (Chicago: The University of Chicago Press, 2017). According to Mazzarella, it was Marcel Mauss in *A General Theory of Magic* (1902-03) who first "described ritual specialists as protopublicists, mana workers who draw on 'the collective forces of society'." (*The Mana of Mass Society*, 33). A decade later sociologist Émile Durkheim in *The Elementary Forms of Religious Life* (1912) "asked how the potential of mana, as harnessed in 'primitive' ritual, might similarly be derived, on a much wider scale, from the energies of urban crowds." (*The Mana*

of Mass Society, 33). But it was Bronislaw Malinowski, father of modern fieldwork anthropology, who directly compared primitive magic to modern advertising. In the second volume of *Coral Gardens and their Magic* (1935) Malinowski argues that "the advertisements of modern beauty specialist, especially of the magnitude of my countrywoman Helena Rubinstein, or of her rival, Elizabeth Arden, would make interesting reading if collated with the formulae of Trobriand beauty magic." (*The Mana of Mass Society*, 33-34). This insight, and Europe's political climate of the time (mid-1930's), led Malinowski to liken political propaganda to a form of magic: "Modern political oratory would probably yield a rich harvest of purely magical elements. Some of the least desirable of modern pseudo-statesment or gigantic politicanti have earned the titles of wizards or spell-binders. The great leaders such as Hitler and Mussolini have achieved their influence primarily by the power of speech, coupled with the power of action which is always given to those who know how to raise the prejudices and the passions of the mob. Moreover, the modern socialistic state, whether it be painted red, black or brown, has developed the powers of advertisement to an extraordinary extent. Political propaganda, as it is called, has become a gigantic advertising agency, in which merely verbal statements are destined to hypnotize foreigner and citizen alike into the belief that something really great has been achieved." (Quoted by Mazzarella, 34). The political aspect of magic highlighted by Malinowski will be dealt with in detail in the third chapter when we investigate further on the basis of mass magical operations.

[7] Lev Manovich, *The Language of New Media* (Cambridge: The MIT Press, 2002), x.

[8] One should note the absence of interiority that characterized the Early Middle Ages (500-1050), a period in which law did not emphasize the role of an individual when it came to committing a crime, nor did religion require interior contrition (*contritio*) for a sin but simple reparation for a transgression (*satisfactio*). This attitude began to change in the eleventh century, when monastic orders began to show indisputable signs of interiority. See: *The Discovery of the Individual, 1050-1200* by English historian Colin Morris.

[9] In his foreword to *Abélard et Héloïse: correspondance* (Paris: Union Générale d'Éditions, 1979), Paul Zumthor argues that even if courtly love had already found a poetic expression of its own, "the new topic reached the level of verbal manifestation and begot a new rhetoric, articulated by an original dialectics, whose abstract model was that of the relations between vassal and liege." For Zumthor, while courtly love represents a shift in emphasis of the human experience from the social to the individual, on a more basic level it continues to reproduce the power dynamics of the patriarchal West.

[10] One of the shrewdest responses of the Catholic Church to the Cathar threat was the institution of the cult of the Virgin Mary, dating from this time. In *Love in the Western World* Denis de Rougemont argues that "The Church of Rome was

under no misapprehension regarding the nature of that which our all too authoritative authorities today persist in refusing to see. It correctly gauged the magnitude of the peril contained in the Heresy. There was the notorious crusade, and also the Dominican Inquisition. The extreme and violent tactics employed could not ensure the pulling up of all the roots of the revolt, sinister and innocent alike. But the eminent wisdom the clergy thereupon sought to satisfy by 'orthodox' means was the human craving that had produced the symbolical cult of Woman. From the middle of the twelfth century onwards there was a succession of attempts to promote a cult of the Virgin. It was sought to substitute 'Our Lady' for the 'Lady of Thoughts' of the heretics. At Lyons in 1140 the canons instituted a Feast for the Immaculate Conception of Our Lady. And the monastic orders which sprang up at this time were replicas of the orders of knighthood" (de Rougemont, *Love in the Western World*, 85).

[11] From *Cathars* by Fredric Cheyette, quoted by Morris Berman in *Coming to Our Senses: Body and Spirit in the Hidden History of the West* (Vermont: Echo Point Books and Media, 2015), 204.

[12] Joseph Strayer, *The Albigesian Crusades* (Ann Arbor: The University of Michigan Press, 1992), iv.

[13] Culianu, *Eros and Magic in the Renaissance*, 105.

[14] Here "real world" or "reality" should be taken at a phenomenological level, that is, as a consensual construct created by social interaction that determines the representations by which a society experiences the physical and biological world.

[15] Leon Marvel, *The Physics of Transfigured Light: The imaginal realm and the hermetic foundations of science*, (Rochester: Inner Traditions, 2016), 149.

Prelude

Whither, then, will you poor lovers turn? Who was it who kindled the white-hot flames of your hearts? Who will quench so great a fire? That is the need, this is the labor; I shall answer you soon, but listen.
Marsilio Ficino, *De amore*

Diana, the huntsman and the stag

In the *Metamorphoses* Ovid tells us that Actaeon, grandson of Cadmus, having finished hunting wandered aimlessly through a forest. Accompanied by his dogs, the young hunter found a hidden grotto surrounded by cypresses where water echoed and, led by curiosity, went inside. Unfortunately, it was Diana's sacred hideout, where the goddess bathed with her entourage of nymphs.

> As soon as he entered the grotto, the Nymphs, naked as they were and dripping wet, beat their breasts at the sight of a man, filled the grove with their sudden shrill cries, and crowded around their mistress Diana, trying to hide her body with theirs. But the goddess stood head and shoulders above them.[1]

Diana's embarrassment was overwhelming. "Her face, as she stood there, disrobed, was the color of clouds lit by the setting sun, or of rosy dawn." Unarmed—her spear, quiver and loose bow lay at the edge of the spring—Diana only managed to turn sideways and hide her face. Without arrows, the goddess hurled jets of water at the astonished hunter and, as she soaked the young man's hair, she added the words that foretold his doom.

> Now you may tell how you saw me undressed, if you are able to tell!

Suddenly, Actaeon's head sprouts stag's horns, his neck lengthens and the tips of his ears sharpen, his hands turn into hooves, his arms and legs into stilts, and his whole body is covered with fine mottled fur. Prey to his own terror and amazement, Actaeon begins to run in his new form but soon realizes that he has nowhere to go. He cannot return to his palace and people, for how would they recognize him? How could he explain what had happened? The thought of hiding in the forest fills him with terror. While he hesitates his hounds see him standing at the mouth of the cave and, in a matter of seconds, the whole pack is chasing after him "over cliffs and crags, and inaccessible rocks." Actaeon is chased through the places where he has often given chase, and even if he knows the forest like the back of his hand, he understands that it won't be long before the inevitable happens. Tired, the young hunter stumbles and one of the dogs takes a bite out of his back while another grabs him by the shoulder, and soon "the whole pack gathers and they sink their teeth in his body."

Actaeon wails in pain. There is no place in his body for more wounds, and his cries, which are not those of a man but neither of a deer, resound from the depths of the forest. His hounds call out looking for him as if lamenting that he is not there to admire the death of their prey, unaware that their master is among them and has witnessed—firsthand—everything.

❋

Actaeon's myth is in the province of eros. Both the embarrassment and anger of the deity, and the curiosity and desire of the young hunter, are manifestations of an exuberant eroticism: a secret grotto where a goddess bathes, the chastity of Diana violated by the eyes of a mortal. The myth's driving force is Diana's supernatural beauty, a grace and perfection that should not be admired by human eyes, eyes that must be punished according to the transgression. In an echo of the story of Actaeon, Tiresias—the blind prophet of Thebes—lost his sight after seeing Athena bathing naked (or Hera, or Diana herself, depending on the version). The beauty of a goddess is just not something that human eyes *should* admire, is not even something that *could be* admired with mortal eyes.

It is not beauty in a "cosmetic" sense—the simple fact of having seen Diana disrobed—that sealed Actaeon's fate. Or, rather, it is cosmetic, but in the original sense of the word: *kosmos*, the Greek word from which cosmetic derives, "referred to the right placing of the multiple things of the world... [and] also implied aesthetic qualities such as becomingly, decently, duly, honorably, creditably."[2] This word, according to James Hillman, "was used especially of women in respect to their embellishments," and he tells us that the Stoics used the word to refer to the *anima mundi*, or *psyche kosmou* in greek. Thus, "cosmetic" originally alluded to an order, a proportion that unites and harmonizes all things, a relationship that determines a truth. The cosmos and its cosmetics originally referred to the face of the world which is, simultaneously, the face of the goddess. This is why looking at the face of Diana implies looking at truth in the eyes, contemplating the whole.[3]

Let us return to our scene to confirm this idea. Actaeon wanders aimlessly through the forest, which in Western culture symbolizes the kingdom of the soul and depths of the unconscious, a space characterized by its solitude and immensity. "The dense and obscure character of the forest," explains Victoria Cirlot, "relates it physically to the *silva*, a Latin term equivalent to the Old French *forest*, that since Cicero alluded to the *prima materia*."[4] This primal matter is what the Greeks called *hylé* (forest or wood), which through the term *silva* originates the Spanish word *selva*, "forest" or "jungle." Therefore, to go into the forest, according to Cirlot, entails

> an immersion in the matter that alchemy has set as a stage within the process of elaboration of the philosopher's gold: the so-called *nigredo* or blackening. From the intimate, inner and psychological point of view, the forest is the place of the soul's operations, of inner transformations and purification.[5]

Actaeon thus wanders through the realm of the soul, a "place" made of primordial matter (wood), and there stumbles upon the vision of Diana's nakedness. The young hunter has achieved something forbidden to most humans: He has seen the soul of the world embodied in the goddess of the hunt, and because of this he must be hunted. From this point of view, Actaeon's myth is a tale of psychological transformation, of the passage from one existential condition to another, and that is precisely how it is interpreted by a key character of this study: Giordano Bruno.

In his *Heroici Furori* (*The Heroic Frenzies*), a work in the form of dialogue dedicated to the various facets of erotic frenzy, Bruno offers a beautiful sonnet about Actaeon's myth:

> The youthful Actaeon unleashes the mastiffs and the greyhounds to the forests, when destiny directs him to the dubious and perilous path, near the traces of the wild beasts.

> Here among the waters he sees the most beautiful countenance and breast, that ever one mortal or divine may see, clothed in purple and alabaster and fine gold; and the great hunter becomes the prey that is hunted.
>
> The stag which to the densest places is wont to direct his lighter steps, is swiftly devoured by his great and numerous dogs.
>
> I stretch my thoughts to the sublime prey, and these springing back upon me, bring me death by their hard and cruel gnawing.[6]

According to Ioan P. Culianu, in order to understand the psychological transformation to which Bruno alludes, we must imagine in the same picture "a goddess emerging half naked from the water and a hunter changed into a stag and devoured by his own dogs."[7] In this image Diana should be made of alabaster, her breasts of purple and her hair of fine gold, for symbolically, "the alabaster of her complexion is symbolic of divine beauty, the purple of active power, and the gold of divine wisdom,"[8] attributes demanding the contemplation of those who seek true knowledge. For Bruno, the mastiffs and greyhounds—the latter faster, the former more robust—symbolize the subject's will and his or her discursive intellect, while the young huntsman "represents the intellect intent upon the capture of divine wisdom and the comprehension of the divine beauty,"[9] a beauty that apart from its aesthetic value reveals a profound truth.

The intimate relationship between the hunter and its prey, simultaneously absent and present in the figure of Actaeon, also reveals an interesting Latin etymology: the common origin of *venator*, hunter, and *venatus*, hunted, which originates "venado," the Spanish word for deer. These two words come from the Indo-European root *wen-*, which expresses desire, effort and searching, and from whence also comes the name of *Venus*, the goddess of love and beauty. The searching implied in this root, the fervent desire for prey, is the origin of the hunt, and it is through this action that Actaeon passes from being the subject, *venator*, to being the object, *venatus*, of his intellect and his will. Thus, the young hunter

> who with these thoughts, his dogs, searched for goodness, wisdom, beauty, and the wild beast outside himself, attained them in this way. Once he was in their presence, ravished outside of himself by so much beauty, he became the prey of

his thoughts and saw himself converted into the thing he was pursuing.[10]

So far we have approached all the characters of the myth except the one that occupies the central place, the very axis of the story: Diana. As the agent of Actaeon's transformation, Diana represents the sensible countenance of the world, the visible face of nature. "It is not possible to see the sun," Bruno writes, "the universal Apollo, pure light in its best and highest form. It is possible, however, to see his shadow, his Diana, the world, the universe, nature which is inside things, which is the light within the opacity of matter, shining in the darkness."[11] Diana, understood as nature in its purest—that is, virginal and "wild"—state is, like Venus, the embodiment of desire and beauty.

Beauty in this way becomes intrinsically linked to the Greek idea of the cosmos to which I referred above. The "cosmetic" is impossible in the absence of a face of the world (i.e. a goddess) that is perceived as beautiful. Likewise, our perception of the world is impossible in the absence of beauty as the central element of its manifestation. This idea of beauty as one of the central elements of the cosmos goes back to the *Phaedrus*, in which Plato affirms that beauty shines

> among the other objects; and now that we have come down here we grasp it sparkling through the clearest of our senses. Vision, of course, is the sharpest of our bodily senses, although it does not see wisdom. It would awaken a terribly powerful love if an image of wisdom came through our sight as clearly as beauty does, and the same goes for the other objects of inspired love.[12]

The erotic implications of this passage are striking: what Plato suggests is that while we cannot perceive wisdom directly, we can glimpse it through the brilliance of beauty. This is why, as James Hillman writes, "all things as they display their innate nature present Aphrodite's goldenness; they shine forth and as such are aesthetic … Visible form is a show of soul. The being of a thing is revealed in the display of its *Bild* (image)."[13] In Hillman's words, beauty is *the very sensibility of the cosmos*.

The answer to Ficino's questions with which I opened this prelude (Who was it who kindled the white-hot flames of your hearts? Who will quench so great a fire?), lies in the contemplation of the face of the goddess/world: "The glory and glow of His countenance […] whether in the [...] Soul, or in the material world, is to be called universal Beauty, and the desire for it is to be called universal Love."[14] It is in this universal form of eros, which extends throughout creation and desires fervently to return to its source, where we find the fundamental affinity that holds the cosmos together. In this sense, Robert Musil argues, love is "no longer a mere emotion but a transformation of a person's whole way of thinking and perceiving."[15] It is this form of eros that turns the young hunter into the hunted, making him the object of his own subject.

What are the implications of this understanding of Venus/Diana for Actaeon's myth? Contemplating Diana naked through the eyes of eros implies the young huntsman's return to the divine, his transformation into the ultimate object of his desire—the goddess/world—which can now be witnessed in its entirety. To be devoured by the hounds of will and intellect means to die to mortal sight and be born with new eyes, divine eyes like those of Tiresias or Homer's. "The sight of the mind," Plato reminds us in *The Symposium*, "begins to see sharply when that of the eyes starts to grow dull."[16]

The subtle inner landscape described by Bruno in his sonnet rests, on the one hand, on his profound knowledge of magic and the art of memory and, on the other, on his insight into what we would now call psychology and which at that time was part of the magical arts. For Bruno, this discipline, understood as a form of manipulation of the countenance of the cosmos/Venus, was an essentially erotic affair, an idea formulated by Marsilio Ficino—architect of the Neo-Platonist Renaissance during the early fifteenth century,— who declared that *love is a magician*.[17] This is why it is not at all surprising that Ficino uses the Latin word *rete*, which means mesh or net, and also the term "hook," to describe the *modus operandi* of magic. Just as a lover sets its nets to bind its beloved (the *venator/venatus* relationship), Venus weaves the immense web of beauty and desire in which we live and die. Thus, we must hunt Venus/Diana or be smitten/hunted by her, which implies yielding to a life trapped in her spell.

The idea of reality as a magic spell has a intriguing precedent outside Western culture: the Hindu concept of Maya. Since the pre-classical period in India (900-100 B.C.). Maya has been understood as a kind of spell or enchantment that envelops the world, preventing us from witnessing the true nature of reality. In Buddhism, it is taken as an illusion or a deception that stems from desire, a veil that must be torn to see the world in its ultimate essence, to be able to contemplate it in its totality. Maya, however, was not always understood in this way. During the Vedic period that preceded the pre-classical era, this term was used in the sense of a great force or power, a type of divine will. Maya is never quoted as the origin of a deception or the cause of ignorance in any of the Vedas. In fact, scholars like Monier-Williams argue that this term originally alluded to an extraordinary wisdom and power reserved for the gods.

From this point of view it is not surprising to find that both "maya" and "magic" arise from the same Indo-European root, *mā*, which means "to limit" or "to measure." "From *mā*," argues sanskritist Franco Rendich, "came the terms 'matter' or rather 'substance defined by a limit', 'measure,' that is, 'what determines a limit;' 'mother', or rather 'she who deals with the the limits of human life.'" From this we can deduce that "maya" should be understood as "the visible and finite reality of the infinite universe perceived by our senses, and, thus, deceptive and illusory."[18] Rendich adds that from "maya" originate other Sanskrit terms such as *mayin*, skilled in enchantments —a term applied to the god Varuna because of his capacity to make rain— *mayu*, sorcery or witchcraft; an *maga*, magician or solar priest. After passing to Greek and Latin this root transforms into words like *mágos*, enchanter or magician, and *magica ars*, magic art. Thus, "maya" is the name of the art of the magician, as well as the illusion that he or she creates.[19]

But let us return to the relationship between love and magic. The erotic worldview developed by figures such as Bruno, Ficino and Giovanni Pico della Mirandola was influenced by Islamic Neo-Platonism—a highly sophisticated intellectual milieu in which the works of Plato, Aristotle and Empedocles crossed paths—which entered Europe via Spain during the twelfth century.[20] Empedocles of Agrigentum's treatment is especially noteworthy here, for, it is worth noting that unlike the West, the Islamic world still regarded this philosopher as a *iatromancer* (that is, a healer, *iatros*, and diviner, *mantis*): a powerful shaman who created a form of medicine whose principles could be applied with equal ease to the magical arts. As Culianu notes, "magic in late antiquity—whose principles reappear, perfected, in magic in the

Renaissance—is but a practical continuation of the empedoclean medical theories as reelaborated by the Stoics."[21] Part I, forthcoming, explores how these same links, binding magic and medicine, persisted in some form or another until the early nineteenth century

While the idea of Empedocles as both shaman and magician was gradually lost in our tradition, the erotic character of his magic retained its essence. The great contribution of Empedocles to the history of Western thought was his theory of the four elements that give rise to the world when they unite in *philotes*, love, or disintegrate in *neikos*, dissension. As a principle of universal union, *philotes* is yet another face of the vast net of beauty and desire that Venus has woven for us, which is why in Renaissance magic "Love is the name given to the power that ensures the continuity of the uninterrupted chain of beings ... Because of eros, and through it, all of nature is turned into a great sorceress."[22] A sorceress whose central act (*maya*), is the beauty which shines forth from the countenance of the goddess.

---

[1] Ovid, *Metamorphoses, trans.* Stanley Lombardo (Indianapolis: Hackett Publishing Company, 2010), 70.

[2] James Hillman, *Thoughts of the Heart.* Accessed, April 15, 2018, at: http://www.compilerpress.ca/Competitiveness/Anno/Anno%20Hillman%20Thoughts.htm

[3] The misogynistic character of the conversion of the female figure into the sensory representative of the divine will be examined in the next chapter.

[4] Victoria Cirlot, *Figuras del destino. Mitos y símbolos de Europa medieval* (Madrid: Ediciones Siruela, 2005), 43. (Author's translation).

[5] Cirlot, *Figuras del destino*, 43.

[6] Giordano Bruno, *The Heroic Frenzies.* Accessed, April 15, 2018, at: https://www.bibliotecapleyades.net/cienciareal/bruno/furori4.htm

[7] Ioan P. Culianu, *Eros and Magic in the Renaissance* (Chicago: The University of Chicago Press, 1987), 74.

[8] Culianu, *Eros and Magic in the Renaissance*, 74.

[9] Bruno, *The Heroic Frenzies.* Accessed, April 15, 2018, at: https://www.bibliotecapleyades.net/cienciareal/bruno/furori4.htm

[10] Bruno, *Heroic Frenzies.* Accessed, April 15, 2018, at: https://www.bibliotecapleyades.net/cienciareal/bruno/furori4.htm

[11] Culianu, *Eros and Magic in the Renaissance*, 75.

[12] Plato, *Complete Works*, edited, with introduction and Notes, by John M. Cooper. 528.

[13] James Hillman, *The Essential James Hillman: A Blue Fire* (New York: Routledge, 1989), 302.

[14] Marsilio Ficino, *Commentary on Plato's Symposium* (University of Missouri, 1944), 170.

[15] Robert Musil, *The Man Without Qualities* (London: Picador, 1995), 609.

[16] Plato, *The Symposium*, translated by R.E Allen (New Haven: Yale University Press, 1993), 165.

[17] Ficino, *Commentary on Plato's Symposium*, 199.

[18] Franco Rendich, *Comparative Etymological Dictionary of Classical Indo-European Languages* (San Bernardino: Personal Edition, 2015), 398.

[19] Joseph Campbell, *The Mythic Image* (Princeton University Press, 1974), 52.

[20] The influence of Neoplatonism and the Islamic magical tradition in Renaissance magic is particularly evident in the *Picatrix*, a treatise on astral magic attributed to the Andalusian scholar al-Madjritî and translated into Latin at the court of Alfonso X, which is indispensable for understanding Marsilio Ficino's magical practices. But even more penetrating than the influence of this text is the treatise *De radii* by astrologer and philosopher al-Kindî, wherein Ficino borrows the idea of universal radiations emanating not only from the stars but also from the elements and, indeed, from all the existing objects. According to al-Kindî's theory, we are all in the midst "of an invisible network of rays coming from the stars as well as from all earthly objects. The entire universe, from the most distant stars to the humblest blade of grass, makes its presence known by its radiations at every point in space, at every moment in time; and its presence, of course, varies according to the intensity and mutual influence of the rays of the universe, so that there cannot be two things truly identical to one another." (Culianu, *Eros and Magic in the Renaissance*, 120). Ficino, like a true Platonist, gave the generic name of eros to these radiations, originating the conception through which Giordano Bruno would develop his brand of erotic magic.

[21] Culianu, *Eros and Magic in the Renaissance*, 8-9.

[22] Culianu, *Eros and Magic in the Renaissance*, 87.

Part I. The Bond of Bonds

Fifth Century B.C. to Nineteenth Century A.D.

[…] one can understand and explain how interaction occurs not only between things which, to the senses, are near each other, but also between things which are far apart. For, as was said above, things are united by a universal spirit which is present as a whole in the whole world and in each of its parts. […] all action comes from quality and form and ultimately from soul. The soul first changes the dispositions, and then the dispositions change bodies. Thus, bodies act on distant bodies, on nearby ones and on their own parts, by means of a certain harmony, joining and union which comes from form.

Giordano Bruno, *De Magia*

1. Eroticism and Magic from the Ancient World to the Renaissance

your sweet laughter, something which robs miserable me
of all feelings: for as soon as I look
at you, Lesbia, no voice remains in my mouth.
But the tongue is paralyzed, a fine fire
spreads down through my limbs, the ears ring with their
very own sound, my eyes veiled
in a double darkness.
Catullus, *51*, 5-12

Lovers have nothing new to say to each other; nor do they actually recognize each other; all that a lover recognizes is the indescribable way in which he is inwardly activated by the beloved.
Robert Musil, *The Man Without Qualities*

Eros and the pneumatic economy

Our story begins in the fifth century B.C., when Empedocles of Agrigentum roamed Sicily and southern Italy as a travelling healer and diviner. In his *Lives and Opinions of Eminent Philosophers*, Diogenes Laertius tells us that at that time the city of Selinunte was afflicted by a plague caused by the stagnated waters of a nearby river, which caused the death of many of its inhabitants and made it difficult for the women to deliver. Empedocles, who had heard of the situation from the neighboring Agrigentum, traveled to Selinunte and saved the town by diverting two adjoining streams that he channeled into the river to purify its waters. After witnessing the recovery of the river, all the city's inhabitants worshiped him "as if he were a god."[1] This legend is an echo of one of the twelve works of Heracles, in which the most admired Greek hero cleaned the stables of King Augeas by diverting the course of two rivers. Far from a gratuitous detail (or excessive praise), comparing Empedocles with Heracles adhered to a tradition that saw this hero not only "as a saviour, but, more succinctly, as an agent of purification of any contagion, that liberated from disease and rescued from pest."[2] The figure of the purifying *iatromancer* will reappear in this study in the most unexpected of disguises.

Thanks to his reputation as a semi-divine being capable of deeds reserved to the gods and heroes of old, Empedocles became—both for the Arab world and for the peoples who inherited Greco-Roman culture—an authority on magic, philosophy and medicine: disciplines that at the time were not clearly delimited. By virtue of his enormous prestige his medical system became fundamental to the study of light and vision, and his influence persisted, in various forms, until the seventeenth century.

In *Poem* Empedocles conceives of vision through the idea that the goddess of love fashioned our eyes out of the four elements and

> wrought them with the dowels of love
> when they first grew together in the devices of Kupris [Aphrodite]
> As when someone planning a journey prepared a lamp,
> the gleam of blazing fire through the wintry night,
> and fastened linen screens against all kinds of breezes,
> which scatter the wind of the blowing breezes
> but the light leapt outwards, as much of it as was finer,
> and shone with its tireless beams across the threshold;
> in this way [Aphrodite] gave birth to the rounded pupil,
> primeval fire crowded in the membranes and in the fine linens.
> And they covered over the depths of the circumfluent water
> and sent forth fire, as much of it as was finer.[3]

For Empedocles, the brightness of Aphrodite is not the only source of light in the cosmos; rather, the eyes also radiate light from within the human body—a divine light taken from the primordial hearth of the universe. It is in the encounter between these two lights that our world arises: the realm of desire that Aphrodite has woven for us. In addition to offering a dialectic to explain how we perceive the world, the Empedoclean idea of vision also reveals a fundamental matter: a participative posture in which the eyes of the body and the eyes of the spirit take an active part in the formation and reception of the images coming from the outside world.[4]

The world in which this theory was formulated was radically different from ours. For the human of classical and late-antiquity, both the eyes of the body and the eyes of the spirit participated in a function that we would now call "physiological," revealing the enormous distance that separates our way of perceiving the world from that of our ancestors. The latter is a form of perception which, in the words of Owen Barfield, cannot "perceive the material merely as such: which in perceiving its environment, perceives at the same time an immaterial within or through, or expressed by it."[5] In the world of our ancestors, light was a phenomenon with mystical nuances, and perception a function that went beyond the strictly corporeal. The result of this configuration was a subtle physiology that fused the functions of the organs of the body with the functions assigned to the spirit.

This framing of physiology persisted and a century after Empedocles's theory of vision was adopted by Plato, who reformulated it in a more systematic fashion, which physicist Arthur Zajonc describes as a state in which:

> the interior light coalesces with daylight, like to like, forming thereby a single homogenous body of light. That body, a marriage of inner light and outer, forges a link between the objects of the world and the soul. It becomes the bridge along which the subtle motions of an exterior object may pass, causing the sensation of sight.[6]

Plato is very clear in stating that when the fire of the eye, the inner light, comes into contact with the fire of the outside world, it transmits its movements through the whole body until they reach the soul. The eyes are not only the point of departure of the inner fire, but also the point of entry through which we are penetrated *by* the external fire. Thus, "once the link is formed, the message may pass, like Iris, Homer's messenger goddess, from one world to the other."[7]

Like any other form of dualism, this scheme posed an structural problem. Because Platonism strongly emphasized a body-spirit division, but at the same time assumed that these two principles acted together, it became necessary to find a link that tied the corporeal to the incorporeal. To this end Aristotle devised an organ that reconciled the breach between the sensible and the intelligible, a first instrument, or *proton organon*, located in the heart. This instrument, which was "composed of the same substance—the spirit (pneuma)—of which the stars are made,"[8] was subtle enough to approach the immaterial soul, and at the same time corporeal enough to be able to enter into contact with the sensible world.

It was the primary organ of communication between the corporeal and sidereal realms. Between body and soul.

The function of the *proton organon* was twofold: since body and spirit belonged to completely different realms —the body made up of the four elements; the spirit or pneuma, of the quintessence that composed the supra-lunar world— the *proton organon* was both the instrument through which the soul transmitted all the vital activities to the body (including intellection, movement and growth) and also the body's way of capturing the sensations from the five senses and translating them into *phantasms* or images that could be understood by the soul.[9] According to Culianu this *sensus interior*, or Aristotelian common sense, became "a concept inseparable not only from scholasticism, but also from all Western thought until the eighteenth century."[10] The functions of this Aristotelian *pneumatic apparatus* were not limited to vision, but rather extended to the rest of the senses, forming a complete theory of sensible knowledge.[11]

The Stoic school developed a theory of perception related to the Aristotelian theory but with some additions and modifications that are relevant to our context. The Stoics renamed the *proton organon* "*hegemonikon*," a "syntheziser" located in the heart, that "received all the pneumatic currents transmitted to it by the sensory organs and produced the 'comprehensible phantasms' aprehended by the intellect."[12] However, for the Stoics perception did not rest exclusively on what went in through the eyes; it was also vital what came out of them. Culianu comments that according to Chrysippus of Soli (*ca.* 279-206 BC),

> the perception of an object would occur by means of a pneumatic current which, taking off from the hegemonikon, goes toward the pupil of the eye where it enters in contact with the air situated between the organ of vision and the perceptible object. The contact produces in the air a certain tension which spreads in the shape of a cone whose summit is in the eye and whose base delimits our visual field.[13]

In a manner similar to Empedocles's fire of the eye, the pneuma of the Stoics went out through the pupils, creating a bridge between the inner and outer world, but it did so taking into account the surrounding air and the distance between the eyes and the perceived object, thus determining a sort of rudimentary "visual field." Here I should point out that the Stoic scheme offered an explanation that was not clear in the empedoclean version: It was the pneuma that transported the image of the object through the eyes and back to the *hegemonikon*, where the *phantasmata* then established themselves, as ethereal images that could be understood by the soul of the individual (i.e., by his intellective spirit). This intimate relationship between these phantasms of the mind with the pneuma, their natural medium, led to the latter being characterized as a mirror through which the images captured by the senses were reflected.[14]

Through what mechanism was the pneuma a suitable medium for the translation of the sensory images into phantasms comprehensible by the intellect is not a question with a clear answer. We can, however, deduce an affinity between these images and the spirit by virtue of their shared incorporeal nature. Perhaps the most complete, and simultaneously intricate definition of pneuma is given by Marsilio Ficino in *De vita's* third book, when he states that it is

> a very thin body, almost nonbody and already almost soul; or almost nonsoul and almost body. In its composition there is a minimum of a terrestrial, a little more of an aquatic, and still more of an aerial nature. But most of it partakes of the nature of stellar fire ... it is altogether shiny, hot, humid, and invigorating.[15]

Pneuma, Ficino further tell us, is "sanguineous, pure, subtle, hot and shiny. Produced by the thinnest blood by the heart's heat, it flies away to the brain and enables the soul to use actively both internal and external senses."[16] Apart from providing a theory of perception and cognition, the pneumatic currents that circulated throughout the body, carried by the subtler portion of the blood, were used to explain other bodily activities such as mobility and the production of voice and sperm. These two emissions, voice and semen, were considered as "the only two modalities through which the spirit leaves the body *in an observable way*,"[17] so that an abundant loss of sperm should affect the voice and the spirit. The notion of a relationship between pneuma, semen, and voice is also found in traditional Chinese medicine, in which a constant and abundant emission of sperm can damage the spirit (*shen*) and lead to death. By virtue of this very relationship, a loud and resonant voice is taken as an indisputable sign of a healthy and vigorous spirit.

Subsequent to Galen of Pergamum (*ca.* 129-201 AD), the idea of the pneumatic apparatus was linked to two interrelated organic systems: a subtle one that established the faculties of the soul, and an anatomical one that described the movements of perceptual processes inside the organism. In the first system, the soul was divided in three parts:

> The rational or intellective soul, eternal, incorruptible, or immortal; the sensitive soul composed of spiritual substance; and the vegetative soul. The vegetative soul is common to men and plants, the sensitive soul is common to man and animals, while the intellective soul belongs to man alone.[18]

While the vegetative soul was responsible for the generation, conservation and growth of the body, the sensitive soul was in charge of perception, a faculty centered on the liver which was then transmitted to the body through the venous circulation. The sensitive soul also had a vital or spiritual function centered on the heart, which spread throughout the organism via arterial blood. This function, also called *vital spirit*, vivified the body and by being purified in the cavities of the brain became an *animal spirit* which, as it filled the nerves, irradiated through the whole body, producing sensitivity and movement.

If, from our current point of view, it seems that this scheme underestimates the role of the brain, the idea was that in this organ resides the *inner sensus* and the *virtus imaginatiua* which received the pneumatic currents transmitted through the blood and the nerves. It was this imaginative faculty that translated the impressions of the senses into phantasms that could be understood by the spirit.[19] Since the pneuma circulates with the blood through the veins and arteries, alterations to this pneumatic circulation, Giorgio Agamben argues, "produce disease: if the blood is too abundant and invades the arteries, thrusting the pneuma toward the heart, the result is fever; if, on the contrary, the pneuma is pushed so that it accumulates at the extremes of the pneumatic vessels, there is swelling."[20] During late antiquity the circulatory system was understood as a vast network that carried not only blood but the spirits needed to animate the body.

According to the great Persian scholar Avicenna (*ca.* 980-1037 AD), the inner sense that processed the sensory phantasms was composed of five "virtues" or powers that corresponded to the five cavities of the cranium: *phantasy* or common sense, "placed in the first cavity of the brain that receives in itself all the forms that are impressed on the five senses and transmitted to it;" *imagination* or "the force placed in the the extremity of the forward cavity of the brain, which holds what the common sense receives from the senses and which remains in it even after the removal of the sensible objects;" followed by the *cogitative* power, located in the medial cavity of the brain which "composes according to its will the forms that are in the imagination with other forms;" the *estimative* power has its seat in the summit of the medial cavity and "the insensible intentions that are found in individual sensible objects, like the power that permits the lamb to judge that the wolf should be avoided;" and finally, the *reminiscent* power, which is located in the posterior cavity and "retains what the estimative power apprehends from the insensible intentions of individual objects."[21]

What Avicenna presents in this quintuple gradation of the *sensus interior* is "a progressive 'disrobing' (*denudatio*) of the phantasm from its material accidents,"[22] which takes it from the sensible to the spiritual and mnemonic. This pneumatological system appears in multiple versions in the course of medieval thought, and, Agamben tells us, "can be compared [...] with those musical compositions referred to as 'variations on a theme'"[23] which, despite the transpositions and divergences, maintain their original identity. Paradoxically, though, this identity lies largely in the ambiguity implicit in the idea of phantasm. Understood as a mental image with effects reaching not only the level of perception but that of social construction, the phantasm exists in the twilight between the objective and the subjective, the material and the immaterial, a zone of indistinction between reality and unreality. This is why the phantasm pulls us towards the twilight from whence it comes: Its central action is to drag us into the shadow of the world.

The phantasms of hysteria and melancholia

The physio-psychological system I have described thus far was closely related to the humoral theory in use in our tradition since Hippocrates (ca. 460-370 BC). The four humors in question are: yellow bile, phlegm, blood and black bile, or *cholos melaina* in Greek, which originates our word "melancholy." These humors were related to the seasons, the elements and different viscera. When either one of these humors prevailed over the others it gave rise to the four classical temperaments: choleric or bilious, phlegmatic, sanguine and melancholic. Along with sleep, faintness and solitude, melancholy was regarded by

Ficino as one of the seven *vacatio*, or exemptions in which the bond between soul and body weakened allowing the former to separate from its physical sheath and acquire gifts such as premonition or clairvoyance. As a form of *vacatio* it was believed that the melancholic temperament was given to certain special faculties. Albertus Magnus (ca. 1200-1280 AD) considered that the so-called hot or smoky melancholy (*fumosa*)—one of the two types of bile—had two main effects on the subject's phantasmic activity:

> The first consists in the *mobility* of the phantasms within the subtle organism: the second, in the great capacity of phantasms to stay *impressed* upon the pneuma. This brings with it, besides a prodigious memory, an extraordinary capacity for analysis. This is why, Ficino tells us, "all the great man who have ever excelled in an art have been melancholic. Either because they were born so or became so through assiduous meditation."[24]

Ficino, of course, was a melancholic. This aptitude for contemplation and metaphysics was known as *tristitia salutifera* (healthy sadness) or *tristitia utilis* (useful sadness) because it became the "golden goad of the soul" that impelled the melancholic in his quest for the divine. The sadness that characterizes melancholy was occasionally accompanied by another very particular characteristic: the melancholic were deeply sexual and given to lasciviousness. The abbess and mystic Hildegard of Bingen (1098-1179 AD) argued that the melancholic are "excessively libidinous and, like donkeys, overdo it with women. If they desisted from this depravity, madness would result ... their love is hateful, twisted and death carrying, like the love of voracious wolves ... they have intercourse with women but they hate them."[25]

This disregard, hatred, and fear of women—as alive now as it was back then—can be found in another manifestation of the melancholic temperament, hysteria, which for many centuries was wrongly regarded as an exclusively feminine condition and characterized as a "melancholy of the uterus." In the Eber papyrus (ca. 1500 BC), one of the oldest extant medical documents, we find the first description of hysteria as a disorder caused by a "floating uterus" that spontaneously moved around the female body. Hippocrates was the first to use the term hysteria, referring to the *hysteron* or womb, and insisted on the Egyptian notion of a restless uterus, but added that the cause of the condition were the "poisonous stagnant humors which, due to an inadequate sexual life, have never been expelled."[26] Because the Hippocratic system posited the female body as cold and humid, it was believed that the uterus was more susceptible to disease, "especially if it is deprived of the benefits arising from sex and procreation, which, widening a woman's canals, promote the cleansing of the body."[27] The beneficial sexual act for women was, as androcentricity would have it, heterosexual.

In the *Timaeus*, Plato tacitly seconds the opinion of Hippocrates and affirms that when this organ "is a long time fruitless beyond the due season, is distressed and sorely disturbed; and straying about in the body and cutting off the passages of the breath it impedes respiration and brings the sufferer into the extremest anguish and provokes all manner of diseases; until the passion and love of both unite them."[28] The Hippocratic treatment for hysteria is rather obvious: if the cause of the condition is an inadequate sexual life that contributes to the accumulation of pernicious humors—which in most cases entails a repressed or uncontrollable eros—women should resume their sexual activity and the convulsive symptoms or the paralysis and paresthesias that characterize hysteria will cease gradually. The other part of the treatment follows the Egyptian advice: the womb should be returned to its place by means of acrid or fragrant odors placed on the face and genitals; thus, if the uterus has been displaced upwards, pleasant smells should be put near the vagina and unpleasant odors under the nose; and viceversa if the womb has descended to the pelvic floor.

From the writings of Hippocrates and Galen, hysteria was identified exclusively with an irregular or abstinent sexual life, but the role that man could have in the development of the disease is never discussed, as neither is the fact that women have to endure unequal social conditions all their lives. With the exception of Soranus of Ephesus, a Greek physician active in Alexandria in the second century AD who claimed that most female disorders were the result of the toils of procreation and encouraged sexual abstinence, the androcentric approach is maintained during the following nineteen centuries: we find it in Avicenna (ca. 980-1037 AD) as well as in the Andalusian Jew Maimonides (1135-1204). In fact, it is through them that the ideas of Hippocrates and Galen extend to the medical schools of Salerno and Montpellier and from there to the rest of the continent.

The idea that abstinence or sexual repression is the cause of hysteria figures in the thought of Trota of Salerno (twelfth century), considered the first female doctor of Christian Europe, who revealed a particularity in the situation of women that persists in the present: given the intimate nature of sexual disorders, many women do not reveal the source of their problems to their doctors out of shame or fear of judgment. The so-called *sanatrix salernitana* practiced in the medical school of her city but was discredited by her male colleagues and her work and identity were practically forgotten until the late twentieth century. Given this deplorable way of treating women, it is not surprising to note that in medical texts of the time they were not described as "patients" but as the cause of an melancholic condition in the male called *amor hereos*, which I will describe in more detail later on.

Hildegard of Bingen, whom I have already quoted in reference to male melancholy, "resumes the 'humoral theory' of Hippocrates and attributes the origin of black bile to the original sin. In her view, melancholy is a defect of the soul originated from Evil and the doctor must accept the incurability of this disease."[29] Although discouraging in this regard, Hildegard reclaims the role of women in society by asserting that "Adam and Eve share responsibility with respect to original sin, and man and woman—sexually complementary—are equal in front of God and the cosmos."[30] Of course, such an ideal of gender equality was disrupted by more influential thinkers such as St. Thomas Aquinas (1225-1274 AD) who, reviving some of Aristotle's ideas, ("as regards the individual nature, woman is defective and misbegotten...") summarizes the Western attitude towards women. From this time until the eighteenth century, hysteria, still understood as an exclusively female condition, was associated with witchcraft and demonic possession, sending tens of thousands of women to the stake.

It is essential to note that this hatred and fear of women found a covert expression in courtly love, a product of the greatest melancholic and poetic minds of its time, and is related to the appropriation, by Occitan poetry, of Gnostic themes latent in Islamic neoplatonism and the Cathar heresy. German psychologist Horst-Eberhard Richter alluded to this circumstance in a passage worth quoting in full:

> Courtly love was a typical manifestation of a form of behavior often exhibited by men in the course of Western history.

> Although in the real world women were oppressed, men enjoyed exhibiting devotion—a devotion largely confined to the realm of narcissistic fantasy—to a maternal feminine figure who possessed the idealized attributes of an angel or the Madonna ... The traits of an angelic innocence and chaste maternity celebrated in the cult of the Blessed Virgin Mary—a cult frequently echoed by the poets of courtly love—were the feminine qualities venerated by men, whose one-sided, distorted ideal of woman enabled them, in fantasy, to adopt towards women a role of passive devotion. Men's exaltation and aesthetic glorification of this fantasy-image of a phantom woman, which continues to crop up in later centuries, for example in German Romanticism, was at bottom a clever strategy for denying the reality of woman's social position, which was the direct opposite of that implied by the Romantic cult.[31]

The narcissistic fantasy to which Richter refers is an idealization of the woman which turns her into a "fantastic" image that penetrates the male pneuma. But in reality man is not worshiping woman *as she is*, he is idolizing his own ideal of divinity. The medieval lover is not in love with a potential partner, he is in love with love itself. This narcissistic view of the woman as a celestial being is a covert way of coming into contact with a set of psychological traits that man has been repressing since late antiquity: the vulnerability and devotion necessary to enter into communion with the divine.[32]

The narcissistic character of courtly love is even more evident if one considers the importance that this poetic tradition gave to Narcissus, not only as an incarnation of love itself, but of love of an image, that is, love of a phantasm. In fact, Narcissus's *miröers perrileus* (dangerous mirror) is identified with the Fountain of Love, a motif that figures prominently in Gillaume de Lorris's *Roman de la Rose*, in which the fountain is the place where Love lurks and anyone who looks into it is destined to fall in love. The motif of the fountain understood as a water mirror has a curious relationship with the theory of vision originated by Empedocles, for in both the eye and the fountain it is the watery element that dominates, "such that in [the eye] are inscribed the forms of sensible objects, as in a mirror."[33] The eye acts as a mirror which reflects the image of the beloved in its watery element; we fall in love looking at the fountain in the eyes of our loved ones.

However, warns Agamben, it is necessary to differentiate between our current notion of narcissism and that of the Middle Ages: "we are so accustomed to the interpretation of the myth given by modern psychology, which defines narcissism as the enclosure and withdrawal in the self of libido, that we fail to remember that Narcissus was, after all, not directly in love with himself, but with his own image reflected in the water, which he mistook for a real creature."[34] The fact that by falling in love with his own image, Narcissus served as the model of an erotic dynamic that emphasized on the "fantastic" over the real, made the medieval human prone to a form of idealization that led him away from the real world and in pursuit of a reunion with the divine, a characteristic feature of both Gnosticism and of the poetry of Dante and Petrarch which derived from the work of the troubadours.

This tendency towards idealization is also palpable in the importance that medieval literature gave to allegory— understood as both literary device and genre—and to the names of things in general. "The name of Love is so sweet to hear," says Dante in *Vita Nouva* "that it seemeth to me impossible that its action in most things be other than sweet, in as much as names are sequent to the things named, even as it is written, *nomina sunt consequentia rerum.*" The indissoluble bond between a thing and its name would seem to repeat itself in the bond between a thing and its image. If the image remains an intra-psychic reality, we speak of a phantasm, if it is externalized as a literary device it becomes allegory.

How was it that woman ended up becoming one of the "official" images of divinity in our culture is a difficult matter to determine. For Morris Berman, this issue lies in that

> Christianity, from very early days, sought to extirpate dualistic and pagan beliefs, which included the worship of the Great Mother, Sophia (wisdom), or Woman as a prophetic being. The result of this was not the elimination of these beliefs, but the driving of them underground. In this process—a process that Joseph Campbell has called "the collapse of the mythological layer"—the archetypal level of the ancient worship got dislocated, and a kind of category error occurred: the ordinary woman, as love object, came to be experienced as Sophia; or in Jung's terminology, as the anima. In this way romantic love, as a profane form of archaic religious experience, began to spread through Western culture.[35]

Thus, rather than a genuine manifestation of earthly love, the image of the feminine as the sensible face of the divine is an expression of man's spiritual search (and man's only), and as such is a sublimated form of exclusion that has served for centuries so that the male psyche does not have to assume all the ways in which women are discriminated in our society. In the West the image of women, and of the feminine in general, has become the fetish of an unattainable deity that has retreated to the transcendent sphere. This, in fact, is the defining characteristic of any form of fetishism: an object or image that by a psychological dislocation represents, in the words of Agamben, the presence of an absence, "both symbol of something and its negation."[36] Seen from this point of view, it is not strange to find that this fetishistic dynamic is closely related to melancholy, since what the mystic and the melancholic poet seek in their contemplation is precisely what they cannot obtain: carnal satisfaction in the union with the beloved. The fetishistic character of the relation between the subject and his unattainable phantasms will emerge once again in the second part of this study.

In the myth of Actaeon—the prototypical expression of this understanding of the feminine—the fetishization implicit in understanding the world as the countenance of the goddess extends to its main character, in whom the hunter and the hunted are simultaneously present and absent, so that Actaeon himself is the presence of an absence and the absence of a presence. Thus, we can posit that viewed from the inside, from the point of view of the mind or inner world, Actaeon's myth is a story of psychological transformation, while viewed from the outside, from the point of view of the world, it is a process of fetishization of the individual and the world. This external view of Actaeon/fetish is the model of the other fetishes that we will find in this study.

Catharism, courtly love and the *Dolce Stil Novo*

As I mentioned in the introduction, Catharism —a dualistic Gnosis that flourished in southern France and northern Italy in the twelfth and thirteenth centuries— is considered by some historians as one of the decisive influences of courtly love. Like many Christian gnoses, the Cathar doctrine was characterized by a strong anticosmism (the idea that the world is bad and impure), and antisomatism (the idea that the body is bad and impure) that condensed in three specific habits: *encratism*, or the abandonment of marriage and abstention of sexual relations, which were considered to perpetuate Satan's creation, who fulfills the function of a Demiurge, or secondary deity that causes the spurious creation we inhabit; *vegetarianism*, to avoid assimilating the corrupt element of creation present in the flesh of animals; and *antinomianism*, or disobedience of the civil and religious laws, because they were understood as an extension of Satan's creation. Needless to say, these demands were far too burdensome for most believers, and only a small group, the *perfecti*, observed them fully, while the rest did so partially and according to their capabilities. As can be deduced from this set of rules, as a doctrine the purpose of Catharism was to escape the corrupt creation of Satan/demiurge to ascend to the spiritual realm where the true deity inhabited.

Now, how was it that a puritan sect opposed to the idea of sex ended up influencing courtly love, and through it the whole erotic attitude of the modern West? Although Cathar doctrine openly condemned marriage, it admitted in some cases libertinism, a radical form of antinomianism that opposed the catholic custom according to which sex was only permitted within marriage and for exclusively reproductive purposes. Given this proviso, the fact that sometimes believers succumbed to the pleasures of the flesh, if not celebrated, was admitted and accepted publicly, "provided that it not bear the legal seal of marriage, because it was more weighty to make love to a wife than to another."[37] The possible antisocial and anti-demographic consequences of such licentiousness worried and enraged the Catholic Church and a huge military campaign, the Albigensian Crusade, was launched with the purpose of exterminating the Cathar heresy. As I mentioned before, the Inquisition was created for this very purpose. Apparently, the encratist, libertine and antinomian attitudes—simultaneously opposed to marriage as well as to civil and ecclesiastical laws— trickled down to the troubadours of Occitania. The first rule of courtly love, consigned by Andreas Capellanus in his *De amore*, goes: "marriage is no real excuse for not loving."

It is not my intention to argue for an exclusive Cathar influence in courtly love when there is ample evidence that other sources, such as Arabic poetry, Neo-Platonism and the Marian mysticism of Abbot Bernard de Clairvoux (1090-1153), could have had an equally important impact. However, sometime in the early twelfth century the troubadours began to "code" an asymmetric form of love between a young knight and a married woman, so that it took place within a socially accepted framework. Over time, this led to a situation in which the beloved, in principle attainable, became an idealized figure, which was to be turned into *phantasmata*, as in the case of Beatrice for Dante and Laura for Petrarch. The prototype of this deliberately "star-crossed" love was that of a knight for the wife of his king. In favor of the Cathar hypothesis, it is worth asking: what could be more libertine and antinomistic that desiring, not your neighbour's wife, but your own liege's?

Denis de Rougemont argues that the true purpose of the Occitan troubadours was to spread the Cathar doctrine, now disguised as a form of love whose real purpose, rather than the consummation of earthly love, was the exacerbation of the lover's passion through the figure or phantasm of the beloved (the narcissistic fantasy described by Richter) with the purpose of ascending the spiritual heights and thus escaping the world. Passion—from the Latin *passio*, "suffering"— through bodily denial and torment was, from the beginning of the Christian era, one of the favorite techniques of Christian mystics and ascetics to bear witness to their faith and return to God. As in the case of innumerable Christian martyrs,[38] the logical end of the erotic/spiritual project of Occitan troubadours was the death of the lovers (or at least of one of them), for only through death one can be separated from the body and return to the true god.

But let us continue with our account of the development of the pneumatic apparatus. The general idea of an organic system that collects the images from the outside world and translates them into *phantasmata* that can be assimilated by the memory and the intellect, persisted in the medicine of Galen of Pergamum and from there crossed over to the Islamic world, where it was adapted by Avicenna and later on regained its prevalence in Europe during the Renaissance of the twelfth century through Latin translations of Arab authors. It was in the refined Islamic cultural milieu where the pneumatic theory of late antiquity would receive an important impulse. From about the eighth century onwards, the hypostatization of women and its transformation into a divine and inaccessible figure, whose psychological basis I just mentioned above, began to figure prominently in Arab mystical poetry. A couple of centuries later we find the Sufi poet Sanâ'î representing a "*Madonna Intelligenza* hidden behind the features of a woman [as] the pilgrim's guide in the cosmos of the Neoplatonists of Islam"[39]. By the thirteenth century, in the middle of the Islamic renaissance, Andalusian mystic sufism led by the poet Ibn 'Arabî of Murcia took the idealization of women to a point where intelligible beauty began to manifest itself in the sensitive beauty of women, thus revitalizing the idea of the world as the countenance of the goddess. It is not by chance that the word "unfaithful" (now obsolete and replaced with infidel) is used for those who have betrayed their beloved or their God alike.

The similarity of these ideas of Arab poetry and mysticism with the love of the Occitan troubadours is remarkable, and although the line of transmission is not entirely clear (the presence of William of Aquitaine, one of the first troubadours, in the Spanish Reconquista gives credence to the influence of Arabic poetry), we can deduce that during the twelfth and thirteenth centuries eastern Spain and southern France acted like a huge crucible where Islamic, Gnostic and Neoplatonic influences intermixed nourishing the poetry of the troubadours. It is worth mentioning that the antinomian attitude of the believer in love, the courteous habit of assuming frivolous or openly licentious behaviors (or at least pretending to do so), would seem "presaged by the sufi attitude called *malâmatîya*, which consists in 'concealing holiness beneath apparent licentiousness of behavior'."[40] What we do know for certain is that Eleanor of Aquitaine spread the ideals of courtly love when she became queen consort of France by marrying Louis VII. Her daughter, Marie of Champagne, was the benefactor of Chrétien de Troyes (1130-1191), whose novels presented some of the ideas of the southern troubadours. In fact, the term *amour courtois* was coined in the late nineteenth century by Gaston Paris to refer to the love of Lancelot and Guinevere, immortalized for the first time by de Troyes in *The Knight of the Cart*. The emergence of these ideas in northern Italy reinforces the narcissistic idea of woman as an angel or a bridge to God that would reach its apotheosis in the image of Beatrice as Dante's guide in his passage through Paradise.[41]

Now, since courtly love is a means to cross over to the divine, it should not be satisfied in the flesh. As in the *Roman courtois* of the twelfth century, it must either be an impossible relationship (the knight's love for an unknown lady or his queen) or it must be outright denied because satisfying it would immediately make it descend from the sublime and divine to the trivial and mundane. Thus, the believer in love tries to "obtain not the favors but rather the contempt of the beloved so that this may increase her unattainability."[42] Of course, this attitude leads to a pathological form of eroticism in which the female phantasm invades the lover's pneumatic apparatus occupying all his thoughts and imaginations, a neurotic search for the image of the beloved that, in psychoanalytical terms, leads to a defective form of transference in which idealizations (or phantasms) prevail over reality.

The love between the subject and his *phantasmata*, which, on another level is the infatuation between man and his ideal of divinity, is essentially a narcissistic and autistic structure which has served as the hidden prototype for our culture's magical operations. The erotic dialectic that underlies the Western ideal of love could be represented as a pneumatic circle whose poles cycle perpetually from the subject to his phantasms:

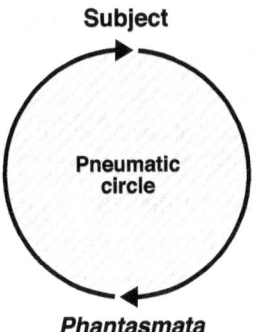

The pneumatic circle is, in essence, an enclosing of twilight, that zone of indistinction between objective and subjective and real and unreal, where the phantasms dwell. Its intensification and sublimation implies its rupture and the flight of the subject to the supra-lunar spheres of the cosmos, as in Dante's journey to the Empyrean. On the other hand, man's confinement in the pneumatic circle, which had already been described by Avicenna under the name *'ishq*, was known in Europe as *amor hereos*, probably because of the *heros*, which according to an old tradition were "evil aerial influences, similar to devils."[43] Bernard de Gordon (ca 1258-1318) tells us that this disease takes place

> when someone is seized by love for a woman, he strongly conceives of her form, her figure, and manner, because he thinks and believes that she is the most beautiful, the most

venerable, the most extraordinary, and most endowed in body and soul; and because he ardently desires her, without measure or hesitation, thinking that if he could satisfy his desire, he would reach his blessedness and his happiness. And so altered is the judgement of his reason that it continually imagines the form of the lady and abandons all of its activities, such that, if someone speaks to him, he scarcely manages to understand. And as he is in incessant meditation, his condition comes to be defined as a melancholy affliction.[44]

The most extreme symptoms of this disease are "lack of sleep, food and drink. The whole body weakens except the eyes," which refuse to waste away as if they wished to attract more of the beloved's phantasms, no matter the consequences. According to Aragonese doctor Arnaldo de Villanova (1235-1611) the phantasms of *amor hereos* "flow 'copious and almost boiling' to the central cavity of the brain, which does not succeed in cooling them, "such that they confuse the judgement and, as it were inebriating it, deceive men and lead them astray."[45] The boiling humor that Villanova refers to is the same heat and dryness that Albertus Magnus took as one of the main characteristics of smoky melancholy. In the most serious cases of *hereos*, the lover's soul, his pneuma, is hopelessly displaced by the phantasmata of the beloved until, like an empty shell, he wastes away and dies. "... I am so pleased to want thus that I suffer agreeably, and have so much joy in my pain that I am sick with delight," writes Chrétien de Troyes.[46]

In its less harmful aspect, *amor hereos* creates a curious pneumatic dynamic masterfully expressed by Dante in the sonnet XIV of *La vita nuova*:

> With the other ladies you mock my looks,
> and do not think, lady, why it is
> that I am seized by such a strange appearance
> when I gaze upon your beauty.
> If you knew, Pity could not be
> held from me in the usual way,
> that Amor, when he finds me so close to you,
> gains so in boldness and temerity,
> that he sets upon my frightened spirits,
> and some he kills, and some he scatters,
> till only he remains to gaze at you:
> so that I change to another form,
> but not so that I cannot then still hear

the wail of those tormented scattered ones.
(Trans. by A.S. Kline)

Dante is transformed, transfigured into "a strange appearance" just by looking and being watched by his beloved. His strange, "upset," countenance, is the subject of mockery among the girls who do not understand the effect of Beatrice's phantasm upon penetrating his pneumatic apparatus and attacking his senses. The effect of these *phantasmata* on the sense organs is even clearer in chapters X and XI, when Beatrice denies the poet "her marvellous greeting," in which Dante puts all his happiness. Wherever he saw Beatrice and could expect to simply be observed by her, Dante felt that

> a spirit of love, suppressing all the other spirits of the senses, made the weak spirits of vision scatter, and said to them: 'Go and honour your lady', and it remained so in their place. And whoever had a desire to know Love, could have done so by watching the trembling of my eyes. (Trans. A.S. Kline)

Dante's animal spirits, the pneuma that synthesizes perceptions from the outside world and brings them to the heart, are conquered and scattered by the vision of his beloved Beatrice. The eyes and countenance of the poet, disturbed and livid, are the perfect expression of the believer in love, which reaches its highest point in the father of the Italian language. We see here how the countenance of the goddess of love and hunting has taken hold of the human soul through the eyes, which in the old days would have lost their light before the intensity of the vision. By Dante's time the pneumo-phantastic doctrine had reached its maximum expression and, through it, the poets of love found a way to reunite with the divine through a complex erotic/pneumatic ritual. As this marks the end of a section.

As a theory of perception, the pneumatic apparatus of empedoclean origin assumes that the only way to acquire sensible knowledge is through the images captured by the pneuma that leaves the sense organs and is carried back to the *hegemonikon*, which then procedes to centralize these sensations and translate them into phantasms comprehensible to intellect and memory. The importance of the "imaginal" nature of the medieval world should not be underestimated. In this regard it is important to bear in mind that prior to the modern era the human did not think in an analytical or causal way, and therefore, says Owen Barfield, it would be true, perhaps truer, to say that they *perceived* in images as to say that they thought them. What we perceive as things they perceived as images... The difference between an image and a thing lies in the fact that the image presents itself as an exterior expressing or implying an interior, where as a thing does not.[47]

Now, since in the pneumatic scheme the soul has primacy over the body, the "phantastic" images have absolute primacy over the word which is, so to speak, an "incarnated" image.[48] Image precedes understanding and speech as well as all forms of linguistic thinking. Hence Culianu proposes the existence of two grammars: the first, primordial and fantastic, and the second, a derivative we use after having translated the images into words to communicate them verbally.[49] The sensory images converted into *phantasmata* were understood as the very language of the soul. This preponderance of the imaginal over the linguistic helps to explain the vulnerability of the premodern human to the assaults of the surrounding pneumatic currents, those curses and "arrows of love" shot by the looks of enemies and loved ones alike. The pneumatic apparatus accounts for both the dynamic of falling in love as well as for spells such as evil eye. "Love is, in turn, magic," says Culianu, "since its processes are identical to magic processes."[50]

By the end of fifteenth century Marsilio Ficino had described an intricate erotic dialectic similar to that of *amor hereos*, which will be of great importance for the central theme of this study. According to Ficino, in every pneumatic operation there are at least two parties: the subject and the object. The subject is the recipient of the pneumatic influences, the lover who receives the image of the beloved, while the object, the beloved, is the one that upon entering the lover's heart as a sensory image becomes a phantasm that invades the latter's pneuma, displacing it. In Ficino's work we see how "the object is changed into the subject ousting the subject who, tormented by the anxiety of prospective annihilation due to being deprived of his state as subject, desperately claims the right to a form of existence."[51] What has happened is this: the soul of the lover has been completely occupied by the phantasm of his beloved so that, henceforth, the phantasm *becomes* the soul itself. The lover has been devoured and has, like Actaeon, "been changed into the object of his love."[52] As in *amor hereos*, the victim of such an unrequited love may languish and, if left untreated, eventually die.[53] A quote from Ficino recorded in *De amore*, his commentary on Plato's *Symposium*, briefly summarizes this erotic dialectic:

> The lover carves into his soul the model of the beloved. In that way, the soul of the lover becomes the mirror in which the image of the loved one is reflected.[54]

If the lover is reciprocated by his beloved, the reflection of the latter in his soul and vice versa opens the possibility for the spiritual rebirth of both parties in the other's soul. With Ficino's formulation the pneumatic circle has become a double mirror where the lovers contemplate each other:

> In fact, there is only one death in mutual love, but there are two resurrections, for a lover dies within himself the moment he forgets about himself, but he returns to life immediately in his loved one as soon as the loved one embraces him in loving contemplation. He is resurrected once more when he finally recognizes himself in his beloved and no longer doubts that he is loved. O, happy death, which is followed by two loves. O, wondrous exchange in which each gives himself up for the other, and has the other, yet does not cease to have himself.[55]

The reciprocity implicit in this dynamic ends up dissolving and sublimating the pneumatic mirror, the ocular analog of the Fountain of Love, after which the souls of both lovers can ascend to the divine.

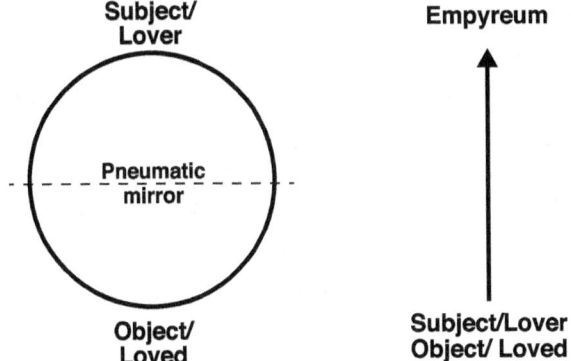

Unfortunately, with the passage of time, the mystical flight implicit in this dialectic would give way to a form of erotic autism which takes place exclusively in an enclosed pneumatic circle, a structure that, as we shall see in the second part, will find its true potential in market economy. This condition is the basis of a form of narcissism which, having crossed over to the modern world, no longer leads to the death of the lover and his potential resurrection in the beloved—or to an ascent to the outer spheres of the cosmos—but to a way of life abstracted from itself and emptied of true will and spirit. When we overlook that this dialectic was in fact a way back to the divine, as is the case in our time, going down this path, Denis de Rougemont tells us, "is no more that an exaltation of narcissism. It is intended to achieve not *liberation* from the senses, but a painful *intensity* of sentiment. Intoxication by the spirit." [56] The compulsive search for an emotional "high," so common nowadays, is a *cul-de-sac* that confines the subject in an erotic dimension that exists only in itself and which cannot not offer a way out; a circumstance shrewdly exploited by advertising and modern media.

The metaphor of the pneumatic apparatus as a mirror is taken up again by Giovanni Pico della Mirandola, a disciple of Ficino's, who, using his teacher's jargon, speaks of the soul as located between the sensible world and the intelligible world —which is why it is called *copula mundi* or *nodus mundi*— and therefore able to reflect these two realms as a sort of double mirror, a *Janus bifrons*. However, Pico's main contribution to our theme is his idea of the *mors osculi* or *morte di bacio*, death through a kiss of the beloved that elevates the lover to the most sublime spiritual heights. For della Mirandola "the lover is the symbol of the soul, the beloved is the intelligence [the divine intellect or angelic mind] and the kiss is the ecstatic union. The oral kiss, *bacio*, among all the postures of corporal love, is the last and the most advanced that can appear as a symbol of ecstatic love."[57] Thus, according to della Mirandola, the *Morte di bacio*

> signifies the intellectual *raptus*, during which the soul is so firmly united with the things from which it has been separated that, on leaving the body, it abandons it completely.[58]

Death through a kiss has many faces. On the one hand it reflects the Cathar ritual of the *consolamentum* through which an aspirant was initiated into the order, a symbolic form of death to the world which was considered to be the creation of the Demiurge Satan. Within courtly love this ritual becomes the *consolament*, the first and usually only kiss that the lady bestows on a knight when he swears eternal fidelity and embarks on his road of passion which, if carried out in full, can only have a fatal ending. The last great expression of the *mors osculi* appears in

Shakespeare's *Romeo and Juliet*, where the son of the Montague family, after drinking the poison[59] says:

> Here's to my love —O true apothecary! Thy drugs are quick.—
> Thus with a kiss I die.

For a consummate mystic like Pico the *morte de bacio* is an expression of the myth of Tiresias in which seeing Athena or Diana bathing naked, "a terrifying vision of the intelligential world," the young prophet has witnessed directly the divine beauty that is the source of true wisdom. Like Tiresias or Actaeon, it is necessary to die to the life of the senses—the purpose of the cortois *consolament* and of the *morte de bacio*—in order to ascend to the truths of the intelligible world.[60]

Magic and the structure of the universe

Before moving forward I must point out an essential matter regarding the nature and the role of magic in the premodern world. In this context magic took advantage of the connection between all things implicit in the idea of *Anima mundi*, it was a type of activity continuous with the very structure of the universe. Thus, Giordano Bruno tells us:

> magicians take it as axiomatic that, in all the panorama before our eyes, God acts on the gods; the gods act on the celestial or astral bodies, which are divine bodies; these act on the spirits who reside in and control the stars, one of which is the earth; the spirits act on the elements, the elements on the compounds, the compounds on the senses; the senses on the soul, and the soul on the whole animal. This is the descending scale. By contrast, the ascending scale is from the animal through the soul to the senses, through the senses to compounds, through compounds to the elements, through these to spirits, through the spirits in the elements to those in the stars, through these to the incorporeal gods who have an ethereal substance or body, through them to the soul of the world or the spirit of the universe; and through that to the contemplation of the one, most simple, best, greatest, incorporeal, absolute and self-sufficient being. Thus, there is a descent from God through the world to animals, and an ascent from animals through the world to God.[61]

By virtue of its connection with the natural order of the cosmos, magic is the most efficient way of channeling its powers (gods, astral demons and elements) either for worldly ends, the manipulation of the forces that control the human world, or elevated ones, to ascend by the Great Chain of Being to the One, God.

The descent of the soul into the world—the incarnation of the pneuma—and its subsequent ascent —the return of the soul to divinity— is one of the key themes of Renaissance magic and, in fact, of its Hermetic, Gnostic and Neoplatonic sources. The particularities of the soul's journey through the planets change from tradition to tradition. For example, "whereas, for Aristotle, the pneuma was just a thin casing around the soul, for the Stoics, as well as for the doctors, the pneuma is the soul itself, which penetrates the whole human body, controlling all its activities."[62] This discrepancy lies in that while for Aristotelian tradition the sidereal pneuma —that is, the *proton organon*, which is made of the same matter as the stars— is innate and transmitted in the act of procreation, in other traditions such as the Gnostic and Neoplatonic the pneuma acquires its sidereal "vestments" as it descends through each of the planets.

For the Gnostics, this descent through the heavenly spheres implies the assimilation by the soul of "increasingly material concretions that link it to the body and to the world here below,"[63] whereas for the Neoplatonists, it implies the acquisition of certain qualities, such as the contemplative faculty, the intelligence and the faculty of procreation and growth, which will again be deposited on the planets on the way back to the empyrean. Whether we talk of increasingly corrupt (material) essences, or of qualities of the soul, most traditions agree that in its descent through the celestial spheres the pneuma picks up the substance of each of the planets—which is then imprinted like a seal and gives it its individual character. This idea establishes a clear continuity between the human temperament and its situation in the cosmos and sets the ground where magical operations take place: in a world where the individual soul is connected to the planets that form the scale of nature—the great chain of being—it is impossible not to imagine human will as connected to the very structure of the Cosmos.

The descent and eventual ascent of the soul through the celestial spheres figures in many premodern traditions. In India, for instance, the gate of the souls is the moon. According to indologist Alain Daniélou:

> The Moon, as presiding deity of the watery element, rules over the tides of the sea. The sphere of the Moon is the reservoir of rain water... The subtle beings, coming from the heavenly

worlds, have to cross the sphere of the Moon, as they come down to the Earth with rain water. This is how the wandering souls seeking incarnation enter first into plant life and then into animals and men.[64]

In Vedic mythology the moon is presented as the abode of migratory spirits and ancestors, an idea that we will briefly find again in another historical context. In its role as regent of the aquatic element the full moon is associated with the cup soma, from which only the bravest brahmins can drink. At the level of the subtle physiology of the human body, which is intimately tied to the physiology of the cosmos, the cup of soma is understood as a cup of sperm, which is the substance of the mind and the organ of thought of the Cosmic Man or *Purusa*. In this sublimated aspect, which can only be accessed by the most expert yogis and brahmins, the moon/semen is a representation of conquered sexual desire and is composed of the bones of *Kāma*, the god of desire and lust.

The very same idea reappears in the Renaissance in the *Memory Theater* of Venetian mage and philosopher Giulio Camillo, in which the cup of sperm is transformed into the cup of Bacchus. Camillo explains that

> the souls that come into this world descend through the gate of Cancer and, in their way back, ascend through the gate of Capricorn. In fact, the gate of Cancer is called the gate of men, and the gate of Capricorn the gate of the gods, for it is through it that men return to divinity...[65]

The constellation of Cancer, explains Camillo, is the abode of the moon and in passing through its door, the souls "drink from the cup of Bacchus and forget about about all the things up there ... depending on whether each one drinks from it in greater or lesser quantity."[66] The path of ascent expresses the Platonic idea of *anamnesis*: by drinking from the cup of Bacchus—which now holds the drink of vanquished desire, the crushed bones of the Kama/Bacchus—the individual pneuma may remember its divine essence and reacquaint itself with the One.

The idea of ascent through the planets is central to the magic system of Giordano Bruno. This thinker and magician argued that the magical and divine rituals of his particular brand of hermetic religion were the natural way to ascend "to the height of the divinity by the same scale of nature by which the divinity descends to the smallest things by the communication of itself."[67] Yet, his system differs crucially from the rest of the Renaissance magical tradition. For the nolan, the One, the divine, is not above or outside of the world, beyond the celestial spheres, but coexists with us in the natural world. *Natura est deus in rebus,* nature is God in all things. This idea has a fundamental implication for our subject matter. If divinity is immanent, the legitimacy of the objectives of magic is not dependent on how mundane or elevated they are, the higher goals of the magician may be immanent as well. Thus, if the destruction of the old geocentric order divided in a supra-lunar sphere (transcendent and composed of quintessence) and an infra-lunar sphere (immanent and composed of the four elements) had its *coup de grace* with the heliocentric theory of Copernicus, the attitude that led to the overestimation of immanence—the typically modern reification of matter that makes modern science possible—was already latent in Giordano Bruno's hermetic philosophy.

The literal search for power and control over the elements that characterizes modern science finds its prefiguration in the Brunian idea of magic which, by proposing a radical form of immanence, ended up becoming a form of "technological magic" that tends to degrade the role of imagination and represent the world as an accumulation of inert matter that can be analyzed and quantified in a rational way. Only in this environment could magic turn into psychology and psychology into control. From this perspective, how strange is it to find that modern society's methods of mass-control can be traced back to Renaissance magic?

The hunter of souls

It is precisely Bruno, in his role as renewer of the magical tradition initiated by Ficino, who offers the most refined and decisive expression of Renaissance erotic magic. The idea of Bruno's magician is that of a hunter of souls (*animarum venator*) who casts his nets and lures his prey, actions that as we have seen, are intimately related to the act of falling in love. The scheme that Bruno presents in works such as *De Magia* and *De Vinculis in Genere* offers us a psychology of sorts derived from the erotic possibilities between individuals, a surprisingly modern idea. Even more disconcerting is Bruno's intention of not only establishing which bonds bind individuals to each other, but also which bonds are useful for binding the masses. For this reason Culianu argues that Bruno was the first to exploit the concept of magic to its ultimate conclusions, envisaging the "science" as an infallible psychological instrument for manipulating the masses as well as the individual human being. Awareness of the appropriate "chains" (*vincula*) enables the magician to realize his dreams of universal Master: to control nature and human society.[68]

The scope of Bruno's ideas is astonishing at the very least. While Machiavelli offers us his discernment about political manipulation, Bruno weaves an insightful analysis of psychology in general, the motivations and biases of both individuals and masses, so that we can deduce the best way to manipulate them. But perhaps the most striking feature of the *De Vinculis* is the manifest way in which Bruno puts himself in the place of the manipulator. Since then most treatises on mass psychology, such as Gustave le Bon's and Sigmund Freud's, which we will discuss in a later chapter, have always had the purpose of determining "the psychological mechanisms operating within a crowd that influence its make up, not to teach *how to control a crowd.*"[69] The most notable exception to this rule is probably the work of Edward Bernays, Freud's North American nephew and the father of public relations.

But let's start from the beginning, with the hunting of a single prey. At its most basic level both the lover and the Brunian magician use their "talents to gain control of the pneumatic mechanism" of his victim.[70] For Bruno the act of ensnaring or catching a prey through baits or pneumatic lures is called "bonding," *vincire*, and the bonds created between the lover/hunter and the beloved/hunted are "bonds," *vincula*. Traditionally, these bonds were characterized as *arrows with pneumatic tips* that fly from the bow of the God of Love towards his prey, or from the lover towards the beloved. Regarding the first case, in the *Roman de la Rose* we read that Sweet Looks—the allegory of the lover's eyes—keeps two bows for Love along with ten arrows, five for each of them. The first bow, beautifully carved in flexible and light wood, shoots five golden tipped arrows:

> Sharpest and swiftest of the arrows five—
> The one best feathered and the one most fair—
> Was beauty called; Simplicity was the one
> That sorer wounds, in my opinion;
> Another was independence named,
> Feathered with valour and with courtesy.[71]

In addition to these virtues de Lorris adds Company and Fair Seeming. Each of these arrows of love is a bond through which the lover binds the beloved to manipulate him or her. The arrows of the second bow, made out of a wood full of knots are: Pride, Villainy, Shame, Despair and New Thought, and are used to break the spells of love. It is important to mention that of the first five arrows, Beauty and Simplicity are shot through the eyes of the unfortunate protagonist while the remaining three enter through the heart and the side. All the pneumatic tips remain inside the body of the Lover. Some decades later Guido Cavalcanti, Dante's best friend and mentor, wrote of his beloved Vanna:

> This virtue of love, that has undone me
> Came from your heavenly eyes:
> It threw an arrow into my side.

The operation of bonding the beloved is, thus, implacable. Whoever bonds, Bruno tells us,

> does not unite a soul to himself unless he has captured it; it is not captured unless it has been bound; he does not bind it unless he has joined himself to it; he is not joined to it unless he has approached it; he has not approached it unless he has moved; he does not move unless he is attracted; he is not attracted until after he has been inclined towards or turned away; he is not inclined towards unless he desires or wants; he does not desire unless he knows; he does not know unless the object contained in a species or an image is presented to the eyes or to the ears or to the gaze of an internal sense.[72]

The similarity of the sequence of events described by Bruno with the emotional struggle of an amorous conquest could not be clearer. In essence, it is through these bonds and pneumatic lures that the magician must impose his will on the beloved, the prey of the magical operation, creating a kind of subjugating desire that has it renounce his or her will. Given this openly erotic character, it is important to point out another etymology related to the *Venus/venator/venatus* complex that will serve to clarify the importance of desire in the scheme presented by *De Vinculis*: "will" in English as "volonté" in French, "volontà" in Italian and "voluntad" in Spanish come from protoindoeuropean root *wel-*, which in Latin gave rise to the words *volo*, "desire," and *voluptas*, "pleasure." What does our will expect but to find pleasure and satisfaction? This root reveals that the relation between the will and the world of the pleasure and desire of Venus/Maya is inscribed in the very meanings of our linguistic family.

It should be noted that in the Vedic world this same idea was expressed through the word *kāma* —which we discussed in the previous section in reference to the hindu god of lust—and which originates in the root *kam*, "to desire" or "to love" and was regarded as the prime source, the seed of the universal mind. In this respect, the tenth mandala of the Rig Veda tells us:

> In the beginning, desire [*kāma*] then rose, which was the first seed of the mind. By peering into their hearts, the wise men in their wisdom discovered the link between being and non-being.[73]

In Vedic cosmogony desire, *kāma*, is the primordial bond—the link that binds existence with non-existence and makes the perception of the world possible—an idea that in the West manifests itself as the countenance of the goddess. For this reason, the bond of bonds, *vinculum vinculorum*, is eros in the broadest sense of the term, a desire ranging from the simplest physical and sexual pleasure to authority, wealth, power and supremacy. At its most basic level, says Bruno, "the kind of proportionality which we regularly experience in eating and in sexual intercourse is found in every act of bonding. For we are not attracted and bonded by these desires and loves at all times, or in the same way, or in the same degree, or with the same variations of time."[74]

Here the empedoclean legacy of Bruno's magic becomes evident once again. Bruno himself argues that

> all affections and bonds of the will are reduced to two, namely aversion and desire, or hatred and love. Yet hatred itself is reduced to love, whence it follows that the will's only bond is Eros. It has been proved that all other mental states are absolutely, fundamentally, and originally nothing other than love itself. For instance, envy is love of someone for oneself, tolerating neither superiority nor equality in the other person [...] We can say the same of the other mental states. Hatred is non other that love of the opposite kind, of the bad; likewise, anger is only a kind of love.[75]

Bruno talks of this universal form of eros as a great web of bonds "which cannot be designated by one name" and to which he refers tentatively as the "hand which binds." This "force of attraction," the bond of bonds, is described as that which

> adorns the mind with orderly ideas; which fills the soul with sequential arguments and harmonious discourse; which makes nature fertile for various seeds; which structures matter in innumerable ways; which vivifies, soothes, caresses and activates all things; which orders, generates, rules, attracts and inflames all things; and which moves, reveals, illuminates, purifies, pleases and completes all things.[76]

Now, if all human emotions can be encompassed by a universal law of attraction, by Eros, it would be theoretically possible to manipulate any affect by following certain magical operations that function coherently within the social and psychological spheres. This is the basic premise of the *De Vinculis*: each and every thing can be manipulated through operations that meet a specific desire. It is important to note that there is no single erotic bond that, when applied in the same way, works equally and with the same effectiveness for the everyone. Each individual must be manipulated according to their individual condition:

> Therefore, different individuals are bonded by different objects. And even though the same object bonds both Socrates and Plato, it binds each of them in a different way. Some things excite the masses, other things affect only a few; some things affect the male and the manly, other things the female and the feminine [...] there is no one and simple factor which can please everyone or satisfy all things, much less does any one thing satisfy different persons or one person at different times.[77]

If this is the case, how can a mass be manipulated? The mechanism is subtle but extremely efficient. The most general bond is the beauty of Eros, from which nothing can escape for "it contains and seeks out all things; it is desired and pursued by many because it invigorates with different types of bonds."[78] However, Bruno warns that

> Nature has distinguished, dispersed and disseminated the objects of beauty, goodness, truth and value in its own way. And, as a result, different things can bind for various reasons and for different purposes.[79]

More than a deficiency, the existence of a single primordial bond is a huge opportunity. The fertility of eros, "which moves all things," is the circumstance that allows the hunter of souls to identify and understand

1. Eroticism and Magic from the Ancient World to the Renaissance

which bonds bind which people, and which bonds can bind the masses. Thus,

> the one who is found to be happy and skilful in more ways and at more levels will bind more things, will rule in more ways and will win out over more people of their own species.[80]

Therefore, the hunter with the most general attributes will be able to cast bonds that will target a greater number of individuals. Not without good reason Bruno asserted that "indeed, it is easier to bind many rather than only one."[81] Now, just as the phantasm of the beloved invades the lover's soul, the images the magician uses to bind his victims penetrate the pneumatic apparatus through the sense organs. In essence, a magical operation is an irruption in the pneumatic circle that reinforces the relationship between the *venatus* and the phantasms that the hunter wishes to implant in his or her psyche. This operation creates a *circle of erotic resonance* that acts as a zone of confluence between the phantasms of the hunter and the hunted:[82]

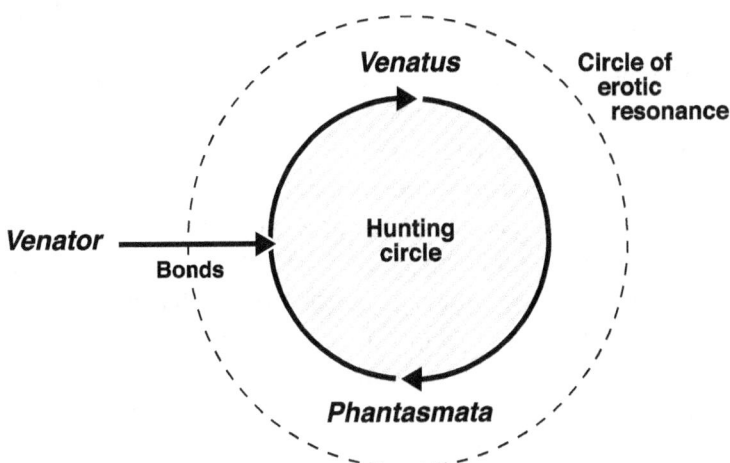

Now, if we take the circle as the symbol of the cyclical time of myth, which is characterized by an order, if not not necessarily matriarchal, at least more feminine than the overt patriarchy of our rational structure, we will see that the act of "magic hunting," whose goal is enclosing the prey within a pneumatic circle, consists basically of confining the victim *in an artificial version of the mythic circle*, in "feminizing" it, so to speak, in order to manipulate it at will; something that will become more evident when we address the psychology of the masses and consumer culture. If one takes into account that the erotic dynamic described by Bruno has its origin in the poetic interpretation that the troubadours made of Catharism, it is not at all surprising to find that this disastrous application of gender inequality is bolstered on a utilitarian attitude towards women, perfectly exemplified in how the *stlinovisti* or the mystic uses a feminine image or phantasm as a vehicle for his own illumination and salvation.

But let us go back to the act of pneumatic hunting. "There are three gates through which the hunter of souls ventures to bind," says Bruno, "vision, hearing, and mind or imagination. If it happens that someone passes through all three of these gates, he binds most powerfully and ties down most tightly."[83]

> He who enters through the gate of hearing is armed with his voice and with speech, the son of the voice. He who enters through the gate of vision is armed with suitable forms, gestures, motions and figures. He who enters through the gate of the imagination, mind and reason is armed with customs and the arts.[84]

Therefore, in order to bind and manipulate an individual or a mass the Brunian hunter-magician must learn to manipulate images, gestures and behaviors that penetrate the pneumatic apparatus of his prey and seize it stripping them of their will; the pneumatic tips can enter through any sense organ. These bonds should not necessarily be beautiful, as Bruno states in this passage, but simply suited to the specific condition of the prey. "He who wishes to bind believes that reason has neither a greater role nor a more important role than love in binding. That which binds is, rather, a knowledge proportional to the genre."[85]

It is not surprising that the prototypical example of many magical operations is organized religion. In Bruno's system, faith is one of the preconditions for any kind of magic, a quality divided into active faith, which characterizes the operator, and passive faith, which characterizes the object of the operation. The continuity between faith in its active and passive facets makes this attribute one of the most powerful bonds that tie the hunter to its prey: he who wants to be healed, in the case of medicinal magic, or saved, in the case of a religious doctrine, is more susceptible if he or she believes in the effectiveness of the manipulator's magical operations.[86] For this reason, Bruno tells us, those of "humble extraction and mediocre instruction" have always been an easy prey for their masters. In them

> the soul opens in such a way that it makes room for the passage of impressions aroused by the performer's techniques, opening wide windows which, in others, are always closed. The performer has a means at his disposal to forge all the chains he wants: hope, compassion, fear, love, hate, indignation, anger, joy, patience, disdain for life and death, for fortune.[87]

Culianu is not off the mark when he argues that "the christian faith, and all other faiths, are only beliefs of the masses set up by magic processes […] by using effective techniques, the founders of religions were able, in a lasting way, to influence the imagination of the ignorant masses, to channel their emotions and make use of them"[88] for their own purposes.

However, in order for the hunter of souls to produce a kind of desire directed towards his person or sublimated towards an object of devotion of his choice, he must fulfill two principal conditions: first, to be able to recognize the bonds and occasions that could tie him to his prey, and second, he must be immune to the desire he produces and imposes on them. Regarding the first of these conditions, the greatest difficulty is that the bonds are—in contemporary jargon—"processes," and therefore extremely subtle and transitory.

> that which is bound is so barely sensible in its depths, that it is possible to examine them only fleetingly and superficially. They change from moment to moment and are related to the bonding agent like Thetis fleeing from the embraces of Peleus. It is necessary to study the sequence of the changes and how the power of a subsequent form is influenced by its predecessor, for although matter is indeterminate in relation to innumerable forms, still its present form is not equally distant from all the others.[89]

The hunter of souls is, in short, someone capable of foreseeing the general movements in the desire of his victims, of observing and changing their circumstances and, at the same time, telling apart their subtler fluctuations, in both individuals and masses, from their previous iterations. A task whose statistical needs are better adjusted to the capabilities of a focus group or think tank than to a single person.

Regarding the second condition, being invulnerable to desire, this implies that the hunter must take care not to become a victim of his own abilities: the *animarum venator* must be a *connoisseur* and master of his own psyche and its images so that he can control the emotions that come with them. "Be careful not to change yourself from manipulator into the tool of phantasms,"[90] warns Bruno himself. This question is not as simple as refraining from desiring, the magician must desire what his victim desires, he must know desire in the flesh, a matter that Culianu defines as the transitive effect of magic: "to arouse an emotion the manipulator must develop it in himself, whence it will not fail to be transmitted to the phantasmic mechanism of their victim."[91] The trick is to compartmentalize the psyche so that in one "chamber" you can cultivate desires identical to those you wish to impose on the victim, while the other prevents you from succumbing to them by keeping the phantasms at bay. This way the hunter may be "intoxicated with love and totally indifferent to all passion, continent as well as debauche,"[92] a state of the soul that in Bruno's poetry is described as a mixture of fire and ice:

> Of Love the standard-bearer I;
> My hopes are ice, and glowing my desires.
> At once I tremble, sparkle, freeze, and burn;
> Am mute, and fill the air with clamorous plaints.[93]

According to Culianu, "the oxymoron in Bruno's poetry can [...] be explained as indicative of a technique and a practice of a magical kind. We are not dealing with stylistic form but with *concrete* descriptions of controlled psychic functions."[94] Like a *stilnovisti*, the hunter of souls must love and desire but never consummate in order to gain mastery of his own desire and power over his prey. This circumstance, as we shall see in Part III, will be of paramount importance in understanding the effectiveness of modern media.

Bruno's warning about not becoming the object of his own magical operations is related to a very particular feature of his system, namely his recommendation to refrain from ejaculating as a technique to strengthen the magical bonds. This magical practice—far more developed in other traditions such as Tantrism and Taoism—is justified, in Bruno's case, as follows: resisting desire strengthens the bonds by creating more desire; enjoyment of desire weakens them by satisfying them. Regarding the retention of semen—which in the case of the male is equivalent to refusing the culmination of sexual desire—we already observed that this emanation is intimately related to the pneuma (spirit), so that if the semen is retained the operator's pneuma is strengthened and with it the bonds that leave the pneumatic apparatus of the hunter towards that of the victim. "The person who ardently *desires* has the power to attract into his orbit the object of his desire. On the other hand, if he emits the semen, the strength of his desire diminishes, and consequently, the strength of the "bond" is also reduced."[95] The perfect hunter will be the one who can project and stimulate desire in others without actually feeling it.

How to achieve such a state of detachment is not something that Bruno dwells upon. However, he gives us a clue when he states that "the primary reason why each thing is capable of being bound

> is partly because there is something in it which strives to preserve itself as it presently is, and partly because it strives to be completely developed in itself according to its circumstances. In general, this is self-love [*philautia*]. Hence, if one could extinguish self-love in an object, it would be subject to any and every type of bonding and separation.[96]

Thus, the perfect hunter must aspire to extinguish the self-love of his victims and for that he must leave even his self-love behind.

It goes without saying that the demands placed upon the *animarum venator* are practically superhuman. A committed hunter must not only be immune to his own desires —without ceasing to cultivate them assiduously— but must also exercise complete mastery over his psyche, what we would now call the unconscious, to the point of becoming an unquestioned master of his phantasms. To what extent this is possible we could only speculate, but undoubtedly the premodern human counted on many and better psychological tools for the task, among them, myth. In fact, Actaeon's story describes the transformation of the human into Bruno's hunter of souls, someone who has looked desire in the face, who has seen the countenance of the goddess, and therefore has begun to witness the world from a point of view that goes beyond the merely human. An accomplished magician-hunter will necessarily be above the realm of *Venus/Maya*—and will therefore be immune to it—but by continuing to cultivate desire he will be able to transmit it and impose it on the pneumatic apparatus of others.

By now an attentive reader may have begun to put together the pieces that link Renaissance magic with the media establishment that emerged in the early twentieth century, but before goin into this topic we must proceed with our historical journey. Here it is necessary to note that the main circumstance that made Bruno the direct ancestor of one of the two great systems of manipulation of our tradition is that the "modern" and the "premodern" worlds have never really been clearly separated, so that this division—the product of a diachronic approach to the study of history—may well prove to be arbitrary and unjustified. As a historical figure Bruno embodies in a particularly clear way the interpenetration of the magical ideas that underlie contemporary science with certain modes of operation that might be called modern. Its modernity is evident in his way of pursuing power, of asserting himself in the world in an entirely active way that contrasts sharply with the *via contemplativa* that dominated Western thought during the Middle Ages and early Renaissance. Bruno contemplates his *phantasmata* not as an end in itself, he comes in contact with these pneumatic images to control them and to learn to impose them on others and, thus, impose himself in the world.

The influence of magic on modern science and technology has been the topic of historians such as Frances Yates, Morris Berman, Ioan Culianu, H.C. Binswanger, and more recently Leon Marvell. With the secularization of hermetic ideas by the Scientific Revolution—which led to their inevitable collapse into a deep substratum of our culture—we see how the magician's functions begin to be encompassed by figures more in keeping with the new establishment: the hypnotist, psychotherapist and, more recently, the PR man and marketing specialist. The Brunian dream of an "integral magician," to use Culianu's term, ended up unfolding not in the field of magic but in that of modern science. But even more importantly so, with the exclusion and eventual eviction of the magician from popular imagination, magic is reified and acquires new forms within the mechanistic vision that defines the modern world: it becomes steam engine, loom and digital network, forms under which it acquires new levels of efficiency.

In our times Bruno's magician-hunter techniques have been used, probably intuitively and unconsciously, against individuals and societies alike, but in most cases those who manipulate us, our modern hunters of souls, are convinced of the need to implement these instruments of control to guarantee the order and stability of society, if only with the petty pretext of ensuring the continuity of their dominion.[97] In the West this attitude can be traced back to Thomas Hobbes with his notion that outside of the conventions of civilization humans would return to a state of war of all against all (*bellum omnium contra omnes*), an idea that figures prominently in the work of Sigmund Freud and Edward Bernays. What is there to say about this? The road to hell is paved with good intentions; and if not so good, at least convinced of their necessity.[98]

---

[1] Peter Kingsley, *Filosofía antigua, misterios y magia* (Vilaür: Atalanta, 2008), 353. (Author's translation).

[2] Kingsley, *Filosofía antigua, misterios y magia*, 355.

[3] Empedocles, *The Poem of Empedocles: a Text and Translation With and Introduction by Brad Inwood* (Toronto: University of Toronto Press, 2001), 259.

[4] The manifestation of the world understood as Aphrodite's splendour is intimately related to certain metaphysical ideas implicit in our linguistic family. This idea, which involves a "becoming visible" or a "coming forth," comes from the Proto-Indo-European root *bha*, "to shine," which expresses the idea of manifestation and, in time, yielded a large group of words in our modern languages. In Sanskrit this root is related to the voice *bhu*, "to be, to grow, to become" (which gave rise to the verb *to be* in English); and when it came into Greek, transformed into the verb *phúō* "which basically means 'to grow,' 'to produce' or 'sprout' and originally denotes a coming out into the light and becoming presence there." From this verb comes the Greek noun *phúsis* which means "origin," "birth," "form" or "nature" and which produced current words such as "physical," "physiology" and their derivatives. From *phúō* also comes *phaínō*, "bring to light" or "make appear," which gave rise to *phainómenon*, "appearance" and which originated the words "phenomenon," and *phantanzein* ("to make visible", "display,") the latter yielding the word "phantasm," a key concept for the magical system outlined in this study.

[5] Owen Barfield, from the essay "Modern Idolatry" which appears in *History, Guilt and Habit* (Oxford: Barfield Press, 2012), 31.

[6] Arthur Zajonc, *Catching the Light*, 21.

[7] Arthur Zajonc, *Catching the Light*, 21.

[8] Ioan P. Culianu, *Eros and Magic in the Renaissance* (Chicago: The University of Chicago Press, 1987), 4.

[9] The term "phantasm" should be understood in its medieval meaning, that is, as an appearance or image of psychic character and not as an apparition or spectre. To understand this meaning we should note that the word phantasm comes from the proto-Indo-European root *bha* that gives rise to Greek *phaos* "light," *phaínō*,

"to give light" or "render visible", and *phainómenon*, "appearance," which originates our word "phenomenon". Seen in this way, a "phantasm" is an ethereal image, an appearance that manifests itself before the mind's eye.

[10] Culianu, *Eros and Magic*, 5.

[11] Here I should clarify an important point. Unlike Empedocles and Plato, Aristotle did not believe that the mechanism of vision was determined by the flow of an object towards the eye but, in the words of Giorgio Agamben, "as a passion impressed by color on the eye, in whose aqueous element the color reflects itself as in a mirror" (Agamben, *Stanzas: Word and Phantasm in Western Culture*, 75). The metaphor of vision, memory and imagination as a mirror will be fundamental for the theory of sensible knowledge from Late Antiquity to the Renaissance.

[12] Culianu, *Eros and Magic*, 9.

[13] Culianu, *Eros and Magic*, 9.

[14] This understanding of the soul as a mirror goes back to Plotinus, who said: "when the Intellect is in upward orientation that [lower part of it] which contains [or, corresponds to] the life of the Soul, is, so to speak, flung down again and becomes like the reflection resting on the smooth and shining surface of a mirror." (Ennead I)

[15] Quoted by Culianu in *Eros and Magic*, 28.

[16] Quoted by Culianu in *Eros and Magic*, 28.

[17] Culianu, *Eros and Magic*, 101. On the relationship between semen and pneuma in *De generatione animalium* Aristotle says: "In all cases the semen contains within itself that which causes it to be fertile—what is know as a "hot" substance, which is not fire nor any similar substance, but the *pneuma* which is enclosed within the semen or foam-like stuff, and the natural substance which is the pneuma; and this substance is analogous to the element which belongs to the stars." (Quoted by Agamben in *Stanzas*, 91).

[18] Culianu, *Eros and Magic*, 10.

[19] Giorgio Agamben offers the most succinct characterization of the influences that shaped the pneumatic apparatus when he writes that "medieval phantasmology was born from a convergence between the Aristotelian theory of the imagination and the Neoplatonic doctrine of the pneuma as a vehicle of the soul, between the magical theory fascination and the medical theory of the influences between spirit and body." Giorgio Agamben, *Stanzas, Word and Phantasm in Western Culture*, 23.

[20] Agamben, *Stanzas*, 92.

[21] Agamben, *Stanzas*, 78.

[22] Agamben, *Stanzas*, 79. In this quote "accident" maintains the Latin meaning of the word, which referred to that "part of the sacred bread and wine which remained after the *substance* had been transmuted into the body and the blood of Christ." (Owen Barfield, *History in English Words*, 138-139). That is,

the term refers to the material traces of the phantasm resulting from its association with the sensory world.

[23] Agamben, *Stanzas*, 79.
[24] Quoted by Culianu in *Eros and magic*, 48
[25] Quoted by Culianu in *Eros and Magic*, 20.
[26] Cecilia Tasca, Mariangela Rapetti, Mauro Giovanni Carta y Bianca Fadda, "Women and hysteria in the history of mental health," Accessed, April 15, 2018, at: *https:// www.ncbi.nlm.nih.gov / pmc / articles / PMC3480686/pdf/CPEMH-8-110.pdf*
[27] Tasca, Rapetti, Carta and Fadda, "Women and hysteria in the history of mental health," 111.
[28] Plato, *Timeaus* (New York: MacMillan and Co., 1888), 341. That the uterus could "err about the body" reveals the pseudo-material understanding of the philosophy and medicine of the time, which was expressed in a subtle physiology that allowed the "organs" to float around changing its positions in the body. On the other hand, it is important to note that the platonic position regarding hysteria and, indeed, the whole of medicine, is erotic. In *Symposium*, Plato puts the following speech in the mouth of the physician Eryximacus (186c-186d): "In short, medicine is simply the science of the effects of Love on repletion and depletion of the body, and the hall mark of the accomplished physician is his ability to distinguish the Love that is noble from the Love that is ugly and disgraceful. A good practitioner knows how to affect the body and how to transform its desires; he can implant the proper species of Love when it is absent and eliminate the other sort whenever it occurs." (*Symposium*, Hackett Publishing Company, 1989).
[29] Tasca, Rapetti, Carta and Fadda, *Women and hysteria in the history of mental health*, 112.
[30] Tasca, Rapetti, Carta and Fadda, *Women and hysteria in the history of mental health*, 112.
[31] H.E. Richter, *All Mighty: a Study of the God Complex in Western Man* (Claremont: Hunter House, 1984), 79-80.
[32] Here it is important to note that Eberhard-Richer's emphasis on psychoanalysis overlooks the Jungian perspective of the subject. From the point of view of analytical psychology, it is only natural that the repressed attributes of the male psyche manifested in the female figure that Jung called *anima*.
[33] Agamben, *Stanzas*, 80.
[34] Agamben, *Stanzas*, 82.
[35] Morris Berman, *Coming to our senses: Body and spirit in the hidden history of the west* (Vermont, Echo Point Books, 1989), 211.
[36] Agamben, *Stanzas*, 32.
[37] Culianu, *Eros and Magic*, 16.
[38] In fact, the word martyr comes from the greek *martyrion*, "to testify."

[39] Culianu, *Eros and Magic*, 17.

[40] Culianu, *Eros and Magic*, 22.

[41] In *Love in the Western World*, Denis de Rougemont quotes *La escatología musulmana en la Divina Comedia* by Miguel Asín Palacios "from which it is inferred that Dante took as a model the *Libro del viaje nocturno* of Ibn al Arabi, written eighty years prior: this work describes, in fact, the journey through the world beyond, hell, purgatory, paradise, with the same encounters and adventures and many similar characters. It seems that Dante belonged to the order of the Templars, who was in obvious relations with an identical Muslim order in its structure, in several of its rules, and even in dress code: the order of the assaccis, to which Ibn was affiliated. (Taken from the Spanish translation *Amor y Occidente*, this fragment does not appear in the English version. 111)

[42] Culianu, *Eros and Magic*, 19.

[43] Culianu, *Eros and Magic*, 19. The tradition referred to by Culianu is the Neoplatonic theurgy which, influenced by a passage from Plato's *Epinomis*, offers a hierarchy of aerial beings (*aerion genus*) that mediate between gods and men, and that were later interpreted by Hierocles as the angels of the Hebrew and Christian tradition. For a complete summary of this topic, the reader can refer to chapter 15 of *Stanzas* by Giorgio Agamben.

[44] Taken from Bernard the Gordon's *Lilium medicinale*, quoted by Agamben in *Stanzas*, 112.

[45] Quoted by Agamben in *Stanzas*, 115.

[46] Quoted by Morris Berman in *Coming to our senses*, 210.

[47] Owen Barfield, from the essay "The Force of Habit" which appears in in *History, Guilt and Habit* (Oxford: Barfield Press, 2012), 47.

[48] Culianu, *Eros and Magic*, 5.

[49] Regarding the primacy of the phantasm over the word, in *De anima* (420b) Aristotle states that "not all sounds emitted by an animal are words, only those accompanied by a phantasm (*meta phantasias tinos*)—because words are sounds that signify. The semantic character of language is thus indissolubly associated to the presence of a phantasm." (Agamben, *Stanzas*, 76). In Hinduism the process of universal manifestation also starts from the imaginal and ends in the linguistic in a process that "takes place in four stages. First, in the undifferentiated substratum of thought, an intention appears. Gradually this intention takes a precise shape. He can visualize what the idea is, though it is not yet bound to a particular verbal form and we are still searching for words to express it. This is the second stage of the manifestation of the idea. Then we find words suitable to convey our thoughts. This transcription of the idea in terms of words in the silence of the mind is the third stage, the fourth being the manifestation of the idea in terms of perceptible sounds. These four stages are known as the four forms of the word." (Alain Daniélou, *The Myths and Gods of India,* 38) Among the recent incarnations of this idea is the "language of thought" of philosopher Jerry Fodor, which starts

from the idea that there must be certain images or primitive figures in the human imagination that, when combined, would form the basic semantic relations available to our thought.

[50] Culianu, *Eros and Magic*, 87-88.

[51] Culianu, *Eros and Magic*, 31.

[52] Culianu, *Eros and Magic*, 31.

[53] It is in this respect that Ficino compares love as a voluntary form of death: "Insofar as it is death, it is bitter, and insofar it is voluntary, it is sweet. He who loves dies; for his consciousness, oblivious of himself, is devoted exclusively to the loved one, and a man who is not conscious *of* himself is certainly not conscious *in* himself. Therefore, a soul that is so affected, does not function in itself, because the primary function of the soul is consciousness... Therefore, the unrequited lover lives nowhere; he is completely dead." (*Commentary on Plato's Symposium*, II, Chapter VIII, 144)

[54] Quoted by Culianu in *Eros and Magic*, 31.

[55] Ficino, *Commentary on Plato's Symposium*, 145.

[56] Taken from the Spanish translation *Amor y Occidente* by Denis de Rougemont. This fragment does not appear in the English version.

[57] Culianu, *Eros and Magic*, 57-58

[58] Quoted by Culianu in *Eros and Magic*, 58.

[59] It is interesting to note that the word *veneno*, Spanish for poison, also comes from the root *wen-*, which gave us *Venus*, *venator* and *venatus*. Originally, *venenum* had the meaning of a medicinal potion, good or bad, as well as an "enchantment" or "seduction" that possibly referred to a love potion. The theme of the potion or the filter of love that ends up being lethal, according to the hidden desires of the lovers, is essential in the myth of Tristan and Isolde, and it is a most important influence on Shakespeare's courtly tragedy. On the other hand it is also curious to note that Verona, where the action takes place, was one of the largest Cathar centers in Italy where, according to de Rougemont, there were almost five hundred "perfecti," the highest rank of the order.

[60] Perhaps the last great literary expression of these themes is Goethe's *The Sorrows of the Young Werther* which ties subjects like *amor hereos* with the Strum und Drang movement and German romanticism. Regarding the melancholic personality of the lover in modernity, it is worth highlighting Henry Barbusse's *Hell* and, of course, the existentialist literature of Hesse, Camus and Sartre which centers on the outsider.

[61] Bruno, *On Magic*, which appears in *Cause, Principle and Unity* (Cambridge University Press, 2004), 108.

[62] Culianu, *Eros and Magic*, 9.

[63] Culianu, *Eros and Magic*, 25.

[64] Alain Daniélou, *The Myths and Gods of India* (Rochester: Inner Traditions, 1985), 74. On the subject of the moon as the door of the ancestors, some verses

from the *Brhad-aranyaka* Upanisad that Daniélou cites in his book describe the path of ascent of the souls of the ancestors to the supra-lunar region:
They who through sacrifices, charities, and penance
have conquered the worlds
pass into the smoke [of the funeral pire],
from the smoke into the half month of the waning moon,
from the half month of the waning moon into the
   half year when the sun moves southward,
from this month into the world-of-the-Fathers,
from the world of the Fathers into the moon.
Reaching the moon they become food themselves
and the gods feed upon them,
just as if ordering King Soma (the moon) to increase and decrease.
And once the fruit of their acquired merits is exhausted
they again enter into space, from space into air,
from air into the rain, from the rain into the earth:
Reaching the earth, they become food, are offered
into the fire of man
and the fire of women.
One born, they grow up in this world
and again start the cycles of existence.

[65] Giulio Camillo, *La idea del teatro* (Madrid, Siruela, 2006), 156-57. Author's translation based on the Spanish version.

[66] Camillo, *La idea del teatro*, 157.

[67] Quoted by Frances Yates in *The Art of Memory* (London, The Bodley Head, 2014), 225.

[68] Culianu, *Eros and Magic*, 88-89.

[69] Culianu, *Eros and Magic*, 90.

[70] Culianu, *Eros and Magic*, 88.

[71] Gillaume de Lorris & Jean de Meun, *Roman de la Rose* (New York: E.P. Dutton & Co., 1962), 20.

[72] Giordano Bruno, *A General Account of Bonding*, which appears in *Cause, Principle and Unity* (Cambridge University Press, 2004), 154-155.

[73] Rig Veda, *Mandala X, 129, 4*. Translation by Franco Rendich. Instead of love, I replaced the word *kāma* for desire to maintain a coherent discourse.

[74] Bruno, *A General Account of Bonding*, 153.

[75] *Theses de magia*, quoted by Culianu in *Eros and Magic*, 91.

[76] Bruno, *A General Account of Bonding*, 146.

[77] Bruno, *A General Account of Bonding*, 149-150

[78] Bruno, *A General Account of Bonding*, 149.

[79] Bruno, *A General Account of Bonding*, 149.

[80] Bruno, *A General Account of Bonding*, 149.

⁸¹ Bruno, *A General Account of Bonding*, 168. Just think of the most popular person in a social network, or of the video with most views on youtube to understand the criteria and scope of this type of bond.

⁸² On his essay *The Magic of Mass Publicity: Reading Ioan Coulianu*, William Mazzarella offers some very interesting insights regarding the concept of resonance in regards to magic and mass media, in particular the idea that erotic resonance is not experienced by the conscious mind but unconsciously as a "being overcome by an ecstatic sense of encountering the very thing that I always wanted – except I didn't know I wanted it until that very moment." (*The Magic of Mass Publicity*, 5) Thus, in Mazzarella's view the manipulations of phantasms is an activity that falls largely on the realm of the unconscious, a connection I will elaborate upon in chapters 2 and 3.

⁸³ Bruno, Bruno, *A General Account of Bonding*, 155.

⁸⁴ Bruno, *A General Account of Bonding*, 155

⁸⁵ Bruno, *A General Account of Bonding*, 163.

⁸⁶ The modernity of this concept is startling, since the bond of faith is what we now call suggestion.

⁸⁷ Quoted by Culianu in *Eros and Magic,* 94.

⁸⁸ Culianu, *Eros and Magic*, 94.

⁸⁹ Bruno, *A General Account of Bonding*, 154.

⁹⁰ *Sigillus Sigillorum*, quoted by Culianu, 92.

⁹¹ Culianu, *Eros and Magic*, 101.

⁹² Culianu, *Eros and Magic*, 102.

⁹³ Bruno, *Heroic Frenzies*. Accessed, April 15, 2018, at: *https://www.sacred-texts.com/aor/bruno/the/the105.htm*

⁹⁴ Culianu, *Eros and Magic*, 241. Note 14.

⁹⁵ Culianu, *Eros and Magic*, 101.

⁹⁶ Bruno, *A General Account of Bonding*, 159.

⁹⁷ As easy as it is to fall prey to the temptation of demonizing those with whom we disagree, I would say that the rest of the cases, which I hope are not the majority, are exemplary instances of narcissism and psychopathy. But what would Bruno himself say about it? Among the sentences collected in the *De vinculis*, one stands out for its lucidity in this regard: "There is one type of bonding in which we wish to become worthy, beautiful and good; there is another type in which we desire to take command of what is good, beautiful and worthy. The first type of bonding derives from an object which we lack, the second, from an object which we already have." (*A General Account of Bonding*, 152) Thus, the search for power and domination is encouraged either by lack or by greed, by thirst for power or by its own satiety. Later on, Bruno warns that not it is not only the good what bounds, but also the simple opinion about the good, whatever we believe to be good, dignified and beautiful. Therefore, if our manipulators estimate that power

and manipulation are good, dignified and beautiful, at least in their minds they will be.

[98] It may be of use to clarify that the Hobbesian notion of "war of all against all" is based on a flawed premise. According to the system that Hobbes delineates in *Leviathan*, what human beings most desire is to avoid a violent death and they will do everything within their power to prevent this from happening. "Finding themselves threatened with such a death," says philosopher John Gray, "they will contract with one another to set up a ruler with unlimited power to command obedience. This sovereign —a mortal god, Hobbes sometimes writes— will bring peace to warring humanity." Thus, it is the desire for peace, disguised as the fear of an atrocious death, which would justify the despotic attitudes of our leaders. However, and here is the flaw according to Gray, Hobbes overlooks that humans, flesh and blood humans and not the fictions in his book, rather than flee from violence get used to it; instead of trying to escape a horrible death they normalize it. It is not fear of death—something natural to all forms of life—what sustains our tyrants, it is a much less transcendental and a rather mundane issue: a paralyzing helplessness that prevents us from assuming a position in the world and from understanding the responsibilities that come with it.

2. High Tide in the Sea of Pneuma

Animal magnetism and hypnosis

And first it appears evident to me, that the moon's influence is necessarily greater on the nervous fluid or animal spirits, that on the blood, or any other fluid of the body. For as a fluid is composed of extremely minute, and [...] elastic parts; it must be more easily susceptible of the power of any external cause whatever. Wherefore the moons's action will chiefly regards those diseases, which are occasioned by the vitiation of those spirits.
Richard Mead, *De Imperio Solis ac Lunae in corpora humana (1704)*

The magnetic tide. *The erotic dialectic of magnetic somnambulis*

By the last quarter of the eighteenth century the last vestiges of the magic *weltanschauung* that characterized the ancient and Renaissance worlds were being buried in a lower substrate of the collective memory of the West. Nevertheless, certain traces of this vision still subsisted in the medicine and biology of the time and would only be extirpated after recurrent comings and goings of vitalist and pseudo-magical theories that would be definitively ousted by the linear imaginary of evolution proposed by scientists such as Charles Lyell, Charles Darwin and Alfred Russell Wallace; a vision that gave priority to the abstract aspects of nature over the concrete qualities derived from personal experience that had occupied the premodern mind. Here it is important to remember that the transformation of the magical ideas of the Renaissance into the entirely "scientific" ideas of the modern world is not clear and, as we shall see in this study, many of these magical forms of knowledge reappear time and again, even in our time, with a quantitative and technological emphasis and under the presumptuous disguise of objectivity.

The power of the field of influence of magic in modern science is particularly evident in the figure of Isaac Newton who, throughout his life maintained a close relationship with alchemy.[1] Therefore it is not strange to find that what Newton attributed to gravity, that mysterious form of attraction that keeps everything in its place was, during the Middle Ages, attributed to souls. "Everything from pebbles to planets had a soul," says Patrick Harpur,

> and every soul had a *telos*—an innate goal or aim. The oak was the *telos* of the acorn, which was attracted to the mature form of the oak. The *telos* of all imperfect metals was gold. Objects fell to earth because they were attracted to their natural element. They were 'returning home.' Thus things were held together by their souls; or, in later Renaissance thought, things were interconnected by an underlying soul, the Soul of the World.[2]

This *anima mundi*, the "universal spirit" to which I referred in the fragment by Bruno with which I opened the first part of this book, is one of the most underestimated and definitive contributions of magic to the scientific establishment. In fact Newton, who spent most of his adult life deeply absorbed in his research on magic and alchemy, devised his theory of gravitation from the "hermetic principle of sympathetic forces"[3] which had figured in the scholastic tradition as well as in the brand of hermetic magic revitalized by Renaissance figures like Marsilio Ficino and Pico della Mirandola.

However, Newton, who secretly agonized to find a way to ingratiate hermetic magic with the new physical science he expounded in his *Principia Mathematica*, could not explain what gravity *was* beyond its geometric formulation and its physical effects, something for which his critics soon accused him of trying to introduce an occult quality—in both senses of the term—into his mathematical system.[4] The English genius expressed his doubts in a letter to his friend Reverend Richard Bentley:

> That gravity should be innate, inherent and essential to matter, so that one body may act upon another through a *vacuum*, without the mediation of anything else, by and through which their action and force may be conveyed from one to another, is to me so great an absurdity that I believe no man who has in philosophical matters a competent faculty of thinking can ever fall into it. Gravity must be caused by an agent constantly according to certain laws, but whether this agent be material or immaterial I have left to the consideration of my readers.[5]

It is one thing to publicly accept his ignorance about the ultimate cause of gravity, a matter with which Newton had no problem, since it exempted him from accepting his hermetic influences, and quite another to suggest that gravitational attraction is the product of a "material or immaterial" agent, an ambiguous comment that could easily lend itself to unpopular animist interpretations in post-restoration England; something to mention to friends in private letters but that had to be kept away from the public eye. After 1650 most ideas openly influenced by magic and alchemy had already been seriously discredited by a long and systematic smear campaign initiated decades ago by figures of the stature of Marin Mersenne and Pierre Gassendi. The young Newton, who at that time studied at Trinity College in Cambridge, understood that he must be extremely cautious in divulging his hermetic inclinations. His solution to this situation was "to delve deeply into the Hermetic wisdom for his answers, while clothing them in the idiom of the mechanical philosophy."[6]

Afraid of risking his reputation as the most important scientist of his time or discrediting his work by revealing his magical and alchemical influences, Newton eventually assumed the most politically correct (and pious) position for his time: gravitational forces are the expression of a divine will, "an infinite and omniscient spirit in which matter moved according to mathematical laws."[7] Such infinity and omniscience are the fundamental traits of the soul of the world, stripped of stultifying magical influences and adorned with mathematical law. The transfiguration of *anima mundi* into Newtonian gravity is the first of the "transformations" I outlined in the introduction to this study. A ripple in the pond of time that will spread down to our days.

At this point our narrative moves away from the topic of magic and approaches the history of medicine, one of the fields where its influence in the modern world is more easily appreciated. The doctor, after all, is one of the hypostases of the magician, with whom he shares a close bond that is evinced in the empedoclean *iatromancer*, both healer and diviner.

A century later, in 1766, an astronomer at the University of Ingolstadt who was about to graduate as a doctor of medicine at the University of Vienna, published a thesis titled *De Planetarum Influxu in Corpus Humanum* (on the influence of the planets on the human body). In his doctoral dissertation, Franz Friedrich Anton Mesmer (1734-1815) discussed the influence of the moon and the sun in the tides and proposed that the human also was subject to astral influences that had an effect in the corporal humors and responded with special precision to lunar cycles. According to Mesmer the stars not only influenced each other but also affected "in a similar manner all organized bodies through the medium of a subtle fluid, which pervades the universe and associates all things together in mutual intercourse and harmony."[8] By the end of the eighteenth century the human could still think of himself as belonging to the Great Chain of Being that held the premodern world together.

Although now these kind of statements may seem quaint at best or openly superstitious at worst, the truth is that at the time they were not taken as eccentric, the University of Vienna was one of Europe's most respected centers of study and the ideas Mesmer proposed in his thesis were in keeping with the investigations of Richard Mead, friend and personal physician of Isaac Newton, who proposed the existence of a universal fluid that circulated through the macrocosm and the human body alike. Far from an inappropriate idea, Mesmer "was following in the tracks of some of the most respected scientist of the era."[9]

In his thesis Mesmer occasionally refers to the effects of planetary influences on the human body with the adjective "gravitational," but at other times he speaks of a different kind of force, which he characterizes as

> [...] the cause of universal gravitation and, very probably, the basis of all corporeal properties; which, indeed, in the smallest particles of the fluids and solids of our organism stretches, relaxes and disturbs the cohesion, elasticity, irritability, magnetism and electricity, a force which can, in this respect, be called *animal gravity*.[10]

It should be noted that the word "animal" in the jargon of the time referred to the soul or *anima* and not to an "animal" in the taxonomic sense of the term. What Mesmer was doing was, to some extent, what Newton had not dared to do openly a century earlier: to associate the force of gravity with the souls. But the matter is not so simple. While Newton secretly regarded himself as a magician and alchemist, since the time of his discoveries the European intellectual environment had turned sharply towards materialism, and Mesmer—a stubborn character that once he thought he had found a truth was incapable of letting go of it—far from believing in mystical influences or mysterious fluids, saw himself as a scientist who had discovered a new physical force that could be of great use to medicine.

Another scholar at the University of Vienna, Maximilian Hehl (1720-1792) —a jesuit astrologer at the court of the Empress Maria Theresa and professor of astronomy at this institution— also believed in the influence of the stars on physical health and "used magnets to 'correct' imbalances in the human organism."[11] After contacting Professor Hehl, Mesmer adopted certain elements of his magnetic therapy and began to use lode stones with his own patients, a matter that resulted in that the force that he had formerly called *animal gravity* changed its name to *animal magnetism*. Between 1773 and 1774 Mesmer treated a Miss Oesterline, a young woman who had suffered for years from a "convulsive ailment accompanied by the most cruel toothaches and earaches, and by delirium, mania, vomiting and fainting fits,"[12] symptoms that a century later would be diagnosed by Jean-Martin Charcot like *epileptiform hysteria*. By means of magnets Mesmer set out to create in the body of his patient a kind of "artificial tide" in his vital humors, "presumably on the assumption that her symptoms were in some way due to interference with 'natural' tides"[13] which were governed by the influence of the stars. At first Fraulein Oesterline felt pain and a burning sensation in her body but her condition improved remarkably in a short time.

Mesmer soon realized that magnets were unnecessary for his therapy; his so-called animal magnetism could not be "mineral" magnetism since this phenomena does not visibly affect the soft tissues. Having realized this, he discovered that he could obtain the same results by means of "passes" of the hands over the body of his patients. He soon understood that *animal magnetism* also resided in his body and acted on his patient's body reviving "the impaired circulation (the "tides") of the patient's own magnetic fluid [and] restoring his nervous system to 'harmony' with the universe."[14] 'Magnetism' as in the expression *animal magnetism* became a reference to a force of sympathetic character, a subtle fluid that circulated throughout the community of living beings moving them and bringing them into harmony and fullness. This universal substance would commonly be known by the generic name of "magnetic fluid."

What Mesmer had discovered—or, for the sake of precision, rediscovered—was what the Chinese and the Hindus had known for millennia by the name of *qi* and *prana* respectively, a vital energy which animates the world and is assimilated by breathing (*spirare* in Latin, from which comes our word "spirit") and that in our tradition was known until the Renaissance by the name of *pneuma*. The tides of bodily humors that Mesmer had learned to manipulate are nothing other than the pneumatic currents described by the magical tradition of empedoclean origin. The pneumatic alterations, which for the *Stilnovisti* and Dante constituted a bridge to the divine—the sensory spirits conquered and set in motion by the vision of the beloved— by the eighteenth century had become the source of countless pathologies that began to be studied and categorized by a new type of medicine that focused on the strictly physical symptoms of diseases. However, for Mesmer, more than physical afflictions, many diseases were blockages in the movement of the magnetic fluid within the human body, energetic stagnations due to the absence of what he called *irritability*, which referred to a condition that made the muscles of the body enter into a constant state of contraction or expansion that weakened or impeded the proper flow of animal magnetism.

While Mesmer's ideas were not particularly extravagant for his time, his presumptuous attitude to the effectiveness of his methods, the theatricality of his treatment, and his insistence on having discovered a new physical force, did not win him any friends or allies within the Viennese medical community. His mentor and friend Anton Stoerck became distant and evasive, and Maximilian Hehl, with whom he shared certain therapeutic ideas, resented him after a bitter dispute over who had invented the magnetic plates Mesmer used in his treatment. Seeing his options reduced in Austria, in early 1775 he published a pamphlet that reported his discoveries and which he sent to almost every scientific institution in Europe. He then embarked on a short tour to demonstrate his methods that took him to Hungary, Switzerland and Bavaria, where he was accepted into the Academy of Sciences. By then his marriage to an influential Viennese widow was in ruins so, without much to lose, he decided to close his affairs in the Austrian capital and emigrate to Paris.

Mesmer's fame preceded him and upon his arrival to the City of Lights he found an environment particularly receptive to his therapeutic methods. Why Paris showed such interest in animal magnetism has been a subject of interest among historians of the period. A school of thought, says Alan Gauld, "points to the existence there of a large class of wealthy, bored and indolent persons, over-fed, under-exercised, and prone to constipation, indigestion, hypochondria and the vapours. These individuals threw themselves with enthusiasm upon any therapeutic novelty."[15] Another school points to the thirst of this same class of people for all kinds of occultisms, and although Mesmer allegedly repudiated these pseudo-religious expressions, it is easy to understand that some of his ideas were attractive among mystics and Rosicrucians. In any case, the Parisians were far more open to intellectual and therapeutic novelties than the Viennese, and shortly after installing his practice at the Place Vendôme, Mesmer was forced to acquire larger offices at the Hotel Buillon, in the rue Coq-Héron.

His success among the common people and the higher classes was overwhelming, "patients were so numerous that, even with the help of assistants, Mesmer could no longer treat each one individually."[16] To circumvent this circumstance he invented an apparatus to store animal magnetism, an idea that we will find again in the twentieth century in the work of Wilhelm Reich. The apparatus in question was a wooden tube (*baquet*) containing iron filings and bottles of "magnetized" water from which protruded a number of movable iron rods. The patients took these rods with their hands or touched the affected parts of their bodies with them. The ambience of Mesmer's practice would no doubt have been unbearably extravagant for our modern therapeutic sensibility:

> the spacious rooms, dimly lit and hung with many mirrors (animal magnetism was reflected by mirrors); walls decorated with astrological symbols; luxurious carpets; a background of harmonious music skilfully adapted to the general mood; the patients around the *baquet*, amused, awe-struck or passing into crisis; and moving among the company the stately form of Mesmer in his lilac suit, occasionally directing a dose of animal magnetism at a patient by means of a metal wand or of his singularly potent index finger.[17]

Perhaps the most disturbing aspect of this *mise-en-scène* would be the intense crises that overwhelmed some of Mesmer's patients. The ailing surrounded the baquet touching each other's fingertips in a human chain, but "usually no great time elapsed before one or other of the company would begin to tremble" says Stefan Zweig, then the limbs would start to twitch convulsively, and the patient would break in perspiration, would scream, or groan. No sooner had such tokens manifested themselves in one member of the chain, than the others, too, would feel the onset of the famous crisis which was to bring relief. All would begin to twitch, a mass psychosis would arise, a second and a third patient would be seized with convulsions, and soon a witches' sabbath would be in full swing. Some would fall to the ground and go into convulsions, others would laugh shrilly, others would scream, and choke, and groan, and dance like dervishes, others would appear to faint or to sink into a hypnotic sleep. One need but study contemporary woodcuts to learn the kind of reactions the patients underwent.[18]

Although in the less advanced cases improvement could be immediate, in other patients the symptoms of a crisis could include "tears, laughter, gastric disturbances, coughing, loss of consciousness, and convulsions resembling those of epilepsy."[19] Hysterical or psychotic symptoms as Zweig suggests? undoubtedly to some extent, but anyone who has attended a yagé ritual or a Reiki session will know that such manifestations, and their concurrent crises, are not at all alien to other medical traditions.

As with the pneumatic currents of the Middle Ages and the Renaissance, which circulated through the body with the blood, according to Mesmer these crises occurred when the magnetic fluid made its way through the energetic and physical obstructions and thus reestablished the body's harmony with the cosmos and restored the patient back to health. Testimonies of these healing crises from the point of view of patients are difficult to obtain in the literature of the period, but it is clear that "Mesmer had a very powerful effect on certain people." Upon being touched by him, the Count of Chastenet, a distinguished officer of the French navy who suffered from asthma attacks, was unconscious for more than half an hour. When Chastenet regained consciousness he found that his condition had improved and after three months of treatment was completely cured. The Count de Chastenet spoke of what had happened with his brothers.

The next great figure of the magnetic movement that I will address in this account is Amand-Marie-Jacques de Chastenet (1751-1825), Marquis de Puységur and older brother of the Count de Chastenet, a philanthropist and virtuous aristocrat who, according to the descriptions of his contemporaries, stood out for his simplicity, modesty, generosity, courage and a touch of *naiveté*. His name and that of his two brothers are listed in the Society of Harmony of Paris, an association founded by disciples of Mesmer for the teaching and diffusion of the techniques of animal magnetism. Having completed his introductory courses in 1784, the Marquis de Puységur settled in his estate in Buzancy in the north of France to put into practice what he had learned with Mesmer.

After dealing with a couple of minor cases, the Marquis began to treat a peasant named Victor Race who for days had suffered from an inflammatory condition of the lungs. Race "had pain in his side, was spitting blood, and was greatly enfeebled by fever. After a quarter of an hour of magnetization he fell into what seemed to be a sleep. He then began to talk, loudly, about his domestic worries."[20] Upon seeing the particular state of his patient, the Marquis had a curious idea:

> When I though his ideas might affect him in a disagreeable way, I stopped them and tried to inspire more cheerful ones;... At length I saw him content, imagining that he was shooting at a target, dancing at a festival, and so on. I fostered these ideas in him, and... forced him to move about a good deal on his chair, as though to dance to a tune, which I was able to make him repeat by singing in my mind. By this means I produced in him and abundant sweat. After and hour of crisis, I calmed him down and left the room. He was given a drink, and ... I made him take some soup. The following day, being unable to remember my visit of the previous evening, he told me of his improved state of health.[21]

Victor Race turned out to be a key figure in the development of Animal Magnetism. From the outset this modest peasant exhibited an impressive array of magnetic —that is, pneumatic—phenomena unheard of until then and which Puységur named "somnambulism" for its similarity with this condition. To begin with, the Marquis could have Race start an activity just by thinking about it and putting all his will into it. But despite this Victor did not become a simple automaton. "Though ordinarily a simple and tongue-tied peasant, he would, in the somnambulic state, converse in a fluent and elevated manner, expressing such sentiments of friendship and gratitude that, says Puységur, 'we were unable to restrain tears of admiration and tenderness to hear the voice of nature express itself so frankly'."[22]

Puységur soon discovered that the state of "magnetic somnambulism" was not limited to a greater susceptibility and eloquence, and that everything that happened in this state was "forgotten" while being awake but could be resumed if the patient was magnetized again, as if there were two distinct personalities. Some of the abilities of the *somnambules*, although incredible, are widely documented. Many subjects were able to "see" the inside of their own bodies so that they acquired firsthand knowledge of their condition. They were also able to predict, "with considerable accuracy, evacuations, bouts of pain, the arrival of suppressed periods, and the bursting of abscesses; above all they predicted the dates and times of renewals of symptoms and of cures."[23] When they were put in contact with other patients they were able to perceive the inside of their bodies and could diagnose their condition and tell what kind of treatment they should receive. The somnambules with this ability were referred to as *médicins* or doctors and assisted the magnetizer with the diagnostics and treatments. This kind of extrasensory perception deserves clarification: When the Marquis asked the most educated somnambules about it they answered that more than "seeing" it was a "knowing," a type of *immediate* knowledge, in the sense of being "unmediated." For Puységur this type of clairvoyance was essentially "a faculty of the soul, a faculty which we may suppose to be released in the somnambulic state when other faculties are in abeyance or under external control."[24]

Apart from these phenomena, many *somnambules* claimed that they could perceive the magnetic fluid flowing from the fingers, hair and eyes of their magnetizers, an idea that points towards the premodern notion of an ethereal fluid that moves with vision and conveys the intentions of the operator in the form of pneumatic phantasms. Could we posit that in the state of magnetic somnambulism the pneuma was able to perceive itself and its movements? Another phenomenon reported extensively during this period was the so-called "stomach vision," which consisted, as the name suggests, of the ability of some somnambules to "see" or, rather, to acquire visual perceptions through the stomach region. It is interesting to note that during the deeper phases of somnambulism the pupils of many patients did not react to light, being permanently dilated, but if a playing card or any other object was placed on top of their bellies—and their eyes were covered to avoid any type of deceit—many subjects were able to distinguish it clearly and to describe it to their magnetizers. Some somnambulists could read closed letters or even see objects stored in metal boxes. As a somnambule gained more control over his or her state "the capacity to perceive in visual impressions spreads over the whole outer surface of the body as a common or general sense, and gives the somnambule knowledge of distant objects."[25] As unlikely as these phenomena may seem, later on we shall see a possible explanation for them.

Now, the fact that the Marquis could make Victor Race act in this or that way just by thinking about it—or that other magnetists could move the members of their patients with their own movements as if they were marionettes—offers us the first point of contact between the methods of animal magnetism and Renaissance magic: There must be a transmission of the imaginary phantasms by the Marquis of Puységur that is captured by the pneumatic apparatus of Race, who was in a state sufficiently susceptible to act upon them. This type of connection, or *rapport* in the jargon of the time, is the ideal state to undertake any magical operation: total receptivity on the part of the prey.

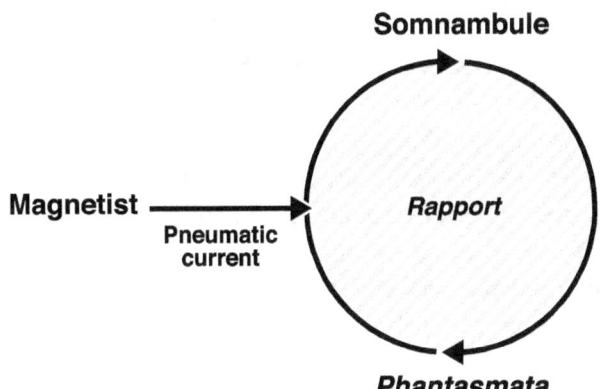

The erotic nature of this situation is rather evident. Many somnambules developed a particular attachment to their "masters," for example Demoiselle M.—the somnambule of Tardy de Montravel, a contemporary magnetist of Puységur's—did not like to be magnetized by anyone else and only allowed him to touch her knees during the process. There was no shortage of somnambules for whom the presence of other people—other than their magnetizers, of course—was disturbing and even disgusting. Apparently, the idea that their patients, particularly women, developed a sexual interest in them did not occur to these respectable gentlemen. What would be the surprise of the Marquis when the mother of one of his patients "began to fear that he was inspiring too strong an attachment in her seventeen-year-old daughter. Puységur found the supposition flattering but incredible."[26] Fortunately, in the case of the Marquis, his simplicity, kindness and commitment to the welfare of his patients prevented any kind of abuse, but abuses certainly were to be had. That such powers were used to seduce young women was only a question of opportunity and lack of scruples. According to a story, Charles Villers—french translator of Kant and amateur magnetist—used his powers to seduce to Lorenza Feliciani, the beautiful wife of Cagliostro.

The eroticism implicit in the operations of animal magnetism is evident on a second front: the role of the magnetizer's will in manipulating the subject's pneumatic currents. If for Mesmer this was possible through "passes" of the hands, for Puységur the important thing was to establish *rapport* between the operator and the subject of the operation. Such a situation implies "the magnetic fluid of the operator and that of the patient mingling to establish a conjoint circulation directed by the operator's will. The operator can then move the patient's body pretty well as he can move his own, *simply by willing the result he desires.*"[27] Magnetic *rapport* may very well be the closest thing to having sex without actually having sex. The role of will —etymologically related to desire (*volo*) and pleasure (*voluptas*)— reappears once again. *Croyez* and *veuillez*, "to believe" and "to desire," were the key words of Puységur's treatment. With his characteristic prudence and common sense the Marquis claimed that he was sure of only one thing about will, namely

> that it is not a physical faculty but a faculty of the free and immaterial soul. The magnetic fluid is so to speak the last, most nearly spiritual, stage of matter, and the will can act directly upon it. Will can thus indirectly act upon other forms of matter, for instance living organisms.[28]

It is important to note that Puységur's description of the magnetic fluid as the state of matter closest to the spirit is formally identical to Marsilio Ficino's definition of pneuma which I quoted in the previous chapter. As in the case of pneuma, the operations of animal magnetism take for granted the existence of a subtle and universal means of transmission, a concept that until the Renaissance was known as *anima mundi*.

The dependence of magnetism on the idea of the soul of the world is even more evident in the figure of Chevalier de Barberin, a Martinist[29] from Lyon and founder of the school of animal magnetism that bears his name. Barberin got rid of the use of the *baquet* and all the other instruments for the transmission or storage of the magnetic fluid, since he argued that the cures arising "from magnetization and somnambulism were the result of will, faith, and an act of God upon the Soul."[30] Barberinist cosmology presents certain Gnostic, Neoplatonic and Hermetic features that explain its affinity with the idea of *anima mundi*. For example, this doctrine holds that all kinds of intelligent beings were created through a series of emanations from God and that man was the last of these, a notion that serves to explain that there are other beings closer to the divine than we are. As in all gnostic mythologies, the body was considered a prison of the soul, which explains why barberinists imagined the human being as being composed of two parts: a real "I" which is a residual spark of the divine, and a "not-I" which is associated with the body and the base instincts.

According to Barberin the magnetic fluid was of two types:

> one corresponding more or less to the fluid of the mesmerists, which accumulates especially round "obstructions" in the body, and another, all-pervasive one, which flows from God, does not accumulate, but may be influenced and directed by human will. It appears to be through this second kind of fluid that magnetic fluid of the first kind is impelled or aided to break down "obstructions," so promoting the cure of disease. Successful magnetizing is thus essentially a matter of an active and properly motivated will, and magnetic passes, wands, etc. have only the function of concentrating the operator's mind. Magnetization at a distance does not depend on any intervening medium. Each real "I" emanates from and hence participates in the Divine and is not truly separate from any other real "I." If an operator meets difficulties he should therefore endeavour by religious exercises to raise himself nearer to the Source from which he and all others have emanated, thus participating in its omnipresence and in its control over the fluid.[31]

The barberinist division of the magnetic fluid into two distinct types slightly recalls the neoplatonic notion of two vehicles of the soul, one sidereal and congenital, that emanates directly from God and is in everyone and everywhere, and another one acquired on the descent by the spheres, which could be manipulated by the magnetists. It is worth mentioning that the Barberinist school became the magnetic faction of the *Bienfaisance*, a Masonic lodge whose members were adept to various forms of ceremonial magic. The encounter between these two movements was essential for the expansion of animal magnetism. "Freemasonry, and its mystical offshoots the Rosicrucians and the Illuminati, flourished widely, and various princes (mainly Protestant ones) were adepts or sympathizers... it seems likely that in Germany, as in France, the masonic network was a channel for the initial spread of mesmerism."[32]

The results of these esoteric associations were not limited to the propagation of the techniques of Mesmer and Puységur, their encounter yielded rather unusual results. It was in the intersection between late-eighteenth and early-nineteenth century mysticism and animal magnetism that a new movement began to grow which would envelope Europe in a frenzy half a century later: spiritism. The magnetic *somnambule* controlled by a human operator is the immediate ancestor of the medium controlled by a spirit. Animal magnetism together with Friedrich Schelling's nature-philosophy and the work of mystics such as Jakob Boehme and Emanuel Swedenborg were some of the formative influences for the new spiritualist movement. Among the pioneers of this current we find Johan Heinrich Jung-Stilling who formulated a system of thought centered on the concept of "ether," which he identified

> both with the magnetic Fluid of the mesmerists, and with the luminiferous ether of physics, (the latter is the vehicle not just for light-waves, but for magnetism, electricity and galvanism). The fact that ether can freely penetrate all material bodies makes it a kind of half-way house between immaterial spirit and matter. It is thus ideally adapted to be the medium through which the rational element in man, his "spirit," can control his body. In fact, Jung-Stilling thinks that man has a duplicate etheric "light-body" interpenetrating the material body and performing just this function.[33]

It is worth noting that the luminiferous ether of eighteenth and nineteenth century physics is yet another transformation of the idea of *anima mundi* which continues to appear time and again under new disguises; a topic that I will discuss in more detail in the intermezzo. In this regard historian Samuel Sambursky argues that pneuma "fulfilled the functions of [the contemporary notion of] physical field by its tensile qualities and by its capacity to give bodies a coherent structure with well-defined physical properties,"[34] a role it continues to fulfill, albeit covertly, to this day.

Here it is important to mention that the ideas of Jung-Stilling and other mystical magnetists brought about an environment in which the contact of the magnetic somnambulists with spiritual beings became more frequent. The mystical faction of magnetism, which unfortunately can only be mentioned in passing, has a curious connection with the magical practices of the Renaissance. In their travels to the afterlife many magnetic sleepwalkers made the same astral journey described by the Hermetic tradition that we discussed in the previous chapter. Stories of ascension talk of contacts with spiritual or angelic beings (the planetary demons of Bruno) and characterize the moon and the planets as the "the probationary homes of departed spirits."[35] Many mystical somnambules, such as the Seeress of Prevorst, claimed to have guardian spirits who guided them in their astral journeys and in their encounters with the inhabitants of the different planets, guides that remind us of the role of the *Madonna Intelligenza* of the Neoplatonic and of Beatrice in the case of Dante.

Regarding the mode of operation of magnetic somnambulism, in a 1785 essay (*Essai sur la théorie du somnambulisme magnetique*) Tardy de Montravel offers an interesting account of the movements of animal magnetism within the human body. In essence, the theory of Montravel reaffirms the existence of a subtle and universal fluid whose obstructions in the human body are the cause of a great variety of diseases. Now, since this "fluid is exceedingly 'elastic' when impelled upon an obstruction it is thrown back from it upon some closely connected part of the body. From there it is thrown back again upon the obstruction, and so on, like a kind of water-hammer... Not surprisingly, convulsions and other kinds of "crisis" may result. When the fluid is reflected back from the obstruction on to the brain, the crisis takes the form of somnambulism."[36] According to Montravel all humans have a "sixth sense" that lacks a specific organ and can be understood as a kind of inner sense of touch that is capable of revealing all kinds of imbalances in the body. When the external senses are inhibited by the magnetic currents coming from the operator, this inner sense springs into action causing the somnambule to be able to perceive the defects in the functioning of his own body. It is interesting to note that, like the *proton organon* of Aristotle and the *hegemonikon* of the Stoics, the inner sense of Montravel takes the perceptions from "the five external senses, and transmits these to the soul or intellectual principle."[37]

The emergence of new theories about electricity in the late eighteenth century gave a new air to both traditional medicine and animal magnetism. Among these are the investigations of Luigi Galvani which suggested that "the action of nerves and muscles was not quasi-hydraulic but electrical in nature,"[38] a matter that offered a new approach to the nature and motion of the magnetic fluid. Galvani's discoveries, later corroborated by Alexander von Humboldt, indicated the existence of an intrinsic animal electricity that was transmitted by the nervous system and created an area of influence or "nervous atmosphere" that extended beyond the anatomical borders of each nerve.[39] In an intellectual environment in which it was argued that organic phenomena would end up being explained in strictly physical and chemical terms, a "force" such as animal magnetism would be revealed, sooner rather than later, as an essentially electrical phenomenon. It is interesting to note that the continuity between the pneumatic apparatus and the nervous system depends to a large extent on the fact that both are constituted for the reception and communication of signals—whether *phantasmata* or electrical impulses—reified to a greater or lesser degree.

The medicine of the time had concluded the existence of two interrelated nervous systems: one "cerebral," which depended on the medula and the brain, and another "ganglionar," composed of chains of ganglia that intertwined at the different plexuses (solar plexus, cardiac plexus...) and were related to different organs. The anatomy of the latter had been discovered throughout the eighteenth century and the habit of the time was to understand it as related to the vegetative and autonomous functions of the organism such as breathing, digestion and heartbeat, so that each major ganglion or plexus was seen as a "small brain" independent from the cerebral nervous system. Under this scheme emerged a series of new explanations about animal magnetism and in particular about the phenomena which characterized magnetic somnambulism.

Carl Alexander Ferdinand Kluge (1782-1844), surgeon and author of an influential book on mesmerism, argued that the therapeutic benefits of animal magnetism originate in the redistribution of the pneuma or vital force in a movement from the cerebral system to the ganglion system, a movement which determines a change in the "control mode" of the organism. As the cerebral system becomes quieter and the ganglion system springs into action the pneuma begins to perform the same functions as during sleep: physical repair and the activation of the imaginative mechanisms. Thus, as the activity of the ganglion system is enhanced, the somnambule begins to experiment

> extraordinary changes [in the] functional relationship within his nervous system. The ganglion system ceases to be a scattered collection of more or less independent "little brains," and develops [...] its own centre [...] This new focus—which is of course the solar plexus—constitutes a centre of perception opposed to that of the brain. Meanwhile, the brain ceases to be the absolute central-point of nervous functioning, and becomes merely one ganglion within an enlarged, but now unified, ganglion-system, or rather, within a whole nervous system now changed into a ganglion system.[40]

The amplified "nervous atmosphere" of this ganglion nervous system could detect "objects in the body's vicinity and conduct information back to the 'communal sense' in the stomach."[41] The fact that this modified nervous system is distributed throughout the ganglion system and simultaneously centered in the solar plexus, not only remembers the structure and movements of the pneumatic apparatus of Galenic-Aristotelian origin, but also offers a possible explanation for phenomena as disconcerting as "stomach vision": in essence, magnetic somnambulism and its "paranormal" effects involve a redistribution of the magnetic fluid, the pneuma, which deactivates the functioning of the outer senses and sharpens the sensibility and activity of the *sensus interior*. However, the historical importance of this conception of the nervous system for our account lies in the following: "the notion that two, largely insulated, kinds of activity may go on simultaneously in the same mind... contains the germs of many subsequent developments in the psychology of the unconscious."[42] The unconscious, that portion of personality that cannot be accessed during wakefulness, came largely from seeing how somnambules could not remember what had happened during the magnetic state once their cerebral nervous system regained control of the body.

The hypnotic tide. *Hysteria, suggestion and hypnosis*

Although they continued to diagnose and prescribe treatments for their own conditions and those of other patients, as we enter the nineteenth century magnetic somnambules become less and less prone to paranormal phenomena such as clairvoyance, astral travel and stomach vision. The magnetic movement moves towards more "rationalistic" positions as it begins to be seriously considered by certain medical professionals and becomes intertwined with phrenology, as was the case of John Elliotson in England and J.S. Grimes in the United States. Meanwhile, spiritism takes on a life of its own and passes from the European continent to the United Kingdom, the West Indies, Brazil and the United States, and then returns to British shores with renewed vigor and ready to take Victorian society by storm.

In the mean time, magnetists such as Abbé José Custodio de Faria (1756-1819), a monk of Indo-Portuguese ancestry who befriended Chateaubriand and the Marquis of Puységur, and Alexandre Bertrand (1795-1831), a prestigious physician from Rennes previously convinced of the theses of Mesmer, begin to critique some of the fundamental ideas of the movement and to offer their own explanations. Abbé Faria is perhaps the first figure to outright deny the existence of the magnetic fluid, to diminish the influence of the magnetizer's will on the somnambulist, and to emphasize what we would now call "suggestion." With these changes in mind Faria invents a new terminology for magnetic phenomena. The magnetic state becomes *lucid dream*, magnetization turns into *concentration*, while magnetizer becomes *concentrator* and the magnetized *épopte*, from the Greek word for "observer." By *concentration*, Gauld tells us, Faria "apparently means a sort of turning of the mind inwards, away from the immediate deliverances of the senses."[43]

Abbé Faria's system is based on the dualism that characterizes most of our tradition's religious expressions:

> Every human being has a body and a soul, intimately bonded.
> In its pure state, the soul possesses intuitive knowledge of

eternal verities, can transcend space and time, etc. But when it is bound up with the human organism these faculties are suppressed, and the everyday consciousness knows nothing of them. At the same time the soul assumes control of the "necessary activity" of the body (heartbeat, breathing, digestion, etc.) Again, the everyday consciousness is unaware of the soul's exercise of this function.[44]

This system, it should be noted, still has very much in common with the medical systems of the premodern world (the soul as an agent of the intellect and bodily functions) and even resorts to the notion of blood as the link between body and soul and the vehicle of the latter within the body, an idea we already saw in Ficino. For Faria the *époptes* or somnambules have thinner blood than most people, a trait that allows the soul to act more freely upon the body or even to fly away from it. However, the Abbé's system introduces something completely new to the discussion of mesmerism: an inkling on the role of the unconscious in magnetic somnambulism.

For Faria, the influence of the *concentrateur* in the *épopte* arises from the mutual trust between the two. The condition of the *épopte* is determined by his suggestibility, which is determined by how liquid his blood is. This circumstance allows for the verbal orders of the *concentrateur*—Faria does not manipulate the magnetic fluid with the hands because he does not believe that it exists— to establish an *intimate conviction* inside the subject. Hence, "once the *concentrateur* has put his subject into a sufficiently abstracted state, shutting out all countervailing influences, his commands or statements, however ridiculous, may profoundly affect his subject's mind, sense, and 'necessary activities'"[45] of the soul. But according to Faria, the *épopte* does not realize that everything that happens during the lucid dream is actually a product of the faculties of his own soul for, as long as it is "embodied, its inner workings remain hidden from him."[46] Faria was the first to give an active role to the the unconscious part of the psyche of the magnetic somnambule, and is therefore considered by many as the precursor of hypnosis.

The denial of the existence of the magnetic fluid reappears in the work of James Braid (1795-1860), a Scottish surgeon at the University of Edinburgh and one of the most important figures in the early history of hypnosis. Through his clinical experience Braid found that it was possible to achieve the state of magnetic somnambulism through the purely physical means that we still associate with hypnosis until today. The act of fixing one's eyesight on a small shiny object placed some ten inches from the face, accompanied by certain verbal indications, usually led to an effort on the subject's attention, which in many cases produced the state described by the magnetists. For Braid this state, far from being the result of the influence of an ethereal fluid, was a product of a change in the circulatory patterns of the brain and spinal cord; an entirely physiological matter. Many conditions, such as pain caused by trauma, muscle spasms, rheumatic disorders and some forms of epilepsy could be treated with great effectiveness by the method devised by Braid. The explanation was that the "quickening" of circulation could be beneficial by "subjecting the brain and spinal cord, and whole ganglion system, to a high rate of excitement,"[47] at which point the circulation could be redirected to the affected limb or organ to release it from the cataleptic state in which it had sunk and have it "wake up."

Even though he did not believe in the existence of the magnetic fluid, Braid was willing to make passes over the body of his patients since he had discovered that these "produce their effects from what is essentially the same cause as that which induces hypnotic phenomena."[48] The trick was to fix an idea in the patient's expectant mind with such force that it could temporarily excite, depress or suspend the function of the sense organs. Upon reaching such a state of concentration the minds of many subjects were "thrown out of gear" and the higher faculties stepped down and gave place to imagination,

> easy credulity, and docility or passive obedience; so that, even whilst appearing wide awake... they become susceptible of being influenced and controlled entirely by the suggestions of others upon whom their attention is fixed... and they consider themselves *irresistibly or involuntarily fixed, or spell-bound, or impelled to perform whatever may be said or signified by the other party upon whom their attention has become involuntarily and vividly rivetted...* [49]

According to Braid, hypnosis would be a state in which the mind is susceptible of being occupied with a single idea or thought that displaces the rest, a notion that we will find again when we speak of mass psychology. And while the erotic factor may seem to have disappeared almost entirely from early hypnotism, it is important to note that such "monolithic fixation" with an idea, or its agent, is essentially the basic mechanism of emotional infatuation, the lover's rapture for his or her beloved, a phenomenon we discussed in the last chapter when we talked about the syndrome of *amor hereos*, in which the object of love takes possession of the soul of the subject dispossessing it. The erotic nature of hypnosis, now intertwined with the hysterical symptoms we discussed in the previous chapter, will reappear surreptitiously in the practice of Jean-Martin Charcot (1825-1893), the father of modern neurology and one of the most respected physicians of his time.

Charcot is the first to openly associate the symptoms of hysteria and epilepsy with some of the phenomena of magnetic somnambulism, which by them was beginning to be called "hypnotic state". Here it is important to mention that after the publication of Paul Briquet's *Traité De_La_Hystérie* (1796-1881) hysteria had ceased to be understood as a condition of exclusively sexual origin and began to be considered as a "neurosis of the part of the brain destined to receive the affective impressions and the sensations."[50] As medical chief of the Salpêtrière, an immense seventeenth-century gunpowder (*salpêtre*) factory converted into a women's hospital, Charcot took over a pavilion where a multitude of epileptic and hysterical patients were treated, an experience that led him to formulate a peculiar theory on the common origin of both conditions. Charcot, who had been instructed in the anatomoclinical school of medicine—known for deriving its conclusions from the comparison of the symptoms of a disease with their respective anatomical lesions—believed that hysteria was a neurological problem and, as such, that it was based on a hereditary predisposition. For Charcot a large number of neurological diseases were inherited and belonged to the then-called "neuropathic family."[51]

It was the observation of the hysterical symptoms of his patients that led Charcott to associate this condition with magnetic somnambulism. In fact, among his patients it was not strange to find that a hysterical attack co-mingled with a hypnotic "attack." Since the hysterical patients of the Salpêtrière shared their ward with the epileptics, the former had become familiar with the attacks of the latter, hence "epileptoid attacks were unusually prominent in the symptomatology."[52] Charcot's hysterical-epileptic attack, also called the *grande hystérie*, was divided into four phases: 1. *epileptoid phase*, which was "a kind of epileptic crisis but more stylized"[53]; 2. *phase of the great movements of the gymnastic type* or "clownism," which began with a tetanic *arc de cercle* in which the subject supports the head and the feet in the ground while arching the back and the legs; 3. *phase de les attitudes passionelles* or *poses plastiques*, in which the subject adopts the typical postures of fear, laughter, ecstasy, pleasure, and other emotions; and the *terminal phase* which was characterized by disorientation and delirium. Although the idea of hysteria as exclusively sexual in origin had already begun to be revalued, it is interesting to note that these attacks could be provoked, or arrested, by "applying pressure on certain hypersensitive points called hysterogens. In women, the region of the ovaries, and in men, that of the testes and the spermatic cord."[54]

Charcot, who had developed an interest in hypnosis since the late eighteen-seventies, discovered that some of his hysterical patients readily sank into the somnambulist state described by Braid and other researchers. Intrigued with the subject he experimented with his patients until he arrived at a typology of the hypnotic state of hysterical origin divided into three phases: 1. *Catalepsy*, which was characterized by "open eyes, mutism, and the immobility of a statue. The body retains the position we give it and the face adopts the corresponding expression. Conversely, if we electrically stimulate a muscle of the face to make it express joy or anger, the body adopts the corresponding posture."[55] For Charcot this phase was a confirmation of the ideas of Julien Offray de la Mettrie, an eighteenth-century philosopher who developed the Cartesian notion of the human as an automaton. 2. *Lethargy*, in which the subject's closed her eyes and fell into a deep sleep. "The body relaxes but simultaneously manifests a 'neuromuscular hyper-excitability': any pressure on a muscle or a nerve causes a corresponding contracture."[56] This "neuromuscular hyper-excitability" is reminiscent of Mesmer's concept of *irritability*, whose absence determined the appearance of blockages in the movement of the magnetic fluid. We can speculate that during this phase of lethargy in which the conscious defenses of the patient disappear, the vegetative nervous system responds in a *natural* way to the doctor's stimuli. After these first two phases, if the subject's crowns were rubbed, some of them would enter a state similar to magnetic somnabulism, from which they awoke with no recollection. During this state, like Puységur's somnambules, subjects were able to "speak intelligently and respond to the hypnotist's verbal or gestural suggestions." Charcot was going down the same path Mesmer had walked a century ago. "But where Mesmer provoked "crises" and disorderly convulsions, Charcot and his assistants achieved a systematic and orderly experimental object that could be repeated at will."[57] In analogy to his *grande hystérie*, Charcot gave this state the name of *grande hypnotisme*.

Given their apparent shared etiology, for Charcot hypnosis rather than Mesmer or Puységur's therapeutic technique became a pathological condition which hysterics were especially prone to. Taking advantage of the fact that with the popularization of railways there was talk of "episodes of paralysis and other symptoms in victims of train accidents," Charcot began to work in a theory in which hysteria was the result of a trauma, such as a mechanical blow that causes tiny lesions in the spinal cord (railway spine). Thus, an accident that produced such an injury would awaken "the latent hysterical background, which would manifest as an attack or a hypnotic state."[58] According to Charcot's theory, physical trauma does not provoke hysteria, it reveals it in those who have a hereditary predisposition to this condition. From this point of view the key to the relationship between hysteria and hypnosis was that physical trauma could lead certain predisposed persons to

> a state of "obnubilation" or "dissociation of the mental unit, of the self," identical to the somnambulist state. The sensation or "traumatic suggestion" takes advantage of the situation to embed itself in the psyche as a *foreign body* or a *fixed idea* and is carried out as an automatism that reflects the "unconscious or subconscious cerebration."[59]

Thus, for Charcot hysterics were individuals who didn't need a hypnotist to be hypnotized, "somnambules whose consciousness escapes the memory and the conscious self."[60] The reason why a paralysis can be suppressed during hypnosis, as Braid and Charcot had demonstrated, is that during this state it is possible to access the unconscious, where the idea or suggestion that produced it in the first place can be eliminated. "Being hysterical means being hypnotizable, easily suggestible. And the other way around."[61] Unfortunately Charcot's theory was discredited when it became apparent that the type of *epileptiform hysteria* on which he had based his work on hypnosis was infrequent outside the unique environment of the Salpêtrière. Charcot's medical demonstrations were confined to a dozen subjects, all of whom, according to Jane Avril—a patient at the Salpêtrière from from 1882 to 1884 for *choreomania* or Saint Vitus dance— had been "trained," not by explicit instructions, but by their interaction with epileptic patients and by the desire to please their physicians. Nevertheless, this matter should not devalue Charcot's contributions to the history of psychology since his theory of hysterical hypnosis paved the way to the idea of a portion of the mind that functions automatically and without conscious control of the individual that would mature in the work of Freud and Jung.

Even if Charcot's theory of an intrinsic relationship between hysteria and hypnosis was not entirely correct in the terms in which it was formulated, it is important to note that the relationship between the seizures and paralysis of *epileptiform hysteria* and somnambulism can be described coherently in pneumatic or magnetic terms, that is, they could be due to the uncontrolled movement of pneuma inside the organism, as it happened during the "healing crises" described by Mesmer and his school.

In this regard, it is interesting to mention the experience of Jane Avril, who learned how to "channel" her condition in the *bals des folles* (crazy dances) that were organized every year in the Salpêtrière and who later became one of the stars of the Moulin Rouge nicknamed *la Mélinite*, for the commercial name of picric acid, a highly explosive chemical compound. In his memoirs Avril describes "the atmosphere of collective emulation that prevailed in the Salpêtrière, the rivalries between patients to attract the attention... the fights that exploded just before Charcot visited the ward..."[62] The protagonists of these hysterical attacks were girls whose illness, Avril says, consisted

> especially in pretending it [...] It was rather comical to me to see how proud and happy they were to be chosen by the "master"! [...] I was always surprised to see such eminent men duped like this, when I, with my dim intelligence, immediately guessed which of these women were putting on a show.[63]

Even if it is quite possible that some of the patients of the Salpêtrière were deceiving their doctors to get their attention—a basic psychological need—both Avril's choreomania and her ecstatic dance routines at the Moulin Rouge are reminiscent of another category of hysterical manifestation: the so-called *mass psychogenic illness* or collective hysteria. It is not absurd to think that in a repressive and unhealthy environment such as a psychiatric ward, with a population made up of hysterical and epileptic patients, these women would be easily "infected" with the symptoms of others; the stylized movements of the first phase of an attack of epileptoid hysteria might as well have their origin in this circumstance: repressed eros, histrionic and out of control pneuma.

Apart from offering an alternative origin to Charcot's theory, this hypothesis offers us a point of departure from the individual to the collective psyche. However, before approaching this subject I should make a brief summary of the school of hypnosis rival to that of the Salpêtrière: the school of Nancy, founded on the work of physician Ambroise-Auguste Liébeault (1823-1904), whose ideas regarding suggestion will give us a better understanding of the bonds that join hypnosis with Freudian psychology.

Liébeault, the son of a peasant family of the Lorraine whose father had earmarked for priesthood, shied away from the profession chosen for him and set out for Strasbourg where, after graduating from the local university, decided to become a rural doctor. A man of extraordinary simplicity and dedication, he spent much of his life tending to the people of his village while developing his own therapeutic method based on different varieties of animal magnetism. The importance of Liébeault for the history of hypnotherapy is invaluable and in fact, several of the techniques that eventually became clichés ("you will go to sleep," "your eyelids are heavy, you are sleepy, very sleepy") are his. It is curious to think that in all probability this extraordinary doctor would have spent his last twenty years of life in relative obscurity had it not been for a fortuitous encounter that we will discuss in a moment.

The idea that suggestion is the central element of hypnosis has its starting point in the work of Liébeault, who understood it as "the influence of the moral body upon the physical body."[64] However, for the purposes of this study, it is vital to explain the understanding of hypnotic operations that Liébeault reached through his medical practice. Rather than resorting to a magnetic fluid, this physician devised the concept of *attention*, understood as a kind of "nervous force" which proceeds from the brain

> and diverges into two broad currents. One of these flows to the cerebro-spinal division of the nervous system, and then yields conscious awareness of sense-impressions, the laying down of

memories, etc. The other flows into the nutritive (autonomic) branch of the nervous system, and is not unusually accompanied by consciousness [...] The flow of attention can be influenced by a stimulus or by a thought or by emotional disturbance, in such a way that it will "move upon a faculty of the brain or one of the sense organs" at the expense of others, or home in upon the nutritive functions.[65]

Liébeault's idea was that depending on the intensity of attention any nerve function could be stimulated or depressed. Thus, while too much attention in certain parts of the nervous system could lead to epilepsy, neuralgia or obsessive ideas, a deficit would result in paralysis and other "nervous debilities." This "nervous force" could be manipulated and redirected by the hypnotist through timely suggestions appropriate to the patient's condition. According to Liébeault, the key to hypnosis was to concentrate the subject's attention on the idea of sleep and then into a "spell-bound" state, or "*charme,*" in his own jargon. "Whereas in normal sleep we withdraw all our attention from the outside world, in this case we fix it upon the hypnotist. It is the phenomenon of *rapport* so well know those who practice animal magnetism. The person is fast asleep, but remains awake with regards to the hypnotist, who can direct attention (the "nervous force") to one or another organic function as he pleases..."[66] The hypnotist completely occupies the attention of the hypnotized.

How was it that this modest rural doctor became the father of hypnotherapy? The story is as follows: in 1881 the Danish hypnotist Carl Hansen passed through Strasbourg and while he was in the region he decided to visit Nancy, where Liébeault had resided for some years. The two worked on a series of hypnotic experiments with ill children, in which apparently thirty six out of forty two kids improved after the experience.[67] By then Hansen was the most popular theater hypnotist in Europe and the news of his collaboration with Liébeault reached Hyppolyte Bernheim (1840-1919), a professor of internal medicine at the University of Nancy who, although sceptic about the supposed effectivity of hypnotic treatment, decided to pay Liébeault a visit.

Bernheim became quickly convinced and used Liébeault's system as the basis for a theory of hypnosis that openly opposed that of the Salpêtrière school. To begin with, he argued that one didn't need to be hysteric to be hypnotized, everyone could be hypnotized to a greater of lesser degree because we are all potentially suggestible; the difference is one of degree not of essence, the key lied in the suggestibility or "credulity" of each individual. In the same manner that not everyone can be bound by the same magical bond, not every suggestion works on everybody. What works, Giordano Bruno would remind us, "is a knowledge proportional to the genre." For Bernheim suggestibility is the primary "inclination of the brain to transform ideas into acts, movements into sensations." Now, if hypnosis is not a pathological condition that only afflicts hysterics, why not use it as a form of therapy to treat pain, paralyses or fixed ideas? Bernheim's program was based on

> seeking the intervention of the spirit to heal the body, such is the role of suggestion applied to therapeutics, such is the goal of psychotherapeutics.[68]

It is worth mentioning that Bernheim's ideas, compiled in *De la suggestion dans l'état hypnotique et dans l'état de veille*, produced a miniature war with the Salpêtrière in which, in the long run, the therapeutic approach of the Nancy school was determinant for its victory. Bernheim showed that it is possible to produce the symptoms of Charcot's *grande hystérie* in non-hysterical individuals and that it is also possible to cause very different symptoms to those observed in the Salpêtrière in clearly hysterical subjects. To demystify that the hypnotic state only occurred in hysterical or "weak-nerved" women, the subjects of Bernheim's study were mostly men. Following Liébeault, Bernheim recognized six degrees of hypnosis: 1. drowsiness; 2. *charme*; 3. and 4. increased drowsiness and loss of relationship with the outside world, appearance of automatic movements that can be imposed or suggested; 5. and 6. light and deep somnambulism of which one awakens with amnesia. It is interesting to note that although not all subjects can reach the state of deep somnambulism, the proportion that do achieve it, approximately one in twenty, "is consistent with modern figures for the incidence of 'deep trance' in hypnotic subjects."[69]

But not everything were disagreements between Nancy and Paris and both schools saw eye to eye on an essential matter. Both Bernheim and Charcot argued that hypnosis brings most individuals back to an "automatic-reflexive-unconscious 'cerebration' (or mental process) that is normally inhibited by higher functions." [70] Indeed, the core of psychotherapeutic hypnosis—the intervention of the spirit to heal the body—was based on the fact that during this state the therapist is able to penetrate the unconscious, to go into the psyche of the patient and implant suggestions in order to help him or her overcome a physical or emotional condition. It was the focus on the unconscious, along with its therapeutic potential, which earned Liébeault and Bernheim a large number of adherents in the German countries.

Among the disciples of the school of Nancy, Josef Breuer, an Austrian doctor and mentor of Sigmund Freud, made some of the most significant contributions to the new discipline. Breuer devised the so-called "cathartic method" in which "while under hypnosis the patient is taken to the psychic precedents of his problem and forced to recognize in what circumstances it took place."[71] According to Breuer, talking with the patient generates a *hypnoid state*, such as an absence or a daydream, in which the psychic mechanism that gave rise to a condition or illness can be emulated via suggestion. Other researchers experiment with this method. Belgian philosopher and hypnotist Joseph Delboeuf (1831-1896) hypnotized a woman obsessed with the vision of her dead son which tormented her day and night and "makes her return to the traumatic scene and verbally 'erases' the memory.

> As soon as I speak, the vision pales, it fades away, disappears... I even challenge her to see it, I make dramatic description of the scene. It's over, there's no bloody phantasm that appears out of nowhere, there are no more screams; the sick person can smile ... From now on it will be known how the magnetizer heals. He places the subject in the state in which the illness had manifested and fights it, now reborn, with words.[72]

In this fragment we can see how the type of inner work that characterized the Brunian magician has crossed over to the sphere of psychology. In essence, this technique allows the manipulation of the patient's *phantasmata*, images that once embedded in the soul—that is, in the pneuma—can torment an individual to the point of threatening his mental and emotional integrity. These phantasms can be eradicated (or "erased," "attenuated" or "blurred" in the literature of the time) by means of suggestions and new phantasms put in their place. The potential of these operations, as the pioneers of advertising and public relations understood very well is, for good or ill, immense. The focus and methods of these modern forms of magic have changed but their operative essence is the same: to penetrate the psyche of an individual or a multitude one must learn to manipulate the images that make up its soul, and the eighteenth and nineteenth centuries offered our tradition the necessary knowledge to make the human more vulnerable than ever to this type of operation.

But the resemblance between magnetism and hypnosis with magic is not limited to merely functional aspects. Seen as a transformation of the "system of magic" that gave rise to Renaissance magic animal magnetism and hypnotherapy share a number of features with erotic magic. There is, for starters, the role of the will and the desire of the operator (*croyez* and *veuillez*), which figures prominently in the Marquis of Puységur's method, as well as the erotic *rapport* between magnetizer and somnambule. The idea of the *anima mundi* that makes all magical operations possible becomes a universal and ubiquitous magnetic fluid, while the *proton organon* is reformulated as a sixth sense or *sensus interior*, available during the magnetic state. On the other hand, what in Bruno is faith in its active and passive facets, in hypnotists like Liébeault, Bernheim and Breuer, merges into an exclusively active idea on the part of the operator: suggestion. This change of emphasis is evident in how a magnetic somnambulist still maintained a two-way relation with his magnetizer, a circumstance that allowed the subject to develop creative abilities impossible during the waking state. This bidirectional relationship—the reciprocity between the operator and the somnambule and between active and passive faith—has completely disappeared in hypnotism. The hypnotized is a simple automaton that "participates" in the operation only marginally and unconsciously.

The age of the masses had begun.

---

[1] In fact, economist John Maynard Keynes was quite surprised when he had the chance to read Newton's manuscripts before they were auctioned by Sotheby's in 1936 and discovered that most of his writings were not about physics and mathematics but about alchemy and occultism. The image of the father of modern physics had been thoroughly cleansed to make it more palatable to our modern sensibility. "Newton was not the first of the age of reason," wrote Keynes, "he was the last of the magicians... he looked on to the whole of the universe and all that is in it *as a riddle*, as a secret which could be read by applying pure thought to certain evidence, certain mystic clues which God had laid about the world to allow a sort of philosopher's treasure hunt to the esoteric brotherhood. He believed that this clues were to be found partly in the evidence of the heavens and in the constitution of elements (and this is what gives the false suggestion of his

being an experimental natural philosopher), but also partly in certain papers and traditions handed down by the brethren in an unbroken chain back to the original cryptic revelation in Babylonia. He regarded the universe as a cryptogram set by the Almighty." (Quoted by Morris Berman in *The Reenchantment of the World*, 118)

[2] Patrick Harpur, *The Philosopher's Secret Fire* (Australia: Blue Angel Gallery, 2002), 206.

[3] Morris Berman, *The Reenchantment of the World* (Ithaca: Cornell University Press, 1981), 124.

[4] Even by mid-eighteenth century Newton's theory of universal gravitation still raised criticisms such as those of Georg Matthias Bose, dean of the University of Wittenberg: "shall action at a distance be granted? will you then prevent a star from acting as a talisman at a distance? Rejoice Melanchthon the horoscope returns." (Quoted by Leon Marvell in *Transfigured Light: The Imaginal Realm and the Hermetic Foundations of Science*, 116.) Voltaire attributed the skepticism of many scientists and philosophers in the continent to a linguistic use: Newton had used the term *attraction*, a word with obvious erotic (and, therefore, hermetic) connotations to refer to the action of gravity. "If Newton had not used the word attraction, everyone in the [the french] Academy would have opened his eyes to the light; but unfortunately he used in London a word to which an idea of ridicule was attached in Paris." (Mandelbrot, *Fractal Geometry of Nature*, 5.)

[5] Quoted by Berman in *The Reenchantment of the World*, 43.

[6] Berman, *The Reenchantment of the World*, 124.

[7] Harpur, *The Philosopher's Secret Fire,* 207.

[8] Franz Anton Mesmer, Quoted by Nevill Drury en *Wisdom Seekers: The Rise of the New Spirituality* (Winchester: O Books, 2011), 16.

[9] Jane Goodall, *Stage Presence* (New York: Routhledge, 2008), 89.

[10] Alan Gauld, *A History of Hypnotism* (Cambridge University Press, 1992), 2.

[11] Drury, *Wisdom Seekers*, 17.

[12] Gauld, *A History of Hypnotism*, 3.

[13] Gauld, *A History of Hypnotism*, 3.

[14] Gauld, *A History of Hypnotism*, 3.

[15] Gauld, *A History of Hypnotism*, 4.

[16] Gauld, *A History of Hypnotism*, 5.

[17] Gauld, *A History of Hypnotism*, 5.

[18] Stefan Zweig, *Mental Healers: Mesmer, Eddy and Freud* (New York: Frederick Ungar Publishing Co., 1962), 56-57.

[19] Gauld, *A History of Hypnotism*, 13.

[20] Gauld, *A History of Hypnotism*, 41.

[21] Puységur, quoted by Gauld in *A History of Hypnotism*, 41.

[22] Gauld, *A History of Hypnotism*, 41.

[23] Gauld, *A History of Hypnotism*, 45.

[24] Gauld, *A History of Hypnotism*, 48.
[25] Gauld, *A History of Hypnotism*, 102.
[26] Gauld, *A History of Hypnotism*, 61.
[27] Gauld, *A History of Hypnotism*, 47. Italics are mine.
[28] Gauld, *A History of Hypnotism*, 48.
[29] Martinism is a form of mystical Christianism that emerged in France in the wake of the teachings of the mysterious theurgist Martinez de Pasqually. It was based on a dualistic mythology which emphasized on the fall of man and the possibility of flowing back to God.
[30] Nicholas Goodrick-Clarke, *The Western Esoteric Traditions: A Historical Introduction* (New York: Oxford University Press, 2008), 180
[31] Gauld, *A History of Hypnotism*, 66.
[32] Gauld, *A History of Hypnotism*, 75.
[33] Gauld, *A History of Hypnotism*, 145
[34] Sambursky, *The Physical World of Late Antiquity*, 3. Quoted by Leon Marvell in *The Physics of Transfigured Light*, 182.
[35] Gauld, *A History of Hypnotism*, 150.
[36] Gauld, *A History of Hypnotism*, 69.
[37] Gauld, *A History of Hypnotism*, 69.
[38] Gauld, *A History of Hypnotism*, 81.
[39] In scientific terms, says Andrea Wulf in *The Invention of Nature*, "it was the Italian physicist Alessandro Volta who proved Humboldt and Galvani wrong, showing that animal nerves were not charged with electricity. The convulsions that Humboldt had produced in animals were in fact triggered by the contact of metals — an idea that led Volta to invent the first battery in 1800." (Wulf, *The Invention of Nature*, 35). Despite this change in emphasis from the pre-scientific to the scientific, the intersection between magnetism and the nascent spiritist movement (or mystical magnetism) gave rise to some ideas that resemble those of the magic of empedoclean origin. For example, the idea of the "nervous atmosphere" becomes, in the work of Heinrich Werner, magnetist, doctor of philosophy and pastor in Württemberg, a *nervengeist* or "nervous spirit" that mediates between the body and soul. Being of psycho-physical nature, this spirit (*geist*) adheres to the soul and constitutes itself as a subtle body that surrounds it, a notion that recalls the Aristotelian idea of the pneuma as an envelope of the soul that I mentioned in the previous chapter and which leads to the "etheric body" so present in New Age mysticism and literature.
[40] Gauld, *A History of Hypnotism*, 106.
[41] Gauld, *A History of Hypnotism*, 155.
[42] Gauld, *A History of Hypnotism*, 158.
[43] Gauld, *A History of Hypnotism*, 276.
[44] Gauld, *A History of Hypnotism*, 276.
[45] Gauld, *A History of Hypnotism*, 277.

⁴⁶ Gauld, *A History of Hypnotism*, 277.
⁴⁷ Gauld, *A History of Hypnotism*, 283.
⁴⁸ Gauld, *A History of Hypnotism*, 284.
⁴⁹ Gauld, *A History of Hypnotism*, 285.
⁵⁰ Quoted by Gauld in *A History of Hypnotism*, 308.
⁵¹ Mikkel Borch-Jacobsen, *Sigmund Freud, Hipnotizador*, which appears in *Sigmund Freud, la hipnosis, textos (1886-1893)* (Bogotá: Arial, 2017), 48. Author's translation.
⁵² Gauld, *A History of Hypnotism*, 308.
⁵³ Borch-Jacobsen, *Sigmund Freud, Hipnotizador*, 49.
⁵⁴ Borch-Jacobsen, *Sigmund Freud, Hipnotizador*, 50.
⁵⁵ Borch-Jacobsen, *Sigmund Freud, Hipnotizador*, 51-52.
⁵⁶ Borch-Jacobsen, *Sigmund Freud, Hipnotizador*, 52.
⁵⁷ Borch-Jacobsen, *Sigmund Freud, Hipnotizador*, 51.
⁵⁸ Borch-Jacobsen, *Sigmund Freud, Hipnotizador*, 61.
⁵⁹ Borch-Jacobsen, *Sigmund Freud, Hipnotizador*, 64.
⁶⁰ Borch-Jacobsen, *Sigmund Freud, Hipnotizador*, 64.
⁶¹ Borch-Jacobsen, Sigmund Freud, Hipnotizador, 64.
⁶² Borch-Jacobsen, *Sigmund Freud, Hipnotizador*, 54.
⁶³ Borch-Jacobsen, *Sigmund Freud, Hipnotizador*, 55.
⁶⁴ Borch-Jacobsen, *Sigmund Freud, Hipnotizador*, 107.
⁶⁵ Gauld, *A History of Hypnotism*, 322.
⁶⁶ Borch-Jacobsen, *Sigmund Freud, Hipnotizador*, 107.
⁶⁷ Borch-Jacobsen, *Sigmund Freud, Hipnotizador*, 110.
⁶⁸ Quoted by Borch-Jacobsen, *Sigmund Freud, Hipnotizador*, 111.
⁶⁹ Gauld, *A History of Hypnotism*, 118.
⁷⁰ Borch-Jacobsen, *Sigmund Freud, Hipnotizador*, 111.
⁷¹ Quoted by Borch-Jacobsen in *Sigmund Freud, Hipnotizador*, 123.
⁷² Borch-Jacobsen, *Sigmund Freud, Hipnotizador*, 124.

3. Eros in the Era of the Multitudes

Le Bon, Trotter, Freud and the libido of the masses

> At the first shrill notes of the pipe,
> I heard a sound as of scraping tripe,
> And putting apples, wondrous ripe,
> Into a cider-press's gripe,—
> And a moving away of pickle-tub-boards,
> And a leaving ajar of conserve-cupboards,
> And a drawing the corks of train-oil-flasks,
> And a breaking the hoops of butter-casks;
> And it seemed as if a voice
> (Sweeter far than by harp or by psaltery
> Is breathed) called out, O rats, rejoice!
> The world is grown to one vast drysaltery!
> So munch on, crunch on, take your nuncheon,
> Breakfast, supper, dinner, luncheon!
> **Robert Browning, *The Pied Piper of Hamelin***

Saint Vitus, possessed nuns and dancing children

Although it can be said that the "society of the masses" begins on July 14, 1789 with the fall of the Old Regime, the possibility of an anonymous human mass had existed *in potentia* since the emergence of the first urban centers in Mesopotamia, the Indus Valley and Egypt during the fourth and third millennium BC.[1] However, while pharaohs, emperors and kings saw in their masses of subjects a simple requirement of the natural order that justified their power, the modern era reverses this circumstance and grants political legitimacy to the multitudes. But before the role of the masses was recognized as fundamental for the proper functioning of society, other forms of congregation, unconscious and involuntary, occasionally seized large portions of the population. Among these manifestations is the so-called *mass psychogenic illness* or collective hysteria, which will allow us to appreciate the confluence of eros, hysteria and hypnosis with the emergence of modern masses. It should be clarified that although the relationship between hysteria and hypnosis is not causal, as Charcot asserted, a historical survey seems to suggest that there is a relationship between mass behavior, the susceptibility that characterizes magnetic somnambulism and hypnosis, and certain "collective hysteroid" states.

For the purposes of this study one of the most significant forms of collective hysteria is *choreomania* or St. Vitus dance, a condition I briefly discussed in the last chapter in relation to Jane Avril, a patient of Charcot's who found her vocation at the *bals des folles* which were organized annually in the Salpêtrière. The story of the saint who gave his name to this condition speaks for itself: Vitus was a Sicilian boy of the fourth century A.D. who was martyred during the Diocletianic persecution, the last and perhaps the bloodiest of the Roman persecutions of Christians. Legend has it that Vitus, the son of a Sicilian senator, was converted to Christianity by his nurse Crescencia and his tutor Modestus and soon began to work miracles. His fame grew so much that it reached the ears of the Emperor Diocletian, whose son suffered from an uncontrollable epilepsy since he was a child. Vitus, who was only seven at the time (twelve in other versions of the legend), healed the Emperor's son, but then refused to make an offering to the gods and it became evident that he, his nurse and his tutor were all Christians. By refusing to recant his faith Vitus was sentenced to die scalded in boiling oil. But just as the young man should have burned in the boiling cauldron, he began to dance in an uncontrolled fashion, infecting Diocletian and his court. In the following centuries Vitus began to be regarded as the patron of actors, comedians, dancers and epileptics, a circumstance that explains why many of the spontaneous processions and dances that happened during the Middle Ages ended in churches consecrated in his name. The figure of Saint Vitus articulates the ideas of healing, dance and collective hysteria in a particularly coherent way which will allow us to associate this last phenomenon both with the movements of the pneuma in the human body and with the healing techniques of animal magnetism.

Among the multitude of outbreaks of choreomania that took place in Europe between the seventh and seventeenth centuries one of the best documented is the "flare-up" of June 1374 in which, suddenly "in dozens of medieval towns scattered along the valley of the River Rhine hundreds of people were seized by an agonising compulsion to dance."[2] The feet of the dancers bled profusely and every single one of them was in a state of trance. In a matter of weeks the mania had spread to the neighboring regions of northeastern France and the Netherlands and it took months for it to disappear completely. A century and a half later, in July 1518, Strasbourg was affected by an outbreak of choreomania when a woman named Troffea began to dance spontaneously in the street infecting thirty four people in the first week, and then four hundred within the first month. A report of the time estimates that this "dancing plague" killed approximately fifteen people daily, some of whom succumbed to heart attacks, strokes or simple exhaustion. From the theoretical framework that I have presented in this study, it is possible to argue that choreomania is a phenomenon in which, given certain psychological pressures, the pneumatic currents stop circulating in their habitual patterns and go out of control producing a state of trance with involuntary and convulsive movements that results in a frenetic form of dance. The pneumatic origin of this type of movement is perfectly possible and the erotic character of dance in general need not be highlighted. The healing crises described by Mesmer and the histrionic phase of Charcot's *grande hystérie* come to mind.

It is important to mention that the epidemics of 1374 and 1518, like most registered cases of choreomania, have something in common: the presence of extreme circumstances that subjected their respective populations to unusual levels of stress and anxiety. In the case of the Rhine Valley, the outbreaks of choreomania overlap with the most affected areas of one the worst floods of the fourteenth century which took place in the first months of the same year. Historian of medicine John Waller comments that the chronicles of the time talk of "the waters of the Rhine rising 34 feet, of flood waters pouring over town walls, of homes and market places submerged, and of decomposing horses bobbing along watery streets."[3] In the decade prior to 1518 the region of Strasbourg was hit by a terrible famine and a succession of exceptionally cold winters that spread all sorts of suffering and illness among the population. "Bread prices reached their highest levels for a generation, thousands of starving farmers and vine growers arrived at the city gates, and old killers like leprosy and the plague were joined by a terrifying new affliction named syphilis."[4] These outbreaks of St. Vitus Dance could be understood as a form of purification, a collective catharsis after a particularly traumatic event for a population. The mechanism would function as follows: a person's pneumatic currents adopts a certain configuration that results in dance-like movements in which the sexual energy begins to flow freely among the population infecting the most susceptible individuals. The mechanism would be similar to that of the Saturnalias and other festivities of the ancient world that still survive in the form of carnivals.

Now, if from a psychological point of view stress is one of the main conditions for the onset of a dance epidemic, communities beset by fear and depression are especially prone to this type of hysteria. Thus, it is not surprising to find that "nuns were disproportionately affected"[5] by ailments of this type. In this regard it is important to mention that at the beginning of the fifteenth century a movement of evangelical reform emerged which called for the recovery of the strictest customs that characterized convents in previous centuries. Some of these cloisters— where nuns were usually turned in against their will or arrived at by circumstances beyond their control— imposed an extremely austere and inflexible regime in which it was only permitted to eat soft food, undergo long fasts and meditate, for hours on end, about the temptations of the devil and the flames of hell. The result: dozens of attacks of collective hysteria in convents across the european continent. One of the most famous cases occurred in 1491 in the Spanish Netherlands, when the nuns of a cloister were possessed by demonic spirits who made them "race around like dogs, jump out of trees in imitation of birds or miaow and claw their way up tree trunks in the manner of cats."[6] In other cases the nuns sank into "frantic deliriums during which they foamed, screamed and convulsed, sexually propositioned exorcists and priests, and confessed to having carnal relations with devils or Christ."[7]

In 1627 Jeanne des Agnes, the mother superior of the convent of Loudun in the region of New Aquitaine, fell in love with a priest of the locality named Grandier. "'When I did not see him', she later confessed, 'I burned with desire for him.' In consequence, Jeanne felt overwhelming worthlessness and guilt. After weeks of painful penance and introspection, she fell into a dissociative state during which she repeatedly accused Grandier of plotting with Satan to make her lust after him."[8] Soon more and more nuns fell prey to a collective delirium, all pointing to the unfortunate priest as the cause of their ills. After an investigation by the Inquisition Father Grandier was condemned to the stake. Apart from revealing the openly erotic character of hysteria, this example allows us to appreciate how "a deep, guilty longing for human intimacy could trigger collective breakdowns. This is in part why, during their possession attacks, dissociating nuns often behaved with alarming lewdness: lifting their habits, simulating copulation, and giving their demons names such as Dog's Dick, Fornication, even Ash-Coloured Pussy."[9] The implicit eroticism in these hysterical crises hardly needs to be emphasized; it is a sudden release of sexual energy that, because it cannot express the conscious or unconscious desires of the psyche, takes the form of a demonic possession in which the pneuma "explodes"—so to speak—producing hallucinations, involuntary movements and sexual postures in order to provide some measure of psychological and physical relief. As in the case of the hysterical patients of the Salpêtrière, an unhealthy environment, lacking opportunities for the development of sexuality, together with the fear, guilt and misogyny that characterizes our tradition, becomes fertile ground for the emergence of all types of individual and collective psychosomatic disorders.[10]

The idea that there is a relationship between collective hysteria and animal magnetism is not new and was looked into in the nineteenth century by Alexandre Bertrand. In his *Traité Du Somnambulisme* (1823) Bertrand makes a comparative study between the symptoms of the nuns of Loudun and those of the Tremblers of the Cevennes, a persecuted Protestant sect, with some of the effects of the healing methods of animal magnetism. It is interesting to note that according to Bertrand, the most suitable patients for magnetic treatment were uncultured peasants, "whose brains have not lost the ability to react upon their organisms."[11] Another group particularly susceptible to magnetism are children, both as the recipients of treatment as well as the administrators of it. The French naturalist and magnetist Joseph Philippe François Deleuze (1753-1835) comments that "children, seven years old, magnetise very well, after they have seen it done. There are instances in which individuals, without any appearance of bodily strength, possess great power for acting upon others..."[12] But it is the susceptibility of children which interests us at this point: "children are very sensible to the action of Magnetism; and it is by them that every candid observer can convince himself, that the imagination is not the cause of these phenomena. On the whole, I would advice those, who wish to know the truth, to examine the effects of this *force* in children and in people of the lowest class who are ignorant even of the name of it."[13]

In this regard, there is an interesting case of choreomania that took place in 1237 in which more than a hundred children from the town of Erfurt in Thuringia spontaneously began to dance and kept on prancing and singing until they reached the neighboring village of Arnstadt. This story bears a striking resemblance to the legend of the Pied Piper of Hamelin which emerged a few years later in the village of the same name. This folklore legend is a particularly clear example of the relationship between pneumatic magic and the susceptibility of the masses. The pied piper can handle the pneuma of animals and humans at will, presenting them with what they most desire. The fragment of Robert Browning with which I opened this chapter describes the desires the piper used to lead the plague of rats into a river.

Even if the children of Erfurt were not manipulated by a leader ("hysterics are individuals who don't need a hypnotist to be hypnotized," Charcot would remind us), it is interesting to note that the figure of the Pied Piper of Hamelin fits in with that of the empedoclean *iatromancer*, who is capable not only of healing but of purifying and rescuing an entire population from a plague. The mysterious piper is, in few words, a magician who knows the secrets of nature (Browning's piper says: "I'm able, by means of a secret charm, to draw all creatures living beneath the sun, that creep or swim or fly or run") and by virtue of this power is a "leader of men."[14] Unlike the people of Selinunte, who worshiped Empedocles as if he were a god, the people of Hamelin refused to pay the pied piper his due, who then changed his colorful outfit for a green hunting uniform (*animarum venator*), enchanted the children of the village with his music and then led them to a cave where they were imprisoned forever. Browning comments that only a lame child was left behind and thus was spared the tragic destiny of his friends. Like the rat of the epigraph, the boy told the people of Hamelin about the promises that came with the piper's spell:

> For he led us, he said, to a joyous land,
> Joining the town and just at hand,
> Where waters gushed and fruit-trees grew,
> And flowers put forth a fairer hue,
> And everything was strange and new;

The sparrows were brighter than peacocks here,
And their dogs outran our fallow deer,
And honey-bees had lost their stings,
And horses were born with eagles' wings;
And just as I became assured
My lame foot would be speedily cured,
The music stopped and I stood still,
And found myself outside the hill,
Left alone against my will,
To go now limping as before,
And never hear of that country more!'

Such are the promises that leaders have always made to their people, largely because the masses have always responded diligently to this kind of imaginary scenarios. From this point of view the Pied Piper of Hamelin would seem a horrendous reminder of the susceptibility of any mass to his unconscious desires.

The crowds and their phantasms

If we can assert that "the age of the masses" has its prefiguration in the hundreds of cases of collective hysteria that took place in Europe between the fourteenth and eighteenth centuries, it is difficult not to realize that the historical event that gives birth to modernity was one of the most imposing and virulent cases of collective hysteria of all time: the French Revolution.[15] "The entire country," says Stefan Zweig,

> was shaken with convulsions far exceeding any that had taken place around the famous baquet. Magnetic cures were replaced by the more lasting cures effected by the guillotine. Princes and duchesses and philosophers of aristocratic birth no longer enjoyed leisure enough for long and witty conversations concerning the magnetic fluid. Séances in castle, palace, or mansion were things of the past; the houses of the mighty were destroyed.[16]

Of course, the kind of hysteria that led to the Storming of the Bastille is far from the St. Vitus dances and the possessions of medieval convents, but it does have something in common with these manifestations: an unconscious and emotional component that prevails over judgment and reflection. This matter, together with the suggestibility of the masses, is at the heart of Boris Sidis and Gustave Le Bon's work, two of the pioneers in the study of mass psychology.

For Sidis, a Ukrainian psychologist naturalized in the United States, the foundation of human social habits is the existence of an unconscious substrate within the mind which "is regarded as embodying the 'lower' and more obviously brutal qualities of man. It is irrational, imitative, credulous, cowardly, cruel, and lacks all individuality, will, and self-control. This personality takes the place of the normal personality during hypnosis, and when the individual is one of an active crowd, as, for example, in riots, panics, lynchings, revivals and so forth."[17] The main characteristic of the unconscious state is suggestibility, which according to Sidis "is the cement of the herd, the very soul of the primitive social group... Man is a social animal, no doubt, but he is social because he is suggestible. Suggestibility, however, requires disaggregation of consciousness, hence society presupposes a cleavage of the mind. *Society and mental epidemics are intimately related; for the social gregarious self is the suggestible subconscious self.*"[18] The main flaw of Sidis's hypothesis is that he understands the subconscious, and its concomitant suggestibility, not as a natural trait of the human mind, but as an anomaly that involves a regression to a lower state of social evolution; a typically nineteenth-century flaw that reappears in the work of Gustave Le Bon.

Le Bon, a French physician of the late nineteenth century, published in 1895 *La psychologie des foules* (*The Crowd: Study of the popular mind*), one of the foundational texts of social psychology and, according to Jesús Martín-Barbero, the "first 'scientific' attempt to think the irrationality of the masses."[19] Le Bon's thesis is based on the following idea:

> Under certain given circumstances, and only under those circumstances, an agglomeration of men presents new characteristics very different from those of the individuals composing it. The sentiments and ideas of all the persons in the gathering take one and the same direction, and their conscious personality vanishes. A collective mind is formed, doubtless transitory, but presenting very clearly defined characteristics. The gathering has thus become what, in the absence of a better expression, I will call an organised crowd, or, if the term is considered preferable, a psychological crowd.[20]

Le Bon's crowd is a *provisional being* essentially identical to a multicellular organism whose global characteristics are different from that of its units. Beyond this biological analogy, it is interesting to note that according to Le Bon a psychological crowd is endowed with a soul and a direction that are determined largely by the race of its members, so that it can be said that there are "Latin" crowds that behave differently from, say, "Anglo-Saxon" crowds. However, the specific traits of any crowd rest in that "it is more especially with respect to those unconscious elements which constitute the genius of a race that all the individuals belonging to it resemble each other, while it is principally in respect to the conscious elements of their character —the fruit of education, and yet more of exceptional hereditary conditions— that they differ from each other. Men the most unlike in the matter of their intelligence possess instincts, passions, and feelings that are very similar. In the case of every thing that belongs to the realm of sentiment —religion, politics, morality, the affections and antipathies, etc.— the most eminent men seldom surpass the standard of the most ordinary individuals."[21] Thus it is through the conscious elements (social circumstances, education, etc.) that individuals are made and through the unconscious that they unite in a crowd.

Here I would like to emphasize that Le Bon's "soul of the race," understood as a type of biological memory, should not be confused with the idea of the unconscious derived from psychoanalysis; the role of any racial notion as a determining factor in human behavior has long been dismissed by sociology and anthropology, in great part due to the disasters it wrought on Germany and Europe during the Third Reich. Even if this is the case, Le Bon's general layout offers an interesting insight into the character of individuals and collectivities that will reappear in Freud's work. Namely that "the conscious life of the mind is of small importance in comparison with its unconscious life. The most subtle analyst, the most acute observer, is scarcely successful in discovering more than a very small number of the unconscious motives that determine his conduct... Behind the avowed causes of our acts there undoubtedly lie secret causes that we do not avow, but behind these secret causes there are many others more secret still which we ourselves ignore. The greater part of our daily actions are the result of hidden motives which escape our observation."[22] And whatever counts for the individual seems only to increase for a crowd.

From the beginning Le Bon makes it clear that the unconscious nature of the masses deserves the lowest of opinions and does not waste opportunity to express it. "In the collective mind," he says, "the intellectual aptitudes of the individuals, and in consequence their individuality, are weakened. The heterogeneous is swamped by the homogeneous, and the unconscious qualities obtain the upper hand."[23] Hence, in a crowd the qualities and aptitudes of its members are not averaged, instead a new set of traits emerge which derive, for the most part, from the unconscious. That being said, it is important to inquire about the causes that give rise to these characteristics. Le Bon cites three in particular. First, a feeling of "invincible power" that arises in an individual integrated in a mass, "which allows him to yield to instincts which, had he been alone, he would perforce have kept under restraint. He will be the less disposed to check himself from the consideration that, a crowd being anonymous, and in consequence irresponsible, the sentiment of responsibility which always controls individuals disappears entirely."[24] The second cause is a "mental contagion" which determines the specific traits of crowds as well as their orientation. Le Bon warns that this phenomenon is easy to verify but remains unexplained. "In a crowd every sentiment and act is contagious, and contagious to such a degree that an individual readily sacrifices his personal interest to the collective interest."[25] In this regard, the pneumatic movements and their relation to collective forms of hysteria may offer a possible explanation.

The third cause is suggestibility, which Le Bon cites as the origin of "mental contagion" and openly relates to a mass hypnotic state. We know today, he says,

> that by various processes an individual may be brought into such a condition that, having entirely lost his conscious personality, he obeys all the suggestions of the operator who has deprived him of it, and commits acts in utter contradiction with his character and habits. The most careful observations seem to prove that an individual immersed for some length of time in a crowd in action soon finds himself —either in consequence of the *magnetic influence* given out by the crowd, or from some other cause of which we are ignorant— in a special state, which much resembles the state of fascination in which the hypnotised individual finds himself in the hands of the hypnotiser. The activity of the brain being paralysed in the case of the hypnotised subject, the latter becomes the slave of all the unconscious activities of his spinal cord, which the hypnotiser directs at will. The conscious personality has entirely vanished; will and discernment are lost. All feelings

and thoughts are bent in the direction determined by the hypnotiser.[26]

Thus, the enormous susceptibility of the masses lies in their dependence on the unconscious, in that their acts necessarily "are far more under the influence of the spinal cord than of the brain."[27] In the medical jargon discussed in the previous chapter this passage refers to the movement that takes place when the pneuma leaves the brain and the central nervous system to activate the ganglions of the vegetative system. As in the case of choreomania, this movement of the individual pneuma —by virtue of its connection with the universal soul or *anima mundi*— synchronizes with the surrounding *pneumata*, causing a *critical mass* which radiates the new pneumatic configuration throughout a group. Thus, a psychological crowd is a provisional being composed of hundreds or thousands of human beings whose pneuma has been redistributed throughout their autonomous nervous systems and which operates, to a greater or lesser extent, unconsciously. Whoever controls this collective pneuma, *the soul of the crowd*, will be able to command it.

Le Bon is categorical when it comes to defining how to achieve such control: "Whatever be the ideas suggested to crowds they can only exercise effective influence on condition that they assume a very absolute, uncompromising, and simple shape. They present themselves then in the guise of images."[28] But it is not only their condition of images, or *phantasmata* in Renaissance jargon, which confers a *venator* power over a crowd. An idea won't be operative until it "has undergone the transformations which render it accessible to crowds, [when] it has entered the domain of the unconscious, when indeed it has become a sentiment."[29] Once an idea or phantasm has finally penetrated into the soul of a crowd it acquires an "irresistible power, and brings about a series of effects, opposition to which is bootless. The philosophical ideas which resulted in the French Revolution took nearly a century to implant themselves in the mind of the crowd. Their irresistible force, when once they had taken root, is known. The striving of an entire nation towards the conquest of social equality, and the realisation of abstract rights and ideal liberties, caused the tottering of all thrones and profoundly disturbed the Western world."[30]

If images are the natural way into the collective pneuma, the "popular imaginary" is the target to which all the efforts of a hunter of souls must be directed. For this reason, says Le Bon:

theatrical representations, in which the image is shown in its most clearly visible shape, always have an enormous influence on crowds. Bread and spectacular shows constituted for the plebeians of ancient Rome the ideal of happiness, and they asked for nothing more. Throughout the successive ages this ideal has scarcely varied. Nothing has a greater effect on the imagination of crowds of every category than theatrical representations. The entire audience experiences at the same time the same emotions, and if these emotions are not at once transformed into acts, it is because the most unconscious spectator cannot ignore that he is the victim of illusions, and that he has laughed or wept over imaginary adventures.[31]

Theatrical representations and, more recently, film and television productions, have been the most effective means of penetrating and manipulating the soul of a crowd. Already by the end of the nineteenth century, Gabriel Tarde, French sociologist contemporary of Le Bon, proposed that mass media, particularly the press, could be useful in controlling the crowds by giving them a common purpose. It is worth mentioning that this collectivization of the phantasm implies the widening of the pneumatic circle, that twilight between objective and subjective and real and unreal, that now encompasses not only an individual but a multitude.

"The power of conquerors and the strength of States," says Le Bon, "is based on the popular imagination. It is more particularly by working upon this imagination that crowds are led. All great historical facts, the rise of Buddhism, of Christianity, of Islamism, the Reformation, the French Revolution, and, in our own time, the threatening invasion of Socialism are the direct or indirect consequences of strong impressions produced on the imagination of the crowd."[32] Now, it is important to bear in mind that it is not only the facts themselves that count "but the way in which they take place and are brought under notice. It is necessary that by their condensation, if I may thus express myself, they should produce a startling image which fills and besets the mind."[33] These *phantasmata* must be emotive, clear images that don't leave any room for interpretation: a victory (the execution of an Arab leader), a defeat (two giant towers collapsing), a crime (prisoners kneeling in a clandestine torture center) or a hope (a boat belonging to an NGO interposed between a whaler and its prey), have always worked wonders when it comes to mobilize the masses or have them give their consent; what is important is that these images take root in the collective pneuma, for once they are assimilated the hunter can operate through them on the unconscious of the crowd. Le Bon is is right when he asserts that "to know the art of impressing the imagination of crowds is to know... the art of governing them."[34]

The relation of this scheme to magic is evident to a rationalist like Le Bon, who warns that even if one does not have the necessary images to manipulate a given crowd, "it is possible to evoke them by the judicious employment of words and formulas. Handled with art, they possess in sober truth the mysterious power formerly attributed to them by the adepts of magic. They cause the birth in the minds of crowds of the most formidable tempests, which in turn they are capable of stilling."[35] Le Bon does not hesitate to assert that the magical power of words is inseparable from the images they conjure but is completely independent of their real meaning, an idea with openly orwellian implications. Giordano Bruno, perfectly aware of this issue, stated that "It is not true... that the power of bonding is derived from what is good rather than from an opinion about what is good."[36] Ideas such as "good" or "true" are irrelevant, a convincing simulation is enough to persuade the masses.

> Words whose sense is the most ill-defined are sometimes those that possess the most influence. Such, for example, are the terms democracy, socialism, equality, liberty, etc., whose meaning is so vague that bulky volumes do not suffice to precisely fix it. Yet it is certain that a truly magical power is attached to those short syllables, as if they contained the solution of all problems. They synthesise the most diverse unconscious aspirations and the hope of their realisation.[37]

"... vagueness has an elevating and magnifying power," Robert Musil reminds us.[38] Thus, when words like democracy and equality—and more recently transparency, sustainability, and social responsibility—are pronounced in an appropriate formula "an expression of respect is visible on every countenance, and all heads are bowed," [39] illusions and unconscious desires begin to simmer in the collective soul. This is why, according to Le Bon, philosophy, despite all its efforts, has never been able to seduce the peoples or to come up with "any ideal that can charm them; but, as they must have their illusions at all cost, they turn instinctively, as the insect seeks the light, to the rhetoricians who accord them what they want. Not truth, but error has always been the chief factor in the evolution of nations... The masses have never thirsted after truth. They turn aside from evidence that is not to their taste, preferring to deify error, if error seduce them. Whoever can supply them with illusions is easily their master; whoever attempts to destroy their illusions is always their victim."[40] As pessimist and arrogant as Le Bon's observation may seem, we must admit that it is increasingly difficult to ignore that it has not been through reason but in spite of it that human civilization has stumbled along like a crowd hypnotized by this or that pied piper.

The susceptibility of a crowd is also related to the "feminization" inherent the act of capturing it within a pneumatic circle, that is, of confining it within an artificial version of the mythic structure of consciousness, a *modus operandi* which, let it be said, is identical to that of any religion.

> The great majority of a nation is so feminine in character and outlook that its thought and conduct are ruled by sentiment rather than by sober reasoning... Since these masses have only a poor acquaintance with abstract ideas, their reaction lie more in the domain of the feelings... And the driving force which has brought about the most tremendous revolutions on this earth has never been a body of scientific teaching which has gained power over the masses, but always a devotion which has inspired them, and often a kind of hysteria which has urged them into action.

Is it at all surprising that the author of this passage is none other than Adolf Hitler?

The most evident consequence of this circumstance is that as psychological crowds we have become slaves to our desires and illusions, to the pipe-dreams that the hunters of souls have riveted in our unconscious. If this idea seems implausible, or if we refuse to accept its proportion of truth, it may be useful to examine the ways in which we are convinced. Le Bon cites three simple procedures: affirmation, repetition and contagion, which can still be verified in the politics and advertising of our day. "Affirmation pure and simple, kept free of all reasoning and all proof, is one of the surest means of making an idea enter the mind of crowds. The conciser an affirmation is, the more destitute of every appearance of proof and demonstration, the more weight it carries."[41] Of course, an assertion does not reach an authentic influence until it penetrates the collective pneuma and for this it must be repeated indefinitely. "It was Napoleon, I believe, who said that there is only one figure in rhetoric of serious importance, namely, repetition."[42] Once an affirmation has penetrated the soul of a crowd and has become revealed truth by means of constant repetition, the mechanism of "mental contagion" that I exposed in pneumatic terms comes into play.

It is important to note that not all leaders are able to impose images on the collective pneuma with the same efficiency, and according to Le Bon the matter lies, almost exclusively, on the prestige they have with the crowd. Prestige, he says,

> is a sort of domination exercised on our mind by an individual, a work, or an idea. This domination entirely paralyses our critical faculty, and fills our soul with astonishment and respect. The sentiment provoked is inexplicable, like all sentiments, but it would appear to be of the same kind as the fascination to which a magnetised person is subjected. Prestige is the mainspring of all authority. Neither gods, kings, nor women have ever reigned without it.[43]

This type of fascination, which "paralyses our critical faculty," is yet another instance of the erotic factor implicit in all pneumatic operations, a phenomenon of the same order than the infatuation that some somnambules, both men and women, developed for their magnetizers. However, the idea that a leader's prestige, social position, or authority is the determining factor in the manipulation of an individual or a crowd— as was the case with many magnetists and hypnotists—was reassessed by later researchers who argued that Le Bon's idea of leadership and his role in manipulating a mass was somewhat narrow-minded. Wilfred Trotter in particular, understood the subject of manipulation of the masses from a completely different point of view.

A physician at the University College hospital and one of the pioneers of neurosurgery, Trotter is remembered for applying biological ideas to the study of the masses. In his best known work, *Instincts of the Herd in Peace and War* (1916) he argues that the gregariousness of our species "is a phenomenon of profound biological significance and one likely therefore to be responsible for an important group of instinctive impulses."[44] According to Trotter, the human tendency to gather in groups, which he calls gregarious instinct, would be at the same level as the three basic instincts of our species: self-preservation, sex and reproduction, and nutrition. Trotter justifies his argument from an evolutionary perspective:

> Changes so serious as the assumption of the upright posture, the reduction in the jaw and its musculature, the reduction in the acuity of smell and hearing, demand, if the species is to survive, either a delicacy of adjustment with the compensatingly developing intelligence so minute as to be almost inconceivable, or the existence of some kind of protective enclosure, however imperfect, in which the varying individuals were sheltered from the direct influence of natural selection. The existence of such a mechanism would compensate losses of physical strength in the individual by the greatly increased strength of the larger unit, of the unit, that is to say, upon which natural selection still acts unmodified.[45]

According to Trotter the main quality of a crowd is its homogeneity, but to ensure the evolutionary advantages that come with it it is necessary that "the members of the herd must possess sensitiveness to the behaviour of their fellows,"[46] in other words, that they are able to recognize their intentions immediately in order to coordinate their activities. This empathic process could be described as the alignment of the individual pneuma in a single configuration that would determine a new extended organism—as it happened in the rapport between magnetizer and magnetized. The virtues of such social configuration are self-evident: "it is clear that the great advantage of the social habit is to enable large numbers to act as one, whereby in the case of the hunting gregarious animal strength in pursuit and attack is at once increased to beyond that of the creatures preyed upon."[47] Rather than a regression to a lower mode of consciousness, as Sidis and Le Bon would argue, our gregarious habits could be the original form of perception of our species and, as such, an integral part of our biological and conscious constitution.

Under these conditions the human individual "not only will... be responsive to impulses coming from the herd, but he will treat the herd as his normal environment."[48] This circumstance would determine the primal sense of well-being most of us feel in the presence of our kind and also explain why we feel uncomfortable and exposed with anything that tends to emphasize our differences with the herd; why loneliness and abandonment are particularly devastating feelings. Now, if the main characteristic of the herd is homogeneity, this is achieved through suggestibility which is, essentially, the propensity to unconsciously align with the prevalent pneumatic configuration of the group. Thus, if a mass is configured at any given moment to take a fortress, the actions and suggestions directed at this purpose will be taken as instinctive and carried out without question; individual will decreases, the conscious self fades away temporarily and everything happens, to put it somehow, "automatically." The mechanism works in a similar way if the mass is primed for a carnival, a football game, a political rally or a Black Friday.

Although suggestibility was understood by Le Bon as an undesirable trait that interferes with the normal operation of the mind when the individual is under the influence of a mass, it is rather a normal condition of human social development, "a necessary quality of every normal mind, continually present, and an inalienable accompaniment of human thought,"[49] as inseparable from the workings of the mind as its subconscious substrate. This fact is of enormous importance because it implies that both individuals and masses are suggestible by principle, but what affects this or that type of individual might not affect a mass and what affects a mass may not affect certain individuals. Giordano Bruno refers to this particularity in the following fragment of the *De Vinculis*:

> We know that there are as many types of bonds as there are types and varieties of beauty. Also, these varieties do not seem to be smaller than the primary varieties of things, that is, the different species. Furthermore, within each species there are different individuals who are bound by different things in different ways. Thus, the hungry are bonded to food, the thirsty to drink, he who is full of semen to Venus; one person to a sensory object and another to an intellectual object; one person to a natural object and another to an artificial one; a mathematician is bonded to abstractions and a man of action to concrete things; a hermit satisfies himself by a desire for what is absent and a member of a family by what is present.[50]

In short, the effectiveness of a suggestion depends on how specific are the bonds it produces. Now, while for Le Bon the suggestibility of the masses depends on "static" factors such as prestige, repetition or contagion, Trotter attributes its effect to the degree to which certain suggestions identify themselves with the "voice of the herd." This "resonance" between a suggestion and the voice of a mass, which is a more "rational" way of referring to the collective pneuma, is referred to by Bruno in this manner:

> A thing [or individual or mass] is bound in the strongest way when part of it is in the bonding agent, or when the bonding agent controls it by one of its parts.[51]

Thus, the essential factor of suggestibility is not the *what* but the *how*, since the what changes from mass to mass and from individual to individual while the how can be identified based on its resonance with the individual or collective pneuma. In essence, to manipulate both masses and individuals one needs to understand how the bonds that affect them at a given moment resonate and develop within them. The trick to manipulation lies in understanding the feedback process between *venator* and *venatus*; achieving this depends on knowing what "moves" the gregarious instinct and how it can be operated upon through symbols.

Here it is important to note that if we are susceptible to manipulation it is not just because of how sagacious and ambitious our leaders are —and let's not fool ourselves, *they are*— but also because of our biological inclination to suggestibility, which has served as the main instrument to gather in communities and more recently in huge masses. In other words: if in the case of our species natural selection acted on the basis of the survival of the crowd and not on that of each individual, it is not at all strange that the gregarious tendency that originally served as an evolutionary advantage ended up becoming a disadvantage for the individual. Thus, from Trotter's point of view, our modern hunters of souls are taking advantage of a natural tendency of the human animal—the suggestibility of the gregarious instinct—which, if set against individual will and freedom, becomes a powerful tool to force consent and to control the population.

Beyond the evident ethical implications of this situation, for Trotter the problem of forcing the consent of a population by means of suggestion is that all the ideas and images generated in this manner appeal to massified individuals as true and natural opinions, and as such as undeserving of reflection. Hence, it is not surprising to find that the masses are characterized by their irrational and sometimes even absurd notions, for the herd refuses, almost instinctually, to think about the way in which these ideas and actions were formed in the first place. A mass is especially susceptible to suggestion because it is naturally, gregariously, primed to accept that certain things *are as they are and it is futile to try and question them*. This "unconscious defeatism" is fertile ground for the leaders of men.

For Trotter the possibility of manipulation and control of the masses by a relatively small group of individuals arises from the demands that the gregarious instinct forces on the individual psyche:

> The element of conflict in the normal life of all inhabitants of a civilized state is so familiar that no formal demonstration of its existence is necessary. In childhood the process has begun. The child receives from the herd the doctrines, let us say, that truthfulness is the most valuable of all the virtues, that honesty is the best policy, that to the religious man death has no terrors, and that there is in store a future life of perfect happiness and delight. And yet experience tells him with persistence that truthfulness as often as not brings him punishment, that his dishonest playfellow has as good if not a better time than he, that the religious man shrinks from death with as great a terror as the unbeliever, is as broken-hearted by bereavement, and as determined to continue his hold upon this imperfect life rather than trust himself to what he declares to be the certainty of future bliss.[52]

Broadly speaking, this conflict between the experience of the individual and the particular set of beliefs of his society, creates a psychological pressure that reaches its peak during adolescence when the subject begins to compare the dissonances between the suggestions of the herd and his own experiences. The result of this process is either a denial of the situation, which produces a "stable" mentality that understands the importance of the demands of the herd and acts accordingly, or a resistance to forget the conflict and deny personal experience, which manifests itself as an "unstable" mentality that does not adapt to the circumstances of the herd. The unstable portion of the population lacks energy, which is consumed in trying to resolve the internal conflict, and is especially prone to skepticism in issues such as patriotism, religion and social status.[53] It is from a small group of "stables" from which our leaders arise, they are those who understand and resonate naturally with the voice of the herd and learn to manipulate the rest of the population, whose skepticism and disenchantment has left them at their mercy. These two types, Trotter tells us, divide society between them, [and] must be regarded as seriously defective and as evidence that civilization has not yet provided a medium in which the average human mind can grow undeformed and to its full stature.[54]

According to Trotter, neither the hunters nor the hunted have ever been close to being either rational or to reaching their true potential as human beings.

From Ficino to Freud. *The phantasms of melancholia and narcissism*

In order to finish putting together our context on the psychological foundations of the manipulation of the masses we must refer to the work of Sigmund Freud who, through his idea of libido, reveals the connection between the erotic magic of the Renaissance and modern psychology. For this we have to go back in time and examine the influence that hypnosis had on his work and his interest, or why not, his fixation, with the erotic component of the human psyche.

With the patronage of a grant from the College of Teachers of the Vienna Hospital, Freud visited the Salpêtrière during the winter of 1885 and spring of 1886 with the intention of continuing his studies of neuropathology. There he became acquainted with the theory of hypnosis and hysteria of Jean-Martin Charcot who, recognizing the talent of the young Freud, allowed him into his social circle, where he met other important doctors and intellectuals of the time. Since then until the last decade of the nineteenth century, Freud would praise Charcot's theory as the revealed truth about hypnosis and hysteria, something that would only change gradually after Hyppolyte Bernheim took him to A.A. Liébeault's practice in Nancy. From then on Freud would flounder between the therapeutic approach of the school of Nancy and the apparent theoretical truths of his Parisian teacher. The conflict, present in his texts and reviews of the time, would only find resolution through the development of a new approach to the treatment of hysteria and neurosis deeply influenced by the "cathartic method" of his mentor Josef Breuer, which I outlined briefly in the previous chapter.

The key to unraveling both the origin of psychoanalysis and Freud's idea of libido as one of the fundamental forces of the human psyche is guarded by one of his most famous patients, Anna von Lieben—

also known as the Baroness von Todesco—his main source of income between 1887 and 1892. A hysteric as few in the history of medicine, Von Lieben was besieged every day by hundreds of fears, embarrassments, anxieties and sexual pecadillos that in most cases manifested themselves with physical symptoms. Hence, if she developed a facial neuralgia it was because "an insult was like a slap in the face." A pain in the chest she explained saying that an incident had "pierced her heart." Hallucinations, insomnia and hyperesthesia were just some of the manifestations of her condition. As her personal doctor, Freud was always to be available, day and night, to tend to her constant fits, which sometimes numbered in dozens. It was with Anna von Lieben that Freud began to elaborate a theory according to which the symptoms of hysteria were symbolizations that took the form of bodily metaphors, which would be psychosomatic in nature. It was during this time that he "learned to interpret word games, to decipher puzzles and occurrences... he learned to psychoanalyze: psychoanalysis was born from the spirit of Anna von Lieben."[55]

Until then Freud had been treating his patients with a hypnotic method that was mainly Charcot's, combined with the cathartic search for traumatic memories he learned from Josef Breuer. Unfortunately the Baroness could not be induced to a state of deep trance with post-hypnotic amnesia and thus she was unable to forget her traumas, many of them from childhood, which she constantly somatized. In any case, Freud had noticed that it was possible for a patient to enter into a deep hypnotic state during which the traumatic memories, the *phantasmata* that originate the condition, were blurred or erased, and yet they would not heal. There was something, Freud speculated, that hindered the recovery of these patients, as if a force remained that "opposed their will to heal."[56] It is from this insight that he came up with a new psychic mechanism to explain hysteria, and in fact, a large number of mental conditions. Every representation, says Freud

> raises a counter-representation, that is, the opposite idea. If I have an expectation or a project, for example, I will also imagine the idea that may oppose that expectation or that project. "It will not work," "I will not get it," etc. Normally these negative and painful ideas are inhibited, repressed by the healthy "representative life," but in the case of neurotic people they become stronger.[57]

According to Freud, this form of self-sabotage is based on the fact that the psychological repression that allows the dissociation of these negative ideas is necessary for a psychological life that if not healthy, is at least "normal." But he warned that in certain types of people like neurotics and hysterics, the more one wants to "ignore, erase, or forget an unpleasant idea, the more it escapes conscious will" and begins to take a life of its own. "This is why," says Freud, "the hysterical delusions of nuns are often obscene, and the fits and tics of well-behaved people are so often crude, because it is precisely these immoral ideas which are most vigorously suppressed..."[58] Anna von Lieben, who at Freud's request kept a diary of her therapy, is an excellent example of the matter. So obscene were some of the entries recorded in it that her son-in-law decided to burn it when the Baroness died in 1900.

The road to healing, Freud decided, was not in making patients forget their traumas, in blurring their *phantasmata*, it was in remembering what they had repressed so that it could be confronted and treated consciously. From this moment on Freud would only induce a very mild hypnotic state that would allow his patients to consciously evoke the events that marked their lives; a state light enough to allow them to recall but deep enough to make them susceptible to the therapist's suggestions.

In 1921, three years after the end of World War I, Freud published a collection of essays, which included *Massenpsychologie Und Ich-Analyse* (Group Psychology and the Analysis of the Ego), a study in which he presented his theory on the psychological mechanisms that underlie the behavior of the masses. Almost four centuries have passed since Marsilio Ficino and Giordano Bruno presented their theories on the erotic operations of magic, and it is with Freud that this set of ideas regains its strength in the West, not as a result of direct transmission—as I hope is clear by now—but through a *field of influence* of which Freud's theory of libido is but another transformation. The coincidences between Freud's ideas and particularly those of Marsilio Ficino are remarkable; to my great surprise the hidden affinities between psychoanalysis and medieval and Renaissance magic-psychology only seem to have been investigated to some extent by Norman O. Brown and Giorgio Agamben.[59]

To explore the conjunction between the Freudian theory of libido and the erotic magic of the Renaissance we must first define the concepts of libido, narcissism and idealization from the point of view of psychoanalysis. With libido Freud refers to "the energy, regarded as a quantitative magnitude (though not at present actually measurable), of those instincts which have to do with all that may be comprised under the word 'love.' The nucleus of what we mean by love naturally consists (and this is what is commonly called love, and what the poets sing of) in sexual love with sexual union as its aim."[60] Freud traces the origin of his libido to Plato's concept of eros and reduces it to the status of "instinct." A better characterization may be that of Stefan Zweig who, in his biography of Freud, talks of libido as a universal and indistinct form of desire that "is the first breath of mental life. As the body craves for food, so does the soul crave for pleasure. Libido, the primal will to pleasure, the unappeasable hunger of the mind, whips us through the world."[61] Indeed, it is in Freud's idea of libido as a universal form of desire where the "coincidences" between magic and psychoanalysis arise.

In regards to narcissism, Freud defines it as an essential stage of the individual's early psychological development during which "the childish ego enjoys its self-sufficiency," and which functions as the primordial mechanism through which every human begins his or her process of identification with the world. This stage is characterized by a psychological absorption in which the infant assumes himself as the center of attention of his parents and consequently of his or her world. As the individual grows, the narcissistic identification is linked to the girl's sexual drive towards her father and the boy's towards his mother, and to the process of identification with the parent of the same sex, a matter that establishes a "mirror" between the sexes and relationships. It is through the narcissistic identification between the boy/father and girl/mother — which simultaneously reflects the sexual desire of the child for the parent of the opposite sex— that the individual begins interacting with the environment and forming affective bonds. In addition to reinforcing emotional relationships between family members and the society at large, these libidinal bonds act in such a way that the individual begins to detect what his family and society value as good. The internalization of the values derived from the family nucleus and the herd form the *ego ideal* (*ichideal*), that represents the standards of behavior to which the individual should aspire.

If we consider the wide diffusion of these psychological mechanisms in the civilized world, it is not at all strange to find that the libidinal character of narcissism and idealization is the psychological mechanism that enables the idea of the woman as an angelic (Beatrice) or divine being (Diana/Venus) that represents the most coveted attributes of the male psyche. The feminine idealizations of courtly love and the *dolce stil novo* can indeed be characterized coherently in psychoanalytical terms. In fact, Freud recognizes a stage of adolescent sexual development in which, as a medieval troubadour, the "man will show a sentimental enthusiasm for women whom he deeply respects but who do not excite him to sexual activities, and he will only be potent with other women whom he does not 'love' and thinks little of or even despises."[62] What we see here is how the libidinal impulse of the individual, originally directed towards the father or the mother, is repressed by a process of idealization that diverts sexual satisfaction to an un-idealized object in order to avoid tarnishing his own *ego ideal*, making it descend to the trivial and mundane.

In *Group Psychology and The Analysis of The Ego* Freud presents an example of the narcissistic mechanism that clarifies its importance for the individual and collective psyche:

> Supposing, for instance, that one of the girls in a boarding school has had a letter from someone with whom she is secretly in love which arouses her jealousy, and that she reacts to it with a fit of hysterics; then some of her friends who know about it will catch the fit, as we say, by mental infection. The mechanism is that of identification based upon the possibility or desire of putting oneself in the same situation. The other girls would like to have a secret love affair too, and under the influence of a sense of guilt they also accept the suffering involved in it. It would be wrong to suppose that they take on the symptom out of sympathy. On the contrary, the sympathy only arises out of the identification…[63]

This example of narcissistic identification and contagion allows us to identify the first point of contact between magic and psychoanalysis. According to Freud, "sympathy"—one of the principles of all forms of magic—is the result of a fundamental process of the human psyche: the narcissistic identification that extends its libidinal bonds producing a network of relations throughout a human group. It was with good reason that Freud affirmed that "the mutual tie between members of a group is in the nature of an identification of this kind, based upon an important emotional common quality,"[64] a quality strong enough to bind the group together. However, before going into mass relations, we must briefly address a particular aspect of individual psychology.

The dynamics of the narcissistic relationship between the ego and the ego ideal are, unsurprisingly, more evident in the melancholic character. When a melancholic, says Freud, loses the object of his love, there arises "a cruel self-depreciation of the ego combined with relentless self-criticism and bitter self-reproaches. Analyses have shown that this disparagement and these reproaches apply at bottom to the object and represent the ego's revenge upon it."[65] It is at this point that the relation between psychoanalysis and erotic magic comes forth, as there are times when the love object "serves as a substitute for some unattained ego ideal of our own. We love it on account of the perfections which we have striven to reach for our own ego, and which we should now like to procure in this roundabout way as a means of satisfying our narcissism."[66] Within this scheme the ego

> becomes more and more unassuming and modest, and the object more and more sublime and precious, until at last it gets possession of the entire self-love of the ego, whose self-sacrifice thus follows as a natural consequence. The object has, so to speak, consumed the ego.[67]

The similarity of the process of "melancholic introjection" with the erotic dialectic of Marsilio Ficino that I addressed in the first chapter is striking. In it we find a mechanism analogous to the process of elaboration of the ego ideal described by Freud that involves the intermediate organ between the body and the soul known as *proton organon* by Aristotle and *hegemonikon* by the Stoics. Ficino calls it *spiritus*, which is the Latin translation of *pneuma*. As the sensory images of the beloved are too coarse to be fixed in the soul, the *spiritus* transforms them into phantasms compatible with its purity. After this depuration has taken place, the soul,

> easily sees the images shining in it as though in a mirror and through them it judges bodies, and this cognition is called by the Platonists sense perception. While it sees these images, it conceives in itself by its own strength images like them, but much purer. Conception of this kind we call imagination and fancy.[68]

For Ficino this erotic dynamic depends upon the condition that the love is reciprocated. However, this correspondence has an external and an internal aspect: the external depends on the reciprocity of feeling, and the internal, that the figure of the beloved, its phantasm, corresponds to what Freud called "ego ideal," a contingency that would allow the introjection and invasion of the lover's psyche.

The phantastic mechanism that transforms a sensory image into a phantasm assimilable by the intellect is a form of "idealization"—or, in Freudian terms, an elaboration of the *ego ideal*—a passage from the sensorial to an "idea" that feeds on the psychological perceptions and expectations of the individual and, in the case of the melancholic, becomes a source of "psychological intoxication."[69] Of course, it should be noted that not all phantasms are idealization in the psychoanalytical sense of the word, but they become such if they correspond to the *ichideal* of the subject.

Now, since in the conversion of the sensory into the fantastic there is a latent idealization, the relationship between the lover and the phantasm of his beloved perfectly reflects the relationship between the *ego* and the *ego ideal*. It suffices to replace *ego* for soul and *ego ideal* for *phantasm* to begin to see the relationships.

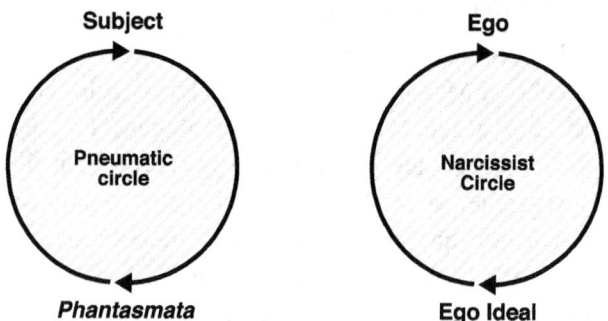

"The phantasm that monopolizes the soul," says Culianu,

> is the image of an object. Now, since man is soul, and since soul is totally occupied by a phantasm (*ego ideal*), the phantasm *is* henceforth the soul (*ego*). It follows that the subject, bereft of his soul, is no longer a subject. The phantasmic vampire has devoured it internally... Metaphorically, therefore, it can be said that the subject has been changed into the object of his love.[70]

What in Ficino's erotic psychology is the phantasm of the beloved, the object idealized by the lover, In Freud becomes an introjected image that has taken hold of the individual's psyche, replacing his ego ideal. Both Freud and Ficino are clear in asserting that this picture is especially observed in unrequited love, the kind of relationship idealized by the *stil novo*, and agree on the conclusion: *the object has occupied the place of the subject*. It is interesting to note that Culianu characterizes the Ficinian erotic dialectic as a form of narcissism, but by focusing his attention on the *phantasm*, on the image of the beloved embedded in the pneuma, and not on its processes, he relates its unconscious character to the analytical psychology of Jung and not with Freud's psychoanalysis.

This erotic dynamic has an important implication for the idea of suggestibility that I have discussed in this chapter. While we are part of a collective tthe libidinal bonds cancel out the feelings of individualism that characterize isolated subjects, they dissolve the narcissism on which the identity of the self is constructed. In a mass, says Freud, "individuals [...] behave as though they were uniform, tolerate the peculiarities of its other members, equate themselves with them, and have no feeling of aversion towards them. Such a limitation of narcissism can, according to our theoretical views, only be produced by one factor, a libidinal tie with other people."[71] For Freud, it is in this erotic bond, in the unconscious feeling of union and community, where we find the origin of the sugestibility that characterizes all human masses.

From being in love to hypnosis, says Freud, there is no great distance. "There is the same humble subjection, the same compliance, the same absence of criticism, towards the hypnotist as towards the loved object,"[72] a matter that we already examined with regard to magnetic somnambulism. Now, if the mechanism of infatuation and hypnosis is the same, only one thing can be happening: "the hypnotist has stepped into the place of the ego ideal."[73]

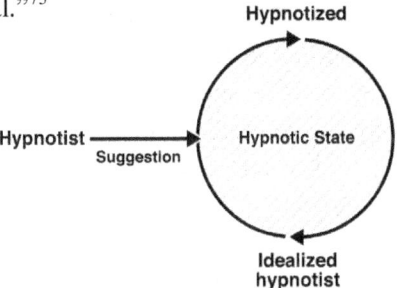

For Freud, the hypnotic relationship is a collective formation of two people that presents one of the key elements of any multitude: the relationship between the individual and the leader. This relationship, like any narcissistic mechanism, is essentially erotic even if its sexual tendencies are not obvious, a fact that allowed Freud to postulate hypnosis as a kind of intermediate libidinal state between being in love and a being in a mass.[74] The leap to understand a crowd as an erotic form of organization is a rather short one: a mass is a *"number of individuals who have put one and the same object in the place of their ego ideal and have consequently identified themselves with one another in their ego."*[75] This common object is either an image that has penetrated and taken root in the collective pneuma, or a leader, a venator that directs the mass through a web of libidinal bonds.[76]

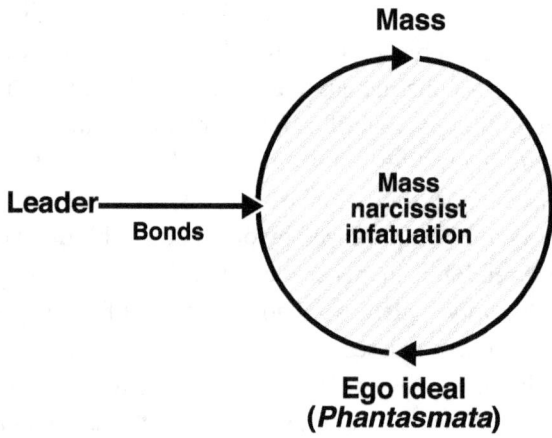

The erotic scheme shared by magic and psychoanalysis leads to the following conclusion: since a crowd "smitten/hypnotized" by its leader pays attention only to him or her, the relationship between the crowd and its hunter is a form of psychological transference. This image recalls the enormous web of bonds "which cannot be designated by one name" that Bruno proposes in the *De vinculis*, and to which Culianu alludes as a "huge apparatus of intersubjective exchanges… a machine of transferences."[77] This being said, it is not surprising to find that just like Bruno before him, Freud understands libido as the bond of bonds, "…a group is clearly held together by a power of some kind: and to what power could this feat be better ascribed than to Eros, which holds together everything in the world?"[78] This idea, of an openly magical character, is the very basis of the empedoclean *philotes* and of the concept of "sympathy," the force of attraction that maintains the universal community in place, the affinity that holds together the realm of desire and illusion of Venus/Maya.

Although Freud can assume a pseudo-magical posture, he is too rational to believe in "mysterious" influences like the magnetic fluid and the farthest he is willing to go is to admit a certain "… mystical element that underlies hypnosis."[79] But the freudian eros is an abstraction, a concept that manifests itself and acts in the world as a "psychic energy" which, if we are honest, is as immaterial and mysterious as animal magnetism itself. Seen in this manner, the transferences of "psychic energy" which form the basis of mass relations could be understood, from a Freudian point of view, no longer as emanations of pneuma or magnetic fluid, but as its "unconscious psychological" aspect, a reduction that conceals their original character and scope. Ideas always end up transforming according to the possibilities of their time.

The bloodbath and horror of the Great War were a definitive influence on Freud and his school to assert that the dynamics between the masses and their leaders were not just a simple form of narcissism and infatuation but the result of a natural tendency towards masochism inherent in every human. It is worth noting that this observation coincides with the masochistic character implicit in the amorous dynamic of courtly love, which was based exclusively on the frustration of the sexual impulse and its constant postponement to achieve a painful sublimation that would lead to an ecstatic union with the divine.

The erotic-narcissistic identification that elevates the lover at the expense of the beloved and allows him to ascend to the divine, becomes, upon entering the terrain of the relationship between mass and leader, a glorious notion of belonging—a secular form of divinization, if we can do with the contradiction—as is clear in the case of Nazi Germany, in which a considerable portion of the population plunged into a state of collective hysteria as they identified (fell in love or replaced their *ego ideal*) with Hitler's project of racial purification. But if the human divinizes itself in its narcissistic identification with its leader, this path entails the torture of having to constantly repress its sexual instinct in favor of increasingly strict social demands, of having to transfer all libidinal energy to the love of the nation or of the party. In these circumstances collective hysteria and neuroses never fail to appear.

According to Freud, this dynamic between mass and leader was subordinated to what he called the death instinct. This concept, which he introduced in his study *Beyond The Pleasure Principle*, was the opposite drive to eros which, when it began to encompass the instincts related to life, reproduction and conservation, was confronted with an unconscious desire for death that nested in the depths of the human psyche. In this essay, one of the most complex and controversial among his students, Freud postulates that sadism corresponds to a sexual form of the death instinct, so that masochism, the "instinct which is complementary to sadism, must be regarded as sadism that has been turned round upon the subject's own ego."[80] In other words, as a toxic form of narcissism in which the subject is left open to the possibility of being hurt and mistreated by his partner (or his leader).

It is this narcissistic background that would determine not only the dynamics of sadomasochism, but also the mass relationships of our culture. According to Freud, it was largely this instinctive need for suffering and death that justified the submissive and obsequious behavior of a mass towards its leader. In other words, the masses unconsciously wish to be punished and suffer at the hands of their tyrant, whom they tolerate patiently as a child who puts up with an abusive or dominant father, or a lover with a thoughtless and disdainful partner. Guilt, an unconscious desire to be punished and the drive towards death supposedly played an essential role in this dynamic. A verse by poet Luigi Tansillo (1510-1568) which describes perfectly the erotic dialectic of courtly love could also be applied to the masses eroticized by a leader: "My sweet pain, new in the world and rare, when shall I ever escape from your burden, since the remedy is weariness to me, and the pain delight?"[81]

In the last decades of his life, Freud proposed that the libido, firmly associated by then to the *pleasure principle*, was subordinated to what he called the *reality principle*, which "does not abandon the intention of ultimately obtaining pleasure, but it nevertheless demands and carries into effect the postponement of satisfaction, the abandonment of a number of possibilities of gaining satisfaction and the temporary toleration of unpleasure as a step on the long indirect road to pleasure."[82] The result of the action of the reality principle was the repression of the violent, selfish and destructive instincts, whose effects Freud considered especially dangerous for humanity; in his concept, World War I was the result of their sudden liberation. Therefore, Freud claimed that human civilization was only possible due to the repression of this set of self-destructive instincts that resided in the unconscious.

But the role of the repression implicit in the reality principle was not limited to merely stopping our species from self-destructing. Given that

> the repressed instinct never ceases to strive for complete satisfaction… No substitutive or reactive formations and no sublimations will suffice to remove the repressed instinct's persisting tension; and it is the difference in amount between the pleasure of satisfaction which is demanded and that which is actually achieved that provides the driving factor which will permit of no halting at any position attained, but, in the poet's words 'presses ever forward unsubdued'[83]

Thus, the denial of pleasure not only prevents the extinction of the human species at the hands of its most basic and violent instincts, at the same time it constitutes the main incentive for the advancement of civilization. For Freud, repression is the civilizing instrument par excellence. If this idea seems logical to our contemporary sensibility it is because it rests on the following premise: the opposition between nature (instincts) and civilization (culture) is absolute and irreconcilable, an idea that is but a corollary of Hobbes' *bellum omnium contra omnes*. Of course, such opposition between instinct and culture has its origin in the typically Eurocentric bias according to which Western culture is the apex of the social and technological development of the human animal. And although Freud can imagine that this state of things is not inherent "in the nature of civilization itself but [is] determined by the imperfections of the cultural forms which have so far been developed,"[84] he assures us—as the good realist he was—that it is more than unlikely that we will ever reach a form of society that, free from this contradiction, can renounce to all forms of coercion.

This being the case, Freud sees in each individual an "enemy of civilization, though civilization is supposed to be an object of universal human interest."[85]

> It is remarkable that, little as men are able to exist in isolation, they should nevertheless feel as a heavy burden the sacrifices which civilization expects of them in order to make a communal life possible. Thus civilization has to be defended against the individual, and its regulations, institutions and commands are directed to that task. They aim not only at effecting a certain distribution of wealth but at maintaining that distribution; indeed, they have to protect everything that contributes to the conquest of nature and the production of wealth against men's hostile impulses. Human creations are easily destroyed, and science and technology, which have built them up, can also be used for their annihilation.
>
> One thus gets an impression that civilization is something which was imposed on a resisting majority by a minority which understood how to obtain possession of the means to power and coercion.[86]

Now, if the human is the "natural" enemy of civilization and its "principal task [...], its actual *raison d'être*, is to defend us against nature,"[87] that is, to defend us from ourselves, in reality there is little hope that the living conditions of the human will ever improve.

This attitude conceals an overwhelming defeatism and, consequently, has been one of the most powerful arguments of our leaders to justify their abuses of power, as it means that we must always depend on a class that directs us and prevents us from descending into the inevitable chaos that supposedly underlies human nature. Seen in this light, the most recent deprivations of civil rights and the sanction of cybernetic surveillance in the fight against terrorism are only a continuation of the repression of those instincts that Freud feared so much.

It is not surprising that, like Le Bon, the father of psychoanalysis understood crowds as the enemies of reason.

> It is just as impossible to do without control of the mass by a minority as it is to dispense with coercion in the work of civilization. For masses are lazy and unintelligent; they have no love for instinctual renunciation, and they are not to be convinced by argument of its inevitability; and the individuals composing them support one another in giving free rein to their indiscipline.[88]

Now, apart from the reasons adduced by Freud, why should humans willingly renounce their instincts, like children subjugated by a controlling father? Doesn't this renunciation imply accepting that the human condition is "monstrous," that, all being said and done, we are an aberration of nature?

Isn't there something evidently wrong with this way of understanding ourselves and our world?

So far we have seen how the fundamental concepts that underlie mass psychological phenomena can be characterized coherently in the terms of Renaissance magic. The libidinal operations delineated by Giordano Bruno in *De vinculis in genere* apply both to what we now call psychological manipulation as well as to what was once known as practical magic. The continuity of these two disciplines, as can be seen particularly in Freud's work, is clear. The transition from the concepts derived from psychology to professions such as public relations, marketing and advertising is direct; each of the above disciplines has openly benefited by the theoretical framework and conclusions of psychoanalysis and other branches of psychology.

While the relationship of a mass with its leader was the main concern of authors such as Le Bon and Freud—a matter as relevant then as it is now—the twentieth century witnessed the birth of a new type of crowd that lacks a manifest leader but whose desires and expectations are constantly managed and manipulated by a new kind of hunter who acts hidden behind new mechanisms and institutions. These masses, which we could characterize as "consumerist," are the product of the democratic world built on the Enlightenment's ideals and have been touted as the culmination of the cultural development of the West; the end product of centuries of social evolution. Such a notion—as "selling" as it is naive—overlooks the fact that the functioning of any democratic society is confronted, sooner rather than later, with a conflict that British Prime Minister Benjamin Disraeli expressed masterfully: "I *must* follow the people, am I not their leader?" In other words, exercising the proper control to govern the masses and, at the same time, having their consent, is a circumstance so unusual as to deserve the name of aberrant. Edward Bernays, Freud's North American nephew and the father of public relations, adds a little bit more irony to Disraeli's already cynical comment: "I *must* lead the people, am I not their servant?"

So far the solution to this situation has been ruthless: the masses must be manipulated, their consent must be manufactured. Noam Chomsky gives this circumstance the name of "spectator democracy," a political system in which the individual only has an active role when called upon to elect or revoke their leaders. The rest of the time the spectators/consumers must recreate passively in the illusions and simplifications that their leaders have woven for their entertainment, renouncing not only to true political participation but also to a true perception of reality. What is the excuse of our leaders? If the herd were not manipulated, they argue, the masses would run out of control and anarchy would ensue, a matter that Harold Lasswell, the father of communication theory, summarized briefly: one should not succumb to democratic dogmatisms which hold that man is the best judge of his interests. Echoes of Hobbes's "war of all against all," the return of the instincts that Freud dreaded so much, resound once again. Now, if this indeed is the case and the fate of the masses cannot be entrusted to them, there is no other alternative than manipulation and the question is what kind or degree is admissible as a tool of social control. If it isn't, and humans should be able to respond for their actions and their destiny[89]—something that we have a better chance to achieve as individuals than as a multitude—then we must react to the game of our hunters and get acquainted with their spells and operations, we must give up being the prey (*venatus*) in a perverse power game that only reveals the extent to which our civilization has descended. Our main problem in dealing with this situation is that as a species we have not achieved a well-established individuality and as a mass we are easily manipulated. Judgement and mass are two states that rarely concur.

If until now I have subscribed to the dialectic between *venator* and *venatus* implicit in the myth of Actaeon is because it is fundamental to understanding the magical operations that underlie modern media. However, Bruno's interpretation as an allegory of psychological transformation, of the encounter between the human and the divine, hardly engages the imagination of our time; therefore, I would like to offer another interpretation better suited to our circumstances. In our quest to weave media networks to predict and control the behavior of our peers we have fallen into them and are being devoured by our own dogs. Actaeon's mastiffs and greyhounds, once hunting instruments, have turned against us. Disguised as smoke screens, echo chambers and disinformation—which we scatter unwittingly and diligently—our dogs sink their teeth in and render us more vulnerable and defenseless than ever.

---

[1] It is interesting to note that the word "mass," derived from the Latin *massa*, (which comes from the Greek *maza*, from the verb *masso*, "to knead") had a magical meaning applied to alchemy. *Maza*, which originally referred to flour dough, was one of the names of *asem*, an alloy of silver and gold that was used to multiply the metals to which it was added (as bread dough increases when yeast is added) and so was called "inexhaustible mass." As for the meaning of "mass" as an agglomeration of people, the first to use it in this sense is Aristophanes in his comedy *Peace*: "O, Poseidon! Well, look at that! What a lovely bunch they make. Stiff and spirited, like beef cakes at a party!" However, this sense of mass as a crowd is absent in the classical period and would only appear again in the eighteenth century in the English *mass meeting* (1733), to extend in the nineteenth and twentieth centuries with expressions such as *mass murder* (1880), *mass movement* (1897), *mass hysteria* (1914), *mass grave* (1918), *mass production* (1920), *mass media* (1923) and, finally, *weapons of mass destruction* (1946). Keeping in mind the magical meaning of the word mass: would it be unreasonable to suggest that modern crowds are a *maza* on which magical operations associated with alchemy operate? A mass that can grow and curdle if the correct additive is added?

[2] John Waller, *Dancing Plagues and Mass Hysteria*, 644. Accessed, April 15, 2018, at: *https://thepsychologist.bps.org.uk/volume-22/edition-7/dancing-plagues-and-mass-hysteria*

[3] Waller, *Dancing Plagues and Mass Hysteria*, 645.

[4] Waller, *Dancing Plagues and Mass Hysteria*, 645.

[5] Waller, *Dancing Plagues and Mass Hysteria*, 644.

[6] Waller, *Dancing Plagues and Mass Hysteria*, 644.

[7] Waller, *Dancing Plagues and Mass Hysteria*, 644.

[8] Waller, *Dancing Plagues and Mass Hysteria*, 645.

[9] Waller, *Dancing Plagues and Mass Hysteria*, 645.

[10] Far from being a past *maladie*, the massive psychogenic disease still occurs in numerous communities in the third world. As with the premodern scenarios, outbreaks of mass hysteria take place in communities that are going through an unusually stressful circumstance. "In modern-day Malaysia and Singapore, for example, factory workers are often drawn from rural communities steeped in beliefs about the spirit world. Those who find it hard to adjust to the regimentation of factory life sometimes enter a dissociative state in which they behave in a

manner shaped by their culture's understanding of spirit possession." (Waller, *Dancing plagues and mass hysteria*, 647).

[11] Alan Gauld, *A History of Hypnotism*, 278.

[12] Edwin Lee, *Animal Magnetism and Magnetic Lucid Somnambulism: With Observations and Illustrative Instances of Analogous Phenomena Occurring Spontaneously*. (London, 1866)

[13] Letter from an unknown doctor to Joseph Philippe François Deleuze (1753-1835). Quoted in *Boston Quarterly Review, Volume 2*, edited by Orestes Augustus Brownson.

[14] In fact, the Pied Piper rids Hamelin of the plague of rats by enchanting them and drowning them in a nearby river, just as Empedocles ridded Selinunte of the plague of stagnated waters by diverting two streams to wash it away.

[15] In *Love in the Western World*, Denis de Rougemont agrees with our analysis of the erotic component of mass movements. The French Revolution, he says, represented "an outburst of passion never before equaled," that is, an unusual explosion of eros "that gave rise to a new form of community: the nation." From this it follows that the nation requires *"that passion shall be translated to the level of the people as a whole."* Now, since passion—which for de Rougemont is the essence of the eros of Courtly love—is actually a form of narcissism, "nationalist ardour is too a self-elevation, a narcissistic love on the part of the collective self. No doubt, its relation with others is seldom averred to be love; nearly always hate is what first appears. But hate of the other is likewise always present in the transports of passionate love. There has thus occurred than a shift of emphasis. And what does national passion require? The elevation of collective might can only lead to the following dilemma: either the triumph of imperialism—of the ambition to become the equal of the whole world— or the people next door strongly object, and there ensues war."

[16] Zweig, *Mental Healers*, 86.

[17] Wilfred Trotter, *Instincts of the Herd in Peace and War* (London: T. Fisher Unwin Ltd., 1921), 26.

[18] Boris Sidis, quoted by Trotter en *Instincts of the Herd in Peace and War*, 27. Italics are mine.

[19] Jesús Martín-Barbero, *De los medios a las mediaciones: comunicación, cultura y hegemonía* (Barcelona: Anthropos, 2010), 27. Author's translation.

[20] Gustave Le Bon, *The Crowd* (Batoche Books, 2001), 13.

[21] Le Bon, *The Crowd*, 16.

[22] Le Bon, *The Crowd*, 16.

[23] Le Bon, *The Crowd*, 17.

[24] Le Bon, *The Crowd*, 17.

[25] Le Bon, *The Crowd*, 17-18.

[26] Le Bon, *The Crowd*, 18. Italics are mine.

[27] Le Bon, *The Crowd*, 21.

[28] Le Bon, *The Crowd*, 36.
[29] Le Bon, *The Crowd*, 38.
[30] Le Bon, *The Crowd*, 38.
[31] Le Bon, *The Crowd*, 40-41.
[32] Le Bon, *The Crowd*, 41.
[33] Le Bon, *The Crowd*, 42.
[34] Le Bon, *The Crowd*, 42-43.
[35] Le Bon, *The Crowd*, 60.
[36] Giordano Bruno, *A General Account of Bonding*, which appears in *Cause, Principle and Unity: Essays on Magic* (Cambridge, Cambridge University Press, 2004), 153.
[37] Le Bon, *The Crowd*, 60.
[38] Robert Musil, *The Man Without Qualities* (London: Picador, 1995), 145.
[39] Le Bon, *The Crowd*, 60.
[40] Le Bon, *The Crowd*, 64.
[41] Le Bon, *The Crowd*, 72.
[42] Le Bon, *The Crowd*, 72. That Napoleon, who has been regarded as the mold of the modern dictator, would have attached such importance to acting as an essential means to the manipulation of the masses is rather telling. In this regard, René de Chateaubriand branded Napoleon an "actor and comedian, even with the passions that he lacks: he is always on stage; in Cairo he is a renegade who boasts of having done away with the papacy; in Paris he is restorer of the Christian religion; Sometimes he is inspired, sometimes he is a philosopher." (Chateaubriand, *De Bounaparte y de los Borbones*, Barcelona: Acantilado, 91. Author's translation).
[43] Le Bon, *The Crowd*, 75-76.
[44] Wilfred Trotter, *Instincts of the Herd in Peace and War* (London: T. Fisher Unwin Ltd., 1921), 20.
[45] Trotter, *Instincts of the Herd in Peace and War*, 22.
[46] Trotter, *Instincts of the Herd in Peace and War*, 29.
[47] Trotter, *Instincts of the Herd in Peace and War*, 29.
[48] Trotter, *Instincts of the Herd in Peace and War*, 30.
[49] Trotter, *Instincts of the Herd in Peace and War*, 27.
[50] Bruno, *A General Account of Bonding*, 168-169.
[51] Bruno, *A General Account of Bonding*, 157. (Parenthesis is mine)
[52] Trotter, *Instincts of the Herd in Peace and War*, 49.
[53] Here it is important to highlight that for Trotter the manifestations of mental instability "are not diseases of the individual in the ordinary sense at all, but inevitable consequences of man's biological history…" It is only when these manifestations surpass a certain threshold that they become true mental pathologies. Needless to say, most humans are a mixture of the two types

described by Trotter and only a minority could be described as completely "stable," normopathic, or completely "unstable," schizophrenic.

[54] Trotter, *Instincts of the Herd in Peace and War*, 60.

[55] Mikkel Borch-Jacobsen, *Sigmund Freud, Hipnotizador*, which appears in *Sigmund Freud, la hipnosis, textos (1886-1893)* (Bogotá: Arial, 2017), 144. Author's translation.

[56] Borch-Jacobsen, *Sigmund Freud, Hipnotizador*, 154.

[57] By 1920 this obstacle, which was initially described as a counter-representation, became the "death instinct" which Freud introduced in his essay *Beyond the Pleasure Principle*.

[58] Borch-Jacobsen, *Sigmund Freud, Hipnotizador*, 156.

[59] In *Stanzas, Word and Phantasm in Western Culture*, Giorgio Agamben comments: "it is probable that contemporary psychoanalysis, which has reevaluated the role of the phantasm in the psychic processes and which seems intent on considering itself, always more explicitly, as a general theory of the phantasm, would find a useful point of reference in a doctrine that, many centuries previously, had conceived of Eros as an essentially phantasmatic process and had prepared a large place in the life of the spirit for the phantasm."

[60] Sigmund Freud, *Group Psychology and Analysis of the Ego*, which appears in *The Standard Edition of the Complete Psychological Works of Sigmund Freud, Volume XVIII*,

[61] Zweig, *Mental Healers*, 332.

[62] Freud, *Group Psychology and Analysis of the Ego*, 57.

[63] Freud, *Group Psychology and Analysis of the Ego*, 51-52.

[64] Freud, *Group Psychology and Analysis of the Ego*, 52-53.

[65] Freud, *Group Psychology and Analysis of the Ego*, 54.

[66] Freud, *Group Psychology and Analysis of the Ego*, 58.

[67] Freud, *Group Psychology and Analysis of the Ego*, 58.

[68] Marsilio Ficino, *Commentary on Plato's Symposium* (University of Missouri, 1944), 189.

[69] The Freudian mechanism of narcissism and idealization is evident throughout Ficino's *De Amore*. In her preliminary study of her edition Rocío de la Villa Ardura sums up the matter: "In other words, the lover attracted by his resemblance to another—for both have been formed responding to a common ideal—perceives the concrete image of the beloved, and through imagination, which brings perfection to the deficiencies and deformations still existing in the beloved compared to the model, is when the soul remembers that common, already abstract ideal."

[70] Ioan P. Culianu, *Eros and Magic in the Renaissance* (Chicago: The University of Chicago Press, 1987), 31. Parenthesis are mine.

[71] Sigmund Freud, *Group Psychology and Analysis of the Ego*, 102.

[72] Freud, *Group Psychology and Analysis of the Ego*, 114.

[73] Freud, *Group Psychology and Analysis of the Ego*, 114.

[74] This erotic character of the masses is beautifully portrayed by Charles Baudelaire, so familiar with the Parisian crowds of his time, in his prose poem *Crowds*: "What men call love is a very small, restricted, feeble thing compared with this ineffable orgy, this divine prostitution of the soul giving itself entire, all its poetry and all its charity, to the unexpected as it comes along, to the strangers as he passes." (Baudelaire, *Paris Spleen*, 20.)

[75] Freud, *Group Psychology and Analysis of the Ego*, 116.

[76] In *Love in the Western World*, de Rougemont arrives, by a different route, to a similar conclusion: "and, more over, let me stress one striking feature. The masses respond to the dictator in a particular country *in the same way* as the women to the tactics of suitors"

[77] Ioan P. Culianu, *Eros y magia en el renacimiento, 1484* (Madrid: Ediciones Siruela, 1999), 103. This last phrase does not appear in the English edition and was translated from the Spanish version.

[78] Freud, *Group Psychology and Analysis of the Ego*, 92.

[79] Mikkel Borch-Jacobsen, *Sigmund Freud, Hipnotizador*, which appears in *Sigmund Freud, la hipnosis, textos (1886-1893)* (Bogotá, Arial, 2017), 148.

[80] Sigmund Freud, *Beyond the Pleasure Principle* (New York: W.W. Norton & Company, 1961), 48.

[81] Quoted by Giordano Bruno in *The Heroic Frenzies*.

[82] Freud, *Beyond the Pleasure Principle*, 4.

[83] Freud, *Beyond the Pleasure Principle*, 36.

[84] Sigmund Freud, *The Future of an Ilusion*, which appears in The *Standard Edition of the Complete Psychological Works of Sigmund Freud, Volume XXI*, 6.

[85] Freud, *The Future of an Illusion*, 6.

[86] Freud, *The Future of an Illusion*, 6.

[87] Freud, *The Future of an Illusion*, 15.

[88] Freud, *The Future of an Illusion*, 7.

[89] In his classic study *Propaganda* French philosopher and sociologist Jacques Ellul comments on how "the individual is of no interest to the propangandist; as an isolated unit he presents much too resistance to external action." The solution that propaganda, either state or corporate, gives to this problem is quite simple "the individual is never considered as an individual, but always in terms of what he has in common with others, such as his motivations, his feelings, or his myths. He is reduced to an average; and, except for a small percentage, action based on averages will be effectual." (Ellul, *Propaganda*, 6-7) Thus, the question is how to achieve an individuality that allows us to stay outside the average of the manipulated population.

Intermezzo

> The war was lost the treaty signed
> I was not caught I crossed the line
> I was not caught though many tried
> I live among you well disguised
> I had to leave my life behind
> I dug some graves you'll never find
> The story's told with facts and lies
> I have a name but nevermind
> Nevermind
> Nevermind
> The war was lost the treaty signed
> There's truth that lives and truth that dies
> I don't know which so nevermind
> **Leonard Cohen,** *Nevermind*

Ecology, cybernetics and the anima mundi

Two fundamental magical notions underpin the mentality of the modern world: the first is a teleological notion of progress that underlies a good deal of the sociological, historical and economic theories of the nineteenth century, a violation to modern rationalism which, according to some scholars, would also afflict evolutionary biology. Regardless of whether we speak of a dialectic between classes that leads to a new socioeconomic structure, of human history as an objective account with a discernible purpose or, why not, of the ability of a species to adapt to its environment, the mechanism is the same: the goal has always been there, the question is to fulfill a destiny that has been laid out in advance. One of the most insidious forms of this magical legacy—turned into determinism in a myriad of fields—is evident in the basic assumption of the market economy since its introduction in the Victorian era.[1]

British philosopher John Gray briefly summarizes the situation:

> The thinkers of the enlightenment, such as Thomas Jefferson, Tom Payne, John Stuart Mill and Karl Marx never doubted that the future for every nation in the world was to accept some version of western institutions and values. A diversity of

cultures was not a permanent condition of human life. It was a stage on the way to a universal civilization. All such thinkers advocated the creation of a single worldwide civilization, in which the varied traditions and cultures of the past were superseded by a new, universal community founded on reason.[2]

Underlying this vision of a universal society—a "globalized" world in our current terms—is the idea that human societies evolve in a single direction, specifically towards a type of liberal democracy regulated by the market. It is this socioeconomic *telos*, as alive now as it was in the mid-nineteenth century, that produced an idea as obtuse as Francis Fukuyama's *The End of History and The Last Man*, who asserted that neoliberalism was the culmination of the socio-cultural evolution of our species, its most refined and ultimate form of government. The most blatant apology to free-market capitalism.

It is worth noting that the magical atmosphere that surrounds market economy goes beyond a teleology transformed into determinism. For the Swiss economist and philosopher Hans Christoph Binswanger the drive of modern economics, and particularly market economy, to unlimited growth is actually a modern transformation of alchemy:

> It is not vital to alchemy's aim, in the sense of increasing wealth, that lead be actually transmuted into gold. It will suffice if a substance of no value is transformed into one of value: paper, for example, into money. We can interpret the economic process as alchemy if it is possible to arrive at money without having earned it through corresponding effort: if the economy is a top hat, so to speak, that yields a previously nonexistent rabbit: in other words, if a genuine value *creation* is possible which is not bound by any limits and is therefore, in this sense, sorcery or magic.[3]

Binswanger's argument, based on an alchemical interpretation of the second part of Goethe's *Faust*, is based on the creation of value through the metaphorical use of the two basic substances of the Great Work: mercury and sulphur. In his reading, the philosophical mercury is involved in the creation of paper money, which is equivalent to a process of *solutio* or dissolution, through which the mineral reserves of gold are "liquefied" and converted into "currency." The second step of the Work, *coagulatio* or coagulation, is equivalent to the "solidification" of paper currency by the acquisition of properties or the production of commodities through the application of sulphur to the liquid mercury, which in Faust is represented as the fire that acts as the source of energy of the industrial revolution. The marriage of mercury (currency) and sulfur (property, commodity) represents the alchemical process for the production of *sal* (salt) which, in Binswanger's interpretation, is equivalent to the production of capital in the sense of an actual means of production.

This way of understanding market economy would seem supported by billionaire and investor George Soros who, a couple of years after the publication of Binswanger's book, argued that if alchemy had failed "to turn base metals into gold [it was] because the behaviour of metals is governed by laws of universal validity which cannot be modified by any statements, incantations or rituals."[4] However, instead of base metals and enchantments, economy involves a variety of participants who are "'easily influenced by theories and therefore highly susceptible to the methods of alchemy.' Thus, while alchemy failed as a science, economics 'can succeed as alchemy'."[5]

Apart from this alchemical vision of market economy there is an "esoteric" interpretation of Marxism promoted by philosophers and economists like Robert Kurz, Moishe Postone, and Anselm Jappe that adhere to the viewpoint of the German school of *Wertkritik* (value criticism). Kurz in particular proposes a distinction between the exoteric and esoteric Marx, the first of which would be a result of the political reception of his work in Leninism, and which has become dogma, and the second that "involves the development of a categorical critique of capitalism, a critique that is never brought to completion within Marx's work, [and which] remains much less accessible."[6] The esoteric interpretation of Marxism has developed mainly from two chapters of *Das Kapital*: chapter IV, where Marx speaks of the concept of capital as an "automatic subject" and chapter I, which postulates the fetishistic character of the commodity, a topic that I will examine in more detail in a later chapter.

Regarding the automatic subject, Marx argues that value exists in two main forms, one when it is associated with money (M) and the other when it is associated with commodities (C) as such. So, as autonomous forms,

> the money-form, which the value of commodities assumes in the case of simple circulation, serves only one purpose, namely, their exchange, and vanishes in the final result of the

movement. On the other hand, in the circulation M-C-M, both the money and the commodity represent only different modes of existence of value itself, the money its general mode, and the commodity its particular, or, so to say, disguised mode. It is constantly changing from one form to the other without thereby becoming lost, and thus turning into an automatic subject. If now we take in turn each of the two different forms which self-expanding value successively assumes in the course of its life, we then arrive at these two propositions: Capital is money: Capital is commodities. In truth, however, value is here the active factor in a process, in which, while constantly assuming the form in turn of money and commodities, it at the same time changes in magnitude, differentiates itself by throwing off surplus-value from itself; the original value, in other words, expands spontaneously. For the movement, in the course of which it adds surplus-value, is its own movement, its expansion, therefore, is automatic expansion. Because it is value, it has acquired the occult quality of being able to add value to itself. It brings forth living offspring, or, at the least, lays golden eggs.[7]

In this fragment Marx seems to indicate that the value of a commodity can "transmute" into two "states" or specific modalities, that is, into currency (mercury) or into the commodity itself (sulphur). The value which has "acquired the occult quality of being able to add value to itself" is no other than "money capital which, while being money itself, creates still more money."[8] That this transmutation of value is automatic and that there is no loss between one modality and the other agrees with the alchemical character of market economy which states that *ex nihilo* creation of value is perfectly possible. Now, beyond this relationship between capital and alchemy, it is the "automatic" character of economic value where we find the relevance of magic for our subject.

Here it is important to make plain that the contributions of magic have not been the only ones to have covertly defined the modern world and it is in the intersection of teleological determinism with the "mechanicism" that emerged with the Scientific Revolution where we find the origin of one of the most persistent ideas of our time: the possibility of creating complex self-regulated systems, be it a market economy, a nuclear dynamic between two superpowers or an artificial intelligence. Only by combining the *myth of the machine*—the notion of a system or mechanism that can operate without the necessity of human intervention—

with the *telos* of the ancient world it is possible to imagine a complex system that reaches a state of dynamic and perpetual equilibrium. However, the authenticity of the myth of the machine as an entirely modern contribution comes into question if we look at it from a historical point of view.

One way to clarify this matter is by looking at the evolution of the word "automatic." This term comes from the Greek word *automatos* and originally meant "spontaneous," "which moves by itself" or "which haves a mind of its own," and was used exclusively to designate phenomena of divine character. Homer uses it in *The Iliad* to refer to the tripods of Hephaestus and to the movements of the gates of Olympus. In its original meaning *automatos* did not belong to the human world and always referred to the work of a god or of the natural world, which back then had a will of its own that lay outside of human reach and was thus compatible with the classic ideas of destiny and purpose (*telos*). *Automatos* became *automatus* in Latin, in use in the early years of the Christian era, and appears in English in the sixteenth century as the now obsolete adjective *automatous*, which referred to an "spontaneous" event that happens by "self-will," partly keeping the original meaning. However, with the proliferation of mechanisms that took place during the seventeenth and eighteenth centuries the term took on the opposite meaning and began to refer to an event that happens without the intervention of a mind, specifically the type of behavior characteristic of a machine.

This change of meaning, which echoed a change in the attitude of the human towards their world, gave rise to a new idea: that it was possible to create an "autonomous and automatic whole" by assembling parts and connecting them in a mechanical device. This notion began to gain popularity in the fourteenth century when Nicholas Oresme speculated that "God might have started off the universe as a kind of clock and left it to run by itself."[9] The metaphysics underlying this idea allowed the world to begin to be imagined as an enormous mechanism of divine origin whose functioning could be deciphered if one understood how its parts were assembled, a circumstance that reveals the moment of intersection between premodern teleology and mechanistic determinism. It is in this *mechanism of divine origin* that we find the conjunction of the machine with the third magical notion that underlies the modern world: the *anima mundi*. We see, therefore, that despite its claim to independence, the myth of the machine has never been truly distinct from the idea of the divine.

Earlier we examined how the idea of the soul of the world—which served to explain the innate attraction of beings and objects, their community and their natural place in the cosmos—was transformed into gravity by Newton, a geometrical law that describes the movement and attraction of physical bodies as an infinite and omniscient spirit in which matter moves according to mathematics." With Mesmer this force becomes *animal gravity,* which was later to be characterized as a kind of magnetism, a force of sympathetic character that circulates through the community of living beings moving them and bringing them to harmony and fullness: soul and gravity at one and the same time.

During the late eighteenth and early nineteenth centuries this magical-rational configuration was used to explain the coherence of the universe as well as its physical attributes. The luminiferous ether, which appears in both the mystical and scientific theories of the time, is the most characteristic expression of this configuration. But what for early eighteenth century figures such as George Berkeley was an essentially spiritual ether comparable to the Holy Spirit, by the nineteenth century begins to be reified into a material ether that serves, quite literally, as a medium for the movement of the waves and particles that make up the physical universe. This concept disappeared from modern physics with the introduction of Einstein's theory of relativity, which made it supposedly superfluous when it proved that the movement of light and matter could be described without the need of a single universal framework.

Although the idea of *anima mundi* was apparently banished from mainstream physics, the truth is that it had already penetrated the heart of the modern world centuries ago; the tenacity with which this idea has taken hold of the psyche of our tradition is as surprising as it is suspicious; we seem unable to get away from its "center of gravity." Among the disciplines most influenced by it is biology. Alexander von Humboldt's idea of nature as a interconnected organism of vast proportions was influenced and, simultaneously, influenced Goethe's idea that the only way to understand the natural world as a whole was to experience it through a combination of reason and feeling; an attitude that lies at the core of German and English Romanticism. Following this line of thought, by the late nineteenth century, German zoologist Karl August Möbius (1825-1908) developed the concept of *biocenosis* (from *bio*, life and *koinos*, common) popularly known as "biotic community," to refer to a group of organisms that coexist in a habitat or *biotope* (from *topos*, "place"). The idea of a community of living beings that coexist in harmony and equilibrium is of considerable antiquity and can be traced back to the *anima mundi*, the community of the universal spirit that gives order and cohesion to the cosmos through eros. Marsilio Ficino gives a concise description of this idea in *De amore*:

> Again, all the parts of fire freely and mutually coalesce, and so with the parts of earth, water, and air: so likewise with every kind of animal: animals of the same kind always flock together instinctively. Here is illustrated love for equal and similar things. Who, then, will doubt that love for everything is innate in everything?[10]

Möbius' biotic community—yet another transformation of the soul of the world—is the immediate ancestor of the concept of ecosystem devised by the English botanist Arthur Roy Clapham in the early 1930s and later developed by Sir Arthur George Tansley (1871-1955). One of the most peculiar features of Tansley's thought is "the *lack* of 'splitting' — between Man and Nature, between Nature and Culture. Tansley's principal contributions were, in contradistinction to American ecology, to emphasize the systemic interrelations of human activity and botanical phenomena — he sees no real difference between those ecosystems which are natural and those which are 'anthropogenic'."[11] Given this tendency not to distinguish between nature and culture, Tansley was particularly prone to applying mechanistic metaphors to the natural world. Indeed, his notion of ecosystem was influenced by the idea of the human brain as an electric grid which, he thought, was the way in which the energy exchanges between organisms and their habitat actually took place.[12] Like Nicholas Oresme, Tansley used the most advanced piece of technology of his time as a metaphor for the workings of the world. What he was actually doing was projecting the myth of the machine unto nature, imposing a kind of *anima machinalis* thinking that he was describing it on its own terms.[13]

Tansley's vision of the ecosystem had a profound influence on the work of the brothers Eugene and Howard Odum, who laid the foundations for ecosystem ecology in their work *Fundaments of Ecology* (1953). Howard Odum in particular used ideas from systems theory to describe "the underlying structure of nature."[14] The result was an entirely factitious understanding of the natural world in which ecosystems were literally represented as electric circuits governed by feedback loops that represented the energy exchanges between different species of plants and animals; a crude reduction of the wealth of the natural world that focused exclusively on its functional aspect.

The mutual influence between ecology, systems theory and cybernetics,[15] particularly evident in the work of the Odum brothers, gave rise to a curious way of understanding the place of the human in the world. Since the idea of an ecosystem is really a mechanistic description of the natural world focused exclusively on its functional aspects, the result of this vision was that in disciplines such as cybernetics the organic forms began to be understood in an entirely mechanical way. This was not the original idea, because

> as a general mathematical theory of self-regulating mechanisms, cybernetics would transcend the boundary between machines and organisms. It would not do this by rejecting concepts of purposes, goals, and will (as in behaviorist psychology), but by *expanding the category of "machines,"* via the concept of feedback, to include these notions.[16]

Of course, the procedure through which this *expansion of the category of machines* took place was not to render the systems more "human" but rather to lower the humans by making them more machine-like. Here I should note that, like magic, cybernetics presupposes a continuity between the elements that constitute a system, no longer in a natural or cosmic context but in a mechanical and artificial one. As a consequence, from the perspective of the *anima machinalis* there is no difference between a machine and a living being, organisms are only abstractions, "nodes in networks, acting and reacting to flows of information."[17] Understood as a transformation of the soul of the world, these flows of information, or feedback loops that come and go through the nodes of the system, are nothing but the correspondences and transferences of sympathetic magic, the immense network of eros stripped of its human character and converted into data. The impulse is exactly the same, only the playing field has changed: while magic intended to govern and control the "human-cosmos ecosystem," cybernetics aims to govern and control the "human-machine ecosystem," which is nothing but a functional reduction of the hermetic notion of *anima mundi*.[18] Pneuma become information.

The idea that humans are just another mechanism—a sort of analog machine that inhabits a complex system and operates through feedback cycles—revitalized multiple fields of study, from anthropology and psychology to communication sciences and artificial intelligence. During the Cold War, the notion of government (from greek *kybernao*, "to steer a boat") implicit in cybernetics, became an integral part of the technical and psychological life of the Western world. With the implementation of cybernetics, two essential activities to any form of control became widespread: information processing and reciprocal communication. The first of these, says historian James Beniger,

> is essential to all purposive activity, which is by definition goal directed and must therefore involve the continual comparison of current states to future goals [...] simultaneously with the comparison of inputs to goals, two-way interaction between controller and controlled must also occur, not only to communicate influence from the former to the latter, but also to communicate back the results of this action (hence the term *feedback* for this reciprocal flow of information back to the controller).[19]

It is easy to recognize that the cybernetic dynamic between controller and controlled is a modern echo of the *venator/venatus* relationship that characterizes brunian erotic magic, a transformation in which the magician's role, his personal and emotional factors, are minimized and mechanized. The modern technological world presents itself as a machine that, at its most basic level, reproduces magical processes. Programmed magic.

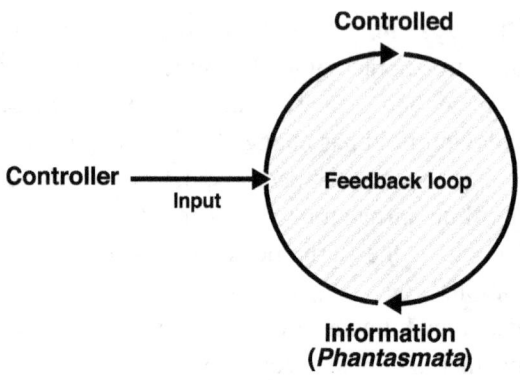

This relation to the idea of *anima mundi* and to the dialectic between hunter and prey allows us to deduce that cybernetics, understood as "the entire field of control and communication theory, whether in the machine or in the animal"[20] which includes "all of the procedures by which one mind may affect another,"[21] is closely related to the magical-heretical system of manipulation I have described so far and, in effect, acts as its technological arm: its main function has been the analysis and application of magical-psychological operations to mass media. For the first time a form of magic uses statistics to account for the efficiency of its operations. As a matter of fact, Norbert Wiener, the father of cybernetics, understood media as a self-regulated system that, ideally, could serve "to 'correct' the actions of a public leader by offering them accurate information about the performance of society as a whole."[22]

The cybernetic account even offers a somewhat impoverished explanation of the teleological behaviors that characterized premodern thought. In 1941, Wiener along with neurobiologist Arturo Rosenblueth and engineer Julian Bigelow developed a theory known as *feedback control* with which they aimed to describe how they could "predict an airplane's future course from information about its present location and velocity. Out of this work came a highly general statistical theory of prediction based on incomplete information."[23] The most interesting part of the paper was its concept of negative feedback or circular self-corrective cycles,

> in which information about the effects of an adjustment to a dynamic system is continuously returned to that system as input and controls further adjustments. In 1943 the three published the landmark article "Behavior, Purpose, and Teleology" which

emphasized comparisons between servo devices and the behavior of living organisms guided by sensory perception. Essentially, they described goal-oriented "teleological" behavior as as movement controlled by negative feedback.[24]

For cybernetics the *telos* of an organism is no longer the fully developed state to which it is naturally "pulled" toward by its final cause, it is a simple behavior with an express goal but lacking *potentia*, or any other purpose beyond the functional. One might ask if this degradation is the price of having entrusted important sectors of knowledge to technologists, the price we must pay to obtain practical and applicable results to one particular area: war.

Eros and modern war

Understanding the role of eros in modern warfare requires going back in time to one of the most evident points of encounter between these two manifestations: courtly love. If implicit to this form of love is a desire for death through passion, a desire whose sole purpose is that of effecting a reunion with the divine, our present cultural construction of love "is linked with a theory of the *fruitfulness of suffering* which encourages or obscurely justifies in the recesses of the Western mind a liking for war."[25] The language we use to describe love is unequivocal: Eros is a young archer who shoots deadly arrows, arrows with pneumatic tips that penetrate the soul of the beloved and invade his or her imagination.

> A lover *besieged* his lady. He delivered *amorous assaults* on her virtue. He *pressed* her closely. He *pursued* her. He sought to *overcome* the final defences of her modesty, and to take them by surprise. In the end the lady *surrendered to his mercy*. And thereupon, by a curious inversal typical enough of courtesy, he became the lady's *prisoner* as well as her *conqueror*. He became a *vassal* of this *suzerain*, in accordance with the laws of feudal warfare, as if it had been he who suffered defeat.[26]

Two things emerge from this fragment. In the first place, it is revealed to us that in the myth of Actaeon—the story of the young *venator*, who ends up as *venatus*—is codified the whole of the erotic, and warlike, dialectic of the West. To love/hunt is to make war and to conquer is, simultaneously, to surrender to the beloved and be transformed into its prey. And second, that the fact that the language in which we express love and war is virtually identical opens the possibility of a natural relationship, that is, "a physiological kinship of the fighting and procreative instincts."[27] However, in light of the discoveries of twentieth-century psychology, this conclusion would seem hasty; the psychological sustenance of our forms of love and war could very well be based on the neurotic deficiencies of the "Western" character and would therefore apply only to our particular form of culture. The study Wilhelm Reich's work I will present in a later chapter will give us important clues in this regard.

Now, although there is no strictly "natural" relationship between love and war, there is a cultural relationship, and this explains the existence of a common rule "applicable to the arts of both love and war—the rule called chivalry."[28] It is in the code of chivalry, in the ideal of a heroic action undertaken by love, where these two expressions converge. The medieval tournament, which also shows the relationship between sport and war, is the area where the erotic joins in with blood and violence. In it appears the custom according to which "a knight carried—like Lancelot—the veil or a fragment of the dress of his lady, and sometimes after the lists handed this to her stained with his blood."[29] Love and courage are displayed simultaneously in hand-to-hand combat. In the medieval tournament the *ethos* of love and war is one and the same thing.

Apart from giving classic war its template, the code of chivalry also gave it its emphasis on aesthetics. The knight adorns himself for battle, his armor, helmet and sword, his plume and banner exalt his social position and dignify his office; to make war is not only necessary, it is something noble and elevated that unconsciously puts man at the service of something beyond himself and brings him closer to the sublime and the divine. War is an art, "an attempt to endow instinct with a kind of correct deportment" or, depending on the point of view, to endow neurosis with a sense of style. In the martial arts that emerged throughout the world during the premodern period, only one trait rivals with functionality and efficiency: the aesthetic factor. In the West it was in fifteenth-century Italy, where the art of war became the expression of a flourishing and profoundly humane culture, where the rights of prisoners were respected during wartime, cities and towns were almost never destroyed and, at times, the duel between the leaders of two armies was enough to finish a campaign. This "civilization" of war, says de Rougemont, is the opposite to its "militarization."

This situation, however, would radically change with the introduction of artillery by the end of the fifteenth century. Little by little, this form warfare would transform

> the inspired and magnificent knights into troops disciplined and uniform. The transformation was going to result in our own day in abolishing every vestige of the passion of making war, as gradually men serving machines became themselves machines and felt neither anger nor pity while performing a few automatic movements intended to deal death at a distance.[30]

Of course, knights despised firearms as a debasement of their art and did so because the technique to impart death from a distance, tells us of Rougemont, "has no equivalent in any imaginable code of love."[31] Eros' arrows require a sensitivity unnecessary to operate an arquebus or a machine gun. The mechanization of the technical means of destruction renders war inhuman and *neutralizes passion*. "The assuaging violence in bloodshed gave place to mass brutality, and rival hordes were hurled at one another, not by the impulse of passionate frenzy, but in obedience of the calculating brains of engineers."[32] This collectivization and dehumanization of war belongs to the same tendency towards automation that turned the *anima mundi* into an *anima machinalis* for which there is no difference between a machine and a living being. According to Walter Benjamin, this same trend led us to the age of the technological reproducibility.

For Benjamin, reproducibility, which is based exclusively on technical means, undermines the authenticity of an artistic work (how can the "original" be distinguished from a copy of a photographic negative?), and in doing so it detaches it from its ritual foundation, which gave it its social and religious function. This secularization of art implies the weakening of its "aura," the halo which gives it its authenticity, which roots it in its cultural context and in reality itself. The mechanization that comes with technique is the main means of this secularization and, indeed, it could be said that what photography and film did to painting, the machine gun and the nerve gas did to honorable war. Artillery and its subsequent developments weaken the "aura" of classical warfare and break the bond with the *passion* that gave it its typical form of expression. Deprived of this aura and its traditional environment, the warrior libido seeks a new scenario, and both de Rougemont and Benjamin agree that politics offered itself as a perfect match.

This insertion of libidinal energy in the field of politics implies its aestheticization, so Benjamin is not off the mark in pointing out that "all efforts to aestheticize politics culminate in one point. That one point is war." [33] Only war "makes it possible to mobilize all of today's technological resources"[34] and allows them to reach their fullness. It was the application of technology to war that changed its face and directed all the forces of the state to the same end. This process turned the states into *war machines* whose end is the destruction of the enemy. After World War I, de Rougemont says, there is no longer talk of "the 'diplomatic fuss' of ultimatums and 'declarations of war' [...] It follows that the defeat of a country could no longer be symbolical or metaphorical—that is, be confined to certain agreed signs—but had to actually be its death."[35] Conquest, which once had its peer in the erotic dialectic, becomes vulgar destruction.

With the secularization and mechanization of art and war we witness a change of historical proportions: the aesthetic aspect of art, its *cosmetic* function as the face of the world/goddess, ceases to be the province of eros and aligns with the political leaders and, through them, with the *war machine*. What clearer image of the aestheticized leader than Leni Riefenstahl's Hitler or Stalin portrayed by actor Mikheil Gelovani? The face of the modern world is the wrath of the Goddess (and not her shame at being seen naked), it is an anger that instead of transforming the hunter into the hunted wants to annihilate him. Modern war is total war, Venus and Diana become Bellona; its method is the totalitarianism of the image.

The battlefield of this new form of war is, according to Giorgio Agamben, "social life in its entirety,

> whose storm troopers are the media, whose victims are all the peoples of the Earth. Politicians, the media establishment, and the advertising industry have understood the insubstantial character of the face and of the community it opens up, and thus they transform it into a miserable secret that they must make sure to control at all costs. State power today is no longer founded on the monopoly of the legitimate use of violence—a monopoly that states share increasingly willingly with other nonsovereign organizations such as the United Nations and

terrorist organizations; rather, it is founded above all on the control of appearance (of *doxa*).[36]

"A Totalitarian State," says de Rougemont "is but the state of war being prolonged and renewed, and then made permanent, in a nation,"[37] that is, maintained by force of aesthetics. Now, if total war annihilates every possibility of passion in human terms,

> politics transferred individual passions to the level of the collective being. Everything that a totalitarian education withheld from individuals was heaped upon the personified nation. It is the nation (or the party) that had passions. It was the nation (or the party) that took over [...] and the rush made unwittingly towards a heroic and therefore divinizing death.[38]

This is the mechanism through which the libido is propagated among the multitudes of a country or a party, and the means through which they begin to be manipulated. In the service of state and politics, aesthetics assumes its cosmetic role, its function as the face of the world, but for this it must pervert itself and become an aesthetic of death. The most evident expression of the alignment of aesthetics with death and modern warfare is Filippo Marinetti's manifesto on the colonial war in Ethiopia:

> For twenty-seven years, we Futurists have rebelled against the idea that war is anti-aesthetic.... We therefore state: ... War is beautiful because—thanks to its gas masks, its terrifying megaphones, its flame throwers, and light tanks—it establishes man's dominion over the subjugated machine. War *is* beautiful because it inaugurates the dreamed-of metallization of the human body. War is beautiful because it enriches a flowering meadow with the fiery orchids of machine-guns. War is beautiful because it combines gunfire, barrages, cease-fires, scents, and the fragrance of putrefaction into a symphony. War is beautiful because it creates new architectures, like those of armored tanks, geometric squadrons of aircraft, spirals of smoke from burning villages, and much more. . . . Poets and artists of Futurism, ... remember these principles of an aesthetic of war, that they may illuminate ... your struggles for a new poetry and a new sculpture![39]

How wrong was Marinetti to think that war gives us dominion over the machine and not the other way around, how far is he from understanding that with the "metallization of the human body" it is more what we lose and what is proportionally gained by the mechanism.

Needless to say, his atrocious manifesto became an important inspiration for the fascist movement that engulfed Italy and the European continent during World War II.

Now, the fact that the mechanization of war weakens its aura and distances it from the sphere of human affairs, converts it—for those of us fortunate enough not to live it in the flesh—in a representation that is witnessed from a distance, a spectacle. Modern war, completely dehumanized, "transmutes killing into 'taking out,' bloodshed into 'body counts,' and the chaos of battle into 'scenarios,' 'game theory,' 'cost benefits,' as weapons become 'toys' and bombs 'smart'."[40] Deployed, the technical means of war can take full advantage of the potential for control and mastery, the ideal of "government" implicit in cybernetics. The *anima mundi* turned into feedback loops becomes the ideal medium for the dialectic of the Cold War, the dialectic of annihilation. At just three minutes from "nuclear midnight"[41], this dynamic is more relevant now than ever.

However, it is important to note that the aura of war is not annihilated by its mechanization and its remnants are lived as a passion not for the extinction of one's own life but for general and indiscriminate destruction. A passion perfectly portrayed by actor George C. Scott in his role of Patton:

> The general walks the field after a battle. Churned earth, burnt tanks, dead men. He takes up a dying officer, kisses him, surveys the havoc, and says: "I love it. God help me I do love it so. I love it more than my life."[42]

The ritual element implicit in the aura of classical warfare—the sacrifice and mortification necessary to ascend to the divine—is perverted in modern warfare and becomes mass sacrifice, genocide and ethnic cleansing, mass suicide and suicide terrorism, final solution. The libidinal energy released in the sexual act, which can be manipulated by magical means, is now released with the ritual immolation of millions of victims; the rite has become secularized and turned into bureaucracy but its essence and yearning remain the same: death. Its energy is also manipulable and modern media is the instrument of its terrifying spell.

The opposition between Eros and Thanatos is factitious, both can push in the same direction. Desire, suffocated by its lack of aura, can contribute to secular death, to oblivion. Aphrodite and Persephone have always been two faces of the same goddess.

The genealogy of the magic system I have constructed thus far could be expressed in two graphics that make reference to the pond of time I mentioned in the introduction. The first shows the development of hermetic philosophy and Renaissance magic from its origins in Empedocles and Plato, (imagine each circle as the impact of a pebble in the water):

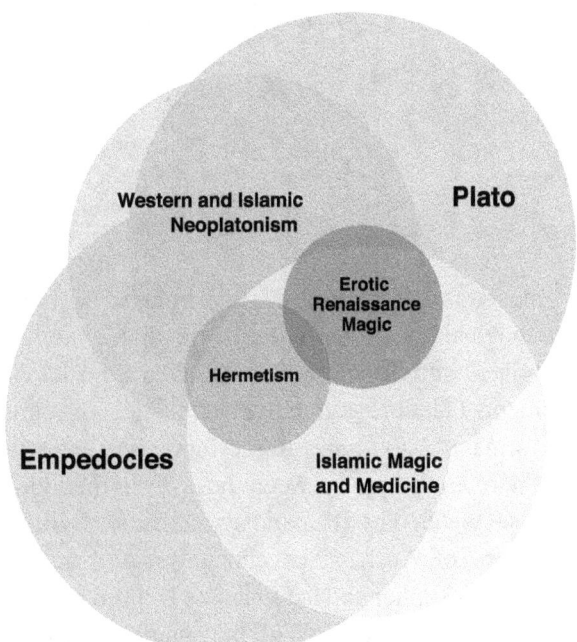

This diagram shows the different *fields of influence* that lead to the system of Renaissance erotic magic. It should be noted that intersections between circles should not be understood as concrete categories but as a mutual zone of influence where new transformations of the original system take place.

Within the field of influence of Renaissance erotic magic we find the subdivisions (animal magnetism, hypnosis and mass psychology/psychoanalysis) to which we have dedicated the first part of this study:

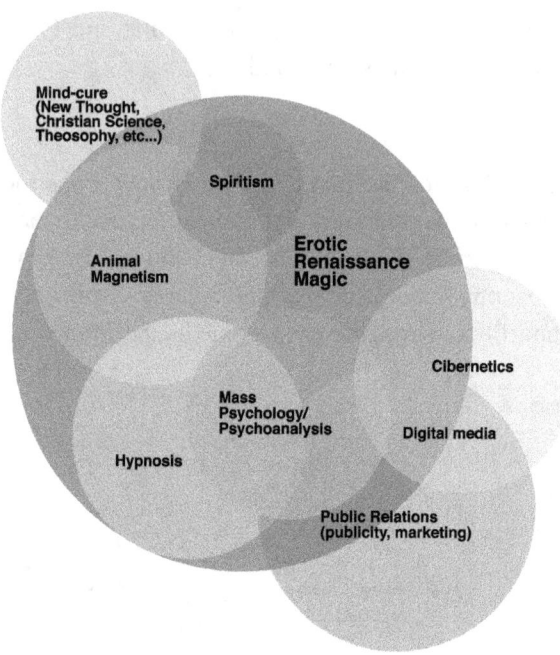

The second and third part of this volume will be devoted to elucidating the magical bonds that underlie the three outer circles: public relations (and related activities), cybernetics and, to a lesser extent, the religious movements that emerged in the late nineteenth century and were categorized as forms of *Mind-cure*. In the fourth and seventh chapter we will delve into the relationships between these disciplines and their recent evolution into *new media*. The fifth and sixth chapters will be devoted to examining the work of Austrian psychoanalyst and scientist Wilhelm Reich and French philosopher and activist Guy Debord and their proposals to counteract the disastrous effects of the magic system that we have examined thus far.

---

[1] In fact, the ways of thinking of Victorian market economy have their origin in *physiocracy*, a school of economic thought founded in France in the eighteenth century which gave rise to the idea of *laissez faire*, a vital concept for all subsequent developments in free market economy. Regarding the expression *laissez faire*, which advocates deregulation and the disappearance of commercial regulations on the part of the state, it is important to note that it originates in the studies of François de Quesnay—one of the founders of the physiocratic school—

on Chinese culture, specifically, on one of the basic concepts of Taoism, *wu wei*, or not-doing.

[2] John Gray, *False Dawn, The Delusions of Global Capitalism* (New York: The New Press, 1998), 2.

[3] Hans Christoph Binswanger, *Money and Magic: The Modern Economy as an Alchemical Process* (London: Quantum Publishers, 2016), 12.

[4] Soros, quoted by Binswanger. vii.

[5] Ibid. From this point of view, how curious is it that Hermes, the god of alchemy, is also the god of commerce?

[6] Neil Larsen, Mathias Nilges, Josh Robinson, and Nicholas Brown, *Marxism and the Critique of Value* (Chicago: M-C-M, 2014), xlvi.

[7] Marx, *Capital: A Critique of Political Economy*. Source: First English edition of 1887.

[8] Binswanger, *Money and Magic*, 33.

[9] Herbert Butterfield, *The Origins of Modern Science* (New York: G. Bell & Sons, 1957), 20

[10] Marsilio Ficino, *Commentary on Plato's Symposium* (University of Missouri, 1944), 148.

[11] Taken from the essay *A nice type of the English scientist: Tansley and Freud* by Laura Cameron and John Forrester, 92.

[12] In *Human Language and our Reptilian Brain* (Cambridge: Harvard University Press, 2000), linguist Philip Lieberman argues that "historically, the most complex piece of machinery of an epoch serves as a metaphor for the brain. The metaphor seems to take on a life of its own and becomes a neurophysiological model. In the eighteenth and nineteenth centuries the brain was often compared to a clock or chronometer. During the first part of the twentieth century the model usually was a telephone exchange, and since the 1950s a digital computer."

[13] This argument is developed by Adam Curtis in the second part of his documentary *All Watched Over by Machines of Loving Grace*.

[14] Curtis, *All Watched Over by Machines of Loving Grace*.

[15] From the Greek *kybernetes* "helmsman or pilot," which also originates the verb "to govern". For the influence of magical, gnostic and hermetic ideas in cybernetics, it is useful to refer to Leon Marvell's *The Physics of Transfigured Light: The Imaginal Realm and the Hermetic Foundations of Science*, particularly the second chapter. Within the framework of cybernetics this influence is particularly palpable in the thought of Gregory Bateson who, for example, in his essay *Form, Substance and Difference* makes a parallel between the Gnostic ideas of Pleroma and Creatura with the idea of map and territory derived from the General Semantics of Alfred Korzybski.

[16] Paul N. Edwards, *The Closed World: Computers and the Politics of Discourse in Cold War America* (Cambridge, MIT Press, 1996), 182.

[17] Taken from the second part of *All Watched Over by Machines of Loving Grace* by Adam Curtis.

[18] In this regard, it is interesting to note that "ecosystem" is precisely the word that Apple chose to refer to the integrated operation of two or more of its devices when they are put online in a home or office environment: a digital ecosystem.

[19] James Beniger, *The Control Revolution* (Cambridge: Harvard University Press, 1986) pág. 8.
[20] Norbert Wiener, quoted by Beniger in *The Control Revolution*, 8.
[21] Claude Shannon, quoted by Beniger in *The Control Revolution*, 8.
[22] Fred Turner, *From Counterculture to Cyberculture* (Chicago: The University of Chicago Press, 2006), 22-23.
[23] Paul N. Edwards, *The Closed World: Computers and the Politics of Discourse in Cold War America* (Cambridge, MIT Press, 1996), 180.
[24] Edwards, *The Closed World*, 181.
[25] Denis de Rougemont, *Love in the Western World* (Princeton: Princeton University Press, 1956), 243.
[26] De Rougemont, *Love in the Western World*, 244-245.
[27] De Rougemont, *Love in the Western World*, 245.
[28] De Rougemont, *Love in the Western World*, 245.
[29] De Rougemont, *Love in the Western World*, 250.
[30] De Rougemont, *Love in the Western World*, 254.
[31] De Rougemont, *Love in the Western World*, 265.
[32] De Rougemont, *Love in the Western World*, 265-266.
[33] Walter Benjamin, *The Work of Art in the Age of its Technological Reproducibility,* featured in *Selected Writings Volume 4, 1938-1940* (Cambridge: The Belknap Press of Harvard University Press, 2003), 269.
[34] Benjamin, *The Work of Art in the Age of its Technological Reproducibility*, 269.
[35] De Rougemont, *Love in the Western World*, 266.
[36] Giorgio Agamben, *Means without End* (Minneapolis: University of Minnesota Press, 2000), 94.
[37] De Rougemont, *Love in the Western World*, 268.
[38] De Rougemont, *Love in the Western World*, 268.
[39] Quoted by Benjamin in *The Work of Art in the Ages of its Technological Reproducibility*, 269.
[40] James Hillman, *A Terrible Love of War* (New York: Penguin, 2004), 3.
[41] With this expression I refer to a hypothetical clock devised by the Bulletin of atomic scientists of the University of Chicago in 1947 to indicate the probability of the total and catastrophic destruction of humanity, whether through nuclear war as well as through climate changes or bio, nano or eco technologies that can produce irreparable damage to the planet, either intentionally, by calculation error or by accident.
[42] Hillman, *A Terrible Love of War*, 1.

Part II. The Magical Bonds in the Modern World

Twentieth Century

This is beginning to feel
Like the long winded blues of the never
This is beginning to feel like it's curling up slowly
And finding a throat to choke
This is beginning to feel
Like the long winded blues of the never
Barely controlled locomotive consuming the picture
And blowing the crows, the smoke
This is beginning to feel
Like the long winded blues of the never
Static explosion devoted to crushing the broken
And shoving their souls to ghost
Eternalized, objectified
You set your sights so high
But this is beginning to feel
Like the bolt busted loose from the lever

TV on the Radio, *DLZ*

4. From the Land of Oz to the Banana Republic

> Human desires are the steam which makes the social machine work. Only by understanding them can the propagandist control the vast, loose-jointed mechanism which is modern society
> **Edward Bernays — *Propaganda (1928)***

> What are those dogs doing sniffing at my feet
> They're on to something, picking up
> Picking up this heat, this heat
> Give me steam
> And how you feel to make it real
> Real as anything you've seen
> Get a life with the dreamer's dream
> You know your culture from your trash
> You know your plastic from your cash [...]
> Whenever heaven's doors are shut
> you kick them open but
> I know you
> **Peter Gabriel, *Steam (1992)***

Consumerism and demiurgy

The last two decades of the nineteenth century saw the birth of a new type of society in the United States. It was a commercial culture completely alien to the rural economies that had prevailed until then in the Western world. In the decades following the Civil War, says historian William Leach,

> American capitalism began to produce a distinct culture, unconnected to traditional family or community values, to religion in any conventional sense, or to political democracy. It was a secular business and market-oriented culture, with the exchange and circulation of money and goods at the foundation of its aesthetic life and its moral sensibility [...] The cardinal features of this culture were acquisition and consumption as the means of achieving happiness; the cult of the new; the

democratization of desire; and money value as the predominant measure of all value in society.[1]

The democratization of desire Leach talks about was the result of two particular circumstances: the rapid industrialization of the United States during the second half of the nineteenth century, and the cult of the new implicit in the foundational myth of this country. If Europe was considered the "old world," America—first the entire continent and then the United States after it hijacked the name in the modern imaginary—assumed the role of its "young" counterpart, a promised land of sorts, naturally plentiful and packed with opportunities where it was possible to thrive and make a new life.[2] This combination of circumstances produced a society in which money prevailed over any other social standard so that it was the laws of the market and the pecuniary values which began to govern all human interactions. A conjunction that contributed, by early twentieth century, to the transformation of North American society from an economy of need to an economy of desire.

With this social and economic transformation, which can be characterized as a rupture with the old methods of production and distribution, human desire took on a new form: a generalized appetite for self-pleasure (*voluptas*) and self-realization through comfort and luxury. This form of desire, previously restricted to the privileged classes, is related to the medieval Latin word *desidium* meaning "idleness, desire, libido," which in turn comes from the classical Latin *desidia* "idleness, laziness." This meaning is still palpable in the English word *desire*, that comes from the Old French *desir* and implies an abandonment and surrender to pleasure. In this respect it is interesting to note that the Spanish word *lujuria* (lust), which comes from the classical Latin *luxuries*, originally referred to an ostentatious and wasteful attitude—a matter in which the late Roman empire excelled—and was only after Saint Augustine that it began to be identified with a sinful excess in a sexual sense. Contemporary North American society is characterized by what I will call *desidia americana*, an abandonment not only to material pleasures, a commercial form of lust (*luxuries*), but by a passive and desiring idleness that must be constantly satisfied. From this point of view, consumer society can be understood as a gigantic magic spell devised by the goddess of love, desire and deceit.

At the time the symbol of this new culture of desire was the department store, which brought together in a single place the cult to consumption and the pursuit of happiness through the acquisition of material goods; a place that embodied more than any other institution the idea of "America" as the land of opportunity.³ From the outset this new society found itself in disagreement with the ethical attitudes promulgated by traditional religion, especially with the most fundamentalist strains of Protestantism which advised virtue, prudence and moderation. Because of this, a new religious attitude was built around the commercial culture which came with its own promises and myths; an attitude in which desire was to be exalted and sin and guilt minimized. As early as 1876, Harper's Bazaar columnist Gail Hamilton exhorted her readers to stop feeling guilty for wanting prosperity and riches: "we all want money and luxury," she said, "we only decry it when we cannot get it […] we ought to enjoy wealth and cease our idle carping against money."⁴

The need to overcome these psychological obstacles led to the formation of new religious sects that were aligned with the objectives and the way of understanding the world of consumer culture. Among the scholars of the time, William James was the first to note this religious attitude. In *The Varieties of Religious Experience* he describes the "mind-cure" movement popular at the time as a deliberately optimistic way of looking at life, whose doctrinal sources can be found in the Gospels, New England transcendentalism, Berkeley's idealism and, in some cases, even Hinduism. But the fundamental characteristic of mind-cure, he says, James tells us, presents a more direct inspiration:

> The leaders in this faith have had an intuitive belief in the all-saving power of healthy-minded attitudes as such, in the conquering efficacy of courage, hope, and trust, and a correlative contempt for doubt, fear, worry, and all nervously precautionary states of mind.⁵

It is from this new attitude that aligns naturally with the commercial interests that arose at the time, that new religious groups such as New Thought, Christian Science and Theosophy began to appear. As a spiritual mentality, William Leach tells us, mind-cure "was wish-oriented, optimistic, sunny, the epitome of cheer and self-confidence, and completely lacking in anything resembling a tragic view of life. In mind-cure there was no darkness, no Melville or Hawthorne, no secrets, no sin or evil, nothing grim or untidy, only the safe shore and "the sunlight of health," in one mind-curer's words."[6] What could be wrong with a worldview that minimizes the overwhelming power of guilt and sin? The same as in all visions that strive to exclude the other side of the coin: a blindness to everything that does not conform to its way of understanding the world and that leads to a sadly one-dimensional humanity.

It is important to highlight that the basic attitudes of mind-cure are related to the development of animal magnetism in the United States. The link between the two movements is Phineas Parkhurst Quimby (1802-1866), a watchmaker from Maine who, after attending a lecture by Charles Poyen (a French magnetist of the Puységur tradition), found his vocation as a hypnotist and magnetic healer. After years of practice, Quimby decided that the effects of his therapies were due to the positive ideas generated in the minds of his patients (a radical variety of "suggestion," in the terms of the school of Nancy), and not to an intrinsic property of the treatment. Noting that the cure came from the eradication of a false idea in the patient's mind ("what could be cured by an idea must also be caused by an idea")[7] Quimby devoted the last twenty years of his life to a form of "mental cure" that depended on the mind-to-mind contact (or *rapport* in Puységur's jargon) with the patient. One of his most famous patients was Mary Baker Eddy (1821-1910), founder of Christian Science who, in life, denied any influence from Quimby's ideas.

For historian Robert C. Fuller, animal magnetism was responsible not only of originating spiritism and Christian Science but of initiating an

> enduring tendency in American religious though. The American mesmerists were the first to encourage popular audiences to abandon a scripturally-based theology in favour of psychological principles said to govern the individual's ability to align himself with a higher spiritual order.[8]

The atmosphere of spiritual independence generated by sects such as Theosophy and New Thought ended up dissolving the ethical doubts raised by the new consumer society in a matter of a couple of decades. The attitude of these sects reflected "in the most committed way the American conviction that people could shape their own destinies and find total happiness. These faiths wanted to make religion work in the modern era, to integrate it with secular and scientific aspirations, and to accommodate it to ever-expanding material desires,"[9] which is why it is only natural to find that their ideologies were congruent with the priorities of the consumer culture.

Although many of the new religions were formally different from each other—Christian Science followed the Gospels while New Thought made use of ideas coming from different religions and Theosophy used occultism and Hinduism—all these varieties of mental healing believed "in 'salvation *in this life*' and 'fullness within time,' not after death."[10] All insisted on the power of the mind and a positive attitude to get what they wanted. "Fear is a 'self-imposed or self-permitted suggestion of inferiority,' wrote one believer, that 'really belongs in the category of harmful' and 'unnecessary things.' It made people ill, keeping them from reaching the true plenitude in the universe,"[11] which by then was already becoming the world of material abundance of consumer culture.

"We are really gods, not sinners"[12] said Swami Vivekenanda, the great spokesman for Vedanta philosophy in the West, while Madame Blavatsky, founder of Theosophy, stated that "god is latent in all individuals," echoing ancient Hermetic and Gnostic ideas that, in their contact with consumer culture, would lead to such trends as the Human Potential movement, New Age and Transhumanism. On the other hand, a new breed of authors of "inspiring" literature (the nineteenth-century ancestor of self-help) such as Orison Swett Marden, urged their followers to "'wake up and stretch [yourselves]… the only thing that keeps us from taking plenty of either money or air is fear'; 'all you desire is YOURS NOW… you are born to dominion and plenty'."[13] Figures such as Marden saw no sense in dwelling on the "dark side" of life or in assigning any benefit to doubt or reflection. For this author humans were "happiness-machines" to which a harvest of good things belonged by birth right; a curious synthesis of mechanicism and "spirituality."

In addition to this sort of "inspirational literature" this cultural environment produced important works in the children literature genre such as Eleanor Porter's *Pollyanna*, a series of novels about an eleven-year-old girl who, in the face of the most abject misery, never stops smiling and spreading "color and light." Following the precepts of mind-cure, Pollyanna does not miss an opportunity to help people reach their true potential. But the most important of the literary works that transpire the influence of the new religious and consumerist attitude is *The Wizard of Oz* by L. Frank Baum (1856-1919). The youngest son of a wealthy

German-American family from New York, Baum worked as a theater writer, salesman, merchant, journalist and window-dresser in his youth, activities that immersed him in the new commercial culture that was then taking hold of the United States. By the turn of the century Baum condensed his experience in his vocation for children's stories. *The Wizard of Oz*, his most famous and successful work, is considered the first children book to break with the traditional theme and emotional tone of its genre and has been called the first American fairy tale. According to William Leach, it is also "one of the most significant cultural documents to come out of the religious turmoil and economic changes of the late nineteenth century,"[14] as well as one of the clearest expressions of mind-cure in literature.

During the second half of the twentieth century *The Wizard of Oz* was the subject of a large number of interpretations that tried to place the work in a wider cultural and political context. Henry Littlefield was the first scholar to treat Baum's story as an allegory of the monetary policies of the late nineteenth century. In his interpretation, the yellow brick road leading to the Emerald City represents the gold standard, which was a hotly debated topic then, and which in 1900, the year of publication of the book, was instituted as the official monetary system of the United States. For his part, historian Quentin Taylor understands the tale as a political allegory in which Dorothy represents the North American people (simple, young and naive), the Scarecrow the late nineteenth century farmers and the Tin Woodman the industrial workers, particularly from the steel industry. In this interpretation the mysterious wizard could be seen as an intriguing politician who uses all sorts of tricks to deceive and win the people's trust.

William Leach, the editor of a critical edition of Baum's novel, argues that *The Wizard of Oz* is an allegory of consumer culture and that its immense success was due to the fact that "it met—almost perfectly—the particular ethical and emotional needs of people living in a new urban, industrial society."[15] In fact, the attitudes of the characters in the book coincide with those cultivated by mind-cure sects, and its plot exalts and normalizes the opulence of large urban centers and department stores represented in the imposing architecture and prosperity of the Emerald City. Now, although the allegorical content of *The Wizard of Oz* is rather novel, according to Leach the basic structure of the book can be found in

John Bunyan's *Pilgrim's Progress*, one of the most important texts of English religious literature, which was very popular among North American Protestants in the first half of the nineteenth century.

In Bunyan's work, Christian, the main character of the story, flees from the City of Destruction (this world), and after many adventures and temptations that threaten his faith he arrives at the Celestial City (Paradise), which streets are paved in jewelery and gold. Likewise, Dorothy's journey takes her from a sad and depressing Kansas to the Land of Oz, where she follows a yellow brick road to the Emerald City whose streets and buildings are covered with precious stones. In this interpretation, the tornado leading Dorothy to the Land of Oz could be taken as a metaphor for the social and economic revolution that transformed late nineteenth-century United States (rural Kansas) into the land of inexhaustible prosperity and abundance that came with the new consumer culture (the Land of Oz).

This structural similarity notwithstanding, *The Wizard of Oz* is far from being a story of spiritual or psychological development like *Pilgrim's Progress*, or even a fairy tale in the strict sense of the term. In the introduction to the original edition of the novel Baum states that

> the time has come for a series of newer "wonder tales" in which the stereotyped genie, dwarf and fairy are eliminated, together with all the horrible and blood-curdling incidents devised by their authors to point a fearsome moral to each tale. Modern education includes morality; therefore the modern child seeks only entertainment in its wonder tales and gladly dispenses with all disagreeable incident [...] It aspires to being a modernized fairy tale, in which the wonderment and joy are retained and the heartaches and nightmares are left out.

By focusing on the entertainment factor of the children genre while excluding its moral side, Baum expressed the mind-cure ideology to perfection. "In the Emerald City and most of the Land of Oz" says Leach "everyone is taken care of. There is little real distress; no significant struggle or conflict; no work to speak of; not much to feel guilty about; and, above all, nothing to fear (even, as it turns out, the wicked witch)."[16] Even when in danger Dorothy is never alone and never acts in an apprehensive manner or is riddled by anguish or despair, her attitude is optimistic and unconcerned and she is always ready to be on her way no matter what obstacles she faces.

The world of Oz, unlike that of other fairy tales, stands out by its abundance of color. The original edition featured a series of illustrations by William Denslow, still marvellous to this day on account of their magnificent use of this resource. Color was used to "accentuate the material and natural abundance of Oz and the Emerald City,"[17] to soothe the children's anxiety and to make them understand that the world is an essentially prosperous place full of happiness.

> In the new consumerist American way, Baum broke the connection between wonderment and heartache. People could have what historically (and humanly) they had never had: Joy without sorrow, abundance without poverty, happiness without pain. Like the other mind-curers, Baum rejected that side of life—the suffering side, the growing-up side—that made the other side worthy of respect and affirmation.[18]

One of the most remarkable features of the Land of Oz is that the rejection of any kind of harshness or negative emotion gives rise to a seemingly friendly and colorful world which nevertheless is particularly sinister in its one-dimensionality. A world in which melancholy, the very engine of mysticism and courtly poetry, has vanished as a social possibility.[19]

The decidedly upbeat tone of *The Wizard of Oz* and Baum's conscious decision to exclude all forms of morality or negativity, does away with the idea of psychological growth implicit in classical fairy tales. Stories like those of Hans Christian Andersen and the Brothers Grimm work because of the intrinsic tension in the situation of the main character, a boy or a girl who is abandoned or mistreated by his or her parents and who must endure—alone and constantly threatened—an adventure whose purpose is to make an allegory of the psychological conflicts that lead to his or her growth and independence. Of course, none of this happens to Dorothy, who has no parents and whose "relationship to her aunt and uncle lacks any kind of intensity or depth; she is an 'eternal' child, protected from the burdens of having to grow up."[20] The result of this situation is that Dorothy does not change at all, she is the same person from beginning to end. As a matter of fact, Dorothy's friends do not change either and the fact that the Scarecrow, the Tin Woodman and the Cowardly Lion are already what they want to be is another of the most revealing instances of the influence of mind-cure in the novel. According to Leach, Dorothy's traveling companions

> are burdened by what mind-curers called "poverty thoughts." The wizard's role is, of course, to give them confidence and to encourage them to overcome their "misery habits." "You have plenty of courage, I am sure," says the Wizard to the Lion. "All you need is confidence in yourself." The Wizard doesn't really grant Dorothy's friends their wishes. What he does, in effect, is to connect the three with what they already are, with their true fullness, or—to use a mind-cure term—with their latent powers.[21]

Now, we must realize that if Dorothy and her friends do not grow throughout the story, it is because they are not their real protagonists. Oz, the mysterious wizard who appears in the middle of the book (and in the middle of the country), is the true center and the only character with a measure of interiority and which goes through some degree of transformation. From this point of view, more than Dorothy's story to return to Kansas, *The Wizard of Oz* is the account of the atonement and redemption of its true protagonist, but fake atonement and redemption, that is. The Wizard may not be a bad man—and he even admits to not being a good wizard—but his circumstances won't allow him to stop being a "humbug" and to constantly resort to deception. When he receives the characters of the story in his palace, he presents himself in a different form before each of them: for Dorothy he is a giant head, for the Scarecrow a lovely lady, for the Tin Woodman a horrible beast and for the Cowardly Lion a huge ball of fire. Curiously, when it is revealed that Oz is an old man without true magical powers but endowed with exceptional technical wit (each of his appearances has a rational and mechanical explanation), the reaction of Dorothy and her friends is not one of anger or indignation; after listening to his story they forgive him and continue to regard him as if he were a great wizard worthy of respect and admiration.

According to Leach the Wizard of Oz is a modern *trickster*, an expert in trades like "advertising, acting, selling, mesmerising, transactions in fictitious goods—on activities that succeeded through illusion and deception."[22] Here we should note that although the trickster figure had a negative connotation and was traditionally associated with Satan—a polymorphous demon who can assume a variety of forms and identities—in the last decades of the nineteenth century this archetype had begun to be "domesticated" in the North American imagination and aligned itself with some of the fundamental characteristics of the new commercial culture.[23]

The portrait that Baum makes of the Wizard and of the story itself, says Leach,

> can be interpreted as a tribute to the modern ability to create magic, illusions, and theater, to do in effect what God and the Devil had done: to make people believe, in spite of themselves. For even though the Wizard is exposed as a charlatan or as a "common man" without any magical powers in the true fairy-tale sense, nevertheless he is very powerful. He is powerful in the modern American capitalist sense, powerful because he is able to manipulate others to do his bidding, to make others believe what is unbelievable, to do what they might not want to do (or to buy what they might not want to buy), and to do it without realizing they are doing it. A superb confidence man, Oz excites a completely misplaced trust, but "the people" adore him anyway.[24]

The effect that Oz's "magic" has on Dorothy and on the multitudes of his country is that of a large-scale deception, a massive fraud. Oz's ability to manipulate the masses is especially evident in the green spectacles everyone must wear when entering the Emerald City so they are not blinded by its radiance and glory. However, upon being exposed, Oz reveals that after arriving in the country and seeing how the locals worshiped him, he ordered them to build a city for him. "Then I thought, as the country was so green and beautiful, I would call it the Emerald City; and to make the name fit better I put green spectacles on all the people, so that everything they saw was green." When Dorothy asks him if everything it's not really green, Oz replies, "No more than in any other city, but when you wear green spectacles, why of course everything you see looks green to you." Although he has no fairy-tale magical powers, Oz's power is to alter and control the way others see the world and this is as powerful a form of magic as any other. It is magic in the Brunian sense of the term. The Wizard of Oz is the first modern transformation of the *animarum venator*, the first hunter/magician whose form of magic is openly related to technology.

It is essential to note that the *trickster* is a fundamental figure in most dualistic religions and particularly in Gnosticism, where it fulfills the role of a demiurge that gives rise to a counter-creation inferior to that of the original god. Like all tricksters Oz's real power is to build secondary realities, to satisfy the desires of others before they know what they are, to envelop them in their own dreams. In this sense the figure of the Wizard of Oz is a very particular literary achievement, for he is

> a benign trickster, a man resembling Satan but with no sinister power, a character to admire and love, not to fear. Baum was telling his readers, through the Wizard, that there is nothing at all to be afraid of; there may be a fraud—a joke—at the heart of the universe, but there is certainly no "real" evil.[25]

This is a very important matter for our study. The fact that there is no genuine evil in the story of Oz implies a reversal of anti-cosmism, the gnostic idea according to which the world is evil and corrupt. This "anti-anticosmism"—which amounts to a commercial variety of pro-cosmism—creates a new and powerful moral illusion: since the Land of Oz does not admit evil or negativity in any form, even the most infamous forms of deception are not seen as reprehensible, they are celebrated as normal and even desirable. This is how the professions based on the typical behaviors of the trickster become vital for the development of the Land of Oz, understood here as the new economy of desire.

If the idea that consumer culture is, at heart, comparable to a fairy tale seems unlikely, the position of John Wanamaker—founder of *Wanamaker's*, one of the first and largest department stores in the United States—speaks for itself. From 1910 this businessman wrote hundreds of editorials for his business in which he portrayed his department store as a fantastic world of abundance and prosperity not unlike the one portrayed by Baum in his Oz books.

Some significant fragments collected by William Leach:

> There is a Garden of Merchandise in Philadelphia where Orchids and hardy annuals of commerce bloom, ever, side by side. This Garden is for all people...

> This Store is an Easter Egg.

> This immense building is not an illusion
> is it easily found
> it is on the road of the people's wants
> it has an everyday fullness
> its fullness is that of freshness

The Store is the Rainbow and the Pot of Gold. You remember Alice Ben Bolt, do you not, and how often we were told that there was a pot of gold at both feet of the Rainbow? A splendid rainbow put me foot down on the corner of Market Street, where this store began, and its other foot was placed on the corner of 13th Street where the Store is now, and today there were some huge golden pots at their feet!

As strange as it may seem, this magical and fantastic component of commercial culture is an essential part of the American dream, which we can now define as an act of demiurgy, a counter-creation of perpetual prosperity and abundance fed by the desire it constantly produces in its subjects.[26]

One of the most important changes that came with the new consumer culture was the definitive separation of the world of production from the world of consumption, a matter that in Marxist theory is considered one of the primary sources of alienation. Until the 1880s, most people in the United States lived in local economies and produced their own clothing, food and everyday objects, an economic unity that vanished quickly after 1890. This division made room for the emergence of a new ideology: consumption became "the 'true realm' of freedom and self-expression, the only refuge of comfort and pleasure, and a place where all wishes were granted and anything was possible."[27] With this change came an unsuspected consequence: once the commercial spaces were separated from the "backstage" of production, the door was opened for them to become "'the stage upon which the play is enacted'"[28]. Consumer culture literally became a spectacle.

The idea of the commercial world as a theatrical spectacle is closely linked to the powers of enchantment of the magical arts and, as such, is the province of the tricksters and demiurges of commercial culture. Regarding this dynamic between spectator and spectacle it is interesting to note that in his persona as a window dresser, L. Frank Baum "recommended the use of a variety of theatrical methods to attract window shoppers. He was not interested in the quality of the goods, but how they looked in a display arrangement. If goods were properly arranged, he argued, 'the show window will sell them like hot cakes even though [they] are old enough to have gray whiskers'."[29] One of the most important consequences of the new way of displaying products was that by breaking up the direct contact between the spectator/consumer and the commodities, the showcase dislocated the relationship between the two; think about the difference between the immediacy of a country market and the impersonal shelves of a supermarket. Touch and smell loose importance as sight becomes the exclusive mediator. According to Leach, the glass display became the most effective way to democratize desire, the goods are there, you can see them, but you cannot touch them unless you enter the store and buy them (or break the window and make a run for it). What you want constantly "looks" at you from the other side of the glass.[30]

The display window has an interesting relationship with the version of the Narcissus myth that appears in the *Roman de la Rose*. Narcissus's eyes reflected the water—the object of his love— become in the *Roman* two crystals at the bottom of the fountain that present the lover with the entire reflection of the garden of delights, a *locus amoenus* (pleasant place) that spellbinds the subject and ties him or her to the water mirror, thus closing the pneumatic circle.

> Just as a mirror will reflect each thing
> That near is placed, and one therein can see
> Both form and color without variance,
> So do these crystals undistorted show
> The garden's each detail to anyone
> Who looks into the waters of the spring.[31]

This literary *topos* finds its modern version in the paradises of luxury and comfort invoked by the land of desire, the two crystals become the commodities that await us behind the glass displays, just like eyes that reflect the totality of the promises that come with consumer culture. If this new culture is intimately bound to erotic desire, is it surprising to find that its ancestor lies in the erotic customs of the West and particularly in narcissism?

Here I should highlight that the relationship between spectator/consumer and spectacle/commodity also recalls the Empedoclean theory of vision which forms the basis of the types of magic I have analyzed in this study. As we saw in the first chapter, this was a bi-directional dialectic in which the encounter of the visual ray that came out of the eye and the external fire that came from the world met and formed a bond between the two parts. In this regard it is quite revealing that John Wanamaker characterized the display windows of his department store as "eyes to meet eyes,"[32] a relationship that establishes a clear pneumatic current between the consumer and the object of consumption, in which the desired objects radiate *phantasmata* that are captured by the ray of the eye of the spectator/consumer. Thus, we can deduce that commercial culture weaves an immense pneumatic web of desire in which the object ceases to be the beloved to become a commodity which, as in the erotic dialectic of the troubadours and Ficino, is also taken as a vehicle of freedom.[33] These eyes/window displays will later on become eyes/screen and, in the digital age, eyes/*live feed*.

But the consumerist version of the pneumatic network of bonds is not merely an application of Bruno's vision. Adapted to the "theatrical" needs of commercial culture, this network of desire acquires a new potential that we might call *demiurgic*: the possibility of creating complete sectors of reality capable of enveloping and manipulating large numbers of individuals. If confining a crowd within a pneumatic circle implies taking it to the zone of indistinction between real and unreal from whence the phantasm emanates, the task of the hunter-demiurge will be extending the limits of this circle, projecting its twilight into the world and thus, bringing the illusion, the negative, into the light.

Of course, at first the images of commercial culture imitated the forms and themes of the *phantasmata* of the pre-modern world. Commercial artists such as Maxfield Parrish used all kinds of Renaissance, Medieval and Classical scenarios for their illustrations, but now the fairies, gods and nymphs in groves and grottos used consumer items such as cameras, light bulbs and soap bars. Although at this early stage of consumer society commercial images had not yet found their own language, Actaeon's hounds had already found a new setting.

During this transition, says Walter Benjamin,

> the creation of fantasies prepares to become practical as commercial art. Literature submits to montage in the feuilleton. All these products are on the point of entering the market as commodities. But they linger on the threshold, they stop halfway. Value and commodity enter on a brief engagement before the market price makes their union legitimate. From this epoch derive the arcades and the *intérieurs*, the exhibition-halls and the panoramas. They are residues of a dream-world.[34]

❃

No matter how many idyllic scenarios and fairy tales the leaders of commercial culture weaved to seduce the new class of consumer citizens, the Land of Oz understood as a commercial paradise was impossible without a radical increase in the techniques of social and economic control. Simultaneous with the consolidation of commercial culture in the early twentieth century, the United States—as well as England, France and Germany—went through another series of changes that historian James Beniger calls the *control revolution*. According to Beniger, this revolution was a direct consequence of the industrial revolution, which accelerated the

> society's entire material processing system, thereby precipitating what I call a crisis of control, a period in which innovations in information processing and communication technologies lagged behind those of energy and its application to manufacturing and transportation.[35]

In broad strokes, the disadvantage between monitoring and communication techniques in relation to manufacturing and distribution of goods produced an explosion in the development of technologies that would contribute to a better control of operational flows in practically all the existing industries and businesses. According to Morris Berman, the control revolution gave rise to a rush "to regulate society and economy in terms of objective criteria,"[36] in an effort to manage the increasing demands of consumer society. With this goal in mind "the United States was divided in four standard time zones in 1884, machinery began to be controlled by feedback devices; and in 1980, punch cards were used to tabulate census data."[37] Along came Henry Ford's assembly line and the emergence of a national system of econometrics. Initially these systems were based on the traditional form of feedback and control, bureaucracy, but they soon began to be reinforced by the appearance of new statistical techniques and the development of new forms of accounting and process monitoring.

In addition to the psychological and socioeconomic changes we have discussed in this section, the consolidation of the new culture of desire brought with it a variety of techniques for controlling mass consumption, such as

> technologies of trademarks, consumer packaging, and mass advertising, all of which gave manufacturers a way of

controlling giant wholesalers and new mass retailers. Advertising became the scientific management of public opinion. Rotogravure sections appeared in newspapers in 1914, neon signs for advertising in 1923, and finally copy research, test marketing, and, of course, broadcasting. The development of feedback marketing techniques (flows of information back to the advertiser) can be dated to 1900.[38]

It is in these information and feedback systems where we find the origin of the impulse towards control which later on consolidated in cybernetics. As we saw in the intermezzo, the totality of these systems is one of the most recent incarnations of the hermetic idea of *anima mundi*; the instruments that emerged from the control revolution are the functional aspect of the network of magical bonds imposed by commercial culture. The transformation of the pneumatic network of Renaissance magic into a digital network follows the general movement of the manipulative impulse: a progression that goes towards greater control of mass phenomena, in which the hysterical-erotic symptoms are attenuated while they spread to ever more numerous groups and take an increasingly personalized character. A movement that, in accordance with the general movement of the economy, goes from the general to the specific and specialized.

In addition to this movement there is subtler one, a tendency to sublimate the material, to abandon the corporeal in pursuit of the phantasm, which translates into a quest to appropriate the unreal and negative in order to feed the real and positive. This trend is easily verifiable in the tendency of consumer culture to invest and lay more emphasis on branding and corporate image—the "soul" of the company—and less on the physical manufacture of consumer goods, its "body," which began in earnest in the last two decades of the past century and has intensified since then as we move into the so-called 'digital era.' "The old paradigm," says Naomi Klein, "had it that all marketing was selling a product. In the new model, however, the product always takes a back seat to the real product, the brand, and the selling of the brand acquired an extra component that can only be described as spiritual. Advertising is about hawking product. Branding, in its truest and most advanced incarnations, is about corporate transcendence,"[39] that is, about getting ever closer to the phantasm.

This tendency has permeated consumer culture since its very beginning. According to Bruce Barton, legendary publicist of the twenties and founder of BBDO, advertising is

> something big, something splendid, something which goes deep down into an institution and gets hold of the soul of it ... Institutions have souls, just as men and nations have souls.[40]

Barton is remembered for recreating the corporate image of General Motors using an idealized American family, which remained in the collective unconscious of the United States for nearly six decades. According to this son of a congregational preacher, the mission of advertising "was to help corporations find their soul."[41] This characterization of the corporation as a "being" or an "organism" endowed with a soul is particularly useful when it comes to imagining the way in which the *phantasmata* of advertising emanate from its deepest layer, from an emotional core of sorts.

But let us go back to the beginning of the twentieth century. As the burgeoning consumer society and its control instruments began to take effect, a new factor emerged in the equation: the methods of production, distribution and control surpassed the population's capacity for consumption. The land of desire began to exceed the expectations of its creators. This issue was detected early on by Edward Bernays, Sigmund Freud's North American nephew and the father of public relations. For Bernays the solution to this situation was simple:

> Mass production is profitable only if its rhythm can be maintained—that is, if it can continue to sell its product in steady or increasing quantity. The result is that while, under the handicraft of the small unity system of production that was typical a century ago, demand created the supply, today supply must actively seek to create its corresponding demand.[42]

More than the production of mass consumer goods, the true challenge of the economy of desire is, in the words of political philosopher Samuel Strauss, "to produce the customers."[43] The real product of the factory of the modern world is not this or that commodity, it's us.

The hand which binds

Edward Bernays was born on November 22, 1891 in Vienna and spent his first birthday on a steamer headed to the United States. His father, Ely Bernays, was married to Anna Freud, the younger sister of Sigmund Freud who, in turn, was married to Ely's sister, Martha Bernays. Thus, Edward was the "double nephew" of the father of psychoanalysis. For many years Freud reproached his brother-in-law, Ely "for having squandered the inheritance of his sisters to provide for an illegitimate child." [44] Ernest Jones, British psychologist and Freud's biographer, asserted that it was not a single illegitimate child but several children and that in fact this circumstance contributed greatly to the ruin of Ely Bernays and to the family emigrating to North America. To add insult to these rumors, Ely was forced not only to borrow money from his brother-in-law to pay for the expenses of the trip, but also to leave his two older daughters with the Freuds while he found a place and a source of income in North America.

Ely managed to establish himself as a grain exporter in New York, and Edward and his sisters grew up in an ostentatious townhouse on Madison Avenue in a privileged environment. However, since Ely's work was subject to fluctuations in international grain markets, money did not always flow steadily, so for his last year of elementary school Edward had to transfer to a public school where he came "into close contact with a cross-section of cosmopolitan New York"[45] and recognized that the society in which he lived was much more varied and complicated than he had imagined. Each person had their own interests and demeanor, each one had to be treated differently.

When the time came to decide his profession, his father, a convinced follower of Theodore Roosevelt's back-to-the soil movement, decided to send Edward to Cornell College of Agriculture, where he was to learn everything necessary to live off the land and collaborate with Ely's business. Unconvinced with his father's decision, Edward finished his career and graduated in 1912 with no intention of pursuing a profession in agronomy. For a short time he had a position related to the import and export of grains and he traveled to Paris where he worked for the gigantic

Louis Dreyfus and Co. decoding telegrams on grain trade. Bored with this job he returned to New York, where one morning he had a chance encounter that would define his professional career. As Bernays himself liked to tell the story: "it all started with sex."

As he boarded the Ninth Avenue trolley Edward ran into Fred Robinson, an old friend from public school, who told him that his father had turned over to him two of his monthly journals, the *Medical Review of Reviews* and *Dietetic and Hygienic Gazette*, and asked him to help him run them. Edward instantly accepted. His great opportunity came a few months after joining when a doctor submitted a review of a play by the French playwright Eugène Brieux entitled *Les avariés* (translated to English as *Damaged Goods*) which dealt with a man with syphilis who after marrying and infecting his partner has a son who also suffers from the disease. Of course, the subject was scandalous as well as an affront to the prudery of the time. The mere fact of publishing the review was a daring move, especially for a magazine aimed at a relatively conservative group such as the medical community. However, convinced of the inherent benefits of being able to speak openly about sex and venereal diseases— an attitude that reflected both Freud's receptivity to the sexual issues and the new North American attitude towards desire—Bernays and Robinson did not stop there. Seeing the opportunity to adding a greater impact and meaning to their work they decided to contact Richard Bennet, an actor who was interested in taking the play to the stage, and offered to finance the production.

Promoting and producing a play with such a controversial topic was not going to be a simple undertaking, but in the process Bernays, who was not prone to give up easily, came up with a formula that he would use countless times throughout his professional career: recruiting the prestige of universally respected men and women to turn a controversial issue into a charitable cause. Bernays founded the *Medical Review of Reviews sociological fund committee* and, leveraging on Bennet's reputation and the benefits of a frank conversation about sexually-transmitted diseases, he brought together celebrities such as of John D. Rockefeller, Franklin Delano Roosevelt and William K. Vanderbilt Sr. The production was a success and once it completed its circuit in the theaters Bennet, who had the rights to the play, broke the partnership with Bernays and Robinson and proceeded to sign a contract to make it into a film in which he had the lead role, and of which there are no copies left today. The two young entrepreneurs were disappointed with Bennet's attitude—in fact, they had already proposed to him to continue working on a series of theatrical productions with similar themes—but every cloud has a silver lining, Bernays had found his true calling.

Enthusiastic about the results of his experiment in show business, Bernays traveled to Paris and then to Carlsbad, a city near Prague famous for its thermal springs, to spend time with his uncle. No record remained on the encounter but "whatever the specifics of their conversation, it is clear that when Eddie returned to New York in the fall of 1913 he was more taken than ever with the Viennese doctor's novel theories on how unconscious drives dating to childhood make people act the way they do. And Eddie was convinced that understanding the instincts and symbols that motivate an individual could help him shape the behavior of the masses." [46] In fact, the manipulation of symbols from a Freudian standpoint would become one of the pillars of public relations discipline as defined by Bernays:

> It is chiefly the psychologists of the school of Freud who have pointed out that many of man's thoughts and actions are compensatory substitutes for desires which he has been obliged to suppress. A thing may be desired not for its intrinsic worth or usefulness, but because he has unconsciously come to see in it a symbol of something else, the desire for which he is ashamed to admit to himself. A man buying a car may think he wants it for the purposes of locomotion, whereas the fact may be that he would really prefer not to be burdened with it, and would rather walk for the sake of his health. He may really want it because it is a symbol of social position, an evidence of his success in business, or a means of pleasing his wife.[47]

Of course, after a century of advertising and psychoanalysis, these conclusions are rather obvious, but in the first decades of the last century they were a particularly powerful insight into consumer behavior.

Throughout his life Bernays maintained a relation that was as close as was possible with his uncle and, in fact, during the economic crisis that hit the German countries after World War I, he helped him to obtain a translation contract for the *Introductory Lectures on Psychoanalysis*, which came as a considerable economic relief at a particularly difficult time for Freud. Although uncle and nephew had some very close and other distant periods, Bernays never missed an opportunity to bring up his kinship with the father of psychoanalysis. But beyond this family bond or the application of certain Freudian ideas to public relations—or the antipathy Freud felt for US culture (America is a mistake, a gigantic mistake is true, but a mistake nevertheless...)—Freud and Bernays shared the same fundamental view of the world: human behavior is subject to the violent underground currents of the unconscious and yielding to these would amount to a general collapse of society, a descent to a state of violence, anarchy and social chaos; a variation of the *war of all against all* formulated by Thomas Hobbes three centuries earlier.

In the case of Bernays this idea was reinforced by his readings of Gustav LeBon, Wilfred Trotter and the journalist and political commentator Walter Lippmann. In his classic *Public Opinion* (1922), Lippmann had concluded that a true participatory democracy was impossible in modern mass societies, whose members "—by and large incapable of lucid thought or of clear perception, driven by herd instincts and mere prejudice, and frequently disoriented by external stimuli—were not equipped to make decisions or engage in rational discourse."[48] The solution to this situation was evident: the bewildered herd, always susceptible of regressing to social chaos, must be governed by "a specialized class whose interests reach beyond the locality."[49]

Bernays's adaptation of Lippmann's ideas was simple and direct, without falling into grandiosity or vague utopian promises. *Propaganda* (1928), his best known book, begins with the following lines:

> The conscious and intelligent manipulation of the organized habits and opinions of the masses is an important element in democratic society. Those who manipulate this unseen mechanism of society constitute an invisible government which is the true ruling power of our country.
>
> We are governed, our minds molded, our tasted formed, our ideas suggested, largely by men we have never heard of. This is a logical result of the way in which our democratic society is organized. Vast numbers of human beings must cooperate in this manner if they are to live together as a smoothly functioning society.
>
> [...] Whatever attitude one chooses toward this condition, it remains a fact that in almost every act of our daily lives, whether in the sphere of politics or business, in our social

conduct or our ethical thinking, we are dominated by the relatively small number of persons [...] who understand the mental processes and social patterns of the masses. It is they who pull the wires which control the public mind, who harness old social forces and contrive new ways to bind and guide the world.[50]

Bernays calls this process of binding and guiding the masses *organizing chaos*, a clear reference to the state of disorder and anarchy, to the chaos implicit in Hobbes' *bellum omnium contra omnes*, which civilization must constantly avoid. However, according to Mark Crispin Miller, professor of media studies at NYU, Bernays' invisible government can also be understood as a heroic elite that shapes the world out of chaos—the primordial state of the cosmos—as God or the demiurge did at the beginning of time. Understood as one of the most important demiurges of commercial culture, Bernays is perhaps the first and clearest embodiment of the trickster archetype as described by William Leach, he is a master at altering and controlling how others see the world, someone capable of creating secondary realities—in themselves spurious and unreal—at his clients' request.

On the other hand, it is rather astonishing that Bernays used the word *bind,* a term with clear magical overtones, to refer to the action of "guiding" or manipulating the perceptions of the masses. Bruno's "hand which binds" is the same invisible hand that "pulls the strings which control public opinion." Indeed, the conscious application of the immense network of bonds described by Bruno in *De vinculis in genere* was possible in a massive scale largely due to the techniques that Bernays learned and refined during his time on the Committee on Public Information, the agency that handled US public opinion during World War I.

According to Miller, this was the first time that governments "systematically deployed the entire range of modern media to rouse their populations to fanatical assent. Here was an extraordinary state accomplishment: mass enthusiasm at the prospect of a global brawl that otherwise would mystify those very masses, and that shattered those who actually took part in it."[51] The Committee's work to "sell" democracy and protect the free world from "Prussian barbarism" was so efficient that once the war was over, Bernays began to wonder whether it would be possible to use the same techniques in peacetime and for commercial and "democratic" purposes. These two categories were, in his mind, as in that of most North Americans of the time, inseparable and more or less equivalent: the freedom guaranteed by democracy is exercised through consumption. If Bernays claimed that his career had started with sex, it could also be said that it began with war. More than democracy and capitalism, it is these two forces, love and war, that would seem inseparable in the Western psyche.

The question was: how to achieve what Lippmann had called "the manufacture of consent"? How to deprive a mass of its will? Like Bruno and LeBon, Bernays had already recognized the power of images and symbols in the behavior of the masses. He knew that it was essential to appeal to the most basic emotions of the individual by any visual, graphic or auditory means, an idea that echoes the doors of sight, hearing and imagination described by Bruno. Following LeBon and Trotter, Bernays understood that the herd does not "*think* in the strict sense of the word. In place of thoughts it has impulses, habits and emotions. In making up its mind, its first impulse is usually to follow the example of a trusted leader. This is one of the most firmly established principles of mass psychology."[52] Now, as the emotions aroused by oratory had worn off after centuries of use and abuse, Bernays recommended parades, rallies and all sorts of performances as a means of obtaining "frenetic and emotional interest" in an idea or a product.

By the early decades of the twentieth century the practice of implanting images—that is, *phantasmata*—in the minds of the masses in order to evoke specific emotions was already widespread. Bernays knew that

> virtually no important undertaking is now carried on without it, whether the enterprise be building a cathedral, endowing a university, marketing a moving picture, floating a large bond, or electing a president [...] The important thing is that it is universal and continuous: and in its sum total it is regimenting the public mind every bit as much as an army regiments the bodies of its soldiers.[53]

His true discovery was realizing that in any complex society the population is divided into countless professional, political and religious groups, and therefore the desires and needs of these groups must be regimented accordingly.[54] But apart from this "militarization" of the soul of the masses—which, as we saw in the intermezzo, is the opposite to its "civilization"—Bernays found out that the essential prerequisite for being able to operate on any mass was to create the appropriate circumstances for an idea to penetrate in the collective psyche and become an emotion. It was to these circumstances, to the particular environment of each situation, where the efforts of the modern hunter of souls should converge.

Until then the way to capture a potential consumer's attention had consisted of a direct appeal to the individual and to the benefits of this or that product or service (YOU, buy this or that, NOW!), so that an advertisement worked like a blunderbuss, it was directed simultaneously and indistinctly to thousands of individuals and to each and everyone of them. However, in this approach each person could offer resistance if he did not feel sufficiently identified with the product or service or simply felt that he or she did not need it. Like Bruno, Bernays was aware that "it is sometimes possible to change the attitudes of millions but impossible to change the attitude of one man."[55]

However, the complexity of modern society offered an opportunity that did not exist in a society based on personal relationships, it made it possible for a *venator* to use regimentation to

> set up psychological an emotional currents which will work for him. Instead of assaulting sales resistance by direct attack, he is interested in removing sales resistance. He creates circumstances which will swing emotional currents so as to make for purchaser demand.[56]

The mere mention of "psychological and emotional currents" evokes the Freudian ideas of libido and transference which, as we have seen, are related to the Renaissance idea of *pneuma* that, in this case, creates a network of libidinal bonds that binds a group of consumers to the wishes of a hunter. Like Bruno, Bernays acknowledged that even if there is not a single bond that, when applied, works equally and with the same effectiveness for everyone, it is possible to eliminate individual resistances by creating an *atmosphere of desire*, a particular circumstance that envelops the public and leads it, albeit indirectly, where the hunter wants it to go. In Bruno's words: "Insofar as that which can be bound is composed of more parts, to the same degree it is less limited to specific bonds."[57]

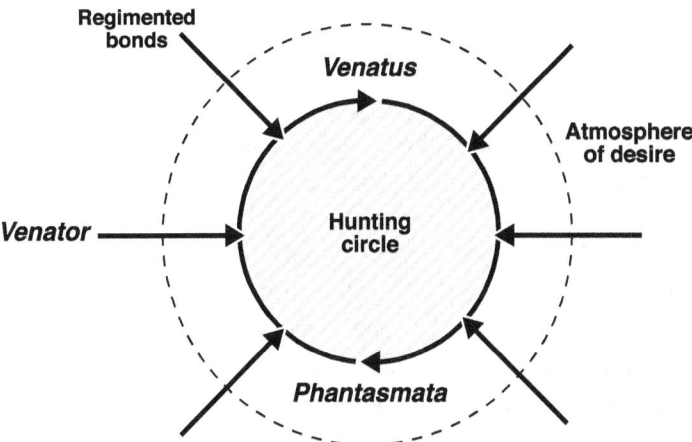

Thus, Bernays embraced the principle of the diversity of bonds that Bruno enunciates as follows:

> Therefore, different individuals are bonded by different objects. And even though the same object bonds both Socrates and Plato, it binds each of them in a different way. Some things excite the masses, other things affect only a few; some things affect the male and the manly, other things the female and the feminine.[58]

One of the clearest practical applications of this principle took place when Bernays was hired in 1935 by the Brewers Association, who were concerned about the influence that the League of Temperance, an association against the consumption of alcoholic beverages, was having on their clientele. Aware that it was useless to try to convince the opposition and, at the same time, win back the brewers' clients, Bernays decided to turn beer into "the drink of moderation." To this end

> he persuaded beer retailers to cooperate with law enforcement to ensure that their product was used responsibly, and he published "evidence" that beer was not fattening and had a caloric value equal to that of milk. He told homemakers that beer would make for a richer chocolate cake; told farmers that brewers were major buyers of their barley, corn, and rice; and told laborers that beer was the one alcoholic beverage they could afford. And he published booklets and wrote letters claiming that beer was the favorite drink of ancient babylonians and the monks of the Middle Ages as well as of George

Washington, Thomas Jefferson, Patrick Henry, and the pilgrims.[59]

Since he understood how each of the interest groups could be manipulated, Bernays used the social regimentation typical of modern society to expand the circle of resonance of these bonds. (See diagram on page 53)

One of Bernays' favorite examples of such an operation was how to sell pianos. Let's say that a brand of musical instruments is interested in launching a new line of luxury pianos and it doesn't know how to market them. The task of the public relations advisor will be to create the right circumstances to swing the demand in favor of the manufacturer.

> He appeals perhaps to the home instinct which is fundamental. He will endeavor to develop public acceptance of the idea of a music room in the home. This he may do, for example, by organizing an exhibition of period music rooms by well-known decorators who themselves exert an influence on the buying groups [...] Then, in order to create dramatic interest in the exhibit, he stages an event or ceremony. To this ceremony key people, persons known to influence the buying habits of the public, such as a famous violinist, a popular artist, and a society leader, are invited [...] Meanwhile influential architects have been persuaded to make the music room an integral architectural part of their plans with perhaps an specially charming niche in one corner for the piano. Less influential architects will as a matter of course imitate what is done by the men whom they consider masters of their profession. They in turn will implant the idea of the music room in the mind of the general public.

> The music room will be accepted because it has been made the thing. And the man or woman who has a music room, or has arranged a corner of the parlor as a musical corner, will naturally think of buying a piano. It will come to him as his own idea.[60]

In this fragment we can recognize all the traits that characterize Bernays' hunting method. In it the authority figures influence the buying decisions of the lower strata of society. Moreover, the circumstance created by the public relations advisor generates an atmosphere with a very particular effect: it causes the consumer to believe that the idea of buying a piano was not implanted in his mind but instead that it was his or her own idea. Why? Because people can easily recognize that they are being manipulated by a direct and isolated stimulus, but to fully grasp a whole atmosphere is something entirely different, it is, so to speak, to stop seeing the trees and start looking at the forest. Now, the function of this atmosphere of desire is not limited to diverting attention from isolated stimuli by dissolving the resistances of each individual, its real function is to propagate the "libidinal energy" throughout the system by creating an environment conducive to the hunter's goals. This atmosphere is the *systemic representation* of Bruno's network of bonds, which now acts as a seed of unreality.

It should be made plain that although Bernays' method was novel, the idea that it was possible to envelop consumers in an atmosphere of desire was already popular by then; the question was not *what* should be done but *how*. The most obvious expression of this attitude may be a speech by radio announcer Helen Landon Cass who, at a convention of window trimmers in 1923, told her audience:

> Sell them their dreams, sell them what they longed for and hoped for and almost despaired of having. Sell them hats by splashing sunlight across them. Sell them dreams—dreams of country clubs and proms and visions of what might happen if only. After all, people don't buy things to have things. They buy things to work for them. They buy hope—hope of what your merchandise will do for them. Sell them this hope and you won't have to worry about selling them goods.[61]

As we saw in the previous section, the idea of creating a secondary reality in order to engage the public is congruent with both the economy of desire and the ideals of consumer demiurgy. "Sell them their dreams…" involves a spectacle, a dramatic representation that captures the attention of the consumer/spectator and circumscribes him to a desire-filled hallucination. This is the maximum expression of the *desidia americana* I formulated at the beginning of this chapter, the abandonment to material pleasures driven by an idleness that must be constantly satisfied.

The passivity of this form of lust greatly facilitates the pneumatic/erotic operations of the modern hunters of souls, a circumstance which Bernays exploited for various purposes. When he was hired in the mid-1920s by the Beechnut Packing Company, a huge bacon producer who wanted to improve its sales after an economic crisis had reduced the contents of breakfasts all over the country, Bernays, seeing that there was no case in trying to steal customers away from the competition, decided to put green spectacles on the whole country and "transform America's eating habits.

> He persuaded a famous New York doctor to write his colleagues asking whether they supported hearty or light breakfasts. Hearty won big, newspapers spread the word, people followed their physicians' advice, and sales roared of the two items most identified with big breakfasts—bacon and eggs.[62]

What is now considered the typical "American breakfast" (fried eggs with two bacon strips) is largely a product of Bernays' imagination. Here I should emphasize that the susceptibility of the masses to these magical operations rests not only on the passivity implicit in their condition—what I have called *desidia americana*—beneath them operates a hysterical and neurotic background which manifests itself as an unconscious and spontaneous inclination to please authority in all its forms, in a way similar to that of a little boy or girl that, above all, wishes to please his or her parents.[63] The "genius" of Bernays mediatic magic was to find the proper way to take advantage of this deficiency.

Aware that it was not always possible to manipulate reality and create the necessary circumstances for a client out of thin air, Bernays became a master at accentuating existing trends and exploiting them for his purposes, a process he called "crystallizing public opinion."[64] Upon being hired by the American Tobacco Company to increase Lucky Strikes' market share among the female audience, Bernays and George Washington Hill, the company's president, had a Machiavellian, or rather Brunian idea: they took advantage that the women's fashion of the day had begun to favor more slender figures and appealed to their vanity. Smoking was good because it helped with compulsive eating, so they came up with the slogan "reach for a Lucky instead of a sweet."

For this campaign Bernays recruited the help of photographers and choreographers who supported the notion that the ideal feminine beauty should have a few less pounds, as well as doctors willing to affirm that the correct way to end a meal was not with a dessert but with a cigarette. Not content with the opinion of these "experts," he flooded the covers of fashion magazines with photographs of slender Parisian models, persuaded several hotels to add cigarettes to their dessert menus and suggested that shelf manufacturers should add spaces designed exclusively to store cigarettes. In Brunian language: since different individuals are subject to different bonds, capturing the attention of a mass requires attacking it from all fronts. Something is perfectly bound, says Bruno

> if it is bound in all its powers and components. Hence, he who binds should count these items carefully so that, in wishing to bind as completely as possible, he can tie up many or all of them.[65]

Judging by the success of the campaign Bernays must have bound plenty of these items. In 1928 American Tobacco Company revenues increased by $32 million and Lucky Strike sales were higher than the rest of the company's cigarette brands combined.

Apart from the pathological obedience of the masses to their authority figures, Bernays realized that the idea of common good was one of the most powerful bonds when it came to manipulating crowds, something he called "hitching private interests to public ones." Examples of this technique abound in his career but perhaps the most infamous of all is the campaign known as "The Torches of Freedom." One year after his work with Lucky Strike, George Washington Hill contacted Bernays again with the following assignment: we succeeded in getting women to smoke, now we need them to smoke in public. If we succeed, we will have doubled our market share. Bernays understood immediately that what prevented women from smoking in public places was a taboo that cast doubt on their reputations. Faced with this problem he went to A.A. Brill, an outstanding Austrian psychoanalyst based in New York known for being Freud's first translator to English. "It is perfectly normal for women to want to smoke cigarettes," Brill told Bernays,

> The emancipation of women has suppressed many of their feminine desires. More women now do the same work as men do. Many women bear no children; those who do bear have fewer children. Feminine traits are masked. Cigarettes, which are equated with men, become torches of freedom.[66]

Brill's argument was based on the idea of "penis envy" that Sigmund Freud had outlined in his 1908 book *On The Sexual Theories of Children*. This concept—thoroughly revised and discredited throughout the twentieth century—[67] supposedly takes place with the discovery of the anatomical difference of the sexes by the girl, who would feel "deprived in relation to the boy and [therefore] wishes to possess a penis as he does."[68] According to Brill, smoking was for women a sublimated way to acquire their own penis and with this to challenge male power. It was then that it occurred to Bernays that if he managed to associate this subliminal challenge with the suffragist movement he could make women smoke anywhere. To do this, he convinced Ruth Hale, a leading feminist, to support the initiative in the press and organized a group of women who would light their "torches of freedom" at the Annual Easter Sunday parade. The telegram sent to the newspapers (and, of course, signed by his female secretary) said:

> in the interests of equality of the sexes and to fight another sex taboo I and other young women will light another torch of freedom by smoking cigarettes while strolling on Fifth Avenue Easter Sunday. We are doing this to combat the silly prejudice that the cigarette is suitable for the home, the restaurant, the taxicab, the theater lobby but never, no, never for the sidewalk.[69]

It is very seldom that the feminization implicit in the act of confining a human group inside a pneumatic circle is so sadly evident. Needless to say, the event was a complete sensation. Ten forward-thinking women responded to Bernays' call and walked down Fifth Avenue while smoking their cigarettes in public. The press and public opinion were delighted with the event, which made headlines in the country's leading newspapers the next day. This was the day when unconscious empathy for a progressive cause was used to sell more cigarettes.

That year, cigarette sales to women increased by 12%.[70]

The banana boat war

In 1870 Lorenzo Dow Baker, the captain of the schooner *Telegraph* which came from the Orinoco Delta bound for Philadelphia, stopped in Jamaica to pick up a cargo of bamboo and have a taste of the island's rum. "While he was drinking, a local tradesman came by offering green bananas; Baker bought 160 bunches at 25 cents a bunch. Less than two weeks later he sold them in New York for up to $3.25 a bunch, a deal so sweet he couldn't resist doing it again. And again. By 1885, eleven ships were sailing under the banner of the Boston Fruit Company, bringing to the United States 10 million bunches of bananas a year. United Fruit was formed in 1899, with assets that included more than 210,000 acres of land across the Caribbean and Central America, 112 miles of railroad, and so much political clout that Honduras, Costa Rica, and other countries of the region became known as banana republics."[71] The social impact of United Fruit Company and its deplorable employment policies changed the face of the Caribbean countries forever. In Colombia, the company's exploitation reached such heights that on December 1928, the Colombian army—threatened by the US State Department with a naval invasion—sent a regiment of three hundred soldiers to the town of Ciénaga to end a strike that had stopped the company's production for months. After days of tension, the regiment ended up firing at a crowd of between two thousand and four thousand people in Ciénaga's central square, killing hundreds of them. It has never been known with certainty how many people died or how many corpses were buried in mass graves or thrown into the sea. "Look at the mess we've got ourselves into," Gabriel García Márquez wrote in *A Hundred Years of Solitude*, "just because we invited a gringo to eat some bananas."

Twelve years after the Banana Massacre, United Fruit was the largest landowner and employer in Guatemala and operated without having to pay any kind of internal tax or tariff for importing supplies or exporting its production. The company had full control of Puerto Barrios, the country's only port in the Caribbean, and had the national rail system at their complete disposal. As if all this were not enough, General Jorge Ubico Castañeda's regime—in power since 1931 after an election in which he was the only candidate to the presidency—gave United Fruit an exclusive contract for exploitation of bananas and allowed the company to pay its workers no more than 50 cents a day. Guatemala was, in short, a *maquila-country*. If the US department stores and supermarkets were the Land of Oz, Central America and the Caribbean became the dumping site that made the yellow brick road possible; the banana republics were that sector of reality that went out of sight after the division between the spheres of production and consumption. As we shall see in the following pages, not even United Fruit's "backstage" was exempt from becoming a sordid spectacle in which the whole of Guatemala transformed in the theater of a new type of media war; the scenario where aesthetics and politics join forces.

Of course, the situation did not take long to explode. In 1944 a series of violent popular uprisings weakened the position of Ubico Castañeda who, in a delicate state of health, fled the country leaving the power in the hands of a military junta that was deposed in the revolution of October of the same year. For the first time political parties were established and popular elections were held. The winner was Juan José Arévalo, a philosopher and educator based in Argentina who had returned to Guatemala earlier that year. Arévalo inherited a country in crisis, 70% of the population was illiterate and 2% of landowners owned three-quarters of arable land. Even so, he did his best to set up education programs and strengthen the democratic system by allowing everyone but illiterate women to vote. Arévalo defined his ideology as "spiritual socialism" and although he granted rights to organize in unions and hold strikes, he banned communist parties. He also broke relations with the government of Franco in Spain and with that of his neighbours Anastasio Somoza in Nicaragua and Rafael Trujillo in the Dominican Republic; his recommendation that Latin America should not recognize and support authoritarian regimes gave him the reputation of being a communist within the region, an unwarranted fame that was exploited by his rivals in the military who tried to overthrow him several times.

In six years of government Arévalo survived some twenty-five *coup d'etats* from his own army. It is not clear whether the CIA or United Fruit indirectly participated in these attempts, but the company was increasingly concerned with the political and social changes the country was going through. During his government the workers of United Fruit went on strike in the plantations and in Puerto Barrios and, for the first time, forced the company to make concessions on their work contracts. In 1951 Arévalo was succeeded by Juan Jacobo Árbenz Guzmán, his defense minister, who was elected by a 50% margin. "If Arévalo was a portent," says Larry Tye, "Árbenz was the realization of the dreaded prophesy."[72] The new government launched a plan to build a highway to the coast, a new port that was not controlled by United Fruit and a hydroelectric station that would allow Guatemala to become independent of foreign service providers. Even if Árbenz's intention was to turn Guatemala into a modern capitalist state, United Fruit, supported by the CIA and the State Department, were bent in portraying his government as a communist regime and an imminent danger to the national security of the United States. It is at this point of the story that Edward Bernays enters the picture.

Bernays had been working for United Fruit since before the fall of Ubico Castañeda's regime, mainly building good will between the US public and the company. To this end, he implemented campaigns to demonstrate the positive effects of bananas on digestion and on the treatment of celiac disease. He also devoted considerable effort to associating bananas with national defense, a variation of his policy "hitching private interests to public ones." With this goal in mind he issued a memorandum explaining how the company's "great white fleet" had been used during the two World Wars to transport rations and troops and set forth the reasons why importing bananas was vital to the United States. His focus on the company's public relations was visionary, "the mission wasn't just to sell bananas [...] but to sell an entire region of the hemisphere."[73] At Bernays' request, Sam Zemurray, the president of the company, restored an ancient Mayan ball court. Around the same time the company premiered an advertising cartoon called *Chiquita Banana*, created by Dik Browne of *Hägar the Horrible* fame. Chiquita, an anthropomorphic banana dressed in a tropical dance outfit, sang songs to educate the North American public on how to prepare and store bananas, which were still not a well known fruit at the time.

In one of his typical moves, Bernays created a front organization to disseminate information on behalf of the company called the Middle America Information Bureau, which, from its very name, was dedicated to presenting an adulterated version of the region. "'Middle America' was a rational and timely expansion of the phrase 'Central America' which by long usage includes only the republics of Guatemala, Honduras, Nicaragua, El Salvador, Costa Rica, Panama and the colony of British Honduras. Middle America would include those countries, along with Mexico and the Caribbean island republics of Cuba, Haiti and the Dominican Republic."[74] According to Tye, this initiative was, to some extent, an honest attempt on the part of Bernays to educate the North American public about a neighbouring region of which they knew almost nothing. However, this educational impulse was by no means altruistic and "all the material released by this office had to be approved by responsible executives of the United Fruit Company."[75] In all, a curriculum on the geography, history and anthropology of Central America and the Caribbean approved by a foreign corporation.

If anything can be said in favor of Bernays in this matter is that, after a visit to Guatemala in September 1947, he wrote a memo warning the board about the bad reputation of the company among the workers:

> Good will of all groups toward the fruit company is poor [...] Ignorance, conscious and unconscious distortions by politicos in power or seeking power, by fellow traveller[s] and communist influences all contribute their part. Guatemala is in a state of transition [...] All these situations complicate [the] issue and make the company vulnerable unless certain things happen. The American embassy might gain more power, or the government and people in authority as well as the literate [members] of the labor unions might recognize the real public interest and economic values of the Fruit Company.[76]

Of course, Bernays' main interest was not the well-being of the company's workers, it was for the company to disguise their attitudes so that the locals could not realize that the "values" of the United Fruit had always been in line with those of the colonialist expansion of the United States in Latin America. Bernays was aware that the larger the company the less likely it is to change its behavior patterns quickly. He did not expect an immediate reaction to his memorandum and he did not get it. What he did get was that the following year they shut down the Middle America Information Bureau. He could have left the company then, but the $100,000 a year they were paying him probably helped to dissuade him. Bernays continued to work for United Fruit, perhaps thinking that he could achieve a gradual change in its attitudes.

But as the Árbenz government launched Decree 900 and began to expropriate uncultivated land from the company to redistribute it among the country's poorest, Bernays' strategy changed radically. No more education about "Middle America" or about the benefits of bananas for digestion, no more restored Mayan ball courts. When his employer's stakes went up in the region, Bernays was more than willing to go to war. And nobody better prepared. Among all United Fruit's public relations advisors, Bernays had the best experience for the task. He had he worked for the Committee on Public Information during World War I, and during the second, advised the army and navy on how best to manage their public relations and disseminate their propaganda. Bernays knew that if the

Árbenz government was to be overthrown, Guatemala could not be portrayed as a developing country in the eyes of the North American public, a republic with a liberal and progressive government, it had to become a threat to US national security, the outpost of a future Soviet incursion into America's backyard. The campaign to overthrow Jacobo Árbenz became one of the first and most successful examples of *black PR*—an expression derived from the military term *black ops*, which refers to a covert operation that is not attributable to any organization or government—and which could equally refer to black magic.

A master at anticipating the social and political trends of his time, in 1951, practically two years before Árbenz's government initiated the expropriations, Bernays wrote a letter to Edmund Whitman, United Fruit's chief advertising officer, pointing out that the recent expropriation of the Iranian government to British Petroleum constituted a worrying precedent: "we recommend that immediate steps be undertaken to safeguard American business interests in Latin American countries against comparable actions there. News knows no boundaries today [...] To disregard the possibilities of the impact of events one upon another is to adopt a head-in-the-sand-ostrich policy."[77] He recommended that the company get a high-level Latin American official to publicly condemn the expropriations and that it hire a lawyer to outline the reasons why the expropriation should be illegal. In short, United Fruit was to launch a media attack that would induce the president and the State Department to pronounce publicly on the matter.

Bernays knew how to take advantage of the ignorance and bigotry that came with the paranoia encouraged by McCarthyism and the Cold War, which unfortunately have survived to this day: if you are not in agreement with the United States and, above all, with its economic interests, you are automatically deemed a "communist;" there are no grays on the political spectrum, you are either with us or against us. This radicalism cannot but question the neutrality of the supposed "center" of the spectrum. Bernays was a lifelong member of the Democrat Party, but how bizarre and ironic is it that Joseph Goebbels, Propaganda Minister of Nazi Germany, had in his library several of his books and that he used *Crystallizing Public Opinion* (1923) in his campaign against the German Jews? In politics it is not only the extremes that meet, fascism is actually spread all over the spectrum.

Always a couple of steps ahead of his prey, Bernays had started planning his media *blitzkrieg* months in advance. By 1950 he had already made a list of ten national magazines such as Readers Digest, Harpers and Saturday Evening Post that could easily be persuaded to publish slightly different but consistent stories about the political crisis in Guatemala from the company's point of view. In similar fashion, stories about the growing influence of the communists in Guatemala began to appear more and more often in the New York Times, New York Herald tribune, Atlantic Monthly, Times and Newsweek. For Bernays it was especially important that liberal magazines such as The Nation would join the effort as he "believed that winning the liberals over was essential to winning America over."[78] From the standpoint of regimentation, understood here as a "militarization" of the public, having the support of these media outlets would enhance the coverage that the bonds had on the population. During this campaign Bernays used his contacts in the press and his considerable reputation and influence to become the biggest source of information on the situation in Guatemala. "A surprising number of respected reporters seemed not to know or care about the orchestration or about the fact that Bernays worked for a firm with huge economic interests at stake."[79]

In order to support his claims to the press, in January 1952 Bernays organized a two-week trip to Guatemala so that a group of Newsweek, Time, San Francisco Chronicle and Miami Herald journalists could see the situation for themselves. Bernays always insisted that journalists were free "to go wherever they wanted, talk to whomever they wanted, and report their findings freely,"[80] but Thomas McCann, a company executive who would later become vice president of public affairs, stated in his biography that these trips, organized and funded by United Fruit, were actually carefully choreographed and regulated by Bernays' public relations team. It was, in a word, a show specially designed to compromise the objectivity of the US press. According to Herbert Matthews—the New York Times reporter who a few years later would reveal that Fidel Castro had not died on the landing of Playa Colorada and was hidden in the Sierra Maestra —"a hostile and ill-informed American press helped to create an emotional public opinion. This, in turn, worked on Congress, and ultimately on the State Department."[81]

By 1953 the influence of the press reached a critical point. John Foster Dulles, Eisenhower's Secretary of State whose law firm had advised United Fruit in negotiations with President Arévalo, and his brother Allen Dulles, the director of the CIA, began to exert considerable pressure within the government. In August of that same year, the National Security Council approved a covert action in Guatemala and in December Allen Dulles launched Operation PBSUCCESS, a plan with a three million dollar budget to overthrow the Árbenz government. The CIA assembled an army of peasants, gave them weapons and money to intimidate the population and created a "rebel" radio station, *The Voice of Liberation*, with the purpose of transmitting propaganda against the Árbenz government and urging the population to join Carlos Castillo Armas, a right-wing military official chosen by the Agency to replace Árbenz once he was deposed. *The Voice of Liberation* transmitted popular music, had an on-staff comedian and its contents were specially designed to lower the morale of the Guatemalan army so that when the time came they did not defend their president. The station claimed to broadcast "from deep in the jungle" when in fact the transmissions were recorded in Miami by Guatemalan exiles and then retransmitted from Central America. As in the case of Colombia in 1928, one of the main deterrents was the idea, propagated by the "rebel" station, that if the Castillo Armas forces were defeated, a US invasion would be inevitable. While Bernays was in charge of public opinion in the United States, the CIA did its part with the opinion of Guatemala.

One of CIA's shrewdest *black PR* moves was to use the influence of the Catholic Church in Guatemala to "raise awareness" among the people of the country about the alleged Communist threat. They talked to a cardinal in New York and convinced him to contact a Guatemalan archbishop. "In April of 1954," a few months before the coup, "a pastoral letter was read in all Guatemalan churches urging all Guatemalans to stand up against 'this enemy of God and country.' The CIA then took this letter and made pamphlets which it later airdropped over Guatemala."[82] On June 18, 1954, Castillo Armas and his rebel forces, divided into four battalions with a total of 480 men advised and trained by the CIA, crossed the border from Honduras and began to sabotage the railroad and the telegraph lines. However, wherever they arrived they were defeated by the Guatemalan army. A force of 160 rebels was repelled by a garrison of 30 soldiers and the battalion that attacked Puerto Barrios was defeated by police and port workers, causing many to flee back to Honduras. Nevertheless, *The Voice of Liberation* transmitted false reports about the movements of the rebel troops that caused many Guatemalans to flee to the countryside. In an effort to regain momentum, the rebels and the CIA sent planes that made a series of light bombing runs that caused little material damage but gave the impression that the Castillo Armas forces were far more powerful than they actually were. "The totality of the effort [was] more dependent upon psychological impact than actual military strength."[83] On June 27, Árbenz resigned from the presidency, left the power to a military junta and went into exile at the Mexican Embassy, where he began a journey that took him to Canada, Switzerland, the Netherlands, France and Uruguay.[84]

The next day, Secretary of State John Foster Dulles went on US national radio and enthusiastically proclaimed that Guatemalans had risen and overthrown the communist regime of Jacobo Árbenz on their own initiative and by their own means. Bernays, in an echo of his "torches of freedom" campaign soon called the rebel forces "the army of liberation," but what is "freedom" in this context but a shell emptied of its original meaning? Freedom to enforce the laws of supply and demand that underlie the Land of Desire?[85] The United Fruit and CIA's campaign against the Árbenz government is one of the most impressive displays of the demiurgical capacity of public relations, a skill undoubtedly based on its magical origins. Taking advantage of the rarified atmosphere that came with the Cold War and McCarthyism, during the early 1950s Bernays enveloped the North American public in a secondary reality through false or deliberately manipulated news to serve his client's purposes. On the other hand, the CIA used similar techniques to cause panic and confusion in the Guatemalan population, thus facilitating the establishment of a regime sympathetic to the economic interests of the United States and the United Fruit Company.

The consequences of United Fruit's manipulations have lasted in Guatemala and the Caribbean long after the demiurgic bubble woven by Bernays and the CIA burst. To begin with, through their appalling actions, United Fruit and the CIA undermined their purpose of instituting a stable and empathetic government to the economic policies of the United States in Guatemala. The next three presidents of the country, including Castillo Armas, died violent deaths, and the reversal of decree 900 was a definite influence on the emergence of communism throughout Central America and the Caribbean. As in the case of Al Qaeda, monsters are created at home. During the polarization a considerable portion of the Guatemalan population organized in several leftist rebel groups that entered into an armed conflict with the subsequent governments of the country. The civil war lasted from 1960 to 1996 and it is estimated that 200,000 people died and a million more were displaced as a result.

As a literary creation, Macondo is a masterful example of demiurgy, its ability to enclose us in a world apart, in an entirely aesthetic dimension, is astounding at the very least. Perhaps by virtue of this capacity, the depiction García Márquez makes of the Banana Massacre reveals the intersection between "real" reality and demiurgic unreality.

Towards the end of the novel, José Arcadio Segundo is among the crowd that had gathered on the town square to protest against the banana company that has exploited the people of the region for years. The army, as in real life, opens fire on the multitude. José Arcadio wakes up face up in the darkness "on an endless and silent train." He is surrounded by corpses packed in the train cars like banana bunches. They are heading towards the sea, to get rid of the bodies like rejected produce. He manages to jump off the train and, in the middle of a tropical downpour, makes his way back to Macondo. In the first town a woman takes him into her house, heats water for his wounds and offers him coffee. After finishing his cup he says:

> "There must have been three thousand of them"
> "What?"
> "The dead," he clarified. "It must have been all of the people who were at the station"

The woman looked at him with pity in her eyes. "There haven't been any dead here ... Since the time of your uncle, the colonel, nothing has happened in Macondo." Upon arriving to town José Arcadio finds that the strike has ended and a pact between the banana companies and the workers is set to be signed.

"The official version," writes García Márquez, "repeated a thousand times and mangled out all over the country by every means of communication the government found at hand, was finally accepted: there were no dead, the satisfied workers had gone back to their families, and the banana company was suspending all activity until the rains stopped."

The demiurgic bubble was already in place and although union leaders continued to disappear, government officials assured their families:

> "You must have been dreaming ... Nothing has happened in Macondo, nothing has ever happened, and nothing ever will happen. This is a happy town."

Macondo is a fictional town twice over, a literary creation that is enclosed in a second unreality bubble where "nothing ever happens." A bubble of apathy and impunity that continues to thrive to this very day.

---

[1] William Leach, *Land of Desire: Merchants, Power and the Rise of a New American Culture* (New York: Vintage Books, 1993), 3.

[2] In addition to the overtly religious tone that turned "America" into the Promised Land and the Biblical Paradise—an ideal assiduously cultivated by the Puritan settlers since the 17th century—it is also necessary to emphasize that the cult of the new implicit in the idea of the land of opportunities led to a marked tendency to utopian thinking. Indeed, the American dream can be consistently described as a form of commercial utopia that seeks to stimulate material desire and abundance through free market economy. In this regard, Walter Benjamin, one of the first philosophers to seek the origin of commercial culture in the Paris of Baudelaire, argues that the new means of production that came with the industrial age manifested themselves in the collective consciousness as images "in which the new and the old are intermingled. These images are ideals, and in them the collective seeks not only to transfigure, but also to transcend, the immaturity of the social product and the deficiencies of the social order of production. In these ideals there also emerges a vigorous aspiration to break with what is out-dated—which means, however, with the most recent past [...] The experiences of this society, which have their store-place in the collective unconscious, interact with the new to give birth to the utopias which leave their traces in a thousand configurations of life, from permanent buildings to ephemeral fashions." (Benjamin, *Paris - Capital of the Nineteenth Century*, 79).

[3] The direct ancestor of the American culture of desire is, paradoxically, France and in particular Paris, where the first urban structures specifically designed for the trade of industrial products emerged. These buildings, known back then as "galleries," made use of new materials such as iron, glass and gas lighting and gave rise to a new kind of passer-by, called *Flâneur* by Baudelaire, which wandered through streets and galleries absorbing the "fruits" of commerce and industry. Almost until the second decade of the twentieth century, American department stores such as Wanamaker's, Macy's and Marshall Field were still taking some of the architectural and decorative traits of nineteenth-century galleries as reference and paid special attention to the trends imposed by French stores such as Galeries Lafayette, Le Bon Marché and Le Printemps.

[4] Quoted by Leach en *Land of Desire*, 22.
[5] William James, *The Varieties of Religious Experience* (Mineola, Dover Publications, 2002), 94-94.
[6] Leach, *Land of Desire*, 225.
[7] Alan Gauld, *A History of Hypnotism* (NewYork: Cambridge University Press, 1992), 193.
[8] Quoted by Gauld in *A History of Hypnotism*, 194.
[9] Leach, *Land of Desire*, 227.
[10] Leach, *Land of Desire*, 228.
[11] Leach, *Land of Desire*, 229.
[12] Leach, *Land of Desire*, 229.
[13] Quoted by Leach in *Land of Desire*, 229.
[14] Leach, *Land of Desire*, 248.
[15] Quoted by David B. Parker, *The Rise and Fall of The Wonderful Wizard of Oz as a "Parable on Populism."* Accessed, October 4, 2017, at: *http://www.halcyon.com/piglet/Populism.htm*
[16] Leach, *Land of Desire*, 251. On this invulnerability, it is interesting to note that Dorothy has a mark on her forehead left by the Witch of the North's kiss. This makes her invulnerable to any type of physical damage.
[17] Leach, *Land of Desire*, 252.
[18] Leach, *Land of Desire*, 252.
[19] This type of fake world lacking in depth has been a recurring theme in American literature and cinema, particularly in the work of Philip K. Dick, and in films such as Peter Weir's *Truman Show*, Alex Proyas' *Dark City*, *Vanilla Sky* by Cameron Crowe (based on *Abre los Ojos* by Alejandro Amenábar) and *Pleasantville* by Gary Ross.
[20] Leach, *Land of Desire*, 256.
[21] Leach, *Land of Desire*, 257.
[22] Leach, *Land of Desire*, 253.
[23] Perhaps the best example of this circumstance is P.T. Barnum, a successful nineteenth century American Performer, businessman and politician, remembered for his *Barnum's American Museum*, where he exhibited all kinds of live shows with curiosities like albinos, giants, dwarves, "exotic women" and all kinds of farces such as the "mermaid of Feejee," a creature composed of the head of a monkey and the tail of a fish.
[24] In fact, it is not surprising to find that Baum himself was a kind of trickster versed in activities such as acting, production and marketing. Since the last decade of the nineteenth century Baum, one of the pioneers in the art of decorating showcases, had published a manual dedicated to this profession entitled *The Show Window*, one of the first publications of its kind in the world. By 1900, the year the year of publication of The Wizard of Oz, Baum also published an updated version of the manual called *The Merchants Record and Show Window*.

[25] Leach, *Land of Desire*, 255.

[26] In *Money and Magic* philosopher and economist H.C. Binswanger elaborates an alchemical interpretation of modern economics based on the second part of Goethe's Faust. Broadly speaking, Binswanger's thesis is as follows: the type of economy that emerged with the industrial revolution is a form of alchemy in the sense that it is capable of transmuting a worthless substance into one with value (simple paper into paper currency). For Binswanger, the changes that took place during the transition from the economy of necessity or subsistence to the economy of desire (the industrial or alchemical economy) were enormous and perfectly reflect the idea of the American dream as a counter-creation of perpetual abundance: "the subsistence economy is adapted to satisfying man's physical needs, which are satiable. Its goals are therefore finite. The industrial economy, on the other had, is adapted to imaginary needs, which can be constantly expanded thorough man's fantasy; these needs are insatiable. Inherent, then, to the industrial economy is an infinite striving. It follows from the striving for money, since money (through the creation of money paper!) can be increased more quickly and more easily than the goods that must be laboriously obtained from the material world. The tendency is therefore first to to produce money and then, tempted or lured by profit, to grant this money additional value as money capital, through a corresponding expansion of imaginary demand and the production of goods this entails. The vision of an ever-improving future is a vital ingredient in the economy of finance and industry. Whatever stands in its way or suggests limitation must be eliminated. By removing these inner limits to its progress, the economy gains increasingly the upper hand and casts the whole world under its spell." (Binswanger, *Money and Magic*, 102)

[27] Leach, *Land of Desire*, 148-49.

[28] Leach, *Land of Desire*, 76.

[29] Joel Spring, *Educating the Consumer-citizen: A History of the Marriage of Schools, Advertising and Media* (New Jersey: Lawrence Erlbaum Associates, 2003), 23.

[30] In *The Flâneur,* Walter Benjamin quotes German sociologist Georg Simmel on how the emphasis on sight over hearing has its origin in a circumstance specific to city life: "Someone who sees without hearing is much more uneasy than someone who hears without seeing. In this there is something characteristic of the sociology of the big city. Interpersonal relationships in big cities are distinguished by a marked preponderance of the activity of the eye over the activity of the ear. The main reason for this is the public means of transportation. Before the development of buses, railroads, and trams in the nineteenth century, people had never been in a position of having to look at one another for long minutes or even hours without speaking to one another." (Benjamin, *The Flâneur*, 37-38). On the other hand, Benjamin agrees with Leach in affirming the importance of glass as the material par excellence of the new consumer culture,

and adds to it other industrial materials such as iron. "With iron," he says in *Paris - Capital of the Nineteenth Century*, "an artificial building material appeared for the first time in the history of architecture. It went through a development whose tempo accelerated during the course of the century. This received its decisive impulse when it turned out that the locomotive, with which experiments had been made since the end of the 'twenties, could only be utilized on iron rails. The rail was the first iron unit of construction, the forerunner of the girder. Iron was avoided for dwelling-houses, and made use of for arcades, exhibition halls, railway stations—buildings which served transitory purposes. Simultaneously, the architectonic areas in which glass was employed were extended." (Benjamin, *Paris - Capital of the Nineteenth Century*, 78).

[31] Gillaume de Lorris & Jean de Meun, *Roman de la Rose* (New York: E.P. Dutton & Co., 1962), 32.

[32] Leach, *Land of Desire*, 39.

[33] However, by not offering a connection with an ideal beyond itself, the idea of "freedom" sold by consumer culture is limited to the autonomy to choose between the options offered by the market (McDonalds or Burger King? H & M or Forever 21?); everything that lies outside of it—that is, the transcendent—is completely out of reach.

[34] Walter Benjamin, *The Arcades Project* (Cambridge: The Belknap Press of Harvard University Press, 1999), 898

[35] James Beniger, *The Control Revolution* (Cambridge: Harvard University Press, 1986) vii.

[36] Morris Berman, *The Twilight of American Culture* (New York: Norton & Company, 2000), 118.

[37] Berman, *The Twilight of American Culture*, 118.

[38] Berman, *The Twilight of American Culture*, 118.

[39] Klein, *No Logo*, 21.

[40] Naomi Klein, *No Logo, 10th Anniversary Edition* (New York: Picador, 2009), 7.

[41] Klein, *No Logo*, 7.

[42] Edward Bernays, *Propaganda* (New York: Ig Publishing, 2005), 84.

[43] Quoted by Leach in *Land of Desire*, 268.

[44] Mikkel Borch-Jacobsen, *Sigmund Freud, Hipnotizador*, which appears in *Sigmund Freud, la hipnosis, textos (1886-1893)* (Bogotá, Arial, 2017) pág. 352.

[45] Quoted by Larry Tye in *The Father of Spin: Edward L. Bernays and the Birth of Public Relations* (New York: Henry Holt and Company, 1998), 117.

[46] Tye, *The Father of Spin*, 9.

[47] Bernays, *Propaganda*, 75.

[48] Taken from the introduction to Edward Bernays' *Propaganda* by Mark Crispin Miller, 16.

[49] Lippmann, *Public Opinion* (New Brunswick: Transaction Publishers, 1991), 310.

[50] Edward L. Bernays, *Propaganda* (New York: IG Publishing, 2005), 37-38.

[51] Taken from the introduction to Edward Bernays' *Propaganda* by Mark Crispin Miller, 11. It is worthy of note that the origin of the term propaganda is religious. This word was coined by Pope Gregory XV who, frightened by the spread of Protestantism, decided to create in 1622 the Office for the Propagation of the Faith (*Congregatio de propaganda fide*) to supervise the evangelical and missionary efforts in the old and the new world. It is also notable that President Woodrow Wilson had urged George Creel—director of the Committe on Public Information—to create an agency to coordinate "not propaganda as the Germans defined it, but propaganda in the true sense of the word, meaning the 'propagation of faith," a comment that brings forth the religious and magical character of North American capitalism. (Taken from George Creel's memoire, *Rebel at Large: Recollections of Fifty Crowded Years*, 158).

[52] Bernays, *Propaganda*, 73-74.

[53] Bernays, *Propaganda*, 52.

[54] The regimentation that Bernays talks about would later become the system the system of "market segmentation" which is, in essence, the recognition of the existence of the variety of bonds and subjects to be bound. With his usual sagacity, Walter Benjamin recognized the ancestor of this segmentation in the Parisian *physiologies* of the first half of the nienteenth century, pocket notebooks that portrayed the different types of people in the city, and which pretended to "divide the Parisian public according to its various strata as easily as a geologist distinguishes the layers in rocks." (Benjamin, *The Paris of the Second Empire in Baudelaire*, 39). The hidden purpose of these physiologies, rather than informing about the new "urban fauna," was to determine in a precise manner the interests of each type of stranger in order to evaluate their behavior and, thus, be able to predict it.

[55] Tye, *The Father of Spin*, 102. Bruno's quote is: "indeed, it is easier to bind many rather than only one."

[56] Bernays, *Propaganda*, 77.

[57] Giordano Bruno, *A General Account of Bonding,* which appears in *Cause, Principle and Unity: Essays on Magic* (Cambridge, Cambridge University Press, 2004), 159.

[58] Bruno, *A General Account of Bonding*, 149.

[59] Tye, *The Father of Spin*, 59-60.

[60] Bernays, *Propaganda*, 78.

[61] Quoted by Leach en *Land of Desire*, 298.

[62] Tye, *The Father of Spin*, 51.

[63] In this respect it is interesting to mention Stanley Milgram's experiment on obedience to authority figures which, through a pretend experiment about the

study of memory, revealed that 61% of subjects, from diverse occupations and education levels, were willing to administer a fatal electric shock to another subject, just because an authority figure asked and insisted upon the task. A good account of Milgram's experiment appears in Lauren Slater's *Opening Skinner's Box: Great Psychological Experiments of the Twentieth Century*. For a fictional account the reader may refer to the novel *The Learners* by Chip Kidd.

[64] Tye, *The Father of Spin*, 24.

[65] Bruno, *A General Account of Bonding*, 164.

[66] Tye, *The Father of Spin*, 28.

[67] The arbitrariness, and patriarchality, of the concept of penis envy was exposed by the neo-freudian psychologist and feminist Karen Horney (1885-1952). According to Horney, men suffered more from womb envy—that is, envy of the female ability to conceive—than females penis envy, whose function would be subsumed by such capacity. Over time, Horney's thesis would also be contradicted by later generations of psychologists and feminists who argued that her concept equated femininity with motherhood.

[68] Jean Laplanche and Jean-Bertrand Pontalis, *The Language of Psychoanalysis* (London: Karnac Books, 1988), 303.

[69] Tye, *The Father of Spin*, 28-29.,

[70] It is important to make plain that the fact that this campaign worked does not rest on the fact that Freud's concept of penis envy was true, as Bernays would have it, but on the correct manipulation of the progressive cause of gender equality and the creation of adequate circumstances for it to penetrate public opinion. Regarding the psychological manipulation of the general public, I should point out the work of Ernest Dichter, an Austrian psychologist naturalized in the United States who founded of the Institute for Motivational Research, where Freudian concepts were openly applied to the world of mass consumption. Dichter was the creator of the focus group, initially a group therapy session about consumer products, where conclusions were drawn about shopping habits and the reasons why a consumer chose this or that product or brand. One of Dicther's most effective jobs was for Betty Crocker Foods, a brand of instant food whose cake mix product was selling below expectations. After a group study for the brand, Dichter concluded that housewives felt an unconscious guilt for using an instant mix, so he recommended a solution of impressive elegance: the housewife should feel like she was participating in the preparation of the product, and for this the instructions should specify that an egg should be added to the mixture, "it would be an unconscious symbol of the housewife mixing her own eggs as a gift to her husband, and so would lessen the guilt. Betty Crocker did it and the sales soared". (Taken from the second part of the documentary *The Century of the Self* by Adam Curtis)

[71] Tye, *The Father of Spin*, 161.

[72] Tye, *The Father of Spin*, 166.

[73] Tye, *The Father of Spin*, 162-163.
[74] Tye, *The Father of Spin*, 163.
[75] Tye, *The Father of Spin*, 163.
[76] Tye, *The Father of Spin*, 164.
[77] Tye, *The Father of Spin*, 167.
[78] Tye, *The Father of Spin*, 168.
[79] Tye, *The Father of Spin*, 169.
[80] Tye, *The Father of Spin*, 170.
[81] Tye, *The Father of Spin*, 177.

[82] Patrick Warren, *How the CIA and Corporate America used propaganda in 1954 to overthrow a democratic nation*. Accessed, April 15, 2018, at: *https://www.scribd.com/document/50930814/How-the-CIA-and-Corporate-America-Used-Propaganda-in-1954-to-Overthrow-a-Democratic-Nation*

[83] Richard H. Immerman, *The CIA in Guatemala: The Foreign Policy of Intervention* (Austin: University of Texas Press, 1982), 161.

[84] Not content with having deposed his government, immediately after the *coup d'etat* the CIA began a smear campaign against Árbenz. When he was allowed to leave the country he was publicly humiliated at the airport where he was arrested, forced to undress in front of cameras and interrogated for an hour regarding some Tiffany's jewelry he had allegedly bought for his wife with government's funds. The defamation campaign lasted from 1954 to 1960.

[85] How ironic is it that the expression "liberation army" is one of the favorite formulas among the leftist rebel groups around the planet?

5. Wilhelm Reich's Modern Heresy

Pneuma in fascism and the natural sciences

The character structure of modern man, who reproduces a six-thousand-year-old patriarchal authoritarian culture, is typifed by characterological armoring against his inner nature and against the social misery which surrounds him. This characterological armoring is the basis of isolation, indigence, craving for authority, fear of responsibility, mystic longing, sexual misery, and neurotically impotent rebelliousness, as well as pathological tolerance. Man has alienated himself from, and has grown hostile toward, life. This alienation is not of a biological but of a socio-economic origin. It is not found in the stages of human history prior to the development of patriarchy.
Wilhelm Reich, *The Function of the Orgasm (1942)*

It must be decided whether nature is an "empty space with a few widely scattered specks" or whether it is a space full of cosmic primordial energy, a continuum that functions dynamically and obeys a generally valid law of nature.
Wilhelm Reich, *Ether, God and Devil (1949)*

During the interwar period our narrative returns to the development of the concept of pneuma and the history of medicine and psychology. In this chapter we take up the thread of the investigations of Mesmer and Puységur and find the clearest modern incarnation of the *iatromancer* in one of the most enigmatic scientific figures of the twentieth century, a man who, like his empedoclean ancestor, synthesizes some of the traits of both the doctor and the magician.

By 1929 one of Sigmund Freud's most outstanding disciples had begun to question some of the basic assumptions of psychoanalysis and dared trying to get this discipline out of hospitals and private practices and take it to the ordinary folk. He affirmed that the *neurotic plague* that allowed the existence of all sorts of dictatorships and fascisms could never be defeated if a preventive stance was not taken in the fight against the neuroses that afflicted modern societies. For this purpose, a radically different position towards human sexuality was to be assumed and, above all, towards the sexual education of the masses. For Wilhelm Reich, Freud's concept of libido had only been a first step in the right direction and, like every first step, it had been rather timid. As in the case of his mentor, his psychological and scientific work reveals an unconscious but profound relationship with the medical tradition initiated by Mesmer that will give us the key to clarify certain characteristic features of courtly love, Renaissance magic and the manipulation of the masses. Unfortunately, his convictions and his impulsive and belligerent attitude against all kinds of fascism, sexism and intellectual hypocrisy earned him great scientific triumphs but led him to be misunderstood and ostracised by his contemporaries; his political affiliations and unorthodox clinical methods made him the object of investigation and persecution by the security agencies of all the countries in which he lived. Reich died with only sixty years in prison and his books and experiments were burned in one of the worst cases of censorship and repression in the history of the United States.

Born into a peasant family from the eastern end of the Austro-Hungarian Empire in 1897, Wilhelm Reich grew up on the family farm in Bukovina surrounded by animals and nature, a circumstance that would deeply mark his approach to science and psychology. Although he was born into a Jewish family, his father Leon, a business-minded man who was excessively harsh with his children and jealous of his wife, did his best to have Wilhelm and his brother Robert grow up in a secular environment. The children were not allowed to play with other Jewish children in their locality and were scolded if they were found speaking in yiddish. Wilhelm and his brother were educated by private tutors for several years to save them the daily trip to the local school. Indeed, in his role as a scientist this type of personalized education along with his experiences on the farm, showed later on as a preference for direct experience that made him a lot more like natural philosophers such as Robert Hooke or Isaac Newton, than to his contemporaries. This preference for the concrete led Reich to a style of psychoanalysis particularly committed to his patients and willing to go beyond their psychological disorders to look into how their social conditions could affect their illnesses and treatment, an attitude sadly absent from the discipline founded by Freud.

From a very early age Reich showed an exceptional interest in sex: he paid special attention to the reproduction patterns of farm animals and in his autobiography he says that he had his first sexual experience at age four when he tried to have sex with a maid who he had heard, or seen, having sex with his boyfriend, and with whom he shared the bed while his parents were traveling. A courageous little boy, Wilhelm asked the girl "if he could 'play' the lover. He stressed to one informant that she permitted him to do so in a very helpful way. Without stimulating him actively, she allowed him to move on top of her."[1] The experience of his early sexuality was fundamental in deciding to associate professionally with Freud; at that time psychoanalysis was the only discipline willing to assert that child sexuality was a fact as well as an essential part of human psychological development.

Reich's life was marked by a traumatic event that took place during his early teenage years and led to a family tragedy. When he was eleven and a half years old, Wilhelm discovered that his mother, Cecilie Roniger, was having an affair with his tutor. At first he noticed that they were finding all sort of excuses to spend time together, but he was not sure if they had had sex or not, until one afternoon when he saw his mother leave the tutor's room blushing and nervous. Later, when he was already practicing psychoanalysis, he published a case study entitled *Über einen Fall von Durchbruch der Inzestschranke* (On the advance of the incest taboo in puberty), in which he recounted his experience posing as a pretend patient. This study accounts, always in the third person, how the impact of his mother's adventure aroused a surge of mixed feelings that he handled as well as a boy his age could. While his father was traveling for three weeks, Wilhelm had the opportunity to observe repeatedly how Cecilie and his tutor had sex. At first, he felt like a spy and persecutor and, simultaneously, as his mother's protector. He wanted to surprise them because he knew that if he did, his mother would immediately give up the affair, but he did not do it because he had read somewhere that lovers got rid of anyone who stood in their way and thought, horrified: "if I discover them, they are going to kill me!" One night while watching them, the anxiety receded and the erotic sensations began to prevail. Then, says Reich, *"the thought came to me to plunge into the room, and to have intercourse with my mother with the threat that if she didn't I would tell my father."*[2]

Once the incestuous feelings rose to awareness, the psychological pressure went on the rise. Wilhelm did not know whether to protect his mother from his father allowing the adventure to continue, as he feared that Leon, an extremely jealous and abusive man, would hurt her; or to side with his father and tell him what was going on, thus ending his torture. He did not understand why his mother preferred the tutor over his own husband and himself, which made him feel betrayed, inadequate and deeply humiliated. To release the pressure, he went to one of the maids in the house and had his first sexual relationship. When his father returned from the trip, Wilhelm apparently suggested that something was going on between his mother and the tutor; Leon questioned him severely until he got the whole truth out of him. Tragedy ensued. Desperate with her husband's incessant psychological abuse, Reich's mother decided to take her life by drinking a household cleaner. It was never clear whether the suicide was actually a wake-up call to force Leon to stop tormenting her; there were more efficient ways to accomplish such a task at home. Her agony lasted for days. Reich's guilt and remorse must have been immense. Until the age of thirty he woke up in the middle of the night thinking "I have 'killed' my mother."[3]

The psychoanalytic implications of Reich's experience are truly overwhelming. To begin with, the fact of having witnessed how his father was displaced by a stranger implies the possibility of a weakening of paternal authority, a theme that will reappear throughout his career. But the most interesting contents of his case come forth in the light of the Freudian interpretation of the Oedipus myth. As in the story, Wilhelm desires his mother sexually, but unlike Oedipus, he does not accidentally kill his father at a crossroads, he unconsciously takes Leon's side and it is the mother who takes her own life. Contrary to the son of Laius and Jocasta Reich, terrified by his actions, does not gauge out his eyes. Like Actaeon or Tiresias, having witnessed the forbidden gave him a new vision of the world, which he developed with an unwavering commitment throughout his professional life. More than a hunter of souls, Reich would become an indefatigable hunter of truth.

The phantasms of neurosis

The tragedy of the Reich family did not end with Cecilie's death. Five years after his wife's suicide, Leon also took his own life by deliberately exposing himself to the winter cold while fishing. He contracted a pneumonia that evolved into tuberculosis and killed him in

1914. His plan was for his children to receive a large insurance policy that he had taken a short time prior to his death, but apparently the insurance company was unconvinced that it was not a suicide and Wilhelm and Robert did not receive a penny. The following year the Russian army entered Bukovina and the Reich brothers had to flee from the family property and go to Vienna to live with their maternal grandmother.

The war was just another horror in Wilhelm's early life, who enlisted in the army and fought on the Italian front, where he experienced for the first time what he called "the machinery of war." But if he had "been apolitical at the start of World War I, he was radicalized by its end."[4] And not merely this, on the front he acquired a notion of destiny and mission that would accompany him throughout his life. Shortly after returning to Vienna and entering Medicine school he joined the youth movement of the Social Democratic Party where he stood out for his radical positions and his fierce arguments with his more moderate friends; by then his experiences had already taught him that no solution ever came from acting half-heartedly. But while radical personalities usually choose a path to which they devoted all their energies, Reich had a restless mind that wanted to encompass the most diverse fields, from political action to sexuality and the natural sciences. Thus, it was his unusual inclination for both science and philosophy that led him to psychoanalysis.

By then Freud's movement, although still harshly criticized by the medical establishment, was beginning to gain a reputation in certain social circles. The improbable mixture of vitalism and mechanism implicit in psychoanalysis—so present in its magical influences—must have been particularly attractive to Reich, who was then studying the ideas of Henri Bergson and agreed with him that the mechanistic approach to science "cut life to pieces before endeavoring to comprehend it."[5] Reich met Freud in 1919 when he visited him to procure some literature for an extracurricular seminar. About his teacher he would later write: "Freud did not put on any airs. He spoke with me like a completely ordinary person. He had bright, intelligent eyes, which did not seek to penetrate another person's eyes in some sort of mantic pose, but simply looked at the world in an honest and truthful way."[6] Freud must have also been impressed with Reich because he allowed him to begin treating patients while still on his last year on the faculty. In the summer of the following year Reich was admitted as a guest member in the Vienna Psychoanalytic Society and, in the fall of the same year, as a permanent member after presenting an analysis of Henrik Ibsen's *Peer Gynt*.

Psychoanalysis owes Reich a coherent methodology for the study of human character that he developed through his work with patients at the Psychoanalytic Polyclinic and the Society's technical seminar. Based on his own experience, Reich began his research on human character by investigating the relationship between the gratification of impulses and their frustration and the links of this psychological response with the impulsive character and the incestuous desires that often appear during adolescence. According to his biographer Myron Sharaf, Reich "posited that impulsive persons often, as small children, initially experienced considerable permissiveness. Then, suddenly, impulse gratification was followed by a belated but 'ruthless' and 'traumatic' frustration."[7] As in his own case, the vast majority of impulsive people analyzed by Reich had started their sexual life prematurely and had fully conscious incestuous desires. Upon reaching puberty these individuals went through intense phases of sexual desire that could not be relieved by masturbation or intercourse as the libidinal organization of the person was deeply affected by feelings of disappointment and guilt. Like Freud, Reich argued that the "identification process had the key to the characterological interpretation of personality" and recognized that the identification with his father was fundamental in explaining his own impulsiveness and fits of rage. As a person extremely aware of his own biases and strengths it is likely that "this awareness of his own conflicts and the environmental matrix within which they developed alerted him to similar constellations in patients."[8]

In the course of his research on character, Reich became aware of the great variety of unconscious resistances that his patients interposed between their psyche and the analyst's advances. During the time he practiced hypnosis, Freud understood these manifestations as a form of psychological defense, a counter-representation of an affect that opposed the will to get better and, later on, as a masochistic manifestation of the death instinct. Reich never fully agreed with the idea of an instinct that impelled people to self-punishment, suffering and death, because such sadomasochistic psychological function would exclude, *a priori*, any real possibility of healing. In Reich's words: "if the overt and covert everyday manifestations of human sadism and brutality were the expression of a biological and, therefore, natural instinctual force, there was little hope for the therapy of neuroses, or for the highly esteemed cultural perspectives."[9] What Freud considered a realistic pessimism was, for Reich, an unjustified defeatism that not only thwarted the task of the psychoanalyst but also justified the abuses of power of the upper classes.

Until then, the study of psychological resistances had focused on the phenomenon of transference which, in the terms that we have developed in this study, could be defined as a pneumato-emotional current that goes from the patient to the analyst. However, Reich noticed that there were multiple "defensive traits" and that these occurred in all patients. Manifestations common to most of them, such as

> rigid politeness, evasiveness, apprehensiveness, and arrogance had originally developed in childhood as a way of warding off strong emotional stimuli from within or without, stimuli once associated with pain, frustration, and guilt. In analysis, they continued to function as a way of blocking strong emotional experiences, now provoked by the unsettling process of analysis itself. The defensive character traits, which in their totality Reich termed "character armor," served to protect the individual against pain, but also served to restrict severely the capacity for pleasure.[10]

Maybe because of his traumatic experience in which the anxiety of witnessing his mother having sex with his tutor became an enormous erotic pleasure, Reich realized that anxiety and emotional pain, as well as euphoria and sexual pleasure may seem opposites in subjective terms but derive their energy from the same biological source. This being the case, he became aware that if the natural flow of a negative feeling is hindered, the human capacity to feel pleasure is also affected. This is how Reich came to the conclusion that self-destructive behavior—what impelled a masochist to seek pain—was not the result of an *unconscious need* to be punished, as is derived from Freud's death instinct, but rather of an *unconscious fear* of punishment, an attitude that inevitably led to fear of pleasure and, in particular, of sexual pleasure. Reich gave this behavior, essential to his theory of character, the name of *pleasure anxiety*, a form of anxiety that owed its existence to the inhibitory action of the character armor and which entailed the denial of the vital processes of the organism.

Soon Reich discovered that most people "reacted with deep hatred to every disturbance of the neurotic balance of their armor"[11] and that this defense mechanism also manifested itself with the opposite emotions to those that could be expected in a certain circumstances. Hence,

> in life situations in which it was necessary to be aggressive, to act, to be decisive, to take a definite stand, the person was ruled by pity, politeness, reticence, false modesty, in short, by virtues that are held in high esteem. But there could be no doubt that they paralyzed every reaction, every living impulse in the person.[12]

From this passage we can deduce that, apart from its defensive function, the character armor has a particular social function: making the individual docile and manipulable. Now, through his emphasis on the concrete, Reich soon realized that the characterological armor of his patients was composed not only of the unconscious psychological defenses whose function was to prevent emotional trauma from being revived, but was intimately related to the somatic responses they showed during therapy. The study of body expressions and facial gestures became an integral part of Reich's treatment, which was drifting further away from the canon established by Freud and his school.

The case of a twenty-seven-year-old alcoholic that Reich treated in the late 1920s serves to illustrate his main ideas and discoveries:

> The general impression given by this patient was marked by the uncertainty of his movements; the forced jauntiness of his walk made him appear somewhat awkward. The attitude of his body was not rigid; rather it expressed submission as if he were continually on his guard. His facial expression was empty and without any distinguishing features. There was a slight shininess to the skin of his face; it was drawn tight and had the effect of a mask. His forehead appeared "flat." His mouth gave the impression of being small and tight. It hardly moved in the act of speaking; his lips were narrow, as if pressed together. His eyes were devoid of expression.[13]

Because of his temperament Reich was an extremely outspoken and firm analyst, to the point that one could say that his treatment was challenging and, from time to time, even aggressive to his patients. Guided by the particular facial expression of the young man, he described it repeatedly until

> a clonic twitching of his lips set in, weak at first but growing gradually stronger. He was surprised by the involuntary nature

> of this twitching and defended himself against it. I told him to give in to every impulse. Thereupon, his lips began to protrude and retract rhythmically and to hold the protruded position for several seconds as if in a tonic spasm. In the course of these movements, his face took on the unmistakable expression of a [suckling] infant.[14]

Reich kept insisting that the patient should not try to repress his bodily reactions and, past a certain point, "the described activity of his face grew more complicated.

> While his mouth became twisted into a spasmodic crying, this expression did not resolve itself into tears. To our surprise, it passed over into a distorted expression of anger. Strangely enough, however, the patient did not feel the slightest anger, though he knew quite well that it was anger.[15]

Given the involuntary nature of these muscular spasms, as he progressed in his research on character, Reich developed a theory in which the neuroses of his patients were the result of alterations in the functioning of the vegetative nervous system, whose origin was in the repression of sexuality. This repression would be particularly effective in cutting off the individual's contact with its core of biological energy, from whence flow both pleasure and anxiety. Reich illustrated the situation in a couple of diagrams that show the flow of energy starting from this biological core which later on divides into bodily sensations and mental impressions:

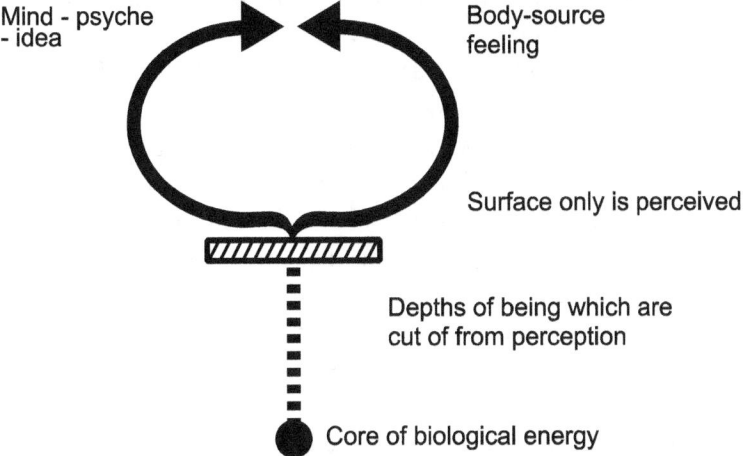

Personality diagram of a neurotic individual
(taken from *The Reenchantment of the World* by Morris Berman)

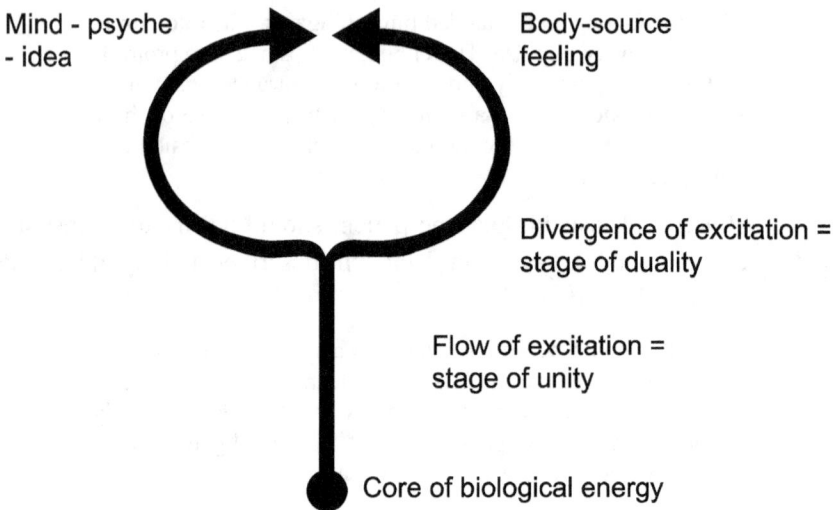

Personality diagram of a healthy individual
(taken from *The Reenchantment of the World* by Morris Berman)

By the late twenties Reich had realized that the defensive function of the character armor was related to the rupture of the individual from its energetic core. After this break took place the armor assumed what the individual could not achieve by his or her own means; thus, the defensive mechanism became unconscious and reinforced the disconnection. The characterological armor manifested itself mainly in the patient's doubts and reservations towards the treatment, "while that which he warded off, i.e., the vegetative excitation, was revealed in the muscle actions of his face,"[16] so that a muscular attitude contained not only the defense but also the affect or feeling against which it was directed.

Contrary to Freud, whose focus was on making "the unconscious conscious by the elimination of the resistances put up against the repressed material,"[17] Reich came to the conclusion that the most effective and direct way to break down these psychic barriers was "destroying the defense forces, not from the psychic but from the muscular side."[18] Instead of concentrating on analyzing the neurotic fantasies of his patients, he opted to attack what he considered their energetic foundation, its source of nourishment.

His patient, who over the course of weeks of treatment had gone from a suckling gesture to a crying facial expression to an angry gesticulation, soon incorporated new movements.

> [He] sat half up on the couch, shook with anger, raised his fist as if he were going to strike a blow, without, however, following through. Then, out of breath, he sank back exhausted. The whole action dissolved into a whimpering kind of weeping. These actions expressed "impotent rage," as is often experienced by children with adults.[19]

During one of this episodes, the patient remembered that his older brother used to intimidate and mistreat him as a child and understood that at that time he had repressed his hatred towards him, who happened to be his mother's favorite. As a tactic to gain the attention and love of the mother, he had overcompensated this hatred by developing a very kind and affectionate attitude towards his older brother, that not only hid his true feelings but later on extended to all his social interactions. In the case of this patient, the powerful and intimidating feelings of anger and hatred towards the brother were repressed within the *character armor*, whose physiological manifestation was a muscular armor that "compressed" these sensations—as well as the physiological sensations associated with sexual pleasure—in the form of spasms. Reich knew that these tonic and clonic muscle spasms were related to the activity of the vegetative nervous system, the key to the matter was that

> the concentration of a vegetative excitation and its irruption reproduced a memory.[20]

Once the patient remembered the emotional origin of his psychological condition and it manifested itself in a somatic fashion, another group of movements and bodily sensations appeared: the facial spasms were joined by a sort of psychosomatic excitation that traveled down to the chest in the form of muscular contractions. When these subsided, there arose a sensation of "currents" towards the lower abdomen. These currents were formally identical to the bodily sensations of the magnetic fluid described by Mesmer and Puységur. Indeed, the type of energy that Reich rediscovered and named *bioelectricity* and, later on *orgone*, is nothing but the pneuma of Medieval and Renaissance medicine and the fluid of the magnetizers of the eighteenth and nineteenth centuries.

But let's get back to the case in question. The tonic spasm of his patient, Reich tells us,

> spread to his chest and upper abdomen. In these attacks, it was as if an inner force lifted him up from the couch against his will and held him up. The muscles of his abdominal wall and chest were boardlike.[21]

By then Reich had already succeeded in making this sensation of currents spread to the lower abdomen and the pelvis producing a series of sexual movements that did not take place with this patient. However, in his case there was another series of muscle contractions that will allow us to link Reich's work with another of the topics of this study: hysteria and mass psychogenic illness.

At this point the patient went through a series of violent contractions and twitching of the legs muscles with an accentuation of the patellar reflex that bends the legs at the knee.

> To my complete amazement, the patient told me that he experienced the twitchings of his leg musculature in a highly agreeable way. Quite involuntarily, I was reminded of epileptic clonisms, and my view was confirmed that in both the epileptic and epileptiform muscular convulsions, we are dealing with the release of anxiety which can only be experienced in an agreeable, i.e., pleasurable manner. There were times in the treatment of this patient when I was uncertain whether or not I was confronted with a true epileptic. Superficially, at least, the patient's attacks, which commenced tonically and occasionally subsided clonically, showed very little difference from epileptic seizures.[22]

From Reich's point of view, the epileptic and epileptiform attacks that we addressed when we spoke of Charcot's theory, would correspond to a sudden release of anxiety that manifested itself as pleasure. This assumption would appear to be correct if we consider that the outbreaks of Saint Vitus dance generally take place in regions that have gone through collective traumas such as pestilences, famines and natural disasters, or in psychologically unhealthy environments such as convents and psychiatric hospitals. Since anxiety and pleasure share their organic basis, an epileptiform attack or an outbreak of collective hysteria would correspond, in Reich's terminology, to the sudden release of repressed anxiety that transforms itself into sexual pleasure as it ripples through the muscular armor.[23] The spasmodic and uncontrollable movements that characterize both the first phases of Charcot's hysteria and Saint Vitus dance would be the anxiety/pleasure accumulated in the vegetative system and converted into clonic seizures or ecstatic dance.

> It has become clear now that the epileptic seizures represent convulsions of the vegetative apparatus in which the dammed-up biopsychic energy is discharged solely through the musculature, with the exclusion of the genitals. The epileptic seizure is an extragenital, muscular orgasm.[24]

In the following weeks, the muscular contractions of Reich's patient began to lose their spastic character and gave rise to another set of strange contractions of the abdomen.

> The upper part of his body jerked forward, the middle of his abdomen remained still, and the lower part of his body jerked toward the upper part. The entire response was an *organic unitary movement*: There were sessions in which this movement was repeated continuously. Alternating with this jerking of his entire body, there were sensations of current in some parts of his body, particularly in his legs and abdomen, which he experienced as pleasurable. The attitude of his mouth and face changed a little. In one such attack, his face had the unmistakable expression of a fish. Without any prompting on my part, before I had drawn his attention to it, the patient said, "I feel like a primordial animal," and shortly afterward, "I feel like a fish."[25]

Reich, who by then had seen this somatic reaction on other occasions, named it *orgasm reflex*, a series of unconscious muscular movements in which the autonomic nervous system takes control of the body. We must add how peculiar it is that this patient spontaneously identified with a fish, an animal which by virtue of its evolutionary stage is endowed with a reptilian nervous system but not a cerebral cortex that would allow it conscious control of other functions such as breathing. As the patient surrendered and gave himself over to the sensations and feelings that came with these movements,

> the somatic sensations of currents increased visibly and rapidly, first in his abdomen, then also in his legs and upper body. He described these sensations not only as currents, but also as voluptuous and "sweet." This was especially the case when strong, lively, and rapid abdominal twitchings occurred.[26]

This release of sexual energy through the loosening of the musculature resulted in a group of somatic manifestations that coincided with those described by Mesmer in reference to the movement of the magnetic fluid. Reich described them as follows: "involuntary trembling and twitching of the muscles, sensations of cold and hot, itching, the feeling of pins and needles, prickling sensations, the feeling of having the jitters, and somatic perceptions of anxiety, anger, and pleasure,"[27] all of them widely documented by eighteenth-century magnetists and known to accompany the crises that preceded healing. The blockages described by Mesmer, Puységur and other magnetists were characterized by Reich as *stasis*, or "overloads" of bioelectricity in specific regions of the vegetative system that were experienced as anxiety, pain or swelling. "Stasis means nothing other than an inhibition of vegetative expansion and a blocking of the activity and motility of the central vegetative organs,"[28] which in the eighteenth century were thought of as "small independent brains" composed of chains of ganglia that interlocked in the solar and cardiac plexuses. These coincidences allow us to postulate a functional identity between Mesmer's idea of *irritability* and the function of Reich's muscular armor, which in both cases prevents the proper flow of magnetic fluid or bioelectricity in the human body. Even the phenomenon of the healing crisis, so common to animal magnetism, reappears in Reich's therapy as

> a state of high charge, when all the body energy is involved in the final effort to shake off disease. Reich noted the crisis in orgone therapy, when the loosening armor allows more and more energy to stream through the body, resulting in an intensification of the symptoms the patient already complained of.[29]

The identity between the ideas of Mesmer and Reich also implies an identity with the typical movements of epileptiform hysteria. In this regard it is not at all strange to find that the *arc de cercle* typical of the second phase of Charcot's hysteria is a form of resistance and, in effect, is the opposite movement, the negative of the sinuous and "concave" movements of the orgasm reflex. From this point of view, this typically hysteric position would be one of the most pronounced expressions of pleasure anxiety.

Through observation of this reflex, Reich came to a conclusion implicit Freud's ideas, but to which he had not dared arrive because of his personality and his desire to secure psychoanalysis' place as a respected discipline. As Freud had already established, the neuroses had a sexual origin and were the result of the repression of the libido. However, Reich went a step further and proposed that the genesis of neuroses was in the fixation of sexual energy in the muscular/character armor, a circumstance that took place due to the inability of most modern humans to achieve a complete release of sexual energy through an orgasm without any conscious intervention, that is, of a *vegetative orgasm*. Reich called this incapacity *orgastic impotence*, which designated not the inability to reach sexual climax, but to achieve a completely natural orgasm that released the sexual energy trapped in the muscular armor, thus attacking the neuroses at their energy source and preventing the formation of new blockages of libido that hinder the adequate flow of bioelectric energy.

Apart from the similarities of his discoveries with animal magnetism and hysteria, Reich identified that one of the greatest sources of orgastic impotence and, therefore, of neurosis, were the fantasies that most people consciously or unconsciously elaborate during sexual intercourse. The mention of the term fantasy is remarkable since it refers us immediately to the medieval and Renaissance idea of *phantasm* as a pneumatic idealization of the beloved. For Reich, "fantasies are opposed to the real experience, for one fantasizes only what one cannot have in reality,"[30] a matter that lies at the center of courtly love, for if the beloved really corresponded to the object of the fantasy, it could replace it, but it would consequently lose the ability of invading the pneuma of the lover as *phantasmata*.

"The more intensively the fantasy has to work to make the partner approximate the ideal," says Reich, "the more the sexual experience loses in the way of intensity [...]"[31] thus becoming a neurotic search for the phantasm or idealization which fetishizes the beloved transforming it in the very image of the unattainable. On the other hand, when there is a *genuine transference* between the parties, that is, when the real-life partner corresponds to the ideal of the lover, there is no possibility of an overestimation or idealization that leads to the formation of pneumatic phantasms. The pneumatic circle starts spinning seamlessly between the lover and the beloved.

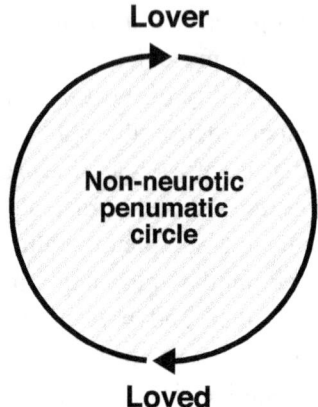

The above means that the amorous dynamic of our tradition stems from a pathological quest that neurotizes the lovers to intensify their feelings, but ends up *alienating them from themselves and from the real world*. This is the legacy of courtly love, a social dynamic that by entrapping the subject in its pneumatic circle, sets it apart from life and from a genuine kind of love. Fantasy "corrupts" sexual desire by making it "virtual" and turning it into a force—in the Latin sense of *vis*—that can be manipulated from the outside, *which is why the phantasm has always been the basic means of individual and mass manipulation*. From Reich's point of view, Bruno's web of bonds is a neurotic transference machine that encourages sexual inequality and repression and leads to pathological forms of desire.

Aside from these insights on the phantasmatic operations of Western culture, it is interesting to note that Reich's theory of masochism can explain the dynamics of religious ecstasy, the Cathar heresy and courtly love. According to Reich this pathology, more than a sexual manifestation of the death instinct, as Freud would have it, was an extreme manifestation of *pleasure anxiety* in which the subject wants to *explode* in order to release an internal tension of sexual nature. This desire to burst—one of the most common descriptions among masochists, both men and women—is actually a covert fear of orgastic relief, the result of the loss of the organic capacity to feel pleasure. The masochist *does not like to feel pain*, as is commonly asserted, what he or she desires and, at the same time fears, is to release the libido contained within the body and constrained by the muscular armor. The only way to provide this release *is through pain*, as if pricking, lacerating or burning the body could finally release the sexual energy contained in it. Now, "since, owing to his pleasure anxiety, the ability to experience gratification through his own initiative and activity is blocked, the masochist anticipates the orgastic resolution, which he deeply fears, as a release from the outside brought about by another person,"[32] and therefore he or she must beg for someone else to torture him or her in order to reach satisfaction against his or her own will. While for hysterics the manifestation of pleasure anxiety is abstinence, which leads to more sexual repression and tension within the organism (and eventually resolves in an epileptiform attack or choreomania), for masochists the increase in sexual tension leads to a continual search for more excitement, which in turn increases the desire for liberation in a terrible vicious circle that can only be shattered through pain.

Reich soon realized that this masochistic dynamic was intimately related to religions such as Christianity and its gnostic variants, which place special emphasis on the suffering and mortification of the flesh.

"Religious ecstasy," Reich tells us,

> is patterned precisely according to the masochistic mechanism. Release from inner sin, i.e., from inner sexual tension—a release one is not capable of bringing about by oneself—is expected from God, an all-powerful figure. Such release is desired with biological energy. At the same time, it is experienced as "sin." Thus, it cannot be realized through one's own volition. Someone else has to accomplish it, be it in the form of punishment, pardon, redemption, etc. [...] The masochistic orgies of the Middle Ages, the Inquisition, the chastisements and tortures, the penances, etc., of the religious betrayed their function. They were unsuccessful masochistic attempts to attain sexual gratification![33]

The religious dynamic that courtly love inherited from Catharism is an expression of a *cosmic masochism* that wishes that sexual energy (sin or impurity) be banished (purified or flogged) not only from the body but from the totality of the material world. It is through this mechanism that the pathological eros of the masochistic vicious circle, always fed by its own phantasms, turns into a neurotic vehicle for the liberation of the flesh.

The phantasms of fascism

By the end of the twenties the gap between Reich's and Freud's ideas had opened up radically, and the imposing and even belligerent attitude of the former—a perpetual source of disagreements with his colleagues—had a negative impact on their reception; his concepts were met with increasing skepticism and discontent by the psychoanalytic community. Additionally, the fact that by then Reich had become a member of the German Communist Party and devoted himself to social activism, did not help at all. If Freud, who became increasingly reactionary and pessimistic over the years, recommended moderation and a measure of sexual repression to guarantee social stability (the repression of destructive and self-destructive impulses implicit in *death instinct*), Reich's revolutionary spirit advocated for the total liberation of libido through the reestablishment of orgastic potency in order to achieve a society in which individuals could naturally regulate their constructive and destructive impulses. In fact, according to Reich, there was a "correlation between the intensity of the destructive impulses and the intensity of sexual stasis,"[34] so that these would not be a natural condition of our species—a biological imperative that made the human naturally violent and destructive, as Freud claimed—but a social pathology related to the sexual repression implicit in Western culture. Hobbes' *war of all against all* is true to the extent that we are a structurally neurotic society, in a sexually healthy society such descent into chaos would not and, in fact, has not taken place. Thus, Reich asserted that "neuroses can be cured by eliminating their energy source, the sexual stasis,"[35] but warned that this could only be achieved outside patriarchy.

To support his position Reich resorted to the work of anthropologist Bronislaw Malinowski, who had studied the matriarchal society of the Trobriand islands, which he described at length in his classic *The Sexual Life of the Savages in North-Western Melanesia* (1929). To Freud's and his followers distress, Malinowski argued that the Oedipus Complex was not universal and that it did not happen in matrilineal cultures such as Trobriand, whose members were "warm, open people, relatively free of the neuroses, perversions and sadism so common in the 'civilized' world."[36] Malinowski also found that a little further to the south, on the Amphlett Islands, there was another tribe that had developed a matrilineal culture with marked emphasis on patriarchal authority which already showed "all the characteristics of the European neurotics (distrust, anxiety, neuroses, suicides, perversions, etc.)"[37] Thus, according to Reich, the mental pathologies of the West originated in "patriarchy, sex negation, and a class division [that] had long ago 'invaded' the natural state of matriarchy, sex affirmation, and primitive communism."[38] To confront this situation Reich founded the Sex-pol (sexualpolitik) social movement for the sexual education of the masses and the Sexual Hygiene and Sexological Research Clinics where individuals and couples received treatment. In addition to offering psychotherapy and sexual counseling, these clinics occasionally organized abortions—a matter which, according to Reich, should be a right for every woman if she did not have the proper means to raise her children or lived in inadequate social circumstances. Needless to say this was a visionary position in the thirties, especially if one takes into account that it entailed serious legal risks.

In his role as an activist Reich was a firm advocate of gender equality and asserted that the relations between the sexes could never be egalitarian if women did not achieve economic independence. He also argued that young people should initiate their sexuality naturally during adolescence—as it happened among the Trobriand islanders and many other matriarchal cultures—that women should participate as actively in courtship as men, and that young couples should be offered all the necessary conditions so that they could develop their sexual life in an environment free of unhealthy fears and taboos. According to Reich, the neurotic plague that afflicted modern societies was the product of the sexual repression that originated and reproduced in the authoritarian family structure, which he considered the basic cell of all fascist states. "The mass plague of neuroses," he asserted, "is produced in the three main stages of human life: in early childhood, through the atmosphere of the neurotic home, in puberty, and finally in the compulsive marriage in its strict moralistic conception."[39]

Before going into the patriarchal process of sexual repression we must make a brief detour to inquire about the socioeconomic origin of marriage and its relationship with patriarchy. According to Reich, patriarchy arose when, contrary to the sexual customs of matriarchies (polygamy, ritual orgies, etc ...), one of the sexes began to suppress the sexual desires of the tribe so that it could acquire power over the rest of the group. To this end, a new custom was instituted that assigned a woman to each man, which was sealed with a contract in which the woman's family had to pay a tribute or dowry that strengthened the position of the male within society. It is from this moment on that human sexuality began to be put at the service of socioeconomic interests under the name of *patrimony*. This patriarchal dynamic is especially effective in suppressing female sexuality and forcing women to assume the roles of wife and mother from whom chastity and fidelity are demanded, very often against their impulses and preferences. In short, the institution of marriage is intimately linked to the idea of monogamy, which required the suppression of the sexual desires of the tribe and was instrumental in dividing society into classes. Thus, we have that the suppression of sexuality, whose main result is neurosis, and the emergence of specialized work and social castes are one and the same phenomenon. Since the new social dynamic required inhibiting the polygamous tendencies of the tribe, the patriarchal monogamous family imposed a regime of sexual repression to guarantee its perpetuation and that of society in general, which over time would become the restrictive morality that characterizes authoritarian societies.

The sexual repression of the patriarchal family begins in early childhood when the boy or girl is subjected to a strict and premature training to clean his or her own excrements—a custom that is virtually non-existent in most indigenous cultures—which sows the first seed of "self-control" from which the vegetative system may begin to be intervened and lose its natural functioning. This first invasion to the vegetative realm prepares the ground for the prohibition of masturbation which, by inhibiting infantile sexuality, destroys the child's relationship with his or her own body and inhibits its independence of action and thought. With his habitual sagacity, Reich understood that "psychic mobility and energy go together with sexual vitality and are its precondition. On the other hand, sexual inhibition is the precondition of psychic inhibition and clumsiness."[40] From this it follows that the search for a sexual partner represents, in both men and women, the fundamental capacity to form social and sexual bonds, that is, to find a place in the world.

According to Reich, the moral inhibition of the child's natural sexuality,

> makes the child afraid, shy, fearful of authority, obedient, "good," and "docile," in the authoritarian sense of the words. It has a crippling effect on man's rebellious forces because every vital life impulse is now burdened with severe fear; and since sex is a forbidden subject, thought in general and man's critical faculty also become inhibited.[41]

In adolescence, with the awakening of libido, the sexual repressions cultivated in childhood intensify, contributing to "psychic stagnation and character armoring."[42] According to Reich, the rather late age in which sexual relations were initiated in his time confirmed the true function of chastity in relation to marriage: "the sooner an adolescent arrives at gratifying sexual intercourse, the more incapable he is of adapting himself to the strict demand of 'only one partner, and this partner for a lifetime'."[43] The purpose of sexual abstinence is to make adolescents submissive and capable of marrying, thus perpetuating the authoritarian and repressive family structure. Of course, the function of sexual repression does not stop there: if we bear in mind that the main objective of abstinence is to make children docile, obedient and dependent, this circumstance is vital when it comes to making them susceptible to unconsciously submit before any authority figure, regardless of whether it is a god, a political figure or a religious leader.[44] In Reich's words:

> [...] morality's aim is to produce acquiescent subjects who, despite distress and humiliation, are adjusted to the authoritarian order.[45]

This process, perfectly diffused in all modern societies, is a *psychic castration* whose main consequence is the appearance of the neuroses that support modern totalitarianisms.[46] Reich was adamant in assuring that this process of sexual repression, which takes place in the bosom of the contemporary family,

> becomes the primary basis of authoritarian ideology by depriving women, children, and adolescents of their sexual freedom, making a commodity of sex and placing sexual interests in the service of economic subjugation. From now on, sexuality is indeed distorted; it becomes diabolical and demonic and has to be curbed. In terms of patriarchal demands, the innocent sensuousness of matriarchy appears as the lascivious unchaining of dark powers. The dionisyan becomes "sinful yearning" which patriarcal culture can conceive only as something chaotic and "dirty." Surrounded by and imbued with human sexual structures that have become distorted and lascivious, patriarchal man is shackled for the first time in an ideology in which sexual and dirty, sexual and vulgar or demonic, become inseparable associations.[47]

Over time, this idea of *dirtiness-body-sexuality* was put in opposition to an ideal of *purity-spirit-chastity* with which the patriarchy identified. It is in this neurotic dualism that Reich found the germ of the fascist philosophies that engulfed Europe in the years leading to World War II.

As a left-wing social leader and activist, Reich was a particularly incisive witness of the rise of National Socialism, of which he made a magnificent study in *The Mass Psychology of Fascism* (1933). Reich begins the book by postulating a tripartite structure of the human psyche: a first and superficial layer composed of the self-control, compulsive kindness and artificial sociability that characterize civilized relationships; a second layer that corresponds to the freudian "unconscious," where the perversions and pathologies product of the stagnation of the natural flow of the libido are stored; and a third, still deeper layer, that serves as the biological core of our species and where a natural sociability and sexuality and the human capacity for action and love operate. Given this structure, Reich argued that

> all discussions on the question of whether man is good or evil, a social or antisocial being, are philosophic game playing. Whether man is a social being or a mass of protoplasm reacting in a peculiar and irrational way depends on whether his basic biological needs are in harmony or at variance with the institutions he has created for himself.[48]

The supposedly essential sadism and evil to which Freud devoted much of his later work was something that Reich simply did not find in his extensive clinical experience. These tendencies were, he assured, pathological manifestations product of the lamentable conditions of the "civilized" human who, throughout millennia had deployed a monstrous socioeconomic structure that acted as a neurosis and alienation machine. It is through an authoritarian education that represses the natural sexual impulses and inhibits the capacities of action and thought, that modern humans ended up becoming a helpless, confused, authority craving creature that, unable of reacting spontaneously, wants to be told what to do, "for he is full of contradictions and cannot rely upon himself."[49] Le Bon, Freud and Bernays were right on this point: the herd is a perpetually bewildered organism, but not because of an inherent condition but because of its psychological conflicts and weaknesses. This, of course, does not mean that the solution is to manipulate them mercilessly with the excuse of safeguarding social order. The solution, as Reich knew, is to make them whole again. His techniques, absurdly overlooked for decades, offer precisely this possibility, the chance to overcome neurosis and attain the well-established individuality we so crucially need.

According to Reich the rise of Nazism depended largely on a deep emotional conflict that divided the German psyche at the time: the longing for freedom and vindication after the socio-economic humiliations that came with the Treaty of Versailles and the fear of responsibility implicit in this freedom. This conflict robbed the German people of its psychic energy, which was consumed in an unsuccessful attempt to find a solution, and ended up paralyzing and delivering them to Hitler who, as a messiah, was willing to assume the dreaded responsibility on behalf of the population. This "paralysis by conflict" was Hitler's main ideological weapon to mesmerize the German masses. In fact, the name "National Socialism" expressed these contradictions by simultaneously appealing to nationalist sentiments and the desire for an inclusive society.[50] On the one hand the Nazis acted according to the revolutionary ethic that brought them to power but their political promises simultaneously tended toward the reactionary ("I am the most conservative revolutionary in the world" the Führer once told the *Hitlerjugend*). They promised to treat the big companies with severity while at the same time granted them benefits; they preached the natural submission of women while advocating their economic independence; they took radical measures against birth control and against abortion as well. This "art of contradiction," says historian Konrad Heiden, "made [Hitler] the greatest and most successful propagandist of his time."[51] More than a way of covering the two extremes of the same magical bond, this ambiguity of Nazi propaganda was aimed at nullifying the possibility of choosing a real position toward the problems of the world, a tactic that, as we will see in the final chapter, will take a even more insidious form in post-Soviet Russia.

Apart from the debilitating contradictions of Nazi politics, the erotic factor implicit in any relationship between a mass and its leader played an important role in keeping National Socialism in power. "One has only to see the faces of the people listening to Hitler," says Sharaf,

> (conveyed so vividly in the documentary films of Leni Riefenstahl) to realize the kind of orgiastic satisfaction the

germans could allow themselves in their devotion to the Führer. This intense libidinal excitation, combined with a sense moral righteousness, was strikingly similar to the atmosphere at religious revival meetings.[52]

The erotic character of the Hitler cult is inseparable from the Nazi ideal of "purity of blood," which acted as a covert catalyst when it came to awakening an irrational fervor in the German masses. For Reich it was clear that all forms of authoritarianism derived their energy from repression and sexual stasis. As one might expect, the Nazi obsession with the purity of blood—which was sustained by a tremendous pleasure anxiety—led to the most common symptom of this disorder: hysteria. In fact, the immense success of the Nazi program of racial purity depended on producing a hysterical reaction to the idea of the contamination of the "aryan blood," in which the pleasure anxiety was transformed, on the one hand, into a virulent reaction against all other races and in particular against the Jewish people, and on the other, in a sexual panic that caused more repression and anxiety; after all, the only way to guarantee a "pure blood" is through celibacy. According to Reich, this ideal originates in the religious mysticism that underlies Nazism which assigns the highest virtues—the *purity-spirit-chastity* polarity—to the Aryan race, while at the same time transfers sensuality—the *dirtiness-body-sexuality* polarity—to the Jewish race, which is then characterized as a threatening source of racial contamination. The portrait of the Jew as particularly lascivious was very common during the Third Reich and agrees with other fascist racisms that characterize the black man as a sexual predator of white women.[53]

Among the hysterical spells of Nazism one is of special interest to our subject. In her *Diccionario crítico de mitos y símbolos del nazismo*, philologist and Germanist Rosa Sala Rose comments on how the identification of Hitler with Parsifal—in particular with the chaste knight of the Wagnerian version of the legend—served to steer the German masses, and especially women, towards collective hysteria:

> [...] it was above all the chastity and sexual purity of the hero what was most carefully cultivated by Goebbels and the other image advisors of the dictator. The fear of female sexuality, which, although atavistic, turned out to be a constant of fascist mentalities, finds a clear reflection in this identification. The Führer, like Parsifal, would sacrifice his personal and family

happiness, for the good of the German people. At the same time, according to a conviction expressed by Hitler himself (significantly shared at the time by the advertising consultants of several movie stars), it was convenient for him to remain single so that his female audience may go on fantasizing of somehow becoming the chosen one. Hence, the existence of his lover Eva Braun was officially kept secret, until their hasty marriage in the bunker on the eve of their suicide procured the young woman a sudden celebrity.[54]

It should be remembered that Giordano Bruno proposes sexual abstinence and the retention of semen as one of the ways to strengthen the magical bonds. How fitting is it to find that, like a *animarum venator*, part of Hitler's magical power depended on a supposed chastity that strengthened the pneumatic webs he cast towards the masses? An essential part of the work of a hunter of souls is to become the fetish of his prey, the image of what they desire but can never attain.

Here it is important to elaborate on some of Nazism's affinities with the Cathar heresy that will reveal another set of even deeper connections with Renaissance erotic magic. To begin with, both Nazism and Catharism originate from a dualism—clearly masochistic and derived from a deeply seated pleasure anxiety—that emphasizes antagonistic pairs such as good/evil, spirit/body and purity/impurity. This opposition of concepts finds its full expression in the idea of a struggle between the powers of light (the *perfecti*/the Aryan race) against those of darkness (the material world/the spiritual decadence of Judeo-Christian culture). The most obvious antecedent of this type of dualism in the Germanic countries is that of the Artaman League, a youth and naturist league of sectarian character founded in 1924. Radical anti-Semites, the Artamans formed communities of farmers who expected that living close to nature would provide them with a purification of the senses.

> They lived in simple lodgings, ate frugally and went out to work singing. Among them ruled almost conventual rules: absolute abstinence from alcohol, nicotine and sexual relations, total obedience to the Führer ("guide") of the group and voluntary acceptance of poverty in order to counteract the excessive refinement of a world supposedly corrupted by materialism. Only racially unimpeachable people were accepted as members.[55]

With the exception of racial purity, this description could be applied without any modification to Catharism. From 1925, the Artamans began to grow closer to the Nazis, who idealized the communion with nature and the idea of an Aryan peasantry. "Much of the later symbolic paraphernalia of the SS," says Sala Rose, "such as the black uniforms, runes, fire rituals, as well as chivalric ideals and elitist spirit, were taken from the artamans by Heinrich Himmler, one of the most prominent members of the league."[56]

Regarding the chivalric ideals of Nazism, we should note the obsession of the SS with the legend of the Holy Grail which, according to the Nazi Germanist Otto Rahn, was a symbol of the "primitive Aryan religion" of which Catharism was the last great expression. In his interpretation "Rahn appeals to the medieval Germanic tradition that makes the Grail a stone fallen from Lucifer's crown (and not the cup that received the blood of Christ after being lanced), who would not be the Evil One, as as Christianity disparagingly affirmed, but the Cathar Luzbel, bearer of light."[57] The fully conscious identification of Nazism with the Cathar heresy justifies its openly anti-Catholic attitude and turns the Albigensian Crusade into the struggle of the Church against the Grail or, in the Nazi imaginary, of the Christian cross against the Swastika.

In light of this identification, it is not surprising to find that Nazism also developed its own versions of the encratism, antinomianism and vegetarianism that characterized the Cathar heresy. Regarding encratism, or the abstention of the sexual relations outside marriage, in Nazism it becomes the abstention of sexual relations outside the Aryan community. Antinomianism, or disobedience of civil and religious laws, reappears in the revolutionary ethic of early Nazism, which reacted violently against the social standards of the Weimar Republic which were considered impure and degenerate. Regarding vegetarianism, like their Cathar ancestors, many senior Nazi officers, like Rudolph Hess and Hitler himself, were vegetarians,[58] an attitude that can be traced to an ideal that held that the natural inclination of the human was towards eating fruits and vegetables and that the consumption of meat was an unnatural degeneration, an idea partly supported by the supposedly scientific notion which held that eating meat stimulated the sexual organs and therefore contributed to having indiscriminate sexual relations, favoring racial mixing.

Considering these similarities it is only natural that Nazism also shared certain traits with Occitan poetry and courtly love. Like these movements, the Nazis promulgated a particular mixture of libertinism and antinomianism when "'aryan' youths were encouraged to have children inside or outside marriage, if they believed that they were begetting them to improve the race."[59] In both cases the purpose of libertinism was to safeguard an ideal of spiritual purity, either by opposing civil and ecclesiastical laws or by engendering a supposedly superior race. It is important to note that, like courtly love, National Socialism developed a form of sexual repression that did not result in outbreaks of choreomania or attacks of epileptiform hysteria but in a prolific production of phantasms that were cleverly manipulated by the Third Reich's hunters of souls.

This set of relationships allows us to expand the thesis of historians such as Hans Maier and Nicholas Goodrick-Clarke who argue that Nazism, more than a political movement, is a *political religion*. In fact, the similarities with Catharism and courtly love suggest that Nazism is a particularly insidious and twisted heir to the Renaissance magical tradition, that it is, at heart, a modern system of erotic magic and that this is the source of its capacity for fascination and its incredible power when it comes to enthralling the masses. "Nazi mysticism," that mysterious and fascinating dimension that many historians have written about, is actually the result of the magical-erotic operations that I have described in this study.

Seen from this point of view, the complete failure of communism to face the threat posed by Nazism was the result of its inability to understand its magical nature. Meanwhile, having entrenched himself in the ego ideal of millions of people, Hitler—in his role of *über-phantasm*—managed to invade and infect the pneumatic apparatus of an entire nation which, trapped in its neurotic armor, fell under the spell of one of the most overwhelming death cults of the modern era. By transforming the passion (*passio*) of lovers, their desire for death and liberation, into the most abject sadism, Nazism, more than any other political or religious cult, embodies the aesthetic of death. In its vortex death acquires a sacred dimension that makes it inevitable to think of the extermination camps as the altars of a huge ritual sacrifice to the goddess of love and war.

Faced with fascism Reich never took into account that the libidinal liberation through violence and discrimination offered by the Nazis was much more powerful than any amount of libido that could be released through a genuine orgastic potency. The sadomasochistic nature of Nazism, palpable in its intense pleasure anxiety, offered a supremely effective way to release the latent sexual energy in the German psyche. However, as in any other form of masochism, the liberation of libido leads to a new cycle of production and accumulation that can only be resolved through an act of extreme aggression that allows a new sudden release, a Saint Vitus of anxiety and violence.

Horrified by the inefficiency of the German Communist Party when it came to stop Hitler's cunning manipulations, Reich continued his work in the Sex-pol movement and founded his own publishing house, *Verlag für Sexualpolitik*, to publish books and pamphlets that divulged a political point of view that affirmed a healthy sexuality based on the education of the german youth and the reestablishment of orgastic potency. The content of these publications and his tireless social activity ended up infuriating not only the nazis but also the leaders of the German Communist Party, who argued that the proletariat did not have any type of sexual disturbance (in their view an exclusively bourgeoisie ailment), as well as the Psychoanalytic Society, which gradually ostracised Reich and his controversial political and therapeutic theories. By 1934 both organizations had expelled him from their ranks.

Eros, orgone, ether

Free from the doctrinal ties imposed by the Communist Party and the Psychoanalytic Society, and harassed by the Nazis, Reich fled Germany and moved to Norway where he reestablished his practice with the help of a handful of colleagues and friends. His research on "the streaming of energy (libido) in pleasure; the reverse movement of that energy in anxiety; and the muscular spasms which, along with the character armor, prevented the free emotional expression of the organism,"[60] were essential for the new phase in his scientific career: the natural sciences.

By then Reich had no doubt that "sexuality and anxiety were manifestations of two antithetical directions of vegetative [...] excitation"[61] and he suspected that this polar structure also underlay all the interactions of the natural world. Based on the work of the German biologist Max Hartmann and zoologist Ludwig Rhumbler, Reich proposed that pleasure responded to a universal movement or tendency to "go towards the world" while anxiety represented the opposite tendency, to "withdraw from the world." Hartmann and Rhumbler had found that by being exposed to a variety of stimuli (electrical, mechanical, chemical, etc.) an amoeba reacted in one of two ways: it either moved toward the stimulus or avoided it or assumed a rigid spherical shape and stilled itself. If there was not stimulation, these two movements of expansion and contraction alternated in a rhythmic and natural pulsation.

The research of Hartmann and Rhumbler allowed Reich to associate his two polarities/movements with the two main divisions of the vegetative nervous system: the parasympathetic system with the reactions associated with pleasure and the sympathetic system with those associated with anxiety. According to this hypothesis, neurosis would be a "sympatheticotonic" condition caused by the repression of sexual sensations in early childhood, as when a child learns to hold his or her breath to inhibit genital arousal according to the wishes of its parents. To advance his hypothesis, Reich took an image outlined by Freud in *Beyond The Pleasure Principle*: "let us picture a living organism in its most simplified possible form as an undifferentiated vesicle of a substance that is susceptible to stimulation. Then the surface turned towards the external world will from its very situation be differentiated and will serve as an organ for receiving stimuli."[62] Reich used this vesicle, a clear analogy to Hartmann and Rhumbler's amoeba, as the representation of a masochist who fears, and at the same time wishes to explode to liberate the libido in a pleasurable sensation ("towards the world") governed by the parasympathetic system. From this configuration we can deduce that the membrane of the vesicle acts as the character armor which, upon becoming rigid, hinders the release of libido during orgasm. In the case of an ill vesicle—that is, a subject whose armor prevents the release of the libido—this energy turns into hatred, annoyance and resentment; in the case of the healthy vesicle—an orgastically potent subject whose armor allows libidinal release—the result is a natural feeling of affection and dedication.

In the course of his research Reich discovered that the electrical potential of the human skin, understood here as the outer membrane of the vesicle, changed if it was exposed to a pleasant or an unpleasant sensation. If the sensation was pleasant, the surface charge increased markedly and, if it was distressing it decreased. The erogenous zones of the body (the penis, vaginal mucosa, tongue, lips, anal mucosa and nipples) were much more variable and capable of producing more charge whether positive or negative. These experiments allowed Reich to postulate an "identity of somatic and psychic processes"[63] and to give libido a physiological and quantitative character, a project that Freud had long abandoned. Like a magnetist in the tradition of Mesmer and Puységur, Reich postulated something that he would corroborate years later in his research on the etiology of cancer: namely, that "organic diseases might be the result of disturbances of the bio-electrical equilibrium of the organism."[64]

His search for a unitary theory of biological energy led him to the conclusion succinctly formulated by his translator Barbara Koopman:

> Since only pleasurable vegetative sensations give rise to an increased surface charge [...] we must assume that pleasurable excitation is the specific process of all living organisms. Other biological processes show this also—for example, cell division, in which the cell shows an increase in [electrical] surface charge coinciding with the biologically productive process of mitosis (cell division). Hence *the sexual process would simply be the biologically productive energy process.*[65]

If the expansive movement governed by pleasure is involved in the most basic of cellular processes, then the most important consequence of the application of Freud's theory of libido would lie outside the scope of psychology: *it was to open a new path to address the problem of biogenesis.*[66] With Reich the idea that Eros is a fundamental and generative force of the cosmos, kept at the margins of Western history since the time of Giordano Bruno, found a way to re-enter our tradition.

If his hypothesis was correct it should be possible to observe it live, to verify it clearly in the simplest of lifeforms: protozoa. To this end Reich went to Oslo's Botanical Institute to obtain amoeba cultures, the most common form of protozoan. The assistant who helped him told him that he should put leaves of grass in water and wait for ten to fourteen days, the amoebas would appear spontaneously. Reich says that he asked naively about the way "the protozoa came into the infusion. 'From the air, naturally', the assistant replied, with an astonished look. 'And how do they come into the air?' Reich asked further. 'That we do not know', the assistant answered."[67] Surprisingly, apparently no one had bothered to ask this question at least since the time of Louis Pasteur, when biologists came to the conclusion that protozoa arise from spores that float in the air and fall into the grass infusion. Textbooks described that the protozoa simply "appeared" in the infusion but nobody thought it important to know *what was happening inside the infusion*. Armed with a microscope, Reich could see how on the edges of the blades of grass appeared vesicles or particles that could not yet be described as protozoa but showed all kinds of spontaneous internal movements. He called these vesicles by the name of *bions* (from the Greek *bio*, "life") and postulated that protozoa developed from the bionic clusters that emerged from the leaves of decomposing grass.

Simultaneous with his experiments with protozoa, Reich had initiated another unusual line of research: the way food transformed into energy. With this goal in mind he put meat, vegetables, milk and eggs in a pot and cooked the mixture for half an hour before taking a sample under a microscope. Initially he thought that he could distinguish the different foods but all he saw was the same vesicles as in his experiments with protozoa: the *bions* seemed to be involved not only in the generation of the most basic forms of life but also in the transformation of matter into energy. That no biologist had described these phenomena was an incredible omission in light of the advances in microscopy. But even more importantly, Reich's thesis ran in the opposite direction to mainstream biology, which held that "life was created once in the far distant past and since then 'all life has come from life'."[68] According to Reich, life not only arose from decaying matter, but this process took place everywhere and all the time.

The onslaught of attacks from his detractors was almost immediate. They contested that the appearance of the *bions* was due to the fact that Reich's infusions were not sterile. By sterilizing the substances that were going to be put into the solution, and the solution itself, the result was the faster appearance of the vesicles and movements that were even more vigorous. They also objected that the movements that were observed inside and outside the particles were physical-chemical and not spontaneous, such as brownian movement, but this definitely could not explain the rhythmic contractions and expansions that happened within the bions. To add to the debate, Reich discovered that bions also arose from inorganic materials such as coal after being sterilized at 1500°C and put into a solution. The biology of that time assured that no germs could survive temperatures higher than 180°C, and even then Reich could observe the same vesicles and the same movements. According to Sharaf:

> Reich's own interpretation was that the preparations contained forms with some life properties. Some kind of transitional organization between the nonliving and the living had been discovered. Reich had succeeded in the laboratory in reproducing some of the conditions for the "natural organization" of living form from nonliving matter.[69]

Reich's experiments with inorganic materials such as coal, earth and sand led him to another curious discovery. "In January 1939, one of his assistants took the wrong container from the sterilizer and, instead of earth, heated ocean sand. After two days there was a growth in the solution which, inoculated on egg medium and agar, resulted in a yellow growth. This new kind of culture consisted microscopically of large, slightly mobile, blue vesicles"[70] which, when observed by microscope, emitted a blue radiation. He called this new type of vesicle SAPA-bion (Sand Packet-Bion).

By then Reich's legal situation in Norway began to get complicated. On the one hand, his detractors claimed that he lacked the experience and basic concepts to conduct scientific experiments in a responsible manner, for which reason he should be denied an extension to his visa, which was about to expire. The controversy degenerated to such an extent that his enemies, partly encouraged by his impulsiveness and belligerence, decided to use details of his psychological treatment that, put out of context, seemed particularly scandalous. For a long time Reich had demanded that his patients enter consultation wearing only underwear, so that it he could observe their bodily responses and the movements of their muscular armor. There was talk of "quackery" and sexual relations with patients. Apart from his group of Norwegian and German friends and researchers, only a couple of public figures came to his defense: Bronislaw Malinowski, who had maintained a cordial relationship with Reich ever since they had been exchanged correspondence, and A.S. Neill, a Scottish educator and founder of the famous Summerhill school. The Norwegian government finally decided to grant an extension to his visa, but Reich had simultaneously been negotiating a US work visa with the sponsorship of a

North American colleague. He abandoned Europe on the last ship to leave Norway before the outbreak of World War II.

Once settled in New England, Reich continued his research designing an apparatus that could contain the radiation of the SAPA-bions to prevent it from dissipating in the air. According to his observations, metals repelled this radiation while organic materials absorbed it, so he proceeded to build a box whose interior walls were metal sheets surrounded by a layer of wood. One of the walls had hinges to be able to put the cultures inside the box and a window through which to observe the radiation. This simple apparatus would later be known as the *orgone accumulator*, the first device to accumulate and conduct bioenergy since Mesmer's baquet, which was curiously built with a similar arrangement of materials. The assumption that this device could contain SAPA-bion radiation turned out to be incorrect but took his investigation in a novel direction. Even if the bion cultures were outside the box, the device itself seemed to attract a bluish radiation identical to the one produced by the cultures. At first he supposed that the radiation coming from the bions had penetrated the metal plates and the wooden panels of the box, which he disassembled, cleaned throughly and then reassembled, with the same result. So he decided to build a new box that he kept carefully away from the cultures and their radiations and which, nonetheless, also presented the same radiation inside.

Baffled, Reich pondered the matter for months until he came to the conclusion that the only possibility was that this radiation was everywhere and that the only thing the device did was to attract it and store it. But if this was true, if there was a form of energy in the atmosphere that could be accumulated so easily, "why wasn't it discovered before?"[71]. It is in his emphasis on the direct observation of the world, in conjunction with the technological advances in microscopy, where we find the probable reason for his discovery. At this stage of his career Reich's unusual scientific approach—that is, unusual for the twentieth century—came to light more than ever. In this regard, his biographer Myron Sharaf quotes Goethe:

> Man himself, inasmuch as he makes use of his healthy senses, is the greatest and most exact physical apparatus; and that is just the greatest evil of modern physics—that one has, as it were, detached the experiment from man and wishes to gain

knowledge of nature merely through that which artificial instruments show.[72]

During a family vacation in Maine, Reich went out to gaze at the night sky over Lake Mooselookmeguntic. He realized that If the theory that the twinkling of the stars was due to light diffusion was correct, it should be the same throughout the sky or even more intense near the moonlight. However, the opposite seemed to be true. When he looked at the stars through a wooden tube, he realized that in the dark blue spaces between them there were vivid sparkles followed by flashes of light. The closer he looked to the moon, the less intense the flashes seemed, the farther away they intensified. It was not an optical illusion because when he observed the scintillation by placing a lens on the end of the tube it appeared magnified. This light phenomenon was the same that he had seen countless times in the accumulator; the energy that this device captured was in fact in the atmosphere. Reich spent the following months doing all kinds of measurements to verify the physical existence of the phenomenon and found that the temperature inside and outside the accumulator varied inexplicably between 0.2°C and 1.8°C. Additionally, the inside of the accumulator registered an electroscopic discharge smaller than the outside. The difference in temperature and electromagnetism was even more pronounced outdoors. He called this form of energy *orgone*, from the proto-Indo-European root *werg-*, which also originated words like organ or orgasm, and originally referred to the energy that is required to perform some work.

Unknowingly, Reich had found an objective way to describe the bioenergy that in our tradition had been known as pneuma and animal magnetism until the nineteenth century and in the East, for millennia, as *qi* or *prana*. And not only this, his research seemed to demonstrate that this vital energy was not a metaphor for cosmic processes, a whimsical notion of unsophisticated minds; it was an objective reality, a physical force with demonstrable effects in the world. In the last pages of *The Function of Orgasm*, Reich describes how atmospheric orgone works in plants and animals:

> The living organism contains orgone energy in each one of its cells, and continuously charges itself orgonotically from the atmosphere by means of respiration. The "red" blood corpuscles are microscopic, orgone-charged vesicles having a

blue glimmer; they carry biological energy from the surface of the alveoli of the lungs to the body tissues. The chlorophyll of plants, which is related to the iron containing protein of animal blood, contains orgone and absorbs orgone directly from the atmosphere and from solar radiation.[73]

With Reich's work the old idea of a community interwoven by Eros, now represented by orgone, found a way to sneak itself once again into the intellectual life of the West, a way that sadly was not only wasted but punished as a modern heresy.

Once he had determined the physical existence of atmospheric orgone, Reich began to extend the scope and implications of his discovery. He soon understood that the fact that orgone was everywhere and that it could be "accumulated" meant that it could be used as a source of energy, a line of research that Nikola Tesla had opened a little over a half century. Like Tesla, Reich understood that orgone inevitably vindicated the notion of the physical ether that Einstein had banished from modern science with his formulation of relativity. This discovery overturned many of the assumptions on which modern physics and biology were built and involved the reassessment of certain ways of doing science that were thought to have been overcome; anathema in the eyes of the modern scientific establishment.

As the insightful observer he was, Reich realized that the emotional movements and bioenergetic expressions of his patients corresponded to the "movements" and "energetic expressions" of the physical world. "To the mechanistic technician of physics," he says,

> The physical functions of nature are seen as split off from the emotional manifestations, as "physics" here and "mysticism" or "religiousness" there. On the other hand, in the well-trained orgonomic observer, these two modes of experiencing nature, otherwise so much opposed to each other, are united into one picture. Here the *physical* does not exclude or contradict the *meaningful*, or the quantitative the qualitative. We are aware that these matters have a deep natural-philosophical significance. The sharp boundary lines between physics and what is called "metaphysics" have broken down.[74]

In the same vein as Mesmer, Reich began to understand orgone as a "substance" that resided both in organisms and the cosmos; the tides of animal magnetism described by Mesmer and his school became a primordial ocean of cosmic orgone. Indeed, like the magnetic fluid of the eighteenth century, orgone could be described as a substance of "sympathetic character that circulates throughout the cosmos giving it harmony and cohesion." Reich's research led him to reacquaint our tradition with the "infinite and omniscient spirit in which matter moved according to mathematical laws"[75] that Newton had enunciated three centuries before. Thus, cosmic orgone is nothing other than a transformation, now objective and quantifiable, of the premodern idea of the World Soul.

As we have seen so far, the idea of the *anima mundi* is inseparable from magic and religion, which is why its reappearance has important implications for these modes of experience. In his clinical work Reich found that during treatment many of his patients remembered a period during early childhood in which they felt fully identified with nature, a feeling of unity that the repressive education of our society destroyed sooner rather than later. The annihilation of the unitary vegetative character of human emotions and the desire to recover it was, according to Reich, the foundation of all civilized religions. Seen thus, "God" would be

> is the mysticized idea of the vegetative harmony between self and nature. From this viewpoint, religion can be reconciled with natural science only if God personifies the natural laws and man is included in the natural process.[76]

"God" can be said to be latent in the vegetative nervous system of every human being, waiting to enter into harmony, that is, resonance with the natural world. Orgonomy, the name Reich gave to the study of orgone, offered a unique opportunity to our culture: to bridge the Cartesian categories of subject and object and close the age-old gap between religion and science, an opportunity that would be thwarted by Reich's usual adversary: fascism, now embodied in the FDA and the FBI.

But why did these government agencies undertake such a persecution? Apart from the deep philosophical and religious implications of his work—which in most cases were misrepresented or misunderstood—the origin of Reich's harassment at the hands of U.S. government agencies has its roots in another of his fields of study, the etiology and treatment of cancer. While still living in Oslo, Reich noticed that a specific type of bion, which he called of PA-bion, proliferated in the presence of another kind of vesicle he called T-bacillus. When he analyzed the blood of healthy individuals he observed that the PA-bions surrounded the dead T-bacilli and realized that the weaker the orgone charge of these bions, the more they multiplied in order to consume the T-bacilli. The cancer cell, he concluded, would be the product of this proliferation of PA-bions. Since cancer seemed to arise in tissues where the cellular orgone charge was low, Reich concluded that exposure to atmospheric orgone could help in cancer treatment. Indeed, the experimental treatment he designed for patients with various types of cancer using orgone accumulators yielded positive results, such as reduction of tumors. Ultimately it was these investigations that put him in the crosshairs of the intelligence and health agencies of the United States.

By the early forties Reich had already been a victim of the intransigence and paranoia of wartime US politics. In 1941, shortly after the attack on Pearl Harbor, he was dragged out of his house at two in the morning by the FBI and detained for three weeks on Ellis Island. He was never offered an explanation for the arrest but since his anti-Nazi and anti-Stalinist reputation was beyond any doubt, the arrest may have had something to do with his positions on sexuality, one of the obsessions of the then director of the Bureau, J. Edgar Hoover. In 1947, The New Republic published an article entitled "The Strange Case of Wilhelm Reich" by Mildred Edie Brady, in which the author suggested, in a simplistic way and without any reference to the details of Reich's research, that the accumulator gave "'orgastic potency,' the lack of which is responsible for everything from neuroses to cancer. Ergo, the accumulator will cure neuroses and cancer,"[77] something that Reich, as a responsible scientist, never claimed.

This article, reproduced by dozens of magazines, became the beginning of a campaign against orgonomy. Two months after the article appeared, the FDA undertook an investigation into the accumulators in which it was suggested that there was some sexual factor in Reich's treatment, as had happened with his opponents in Norway. The FDA interviewed numerous users of the accumulators to collect their perceptions about the effects of the device, none of which gave complaints or negative comments. By the early 1950s, the pressures of the investigation and the unfair persecution of his ideas had taken their toll: Reich's paranoid tendencies—increased by his unresolved psychological conflicts—came to light, his rhetoric took on prophetic overtones and he began to blame colleagues and acquaintances and argue a complex conspiracy against him, which included portions of the federal government, the pharmaceutical sector and the "red fascists," as he liked to call the North American communists.

By the mid-1950s, the FDA had prepared an extensive case against him that included fraud and violation of federal laws and ordered a ban on the manufacture and distribution of accumulators and all types of literature that suggested the effectiveness of the device. Reich decided to represent himself, refused to comply with the conditions of the judge and pleaded not guilty. He was fined for contempt of court for not appearing on the first trial date and, finally, after months of legal proceedings, his foundation was fined ten thousand dollars and he was sentenced to two years in prison. Throughout the trial, Reich maintained that the persecution of his person and his work were unconstitutional and that any scientific research should be free of political and ideological interference. Dozens of accumulators were destroyed and, while he was appealing his sentence from prison, six tons of his books were burned in one of the public incinerators of New York City. Reich died of a heart attack in the early hours of November 3, 1957 in the Lewisburg Penitentiary in Pennsylvania, just eight days before his parole hearing.

Since his death only a handful of scientists and institutions have seriously taken the task of reproducing his experiments to confirm his findings. Reich is probably the only person whose books were burned by both the Nazis and the US government.

---

[1] Myron Sharaf, *Fury on Earth: A Biography of Wilhelm Reich* (Boston: Da Capo Press, 1994), 39.

[2] Wilhelm Reich, *Über einen Fall von Durchbruch der Inzestschranke*. Quoted by Sharaf en *Fury on Earth*, 42

[3] Sharaf, *Fury on Earth*, 44.

[4] Sharaf, *Fury on Earth*, 54.

[5] Wilhelm Reich, *The Function of Orgasm* (New York: Farrar, Straus & Giraux, 1973), 24.

[6] Reich, *The Function of Orgasm*, 35.

[7] Sharaf, *Fury on Earth*, 68.

[8] Sharaf, *Fury on Earth*, 69.

[9] Reich, *The Function of Orgasm*, 153.

[10] Sharaf, *Fury on Earth*, 75.
[11] Reich, *The Function of Orgasm*, 147.
[12] Reich, *The Function of Orgasm*, 147.
[13] Reich, *The Function of Orgasm*, 310.
[14] Reich, *The Function of Orgasm*, 311. The tonic and clonic phases of an epileptic attack correspond to two types of nervous activity. During the tonic phase all the muscles contract, producing a general spasm that is "released" during the clonic phase, when the arms and legs begin to shake quickly and rhythmically.
[15] Reich, *The Function of Orgasm*, 312.
[16] Reich, *The Function of Orgasm*, 312.
[17] Sharaf, *Fury on Earth*, 74.
[18] Reich, *The Function of Orgasm*, 313.
[19] Reich, *The Function of Orgasm*, 313.
[20] Reich, *The Function of Orgasm*, 315. It is interesting to note that during the second phase of Charcot's hysterically rooted hypnosis "the body relaxes but manifests at the same time a 'neuromuscular hyper-excitability': any pressure on a muscle or a nerve causes a corresponding contracture'." This clinical fact seems to indicate a relationship between the musculature and the autonomic nervous system, which if we add the psychological factor could explain how a memory or feeling is fixed on the muscular armor.
[21] Reich, *The Function of Orgasm*, 317.
[22] Reich, *The Function of Orgasm*, 317.
[23] Already in the nineteenth century Charcot had argued that the origin of hysteria lay in sexual dissatisfaction, a matter that he chose not to highlight in his research. Well known is his phrase: «*mais, dans des cas pareils c'est toujours la chose génitale, toujours... toujours... toujours*» (But in such cases it is always a matter of genitality, always ... always ... always).
[24] Reich, *The Function of Orgasm*, 345-346.
[25] Reich, *The Function of Orgasm*, 320.
[26] Reich, *The Function of Orgasm*, 321-322.
[27] Reich, *The Function of Orgasm*, 271. It is worth noting here that Mesmer's first patient, Fraulein Oesterline, who for years had suffered from a "convulsive ailment accompanied by the most cruel toothaches and earaches, and by delirium, mania, vomiting and fainting fits" (Gaul, *A History of Hypnotism*, 3) also felt pain and burning in the body, but her condition improved markedly in a short period of time.
[28] Reich, *The Function of Orgasm*, 348.
[29] Marc Shapiro, *The Creative Process*, quoted in W. Edward Mann's *Orgone, Reich and Eros* (New York: Simon and Schuster, 1973), 93.
[30] Reich, *The Function of Orgasm*, 109.
[31] Reich, *The Function of Orgasm*, 110.
[32] Reich, *The Function of Orgasm*, 253-254.

[33] Reich, *The Function of Orgasm*, 256-257.
[34] Reich, *The Function of Orgasm*, 166.
[35] Reich, *The Function of Orgasm*, 153.
[36] Sharaf, *Fury on Earth*, 138.
[37] Reich, *The Function of Orgasm*, 230.
[38] Sharaf, *Fury on Earth*, 197.
[39] Reich, *The Function of Orgasm*, 199.
[40] Reich, *The Function of Orgasm*, 199.
[41] Wilhelm Reich, *The Mass Psychology of Fascism* (New York: Farrar, Strauss and Giroux, 1980), 30.
[42] Reich, *The Function of Orgasm*, 199.
[43] Reich, *The Function of Orgasm*, 200.
[44] Here we must remember that blind obedience to authority, as a hunter like Edward Bernays knew well enough, is the first and most effective bond in mass manipulation.
[45] Reich, *The Mass Psychology of Fascism*, 30.
[46] Here the objection could be raised that since the 1930s the attitudes towards sexuality have improved and sexual repression is no longer as pronounced, for which reason the source of neuroses would be in the course of being eliminated. However, one should also bear in mind that the vegetative sexual disorder that Reich called *orgastic impotence* continues and will continue to be the sexual norm until radical measures are taken to change the economic and political conditions that impede the natural flow of libido at the individual and social levels.
[47] Reich, *The Mass Psychology of Fascism*, 88.
[48] Reich, *The Function of Orgasm*, 234.
[49] Reich, *The Function of Orgasm*, 234.
[50] Sharaf, *Fury on Earth*, 166.
[51] Quoted by Sharaf in *Fury on Earth*, 165.
[52] Sharaf, *Fury on Earth*, 166.
[53] It is interesting to note that the image of the black male as a sex crazed rapist of white women—a political fabrication to justify racial segregation in the 20th century—was boosted to new heights by the release of D.W. Grifith's film *Birth of a Nation* (1915), which pictured blacks as a regressive cultural force and inspired the rebirth Ku Klux Klan.
[54] Rosa Sala Rose, *Diccionario crítico de mitos y símbolos del nazismo* (Barcelona: Acantilado, 2003), 292. Author's translation.
[55] Sala Rose, *Diccionario crítico de mitos y símbolos del nazismo*, 73-74.
[56] Sala Rose, *Diccionario crítico de mitos y símbolos del nazismo*, 74.
[57] Sala Rose, *Diccionario crítico de mitos y símbolos del nazismo*, 193. The parenthesis is mine. Here it is also important to note that Rahn understood Wolfram von Eschenbach's *Parsifal* as an encrypted document of the Cathar

heresy, which would explain the constant identification of Hitler with this arthurian knight.

[58] Sala Rose, *Diccionario crítico de mitos y símbolos del nazismo*, 394-395. As a curious anecdote, Sala Rose comments that "the day of Baldur von Schirach's wedding, Hitler presented the bride with a note with the culinary instructions that had to be taken into account when he was to visit them: "I eat everything that Nature provides voluntarily: fruit, vegetables, vegetable fats. But I beg to be spared of all that animals only give despite of themselves: meat, milk and cheese. So, from an animal, only the eggs!"

[59] Sharaf, *Fury on Earth*, 165.
[60] Sharaf, *Fury on Earth*, 206.
[61] Reich, *The Function of Orgasm*, 134.
[62] Sigmund Freud, *Beyond the Pleasure Principle* (New York: Dover Publications, 2015), 20.
[63] Sharaf, *Fury on Earth*, 214.
[64] Sharaf, *Fury on Earth*, 214.
[65] Sharaf, *Fury on Earth*, 214. Italics are mine.
[66] Reich, *The Function of Orgasm*, 36.
[67] Quoted by Sharaf in *Fury on Earth*, 218.
[68] Sharaf, *Fury on Earth*, 222.
[69] Sharaf, *Fury on Earth*, 223.
[70] Sharaf, *Fury on Earth*, 223.
[71] Sharaf, *Fury on Earth*, 278.
[72] Quoted by Sharaf in *Fury on Earth*, 279.
[73] Reich, *The Function of Orgasm*, 385. It is worth remembering here that the idea that vital energy enters the body through breathing is present in all cultures that have come to the conclusion of such force. In the West this conclusion is implicit in the Greek verbs *pnein* and *psykhein* and in the Latin verb *spirare*, which denote the idea of breathing or blowing.
[74] Wilhelm Reich, *Selected Writings* (New York: Farrar, Strauss and Giroux, 1973), 426.
[75] Patrick Harpur, *The Philosopher's Secret Fire* (Victoria: Blue Angel Gallery, 2002), 207.
[76] Reich, *The Function of Orgasm*, 358.
[77] Sharaf, *Fury on Earth*, 361.

6. Economy, Neurosis and Spectacle

Capitalism and magic

You will not be able to stay home, brother
You will not be able to plug in, turn on and drop out
You will not be able to lose yourself on skag
Skip out for beer during commercials
Because the revolution will not be televised
The revolution will not be televised
The revolution will not be brought to you by Xerox
In four parts without commercial interruptions [...]
The revolution will not be brought to you by the Schaefer Award Theater
and will not star Natalie Wood and Steve McQueen or Bullwinkle and Julia.
The revolution will not give your mouth sex appeal
The revolution will not get rid of the nubs
The revolution will not make you look five pounds thinner,
because the revolution will not be televised, brother [...]
Gil Scott-Heron, *The Revolution Will Not be Televised (1970)*

Now I'm finding truth is a ruin,
nauseous end the nobody is pursuing.
Staring into glassy eyes, mesmerized.
Mr. Bungle, *Retrovertigo (1999)*

In December 1964, at the campus of UC Berkeley, a group of students protested against what they considered a degradation of the North American educational system. Their leader, Mario Savio, argued that academia had become an autocracy at the service of the military-industrial complex in which the students were simply "raw material" that after being duly "manufactured" would be sold to the university's clients. Some of the protesters carried computer cards punched with legends such as "STRIKE" or "FSM"[1] hanging from their necks, implying that they felt like another product of the military-industrial complex, instruments of death. One of the students stuck a sign to his chest that mocked the instructions of a computer of the time: "I am a student at the University of California. Please do not fold, bend, spindle or mutilate me."[2]

Two years later, by the end of November 1966, students of the University of Strasbourg in cahoots with an obscure group of activists known as *Situationists*, bombarded Professor Abraham Moles, then president of the French Cybernetic Society, with tomatoes. On December 2 of the same year, students sympathetic to the same activist group managed to get themselves elected as leaders of the Strasbourg chapter of the National Union of Students. Their first action was to use the funds of this organization to print a pamphlet in which they proposed its dissolution because, they argued, it "was only a mechanism to integrate students to an unacceptable society."[3]

By May 1968, groups of Parisian students were graffitiing reichian symbols on the walls of the Sorbonne, while in Berlin the youths of the free love communes threw copies of *The Mass Psychology of fascism* to the police. These were the most violent popular revolts so far in the twentieth century and, in the case of Paris, since the Revolution of February 1848. Once again barricades were raised in the working-class areas of the city and the situation almost came to a civil war. Both in Europe and the United States, students and various leftist groups rose against what they perceived as an insidious process of dehumanization resulting from industrial economy. The Situationists were one of the driving forces of the Paris revolts of '68', and their leader, Guy Debord, is an specially clear exponent of esoteric Marxism, as well as of the project of destruction of art by art initiated by the poetry of Charles Baudelaire, a conjunction that will allow us to examine some of the most outstanding magical traits of the twentieth century media project.

Urbanism, play and situation

The son of a pharmacist, Guy-Ernest Debord was born on the outskirts of Paris on December 28, 1931. He lost his father at the age of four and just before the start of World War II his mother and grandmother took him to Nice, which then lay outside the occupied zone. During the war the family assumed an itinerant way of life that took them to Pau in the Pyrénées-Atlantiques, where Guy attended elementary school at the Lycée Louis-Barthou and where, coincidentally, one of his literary heroes had also studied: Isidore-Lucien Ducasse, better known as the Count of Lautréamont, patron saint of dadaism and surrealism, remembered for *The Chants of Maldoror,* a poem in prose with strong Gnostic nuances. After the Liberation of Paris, Debord and his family settled in Cannes, where Guy entered the Lycée Carnot and began reading Arthur Cravan, boxer, adventurer and poet (and also Oscar Wilde's nephew), who disappeared on the Pacific coast of Mexico in 1918.

Young Debord never excelled at school and instead stood out for devoting his time to writing "meticulously crafted letters, full of effusive poetry and revolutionary idealism to his school pals: 'We have been *enfants terribles*. If we become adults we will be dangerous men.'"[4] In *Panegyric*, his autobiography, Debord wrote of those years: "I went slowly but inevitably toward a life of adventure, with my eyes open. I could not even think of studying one of the learned professions that lead to holding down a job, for all of them seemed completely alien to my tastes or contrary to my opinions."[5]

At the 1951 Cannes Film Festival Debord met Isidore Isou, a Romanian artist based in France and founder of *Letterism*, a late avant-garde movement with a penchant for vandalism and provocation. A year earlier, during Easter, a member of the group disguised as a Dominican monk appeared at the Notre Dame pulpit and informed the congregation that 'God was dead'. "This action ended with an attempted lynching, the impostor's arrest, and headlines in all the papers."[6] Isou and company had gone to the film festival to show *Traité de bave et d'éternité* (Treatise on Slime and Eternity) by Isou, a feature film that perfectly fit the group's ambitions: it ran for more than four hours during which the screen remained blank for long periods or only guttural voices seemed to declaim poetry; needless to say, it caused a genuine uproar. Debord couldn't but join the group, after all, he felt "quite at home in the most ill-famed of company."[7]

The letterists, who embraced the iconoclasm of Dadaism and early Surrealism, advocated for the self-destruction of all forms of art; their meeting places were the taverns of the old city, where Debord got his taste for alcohol. "Even though I have read a lot, I have drunk even more," he says in *Panegyric*: "I have written much less than most people who write; but I have drunk much more than most people who drink." More than "works of art," Isou and the letterists constantly came up with new modes of expression, forms that sought to reduce poetry to its last and smallest meaningful component, the letter. The self-appointed mission of the letterists was to finish what Baudelaire did with the stanza and Rimbaud with the verse, they would make art and poetry collapse on themselves creating a new form of expression that did not run separate from real life. This "supersession of art," one of the central ideas of Letterism, would remain with Debord even after he left the group. But if art was to be overcome, "the whole world must be torn down then rebuilt not under the sign of the economy but instead under that of a generalized *creativity*."[8]

One of the favorite aesthetic practices of the letterists was the *détournement* (literally "detour" or "deviation"), an appropriation technique derived from Dadaist collage and the type of distorted quotation used by Marx and Lautréamont, in which a fragment of text or image was adapted to a new use and context, and that as a form of semantic subversion has survived to this day in anti-capitalist collectives like Adbusters and artists like Barbara Kruger and Banksy. Indeed, the bulk of Debord's philosophical work can be understood as a détournement of Marx and Hegel, among others.

Under the letterist banner, Debord produced his first film, entitled *Hurlements in faveur de Sade* (Howlings in Favour of Sade), in which, following the tradition of Isou, the screen alternated between long runs of black and white frames while a voice quoted from the most varied sources. In the first minutes of the film you hear: "Cinema is dead. Films are no longer possible. If you want, let's have a discussion."[9] According to Anselm Jappe, the intention of these provocations was to force the subject to transcend his passivity as a spectator, to incite him to participate in the work, whether through indignation or consent, a tactic that, in Reichian terms, would amount to a shaking of the characterological armor in order to produce a sudden release of energy and activity, a call to action. Debord was not interested in "the search for a new *aesthetic*, on the contrary, he wanted to draw a line under even the most recent art."[10] This attitude put him sooner rather than later in overt opposition to Isou, who he deemed too positive and "artistic," too interested in traditional form and expression. In November 1952, Debord and three other Letterist friends founded the *Letterist International* (LI), an organization of Marxist inspiration with which they planned to finish the Project for the destruction of art by art initiated by Baudelaire almost a century ago.

The radical attitudes of Debord and LI are more easily understood if they are put in context. By the 1950s, the french *avant-garde* had long since lost its initial spark, in fact, surrealism had been absorbed by the bourgeoise and elevated as one of the most important artistic trends of the twentieth century; Dalí and Breton had sold-out, art truly felt dead. On the other hand, the French Communist Party, influenced by Stalinism, "had conducted a veritable reign of terror over the intellectuals, successfully silencing any thinking on the Left that did not correspond to its manuals."[11] In addition to this, during the first part of the decade France went, in the words of Jappe, through a "sudden eruption of modernity." The first television broadcast took place in 1953, in 1955 the first washing machines appeared in the market, simultaneously with the first *grands ensembles*, high-rise apartment buildings for moderate-income families that would soon populate the outskirts of every French city. Paris was changing and Debord and LI watched, between alcoholic binges, as their city was irrevocably transformed.

For Debord the problem with the new urban planning projects was the separation they induced in the population. By the mid-nineteenth century Paris was still a city of the people, until Georges-Eugène Haussmann, prefect of the Seine and "demolition artist" of Napoleon III, "blasted and brutally hacked open medieval Paris, wiping out dirty working-class neighbourhoods"[12] to make room for the *grand boulevards* we know today, a move that evicted the less favored classes from their neighbourhoods "and deprived them of their urbanity, of their 'right to the city'."[13] In a classical example of détournement, Debord mockingly asserted that Haussmann's Paris "was a city built by an idiot, full sound and fury, signifying nothing." The truth, Walter Benjamin tells us, is that Haussmann wanted to secure the city against civil wars, his ultimate goal was to prevent the tactics of barricade fighting in two ways: "the breadth of the streets was to make the erection of barricades impossible, and new streets were to provide the shortest route between the barracks and the working-class areas. Contemporaries christened the undertaking: 'L'embellissement stratégique'."[14]

A century later, a new generation of architects and technocrats led by Le Corbusier would resume Baron Haussmann's mission under the motto *supprimer la rue!* (eliminate the street!), which for them represented the disorderly and unpredictable in any city. Debord would not miss an opportunity to go head on against the Swiss-French architect, whom he said was "more cop than anything else." For Debord his architecture was "life definitely divided in enclosed blocks, in monitored societies; the end of any chance of insurrection and of encounter;

automatic resignation."[15] In this sense, Le Corbusier represents the architectural realization of the panoptic of the English philosopher and social theorist Jeremy Bentham, a type of prison in which all the prisoners can be observed by a single watchman who, by virtue of this jail's structure, is invisible to them. A whole tradition of social criticism initiated by Michel Foucault takes Bentham's panopticon as a sadly accurate metaphor for the obsessive tendency of contemporary states to monitor and control their subjects.

According to Marxist theorist Andy Merrifield, the separations imposed by urban planners implied a compartmentalization "—of activity and people—in the name of efficiency. Everything had its place, its function; work here, residence there, leisure somewhere else. Spaces got hacked up and simplified, people got decanted, experience flattened. Separation meant the compartmentalization of consciousness, an inability for people to understand the totality of their lives. Separation in the city and in activity spelt separation in the mind, alienation, false consciousness, a retreat into contemplation."[16] Here I should highlight two relationships: the idea of compartmentalization implicit in modern urbanism is the architectural expression of social regimentation that Edward Bernays began to apply as a hunting technique since the 1920s. A properly compartmentalized life is a life segmented into potential markets, which gives rise to a society where people can be easily manipulated and directed by specific consumption patterns. This is a society in which the network of magical bonds posited by Bruno can be easily deployed. On the other hand, it is not difficult to see that the inability of most people to "understand the totality of their lives" is, in Reich's terms, inseparable from the physiological basis of neurosis. The modern human's disconnection from its core of biological energy, the very foundation of the neurotic personality, can be characterized as *the separation of the human from itself* (see diagrams in page 215-216) from that which makes him not only an individual but one active and capable of responding for his destiny, and which in its absence leaves him helpless against all sorts of hunters of souls. With Le Corbusier, architecture becomes an instrument of social fragmentation and neurosis ideally suited for the manipulation of the masses by magical means.[17]

Of course, Debord's idea of *separation* is inseparable (so to speak) from the Marxist concept of alienation, a byproduct of industrialization in which as the population is separated from the means of production through the specialization of labor, the possibility of achieving a *full picture* of the vital relationships that make up social life disappears, a situation that entails an inevitable descent into contemplation and inaction, into social passivity.

In his film *Critique de la Separation*, a voice calmly enunciates:

> our age accumulates power and sees itself as rational, but nobody recognizes these powers as their own. Nowhere is there an entrance to adulthood: the only possible transformation is that, one day, this long anxiety becomes a routine dream. Because nobody stops being under surveillance. The question is not corroborating that some people live better or worse than others; but that we all live in ways that are beyond our control.

In response to this situation, Debord and his band of letterists founded *Potlatch*, a magazine designed to divulge the collective concepts of the movement that reached a little over two dozen numbers in four years. The magazine was named after the great festivals of the tribes of the American northwest in which a exchange of gifts in food and drink took place and all the surpluses, which may be used to elevate the status of a chief or a tribe, were purposely destroyed. French sociologist Marcel Mauss popularized the concept in his book *The Gift*, which appealed to Debord because it challenged the capitalist notion of monetary exchange and use value as the basic principles of the economy.

It was in *Potlatch* where Debord presented for the first time the concept of *psychogeography*, which he defined as "the study of the precise laws and the specific effects of the geographical environment, consciously organized or not, on the emotions and behavior of individuals."[18] In practice, psychogeography took the form of a set of creative practices and strategies to explore cities and create new ways of relating to the urban landscape. This discipline is closely linked to the letterist practice of *dérive,* or drifting, a strategy in which a group of people put their daily habits aside to embark on a rapid journey through different urban environments in order to reach new conclusions about the city and the emotions evoked by its different areas. The aim of the *dérive* was the "dealienation" of consciousness by restoring the subject's relations with a unitary and non-separate urban space and, through it, with reality.

One of the most interesting features of this practice appears in the essay *La Théorie de la Dérive*, written in 1956:

> all indications are that the most fruitful numerical arrangement consists of several small groups of two or three people who have reached the same level of awareness, since cross-checking these different groups' impressions makes it possible to arrive at more objective conclusions. It is preferable for the composition of these groups to change from one *dérive* to another. With more than four or five participants, the specifically *dérive* character rapidly diminishes, and in any case it is impossible for there to be more than ten or twelve people without the *dérive* fragmenting into several simultaneous *dérives*.[19]

In this fragment we can appreciate the interpersonal connection that arises in small human groups (two to three people) that reach "the same level of awareness" or, in pneumatic terms, that establish a *rapport* from which a collective mind emerges that can be willingly applied to the achievement of a goal. In time, this emphasis on a collective and productive configuration—a non-linear inheritance of the fruitful relationship between the magnetists and their *somnambules*—transformed into a quest to construct ludic situations that subverted the order imposed by the separation of modern urbanism and induced the individual to claim an active role in the construction of his or her reality.

Thus, play became an essential piece to the search of situations that arose from the practice of urban drifting. Debord's notion of play comes largely from the concept of *homo ludens*, man the player, devised by Dutch historian Johan Huizinga in the book of the same name. In his work Huizinga posits play as a vital cultural activity of our species, both in a civilizing function that shapes competition, law and war, as well as in a cultural function, which is evident in art, poetry, philosophy and myth.

Some fragments from Huizinga's book that are relevant to our topic:

> Inside the play-ground an absolute and peculiar order reigns. Here we come across [a] very positive feature of play: it creates order, *is* order. Into an imperfect world and into the confusion of life it brings a temporary, a limited perfection. Play demands order absolute and supreme. The least deviation from it "spoils the game," robs it of its character and makes it worthless.[20]

All play moves and has its being within a play ground marked beforehand either materially or ideally, deliberately or as a matter of course. Just as there is no formal difference between play and ritual, so the "consecrated spot" can not be formally distinguished from the play-ground. The arena, the card-table, the magic circle, the temple, the stage, the screen, the tennis court, the court of justice, etc., are all in form and function play-grounds, i.e. forbidden spots, isolated, hedged round, hallowed, within which special rules obtain. All are temporary worlds within the ordinary world, dedicated to the performance of an act apart.[21]

Fighting, as a cultural function, always presupposes limiting rules, and it requires, to a certain extent anyway, the recognition of its play-quality. We can only speak of war as a cultural function so long as it is waged within a sphere whose members regard each other as equals or antagonists with equal rights; in other words its cultural function depends on its play quality.[22]

Two points in question arise from these passages. First, play creates an order of its own that isolates it from the world and enforces its own rules—which Huizinga relates openly to the circle, literal or metaphorical, where magical operations take place. Thus, a game can be understood as an activity that by virtue of its internal structure is closely related to magic; play *creates its own pneumatic circle*. Second, play is related to hunting and war which, as we saw in the intermezzo, depend on a structural relationship with the erotic and its magical operations. Thus, we can propose a new pneumatic circle for play in which the players interact with a narrative that creates a barrier between itself and the circle of reality.

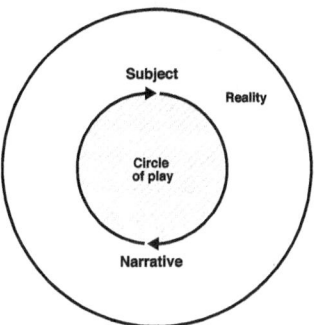

It was the relationship between play and war what drew Debord's attention to Huizinga's book, which he favorably reviewed in *Potlatch*:

play is strategy and, as such, offers a way of establishing rules of engagement, of standing up and waging war against society at large. For Debord the enemy was a world in which "everything that was directly lived has receded into a representation,"[23] and which he referred to as *spectacle*. The way to counteract this state of affairs was through the creation of situations, a situation being "a moment of life concretely and deliberately constructed by the collective organization of a unitary ambiance and a game of events."[24] The construction of situations was the main activity of the *Internationale Situationniste* (IS), successor to the International Letterist, which Debord founded in 1957 with his then wife Michèle Bernstein and Danish painter Asger Jorn, among others.

Given Debord's aversion to all forms of aesthetic—which his detractor Frédéric Schiffter calls a "religious hatred of the image"—the new collective aligned itself from the beginning with the *avant-garde's* project which sought "the dissolution of the border between art and life, the *realization* of art in life and, in short, the elimination of "art" (or aesthetics) as a cultural sphere separate from everyday life."[25] However, according to Giorgio Agamben, it would be naive to think that a situation, in the Debordian sense of the term, is the becoming of life into art or of art into life. A situation, he argues, takes place in a "territory" that is first and foremost *gesture*, that crossroads between life and art, act and power, text and execution. The only way of moving through it is by tracing a pneumatic circle that transcends in its unicity the even larger circle of the spectacle.

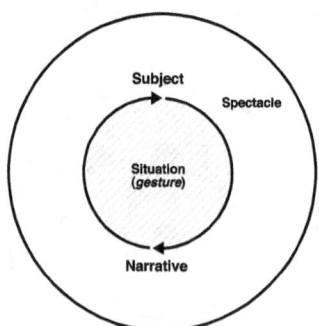

Debord's revolution is essentially magical:

We did not seek the formula for overturning the world in books, but in wandering. Ceaselessly drifting for days on end, none resembling the one before. Astonishing encounters, remarkable obstacles, grandiose betrayals, perilous enchantments — nothing was lacking in this quest for a different, more sinister Grail, which no one else had ever sought [...] We had rediscovered the secret of dividing what was united. We did not go on television to announce our discoveries. We did not seek grants from academic foundations or praise from the newspaper intellectuals. We brought fuel to the fire.[26]

Avant-garde, marxism and magic

Understanding the true extension of the Debordian concept of spectacle, as well as the deeper meaning of the *avant-garde* project, requires delving into one of the fundamental and least-treated concepts of Marx's thought: commodity fetishism. This concept, along with the automatic nature of the commodity that we approached in the intermezzo, forms the basis of what is known as esoteric Marxism.

The question here is, what did Marx understand by fetishism? In his work, the term does not have the sexual sense to which a century of psychoanalysis has accustomed us, and which we will deal with in time. Fetichism is a term that Marx borrowed from the work *The Cult of The Fetish Gods* (1760) by Charles de Brosses, Count de Tournay and friend of Voltaire, which alluded to the most primitive form of religious worship. With this term Marx sometimes referred to how "the nations which are still dazzled by the sensuous glitter of precious metals, and are, therefore, still fetish-worshippers of metal money, are not yet fully developed money-nations."[27] While this fragment correctly characterizes the essence of what Marx had in mind when he spoke of fetishism—the worship of a hidden quality—this idea is not a completely accurate reference to what he would later develop under the name of commodity fetishism.

In the fourth part of the first chapter of *Capital*, entitled "the fetishistic character of the commodity and its secret," Marx comments that the commodity seems at first sight to be a trivial and perfectly understandable thing:

> [...] Its analysis shows that it is, in reality, a very queer thing, abounding in metaphysical subtleties and theological niceties. So far as it is a use-value, there is nothing mysterious about it, whether we consider it from the point of view that by its

properties it satisfies human needs, or that it first takes on these properties as the product of human labour. It is absolutely clear that, by his activity, man changes the forms of the materials of nature in such a way as to make them useful to him. The form of wood, for instance, is altered if a table is made out of it. Nevertheless the table continues to be wood, an ordinary, sensuous thing. But as soon as it emerges as a commodity, it changes into a thing which transcends sensuousness. It not only stands with its feet on the ground, but, in relation to all other commodities, it stands on its head, and evolves out of its wooden brain grotesque ideas, far more wonderful than if it were to begin dancing on its own free will.[28]

For Marx, this mysterious and clearly mystical quality of the commodity arises from its separation into two forms of value: use value and exchange value. The first, which an object acquires by fulfilling a specific human need, and the second, which comes from its capacity to acquire a monetary and, as such, abstract value when entering the market. While the use value expresses "a physical relationship between physical things," the exchange value expresses "the value relation between the products of labour which stamps them as commodities." These products, however,

have absolutely no connection with their physical properties and with the material relations arising therefrom. There it is a definite social relation between men, that assumes, in their eyes, *the fantastic form* of a relation between things.[29]

The mere mention of a "fantastic form" of the commodity gives us a clear idea of what Marx had in mind: a hidden, ungraspable and mysterious quality that any object obtains by acquiring an exchange value in the market and that, by virtue of its immateriality, exerts an enchantment, a *charme*, which renders it closer to a primitive fetish, something infinitely more similar to an image or *phantasm*, than to the physical commodity from which it emanates. On the other hand, the fact that this fantastic form comes from a social relationship between things (in the case of a typical commodity, the amount of work invested in its production), immediately refers us to the idea of the market as a network of pneumatic relationships that I outlined in the fourth chapter. The magical quality that turns window displays "into eyes to meet eyes" (John Wanamaker), does not come exclusively from the separation of the sphere of production from the sphere of consumption—a division that constitutes the very basis of alienation—, it is actually a matter inherent to the structure of the commodity itself.

Thus, the magical aura that surrounds commodities, the very root of their powers of attraction and enchantment, is the product of its dissociation in two simultaneous forms of value which, nonetheless, cannot be perceived simultaneously by the senses. Either its use value is perceived, forgive the redundancy, by using the object, or we get an abstract impression of its exchange value, but as one of those double figures that when viewed from the top down or from the bottom up show the face of a young woman or an old hag, it is not possible to perceive, and above all, to enjoy both forms of value at once. The exchange value that determines the fetishistic character of the commodity usually prevails.

Now, "the transfiguration of the commodity into an *enchanted object*," says Giorgio Agamben, "is the sign that the exchange value is already beginning to eclipse the use-value of the commodity."[30] It is not a mystery that people have never bought goods for their intrinsic utility, but because of the status that emanates from their phantasmagorical aura (*Sell them their dreams, sell them what they longed for and hoped for and almost despaired of having*), a spell that, as it expands throughout the pneumatic network deployed by the capital, leads to the atmosphere of desire that hunters of souls like Edward Bernays learned to manipulate for their corporate clients. What Debord calls spectacle is nothing other than the stream of *phantasmata* that emanate from the immense network of commodities that sustain the capitalist world and form "a pseudo-world apart, solely as an object of contemplation."[31] Achieving this pseudo-reality is tantamount, so to speak, to putting green spectacles on everybody. The spectacle is thus an immense act of demiurgy.

Although Marx's concept of commodity fetishism had arisen from a religious and anthropological concept and lacked an overtly sexual character, Giorgio Agamben has revealed a series of relations between Marx and the concept of fetishism as developed by Freud. The idea of the human sexual attachment to an inanimate object appears for the first time in the essay *Le fétichisme dans l'amour* (1887) by Alfred Binet, a disciple of Charcot at the Salpêtrière. This is the first mention of the word fetishism in relation to human sexuality and the starting point of Freud's theory on the same topic, which he presented late in his career in a brief essay called

"Fetichismus," which appeared in the *Internationale Zeitschirft für Psychoanalyse* (vol. XIII) in 1927. In this text Freud posits that the fetishistic fixation arises "from the refusal of the male child to acknowledge the absence of the penis of the female (the mother).

> Confronted with the perception of this absence, the child refuses [...] to admit its reality, because to do so would permit a threat of castration against his own penis. The fetish is therefore the "'substitute for the woman's (the mother's) penis that the little boy once believed in and [...] does not want to give up."[32]

Thus, in the Freudian sense, a fetish is simultaneously the conscious recognition of a reality as well as its unconscious negation. "Whether a part of the body or an inorganic object, [a fetish] is, therefore, at one and the same time, the presence of that nothingness that is the maternal penis and the sign of its absence. Both symbol of something and its negation."[33] A fetish is, in short, *the presence of an absence*, the positive representation of a negativity. It is worth mentioning that the fact that fetishism is almost exclusive to the male sex suggests that this condition is the opposite pole of the feminization implicit in the act of entrapping a prey in a pneumatic circle. If society must be feminized in order to be manipulated, this operation must be carried out through a predominantly male pathology.

The similarity of the erotic dynamic of courtly love with the Freudian understanding of fetish is evident: the *phantasmata* of the beloved, like a high-heel shoe or a lock of hair, are representations of an absence, of an idealized female figure that depicts the unattainable divinity, in the case of the believer in love; or, in the fetishist's, of a sexual desire that got erroneously *caught* in an object. In fact, according to Agamben, sexual fetishism is characterized by an essentially melancholic feeling:

> [...] the fetish confronts us with the paradox of an unattainable object that satisfies a human need precisely through its being unattainable. Insofar as it is a presence, the fetish object is in fact something concrete and tangible; but insofar as it is the presence of an absence, it is, at the same time, immaterial and intangible, because it alludes continuously beyond itself to something that can never really be possessed.[34]

This feeling of "never being able to possess the beloved object" that governs the melancholic desire of the ascetic and the libertine, of the courtly poet who will never quite reach his beloved, is the same drive that impels the desire of the fetishist as well as that of the compulsive buyer.

The leap that joins these two categories, fetishism and consumerism, is as follows:

> The superimposition of the use-value corresponds, in fetishism, to the superimposition of a particular symbolic value on the normal use of the object. Just as the fetishist never succeeds in possessing the fetish wholly, because it is the sign of two contradictory realities, so the owner of a commodity will never be able to enjoy it simultaneously as both useful object and as value.[35]

Unsurprisingly, the dynamics of fetishism and consumerism share an essential feature. "Precisely because the fetish is a negation and the sign of an absence,

> it is not a unrepeatable unique object; on the contrary, it is something infinitely capable of substitution, without any of its successive incarnations ever succeeding in exhausting the nullity of which it is the symbol. However much the fetishist multiplies proofs of its presence and accumulates harems of objects, the fetish will inevitably remain elusive and celebrate, in each of its apparitions, always and only its own mystical phantasmagoria.[36]

This is why a commodity, like any other form of fetish, can only be enjoyed through a compulsive accumulation that evinces the neurotic character that permeates the totality of the system. What in Reichian terms is "a neurotic search for the phantasm or idealization which fetishizes the beloved transforming it in the very image of the unattainable," takes on the character, with Marx and Freud, of a systemic neurosis that emanates from the fetish/merchandise and infects the world through the pneumatic networks deployed by the capital.

Baudelaire, father of the *avant-garde* spirit, experienced first hand the emergence of the reign of the commodity. As the keen and sensitive thinker he was he understood early on that if the work of art was to survive in the irresistibly seductive world of modern merchandise, it would be because it was able to compete on par with it. Broadly speaking, Agamben argues, the situation was as follows:

> Once the commodity had freed objects of use from the slavery of being useful, the borderline that separated them from works of art —the borderline that artists from the Renaissance forward had indefatigably worked to establish by basing the supremacy of artistic creation on the "making" of the artisan and the laborer—became extremely tenuous.[37]

The work of art as creative endeavor, Baudelaire noticed, was in danger of extinction. The attack came from two fronts. It was not only that the merchandise threatened to completely change the character of everyday objects, in addition to this, the reproduction techniques ruined the idea of originality implied in artistic doing, a theme that Walter Benjamin would later deal with extensively. Baudelaire's solution was as bold as it was risky: if the commodity was to invade daily life, art should not be far behind. For this, the work of art would had to become a commodity of sorts, but one that was not subject to "the tyranny of the economic and the ideology of progress."[38] Thus, art would have to integrate itself into daily life, as the competition had already done, but it had to do so by its own rules. The work of art, Agamben tells us, was to become an *absolute commodity*, a new type of object "in which the process of fetishization would be pushed to the point of annihilating the reality of the commodity as such.

> A commodity in which use-value and exchange value reciprocally cancel out each other, whose value therefore consists in its uselessness and whose use in its intangibility, is no longer a commodity: the absolute commodification of the work of art is also the most radical abolition of the commodity.[39]

The project of annihilation of commodity fetishism devised by Baudelaire took a particular path: the *avant-garde* that inherited its spirit advocated the dissolution of the separation between the spheres of art and life Hence, the late nineteenth century's cry for *l'art pour l'art* was taken as the enjoyment of art for its own sake when, in reality it was, according to Agamben, "the *destruction* of art worked by art."[40]

The dismantling of the artistic edifice was drenched in esotericism and magic from the very beginning, an influence of great importance for art, literature and science long before Baudelaire came into the scene. Goethe, Coleridge, Shelley and Blake drank from these waters, as did the early Balzac, from the hand of Swedenborg. Later on Vasili Kandinsky and Piet Mondrian would join the Theosophical Society and Paul Klee Rudolf Steiner's Anthroposophy, while Kazimir Malevich explored the work of P.D. Ouspensky, the most illustrious disciple of George Ivanovich Gurdjieff. The relations of surrealism with occultism and magic are well documented and, indeed, as the movement slowly fell out of the public eye many of its members embraced mysticism and withdrew from social and political activity.

Mainstream art history has tried to play down the importance of these influences in favor of the *avant garde's* supposedly prodigious creativity. "Perhaps the time has come," says Jacobo Siruela,

> to revise this old cultural cliché, born out of prejudice and misinformation, with less suspicious eyes, which tries to erase from the cultural panorama a rich diversity of underground currents despite the influence they exerted since the eighteenth century on many poets, writers and modern artists and even on scientists, when, apart from any consideration of value, they sometimes turn out to be very necessary to understand the spiritual climate in which many remarkable works of our culture were forged [...]⁴¹

The *avant-garde* project for the transfiguration and dissolution of art opens up an unusual possibility that only Debord and the Situationists developed in full. The *decommodification* of everyday space and objects leads to the creation of a new way of relating to things, of an "unreality" free of the fetishistic alienation that lies hidden within the reality imposed by the commodity. Aware of this *seed of unreality*, Debord and company proposed the construction of situations that would expand this new "territory."

The construction of a new reality—a counter-creation that subverts the metaphysics of capitalism—is a project with overtly demiurgic overtones, something that is not at all surprising if we bear in mind that marxism itself can be understood as a form of gnosticism. This argument was put forth by Austrian philosopher Ernst Topitsch who followed "the gnostic myth of the fall, alienation, and blindness of the humans deceived by the Demiurge down into the Hegelian myth of alienation of the Spirit and then into the Marxist myth of the alienation of humankind through religion and of its salvation through the exercise of 'positive science.' […] in Marx's theory, the place of the gnostic elect is taken by the proletarians, who possess the secret lore of class struggle, as well as a true class awareness as against the false, alienated, or ideoligizing conscience of everyone else."[42]

However, the gnostic character Debord's work is twofold, as one of his favorite literary works, *The Chants of Maldoror* by the Count of Lautréamont—the pseudonym of the french-uruguayan writer Isidore-Lucien Ducasse—is a gnostic goldmine. The heretical component in Lautréamont's work is part of a long lineage of authors that, according to Harold Bloom, begins with Valentine, the poetic genius of the Alexandrian gnostics, and passes through Nerval, Blake, Novalis, Rilke and Yeats, authors in which "gnosticism is indistinguishable from imaginative genius." I venture, says Bloom, "after a lifetime's meditation upon Gnosticism, the judgement that it is pragmatically *the religion of literature.*"[43] He then points out that this religious current generates a type of knowledge that

> frees the creative mind from theology, from historicizing, and from any divinity that is totally distinct from what is most imaginative about the self. A God cut from the most inmost self is a hangman God, as Joyce called him, the God who originates death. Gnosticism, as the religion of the literary genius, repudiates the hangman God.[44]

This rejection of the God of death, the spurious god who stole the creation from the true and ineffable god within, the Gnostic God, implies that the heretical author must assume the role of a creative demiurge, whose natural place in the order of things is that of the perpetual antagonist.

The Chants of Maldoror presents us with a particularly clear exposition of this worldview. The feeling that dictates that you are not to achieve what you desire prevails Lautréamont's work, a consummate melancholic. Maldoror is a supernatural character, a fallen angel trapped in the flesh who calls himself "plunderer of celestial floatsam." With his character Lautréamont draws an exceptional portrait of the Gnostic archetype in two of its facets: on the one hand as an archangel of evil in an unceasing struggle against the *God in The Brothel*, as he calls the God of death, and on the another as a libertine given to outbursts of a strange and perturbing violence. Like a radical antinomist, Maldoror mutilates and perverts to inflict damage on the work of the God in the brothel, so that souls are freed and return to the path of true light, a Luciferian light. The morbidity of his actions is justified.

The world that Lautréamont depicts in his poem is a prison for the human spirit which, deluded, has always believed "[...] that he was filled with goodness mingled with only a minute quantity of evil.

> By dragging out his heart and his life-thread into the light of day I taught him the rude lesson that, on the contrary, he is made up of evil mingled with only a minute quantity of good which the lawmakers have been put to it to conserve.[45]

This minute quantity of good corresponds, in Gnosticisms such as Catharism, to the divine spark that humans inherited from the true God before falling into the damnation of the flesh, and which must be purified and flagellated. This struggle makes Maldoror a Promethean character, a bringer of light that must expose the deceptions of the false God for the whole world to see:

> I shall strike your hollow carcase with such violence that I guarantee to beat out the fragments of intelligence that you would not bestow upon man because you would have been jealous of making him equal to yourself, and that you have impudently kept hidden in your guts, cunning scoundrel, as if you had not known that some day I should ferret it out with my ever open eye, filch it from you, and share it with my fellow men.[46]

Lautréamont's influence on Debord—which implies the latter's covert affiliation to the Gnostic archetype—is particularly palpable in his conception of the modern world as a spiritual wasteland that must be restored to its original splendor and unity. Since only the true God can animate a true world—in the sense of impregnating it with *anima*—the demiurge of modern economy can only give life to a *pseudo-anima*: the spectacle. This phantasmatic delusion represents the creation of the god of death (the realm of commodity fetishism), which must be destroyed in order to return the world to its original condition, to the richness of experience prior to the fall, that is, to the arrival of the commodity and its phantasms. The feeling of being trapped in a spurious creation is essential to understanding the magical aspect of Debord's work.

In his prologue to the fourth Italian edition of *The Society of The Spectacle*, Giorgio Agamben unveils an interesting relationship between Hebrew mysticism and the Debordian spectacle. The point of articulation is the *Shekinah*, "the last of the ten Sefirot or attributes of the divinity, the one that expresses divine presence itself, its manifestation or habitation on Earth: its 'word'."[47] Traditionally, the Shekinah is understood as the feminine moment of divinity, the figure of its presence in the world, a definition that allows us to link the last of the Sefirot with the role of Venus in the Hermetic tradition and with that of Diana in Actaeon's myth.

In a legend that appears in the Talmud "four rabbis, entered Heaven: Ben Azzai, Ben Zoma, Aher and Rabbi Akiba... Ben Azzai cast a glance and died... Ben Zoma looked and went crazy... Aher cut the branches. Rabbi Akiba came out uninjured."[48] Aher's cutting of the branches, says Agamben

> represents the sin of Adam who, instead of contemplating the Sefirot in their totality, preferred to contemplate only the last one, isolating it from the others—thereby separating the tree of science from the tree of life. Like Adam, Aher represents humanity insofar as, making knowledge his own destiny and his own specific power, he isolates knowledge and the word, which are nothing other than the most complete form of the manifestation of God (the Shekinah), from the other Sefirot in which he reveals himself.[49]

The relationship between the Shekinah—which is nothing other than the manifestation of the countenance of the goddess— and the spectacle is as follows: when manifestation is separated from the whole, as it happens with Aher's cutting of the branches, "the revealed and the manifested—and hence, common and shareable—being becomes separate from the thing revealed and comes in between the latter and human beings,"[50] that is, it becomes an autonomous entity that takes on a life of its own and isolates the human not only from the divine but from the world itself. "In this condition of exile, the Shekinah loses its positive power and becomes harmful (the cabalists say that it "sucks the milk of evil")."[51] This malevolent Shekinah, the countenance of the world that starts acting on its own, is the cabalistic figuration of the Debordian spectacle, in which the human, prey of its own desires and ambitions, starts being devoured by them as Actaeon was devoured by his dogs.

Debord's spectacle as demiurgy

It often happens that the staunchest of critics are the best judges of character of their victims. French philosopher Frédéric Schiffter, who wrote the most destructive criticism of the work and person of Debord, entitled *Contre Debord*,[52] convincingly argues that the work of this philosopher is actually a "metaphysical offensive" against modern capitalist society. And he is not wrong. As his Gnostic and esoteric influences show, the attack Debord undertakes against contemporary society is essentially magical: if the spectacle can be considered an act of demiurgy, Debord's and the situationists' response is demiurgy as well. One spell undoes another.

For Schiffter, the core of Debord's thought is an interpretation of Rousseau's ideas of "state of nature" and "good savage," which suggest that the original state of humanity is, in essence, a primitive form of communism (an idea also shared by Wilhelm Reich) which degenerated "when commercial exchange shattered the foundations of the community, needs became artificial, exchanges were commodified and societies became unequal."[53] Whether or not the idea of a kind human nature or, at least, in a state of *tabula rasa* is true, as Rousseau would argue, the inequality and alienation inherent to patriarchal societies based on material progress is an incontestable fact, one needs only to stick the head out the window.

Under this frame of mind, says Schiffter, the commodity appears as a diabolical fetish—from *diabolos*, that which disunites—that desacralizes the world and establishes the kingdom of "generalized separation." So far the criticism is true, the root of Debordian thought is religious and magical, but is this necessarily "wrong"? Debord's iconoclasm, his religious hatred for representation, is the suspicion and aversion of anyone who has realized the political and economic application of the phantasms of the imagination. Beyond this point Schiffter debunks Debord as a resentful hack and his contribution as the hallucination of a despotic alcoholic and charlatan. Alcoholic and despot, beyond any doubt; charlatan, as any drunkard, but in spite of all the flaws one can impute Debord, the fact remains that his work fits perfectly within the magical tradition developed by Ficino and Bruno. On the other hand, the present seems bent on confirming his theories.

When Debord wrote *The Society of The Spectacle*, his most important book and the most rigorous compendium of his thought, the avant-garde and counterculture spirits were heated. By the time it was published in late 1967, they were about to blow. And explode they did. Five months later, in May 1968, thousands of students from Nanterre, the Sorbonne and other European and North American universities manifested their preoccupation with their role in a world that resembled a huge mechanical and ruthless beast. Debord, Merrifield says, "attempted to delve in the belly of the fabulous beast, showing how commodity logistics penetrated new depths of modern life."[54] The logic of how commodity fetishism had begun to dominate human life was clear and simple:

> An earlier stage in the economy's domination of social life entailed an obvious downgrading of *being* into *having* that left its stamp on all human endeavor. The present stage, in which social life is completely taken over by the accumulated products of the economy, entails a generalized shift from *having* to *appearing*: all effective "having" must now derive both its immediate prestige and its ultimate *raison d'etre* from appearances.[55]

Thus, the spectacle is the realm of appearances, an *"affirmation* of appearances and an identification of all human social life with appearances."[56] But this is not a realm we can perceive directly. Like every form of fetishism it is the *positive representation of a negative reality*, or, in Debord's words "a negation [of life] that has taken on a *visible form.*"[57]

According to Andy Merrifield, the difficulty to fully understand the Debordian notion of spectacle is that it "suggests that the separation between appearance and essence (Marx's trusty definition of science) has, like a piece of elastic, been stretched to such degree that these two opposing ends of reality have now snapped and reformed as one. An epistemological duality has recoiled into an ontological unity: essence is really appearance, and appearance really is essence. Society's image of itself *is* the real reality of society, its reality an image; society's form is society's content, its content is its form. It says nothing more than this."[58] Thus, as über-fetish, spectacular reality presents itself as

> an enormous positivity, out of reach and beyond dispute. All it says is: "Everything that appears is good; whatever is good will appear." The attitude that it demands in principle is the same passive acceptance that it has already secured by means of its

seeming incontrovertibility, and indeed by its monopolization of the realm of appearances.[59]

The passive acceptance of which Debord speaks is what I called *desidia americana*, that desiring and passive idleness that must be satisfied by consuming constantly. Now, we can characterize this form of desire (*desidia*)— which more than *americana* has now become global—as the product of commodity fetishism, which restricts human beings to the role of mere spectators. Because of this, Debord calls the spectacle "the sun that never sets over the empire of modern passivity"[60]. It is the very consolidation of the democratization of desire that underlies the so-called "American Dream."

Now, understood as the monopoly of appearances, the spectacle can be coherently characterized as a magic spell, a representation that emerges from the twilight between reality and its negative twin, and which constantly pulls us towards the phantasms. The *phantasmata* that make up the spectacle are "autonomous images" that, like a psychological phantasm, seize the unconscious of an individual, and take on a life of their own, but not in a person's inner world but in the unconscious of a whole society. From a magical perspective, the spectacle is *the externalization of the phantasm*, its passage from the individual unconscious to the collective unconscious where it is consolidated as a double mirror, a *Janus bifrons* that reflects exchange value and phantasms towards the interior of the individual and towards society as well. The spectacle is a *specular structure* that encloses individuals in a perpetual cycle of images and robs them of their psychic energy; a cube whose interior walls are all mirrors. Thus, with the consolidation of spectacular society "the real consumer has become a consumer of illusions. The commodity is this materialized illusion, and the spectacle is its general expression."[61]

Debord's idea of merchandise as a "materialized illusion" is intimately related to the idea of unreality, or *negative reality* I formulated above, which depends on a relationship that treats consumer goods as a sexual fetish, that is, as the presence of an absence. The spectacle is thus an unreality that in its eagerness to represent the unattainable, the negativity implicit in any fetish, leads the whole of consumer society towards the neurotic quest of the fetishist, the believer in love and the Cathar. But while the classical varieties of this form of neurosis could not find a way to capture the negativity of their objects of desire, the owners of consumer culture stumbled upon a way to create a kingdom for the fetish and its phantasms: the free market.

This externalization of the spectacle's phantasms in the marketplace derives largely from a particularity of commodity metaphysics that we addressed briefly in the Intermezzo. In Chapter IV of *Capital*, Marx states that value, whether in the form of money or a commodity, constitutes an "automatic subject" that acquires "the occult quality of being able to add value to itself," that is, to gain value in each market cycle. Thus, when phantasms began to be associated with commodities, a very particular phenomenon took place: these images began to "add value to themselves" according to the status of their base commodities—or, in other words, to acquire exchange value—a process which gave them a life of their own apart from their activity within each individual. Life not only in the psychological sphere but in the economic one as well. *Phantasms became alive in the market*. It is important to make clear that, by acquiring the ability to produce their own phantasms, any product available in the market becomes a *venator-commodity* capable of finding and stalking its own prey.

A great deal of Debord's critique of spectacular capitalism lies in his observation that the mechanisms of modern economy penetrate all the levels of human life, to the point that they become its determining factor. This is why

> the spectacle is able to subject human beings to itself because the economy has already totally subjugated them. It is nothing other than the economy developing for itself. It is at once a faithful reflection of the production of things and a distorting objectification of the producers.[62]

Debord's reference to the spectacle as "the economy developing for itself" alludes to early modernity's idea which states that it is perfectly possible to create a mechanism capable of acting of its own volition and which, as we saw in the Intermezzo, is intimately linked to theology. This *anima machinalis* is the functional principle of ecology, cybernetics and free market economics, of any human ideology that seeks to superimpose an *automatic order* on the world. Now, if the spectacle can be defined as a magic spell, it is a spell of a new variety, an *automatic spell* that adjusts constantly to the needs and changes of its system, which mutates with the fluctuations of the economy. A spell that is, at least to an extent, *self-*

sustaining. In its current phase market economy becomes a gigantic esoteric machine that spews out one commercial spell after another.

The main effect of this magic spell, Debord tells us, is to turn the world on its head, to put its negative facet above the positive and have us sink into a neurotic and fetishistic passivity, a self-absorption in which "the true is a moment of the false."[63] In this inverted world, exchange value has triumphed definitively over use value, making the fetishistic character of the merchandise prevail over its materiality. This world turned inside out has its origin in the separation that Debord fought along with the Letterists and Situationists. A world in which social relationships have been completely undone and exchange value rules over any other way of assigning meaning, in which people have been cut off from their livelihoods and, ultimately, from their own lives; in which "the social relationships between workers and owners, between minimum wage toilers and rich bosses, between third world farmers and Wall Street stockbrokers"[64] have been eclipsed by the hidden logic of the commodity. This is a world in which Marx's "estranged labor," says Merrifield, becomes "estranged life." The society of the spectacle is the moment when the psychological world of the human being, his phantasms, are projected towards the exterior while, at the same time, the external world, represented by the market, invades inner life. "The moment when the commodity has reached the *total occupation* of social life."[65] This moment should mark a turning point in our idea of reality: since the spectacle has turned the world into another commodity, its fetishization is equivalent to the complete fetishization of reality.

Thus, the spectacle is the realm of alienation whose roots sink into "the oldest of all social specializations, the specialization of power."[66] Hence, it is, in any of its degrees of intensity and penetration, one of the byproducts of any hierarchical society, and in particular of those in which power has been monopolized by a specific group that determines the norms of production and social interaction. A system whose intrinsic purpose is the division and effective isolation of in*dividuals* (those who should not be able to be divided), and its by-product neurosis and mental illness.

> Workers do not produce themselves, they produce a power independent of themselves. The *success* of this production, the abundance it generates, is experienced by the producers as an

> *abundance of dispossession.* As their alienated products accumulate, all time and space become foreign to them. The spectacle is the map of this new world, a map that is identical to the territory it represents. The forces that have escaped us *display themselves* to us in all their power.[67]

The key to this matter is separation, which Debord calls "the alpha and omega of the spectacle."[68] Its originary form is "the institutionalization of the social division of labor in the form of class divisions [that] had given rise to an earlier, religious form of contemplation: the mythical order with which every power has always camouflaged itself."[69] Thus, the process of specialization which according to Wilhelm Reich is at the root of monogamy, sexual repression and, ultimately, the current epidemic of neurosis, is the same process that originates the phantasmagoria of the spectacle. On the other hand, Debord's passage hints at an idea as interesting as heretical: namely that the separation of the human from a truly vital form of experience, originating from the core of biological energy, would lay at the origin of the human religious impulse, in which "the sacred justified the cosmic and ontological order that corresponded to the interests of the masters […]"[70]

Given this conjunction between the spectacular and the religious, Debord affirms that "the spectacle is the material reconstruction of the religious illusion."

> Spectacular technology has not dispersed the religious mists into which human beings had projected their own alienated powers, it has merely brought those mists down to earth, to the point that even the most mundane aspects of life have become impenetrable and unbreathable. The illusory paradise that represented a total denial of earthly life is no longer projected into the heavens, it is embedded in earthly life itself. The spectacle is the technological version of the exiling of human powers into a "world beyond"; the culmination of humanity's *internal* separation.[71]

The spectacle, always closed in on itself, is its own fetish and religion. Psychological and economic alienation are not its results, they are its own origin: "its means and ends are identical."[72] Now, Debord asserts that "the reigning economic system is a *vicious circle of isolation*,"[73] this tautological character recalls the autism of the pneumatic circle of Brunian magic in which the flow of psychic energy constantly revolves between the subject and its phantasms.

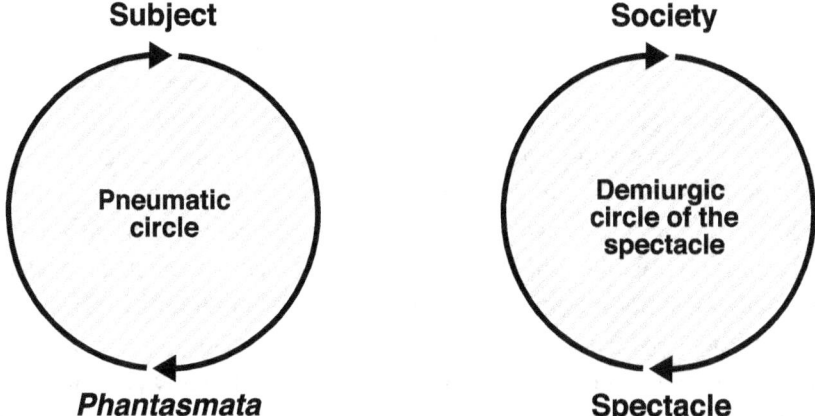

However, with the spectacle, the pneumatic circle becomes a demiurgic circle that envelops the whole of society through commodity metaphysics, a circle in which "the commodity contemplates itself in a world of its own making."[74] Thus, the spectacle becomes a superstructure that feeds on psychic energy, going round the circuit time and again, renewing itself with each new economic offering which, of course, comes with its own *phantasmata*.

"When the real world is transformed into mere images," says Debord,

> mere images become real beings —dynamic figments that provide the direct motivations for a hypnotic behavior. Since the spectacle's job is to use various specialized mediations in order to show us a world that can no longer be directly grasped, it naturally elevates the sense of sight to the special preeminence once occupied by touch: the most abstract and easily deceived sense is the most readily adaptable to the generalized abstraction of present-day society. But the spectacle is not merely a matter of images, nor even of images plus sounds. It is whatever escapes people's activity, whatever eludes their practical reconsideration and correction. It is the opposite of dialogue. Wherever *representation* becomes independent, the spectacle regenerates itself.[75]

Here I should highlight that Reich's opposition to sexual fantasies which induce the individual to embark on a neurotic quest for the beloved via the phantasm, becomes in Debord a radical opposition to representation, which he considers the very antithesis of the richness of experience lived, so to speak, in real time. This conjunction between Reich and Debord's theories, stemming from Marx's influence on both, makes the spectacle the most pervasive and widespread source of neurosis in modern societies.

Now, we should mention that although the spectacle emerged from the specialization of work and the division of society into classes, its main source of sustenance is the psychological energy of its members, more specifically the libidinal discharges that encourage the constant production and consumption of *phantasmata* and commodities. Given the relationship between neurosis and commodity metaphysics, the libido trapped in the pneumatic network of bonds weaved by the spectacle can be understood as a form of *mitigated collective hysteria* in which the crisis is resolved in the form of unrestrained consumption. As in the case of masochism, in which the level of desire and repression escalates constantly, consumption as a pneumatic form of relief only works temporarily and, as the system becomes overloaded with libido, it becomes imperative to release it once again by consuming. This process takes place constantly and only in some particular instances of the calendar consumption is openly ritualized and resembles in its debauchery the Saturnalias of the ancient world and the carnivals of the present. The *Black Friday* is the St. Vitus dance of commercial culture.

As the prototypical economic structure of our time, the spectacle represents "*capital* accumulated to the point that it becomes images."[76] The phantasms of the spectacle are thus a sublimation of their basic substance, which, by going time and again through the retort of market economy, lose their materiality and dissolve into *an all-pervading spirit*. This metaphor culminates the alchemical interpretation of modern economics proposed by H.C. Binswanger, in which the production of capital depends on the transmutation of *philosophical salt* (capital) through the marriage of mercury (currency) and sulphur (property, commodity) via a successive process of *solutio* and *coagulatio*. Once the philosopher's stone of capital is achieved, it takes on a life of its own and starts adding value to itself in each new cycle until it dissipates into a vibratory aura made up of value and phantasm.

6. Economy, Neurosis and Spectacle

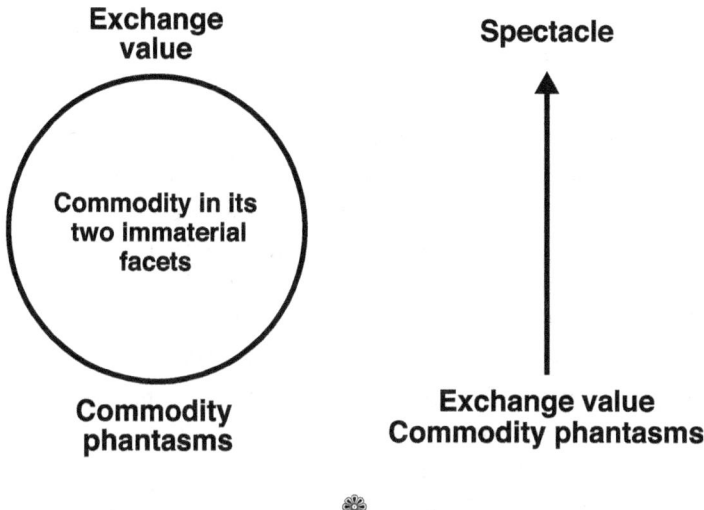

At this point it may be necessary to clarify that the spectacle is more than the fetishization of the totality of commodities present in the market, it is the complete *fetishization of the social reality of modern human beings*. Thus, more than a cluster of images—of *phantasmata* emanating from commodities—the spectacle "is a social relationship between people that is mediated by images."[77] The importance of the spectacle rests not so much in its imaginal nature, but in the relationships that these images impose, which act as a powerful instrument of pneumatic manipulation. In this sense, the spectacle is nothing other than the *economic representation* of the network of desire proposed by Giordano Bruno.

"Understood in its totality," says Debord,

> the spectacle is both the result and the project of the dominant mode of production. It is not a mere decoration added to the real world. It is the very heart of this real society's unreality. In all of its particular manifestations—news, propaganda, advertising, entertainment—the spectacle represents the dominant *model* of life.[78]

The "unreality" Debord talks about is the daily bread of every contemporary society. It takes place wherever the market and the commodity are, wherever the degree of economic and psychological alienation has separated the human from its means of production and, ultimately, from himself. Very gradually, since the mid-nineteenth century the working class, which Marx called *proletariat*, became the victim of a new form of domination and slavery: consumerism. As the market expanded its networks and supply began to exceed demand, the collaboration of the working class became necessary. The worker was freed from the contempt of his masters and, at least in appearance, began to be "treated like a grownup, with a great show of politeness, in his new role as a consumer."[79] To this end, the economy had to absorb the portion of the worker's life it had not yet colonized: leisure time, a move with which it took effective control of all aspects of human life. This is how "alienated consumption became just as much a duty for the masses as alienated production. The society's *entire sold labor* has become a *total commodity* whose constant turnover must be maintained at all cost."[80] In this sense, we have all been *proletarianized*, we all work and, with our earnings, we consume spinning the wheels of commodity, market and spectacle.

The integration of individuals to this system, says Debord,

> means bringing isolated individuals together as *isolated individuals*. Factories, cultural centers, tourist resorts and housing developments are specifically designed to foster this type of pseudocommunity. The same collective isolation prevails even within the family cell, where the omnipresent receivers of spectacular messages fill the isolation with the ruling images—images that derive their full power precisely from that isolation.[81]

The feeling of being surrounded by people and yet completely alone must be one of the most common in the Western world; so widespread as to go unnoticed by its supposed normality. The unreality of the spectacle is the place of collective exile that modern humans have devised for themselves, the "non-place" where our whole social existence takes place, where we all share the delusion of being united through commodities and services, of participating through elections, charities and pop-politics, of leading full lives filled with a unidimensional phantasmagoria, with nothing that we can call truly human apart from its capacity to arouse our most basic desires. The capitalist mode of production which forces "producers to participate in the construction of the world is also what excludes them from it. What brings people into relation with each other by liberating them from their local and national limitations is also what keeps them apart."[82] *Unity in separation*, a phrase with clear nuances of George Orwell's *doublethink* (the act of simultaneously accepting two mutually contradictory beliefs as correct), could be the very slogan of the debordian spectacle.

Now, how did this unreality came into being? The unreality of the spectacle is an *abstract form of space* that emerged with the operations of market economy, it is nothing less than the process of cultural and economic homogenization that we now call "globalization," its spatio-temporal byproduct. With prophetic precision Debord argues that capitalist production,

> has unified space, breaking down the boundaries between one society and the next. This unification is at the same time an extensive and intensive process of *banalization*. Just as the accumulation of commodities mass-produced for the abstract space of the market shattered all regional and legal barriers and all the Medieval guild restrictions that maintained the quality of craft production, it also undermined the autonomy and quality of places. This homogenizing power is the heavy artillery that has battered down all the walls of China.[83]

Thus, spectacular unreality is banal, abstract and homogenous, a spell which gives rise to the non-place which we all inhabit without regard to our language or nationality. The global market has become a space which does not exist and yet—precisely because of its non-existence—contains all the illusions and phantasms which constantly invade us and which we have been conditioned to desire.

As in the case of space, the separation that underlies the spectacle has an essential effect on the category of time. According to Debord, the social appropriation of time is inseparable from the division of the society into classes, so that the power of the ruling class does not consist only of the appropriation of the means of economic production but also of the *temporal surplus value* that results from these means. Thus,

> The owners of this historical surplus value are the only ones in a position to know and enjoy real events. Separated from the collective organization of time associated with the repetitive production at the base of social life, this historical time flows independently above its own static community. This is the time of adventure and war, the time in which the masters of cyclical society pursue their personal histories; it is also the time that

emerges in the clashes with foreign communities that disrupt the unchanging social order.[84]

The importance of the concept of time for capitalism should not be underestimated, it is its basic value unit, the essential and abstract measure with which the effort to manufacture any commodity can be estimated. Moreover, as with space, capitalism has unified time into a single stream composed of equal and abstract fragments, distancing it from human time—a time composed of lived experiences—to turn it into a *time of things*, a commodified time governed by the laws of logistics and production, of supply and demand. "Time is money" is the motto of a society in which human experiences have given way to an experience of time determined by the commodity and the market, a devalued time that "is the complete opposite of time as 'terrain of human development'."[85] This form of time, completely stripped of its qualitative character and imposed by the global market, is the time of the global spectacle.

This commodified time, "an infinite accumulation of equivalent intervals,"[86] is abstract and homogeneous as the notion of space that accompanies it, but above all is "itself a consumable commodity, one that recombines everything that the disintegration of the old unitary societies had differentiated into private life, economic life, and political life."

> The entire consumable time of modern society ends up being treated as a raw material for various new products put on the market as socially controlled uses of time.[87]

Production time creates time for consumption and entertainment, which in turn sustains traditional forms of production and creates new ones. Therefore, Debord argues, commodified time is *pseudocyclic*. In fact, this type of time time is connatural to the *demiurgic circle of the spectacle*, the most recent version of the pneumatic circle. Upon entering this demiurgic circle time starts running in a closed loop sustained by the commodity.

> Pseudocyclical time is associated with the consumption of modern economic survival—the augmented survival in which everyday experience is cut off from decision making and subjected no longer to the natural order, but to the pseudo-nature created by alienated labor. It is thus quite natural that it

echoes the old cyclical rhythm that governed survival in preindustrial societies [...]⁸⁸

This pseudocyclic character of the spectacle coincides with our assertion that the pneumatic circle is a deficient re-elaboration of the mythical structure of consciousness. Now, if the demiurgic circle is a new version of the mythical circle, its social application through the debordian spectacle is the establishment of a new form of cyclical time in which everything happens *eternally* according to the cycles of the market; a constant movement that does not entail change of any kind. Just as the lover is trapped inside a pneumatic circle that binds him to the phantasms of his beloved and prevents him from leaving, the consumers/spectators are bound to the phantasms of the commodity, which keeps them outside reality and prevents them from participating in any significant way. (*I am so pleased to want thus that I suffer agreeably, and have so much joy in my pain that I am sick with delight.*) At the mercy of commodified time, humans themselves end up becoming commodities which, eternalized and objectified by the spectacle, have only one possibility: to continue feeding the system that oppresses and alienates them from reality.

The reason why capitalism has been so effective at halting, subverting or absorbing any economic or social trend that threatens its hegemony is this: keeping people away from reality, locked away in spectacular space and time, is the best and subtlest way to prevent any genuine kind of revolution or lasting social change. Few have captured the ability of the spectacle to absorb any incipient outbreak of discontent or rebellion like disgruntled comedian Bill Hicks:

> I know what all the marketing people are thinking right now. "Oh, you know what Bill's doing? He's going for that anti-marketing dollar, that's a good market, he's very smart." Oh man, I'm not doing that, you fucking evil scumbags! "Ohhh you know what Bill is doing now, he's going for that righteous indignation dollar, that's a big dollar, a lot of people are feeling that indignation, we've done research, huge market, he's doing a good thing."

The ways in which the establishment deprives the population of its ability to disagree are variations of a general *modus operandi*: to anticipate public opinion and then hijack it in order to control it. "Whenever power is seriously in crisis," says Giorgio Agamben, "the media establishment apparently dissociates itself from the regime of which it is an integral part so as to govern and direct the general discontent lest it turn itself into revolution."[89] The absorption of the human capacity to dissent represents the moment of the complete colonization of human individuality by an economic system that imposes a falsified social life; the realm of automatic resignation.

This colonization of exterior (economic) and interior (psychological) life takes place in both right-wing and left-wing regimes. By the beginning of the sixties Debord had already noticed that "the state, irrespective of its ideological stripe, was itself subsumed within this system, and increasingly became a facilitator of spectacular capitalism"[90]. The reason for the omnipresence of the spectacle at both ends of the political spectrum is that, according to Wilhelm Reich, communist states like the Soviet Union were never true state socialisms, "but rigid capitalist states in the strict Marxian sense of the word.

> According to Marx, the social condition of "capitalism" does not, as the vulgar marxist believed, derive from the existence of individual capitalists, but from the existence of the specific "capitalist modes of production." It derives, in short, from *exchange economy* and not from *use economy*, from the *paid labor* of masses of people and from *surplus* production, whether this surplus accrues to the state *above* the society, or to the individual capitalists through their appropriation of social production. In this strict marxian sense the capitalist system continues to exist in Russia.[91]

This being the case, according to Debord the difference between leftist and rightist regimes lies in the specific use of their spectacular tactics, which can be grouped in two categories: the diffuse and the concentrated. The diffuse spectacle, Debord tells us,

> is associated with commodity abundance, with the undisturbed development of modern capitalism. Here each individual commodity is justified in the name of the grandeur of the total commodity production, of which the spectacle is a laudatory catalog.[92]

Thus, the diffuse spectacle presents a unified catalog of *phantasmata* that consumers/spectators can access. However, each of these phantasm/commodities is only a fragment of the totality of the spectacle, whereby the supposed happiness and realization that accompanies its acquisition will always be subject to a subsequent acquisition that brings it closer to the unattainable totality. *Nonetheless, no matter how hard he tries, the fetishist will never manage to get closer to his fetish.*

On the other hand, the concentrated spectacle takes place mainly in left-wing regimes, which Debord calls "bureaucratic capitalism" because of its typical administrative structure. The commodity bureaucracy appropriates, he tells us,

> is the total social labor, and what it sells back to the society is that society's wholesale survival. The dictatorship of the bureaucratic economy cannot leave the exploited masses any significant margin of choice because it has had to make all the choices itself, and any choice made independently of it, whether regarding food or music or anything else, thus amounts to a declaration of war against it. This dictatorship must be enforced by permanent violence.[93]

In the concentrated spectacle phantasms are administered through a central figure that becomes "the guarantor of the system's totalitarian cohesion."

> Everyone must magically identify with this absolute star or disappear. This master of everyone else's nonconsumption is the heroic image that disguises the absolute exploitation entailed by the system of primitive accumulation accelerated by terror. If the entire Chinese population has to study Mao to the point of identifying with Mao, this is because there is *nothing else they can be*. The dominion of the concentrated spectacle is a police state.[94]

The distillation of all pneumatic power into a *phantom dictator* and its implementation through a police state, reveals the point of contact, the hinge so to speak, that joins the concentrated spectacle with the diffuse. While in the concentrated spectacle the scarcity of commodities forces the concentration of all the potential for manipulation in an *alpha phantasm*, in the diffuse spectacle the abundance of commodities, and its phantasms, coalesces in a number of pneumatic figures that fulfil the same objective as the dictator; a fact that leads to the appearance of a new variety of *animarum venator*. Thus, the dictator is the concentrated representation and the analogue of one of the main figures of the diffuse spectacle: the celebrity, who is nothing more than a dictator of opinion; opinion on culture, fashion, culinary, politics, lifestyle, sports and even religion and science. *The celebrity is the hidden point of union between the so-called democratic and totalitarian states.*

The appearance of the celebrity, whose lineage can be traced back to the dandy and the phantasmagoria of the nobilities and royalties of old,[95] does not rest exclusively in his relationship with the dictator. Since the "the general commodity-form continues onward toward its absolute realization,"[96] it was only natural that it would eventually absorb the whole of human life. In this sense, the celebrity represents the complete commodification of the human, which brings together the totality of the spectacle by projecting it into images of socially available roles. Thus,

> as specialists of *apparent life*, stars serve as superficial objects that people can identify with in order to compensate for the fragmented productive specializations that they actually live. The function of these celebrities is to act out various lifestyles or sociopolitical viewpoints in a *full, totally free manner*.[97]

Since it is the human embodiment of the spectacle, the star or celebrity is "the enemy of his own individuality as of the individuality of others,"[98] a consumer that is simultaneously consumed, Actaeon and hound at one and the same time. In its most advanced phase, a celebrity is a human merchandise completely stripped of interiority, a *medium* so to speak, that channels the magical operations that were previously carried out exclusively by the market. In fact, it would not be off the mark to asure that, as a human-commodity, the celebrity has absorbed its metaphysical qualities and given them a human countenance. Moreover, since a celebrity is a human figure that must have emptied itself of interiority in order to become a commodity—let's take Tom Cruise and Jared Leto as prototypical examples—it has made the commodities' magical operations even more effective. *The perfect hunter will be the one who can project and stimulate desire in others without actually feeling it.* Hence, the celebrities' ability to become fetishes for the masses and, by virtue of this attribute, to operate on large sectors of society with the same ease with which political figures and religious leaders had done so in the past.

The appearance of the celebrity is an integral part of the general movement of the modern manipulative impulse: from the collective hysterias of the Middle Ages and early modernity to the revolutions of the nineteenth century and the mass movements of the twentieth, to the emergence of disciplines such as public relations, advertising and marketing, celebrity is one of the most recent steps in the movement that we determined in the fourth chapter, a progression that goes from the general to the specific and personalized, to the control not of groups as such but of individuals *en masse*. As we will examine in the last part, this trend will reach its apex with the arrival of digital technology and social networking, which represent a new level of spectacular colonization.

But one of the most important and far reaching developments of the spectacle in recent years predates its inclusion in the digital realm. It lies in the unification of the diffuse and concentrated forms of the spectacle into what Debord call its integrated form:

> The integrated spectacle shows itself to be simultaneously concentrated and diffuse, and ever since the fruitful union of the two has learnt to employ both these qualities on a grander scale. Their former mode of application has changed considerably. As regards concentration, the controlling center has now become occult never to be occupied by a known leader, or clear ideology. And on the diffuse side, the spectacle has never before put its mark to such a degree on almost the full range of socially produced behavior and objects. For the final sense of the integrated spectacle is this—that it has integrated itself into reality to the same extent as it was describing it, and that it was reconstructing it as it was describing it. As a result, this reality no longer confronts the integrated spectacle as something alien. When the spectacle was concentrated, the greater part of surrounding society escaped it; when diffuse, a small part; today, no part. The spectacle has spread itself to the point where it now permeates all reality. It was easy to predict in theory what has been quickly and universally demonstrated by practical experience of economic reason's relentless accomplishments: that the globalisation of the false was also the falsification of the globe.[99]

From this fragment derive two main issues that we will investigate in the last part. First, the complete penetration of the demiurgic sphere of the spectacle on real life, a matter whose history is intimately linked to the development and appropriation of the twentieth century countercultures; and second, the emergence of the most virulent form of integrated spectacle in a place with a long concentrated tradition followed by the abrupt appearance of the diffuse variety: post-Soviet Russia.

By the beginning of May, 1968, a regiment of the French *mobile gendarmerie* entered the Sorbonne's main square with the intention of interrupting a revolutionary meeting, a fact that, unsurprisingly, heated up a social environment that was were already about to blow. Thousands of students ripped up the cobblestones from the university's square and the adjacent streets and confronted the police. On May 13 groups of situationists and students redecorated the walls of the Sorbonne and Nanterre with dozens of *détournements*. One of the murals read: "humanity will only be happy the day the last bureaucrat is hung from the guts of the last capitalist." The next day the workers of Sud-Aviation occupied the company's factory at Nantes, Renault's union did the same in Cléon. The printing presses stopped the distribution of newspapers in Paris and the workers' councils joined the student councils, "the working class, at last, declared its unequivocal support for the student movement when rank and filers at Renault-Billancourt took over France's largest factory."[100]

By the end of the month, approximately ten million workers had gone on strike, stopping the assembly lines of dozens of factories. The revolution had become contagious, a civil war seemed inevitable:

> alienation was cast-off, momentarily; freedom was real; capitalized time abandoned. Without trains, cars, Metro and work, leisure time was reclaimed, time lived. Students and workers had reclaimed the contingent situation, had acted spontaneously, had created new situations, and realized what no trade union or party could do, or wanted to do. And yet, as quickly as things erupted, they were almost as speedily violently and ideologically repressed, by the state and the bourgeoise.[101]

May of 1968 lost its momentum and disappeared under the brutal pressure of the establishment. By July everything had returned to its normal state of spectacle. Shortly after, Debord began to leave Paris forever. By the early seventies he had settled with his second wife, Alice Becker-Ho, in a rustic chalet in the village of Champot, near Limoges. There, while he was being surveilled by the French security services, he devoted himself to reading, playing war games and drinking; he ended up sinking into the ethilic chasm that had accompanied him throughout his adult life. Over time his alcoholism degenerated into polyneuritis, an affectation of the nerves located outside the central nervous system, which led him to commit suicide. He shot himself in the heart on November 30, 1994.

Life has a curious and sometimes cruel way of commenting on our deeds. There is no way to know if Debord was surprised when Carlo Freccero, a disciple of his "who became head of Silvio Berlusconi's media empire announced that he had learned his craft from Debord's writings."[102] Surely he must have felt disgusted. On the other hand it is not surprising that someone could use Debord's theses for mass manipulation: all one has to do is "turn them around" and do everything one shouldn't. From this point of view *The Society of The Spectacle* is a sort of inverted image of Bruno's *De Vinculis in Genere*, the most complete manual of media manipulation of the twentieth century. If his ex-disciple's declaration would have revolted him, what happened fifteen years after his death would have made him wallow in his grave. In 2009 Debord was declared a "national treasure" by Nicolas Sarkozy's minister of culture who, after preventing Yale University from acquiring his personal archive, called him 'one of the last great French intellectuals.' "For all his sardonic wit," comments John Gray, "he would have regarded his posthumous respectability as final proof that opposition to the spectacle had ceased to be possible."[103]

The Debordian situation as a demiurgic bubble meant to subsume the spectacular bubble had a limited and ephemeral success, its application *en masse*, as evidenced by the May 1968 revolts, seems determined by factors largely unrelated to the will of the individuals involved. Is it possible to refine the technique of the situationists and fight fire with fire against the spectacle? The answer to this question is beyond the focus of this study and, as we will see below, with the arrival of the so-called "digital age" the magical-spectacular techniques have acquired a subtleness and efficiency hitherto unimaginable. These recent developments imply that if the spells of the spectacle have been refined, the alternatives against it must also be refined as well. The onus is on each of us.

¹ The acronym FSM refers to a finite-state machine, a computing model that allows one of a finite number of states at a given time. Examples of this type of machine are vending machines, elevators and traffic lights.
² Quoted by Fred Turner, *From Counterculture to Cyberculture* (Chicago: The University of Chicago Press, 2006), 2.
³ Anselm Jappe, *Guy Debord* (Berkeley: University of California Press, 1993), 82.
⁴ Andy Merrifield, *Guy Debord* (London: Reaktion Books, 2005), 19.
⁵ Quoted in Merrifield, *Guy Debord*, 16.
⁶ Jappe, Guy Debord, 48.
⁷ Jappe, Guy Debord, 48.
⁸ Jappe, Guy Debord, 47.
⁹ Quoted by Jappe en *Guy Debord*, 49.
¹⁰ Jappe, *Guy Debord*, 49.
¹¹ Jappe, *Guy Debord*, 51.
¹² Merrifield, *Guy Debord*, 45.
¹³ Merrifield, *Guy Debord*, 45.
¹⁴ Walter Benjamin, *Paris - Capital of the Nineteenth Century*. Accessed, April 11, 2018, at: *https://www.scribd.com/document/56428348/Benjamin-W-Paris-Capital-of-the-Nineteenth-Century-NLR*
¹⁵ Merrifield, Guy Debord, 46.
¹⁶ Merrifield, Guy Debord, 47.
¹⁷ The architecture of Brasilia, deeply influenced by Le Corbusier's ideas and by far the most radical of all modernist architectural experiments, allegedly provoked an intense feeling of melancholy in some of its residents. This theory attained such currency that in his book *JQ, Brasília e a grande crise* (Jânio Quadros, Brasília, and the Great Crisis), politician and writer Gileno de Carli blames the abrupt and mysterious resignation of President Quadros on the city's architecture. A relevant fragment taken from the Emily Fay Story's dissertation, *Constructing Development: Brasília and the Making of Modern Brasil*: "Never adequately explained by Quadros, de Carli attempts to make sense of the resignation by presenting a psychological analysis of the man, arguing that living in Brasília intensified Quadros's tendency toward depression and solitude and led directly to his decision to resign. Describing Quadros's daily commute from the residential Palácio da Alvorada to his offices in the Palácio do Planalto across the open cerrado (the brazilian savanna), where the open sky was devoid of all life, with not even a vulture to be seen. The twisted shapes of the trees exacerbated Quadros's psychological pain. His downfall therefore came from Brasília itself, which in de Carli's description, "is a beautifully cruel city... A geometric city, rectangular, linear... [M]ontony is imposed by the lack of contrasts... Fabulously beautiful, it is terribly sad." The last words Quadros spoke before embarking on a plane to return to São Paulo, according to de Carli, were: "Damned city. I will

never return here." (Emily Fay Story, *Constructing Development: Brasília and the Making of Modern Brasil*, 142)

[18] Guy Debord, "Introduction to a Critique of Urban Geography." Accessed, April 11, 2018, at: *http://library.nothingness.org/articles/SI/en/display/2*

[19] Guy Debord, "Theory of the Dérive." Accessed, April 11, 2018, at: *http://www.bopsecrets.org/SI/2.derive.htm.*

[20] Johan Huizinga, *Homo Ludens, a Study of the Play-Element in Culture* (London: Routledge & Kegan Paul, 1949), 10.

[21] Huizinga, *Homo Ludens*, 10.

[22] Huizinga, *Homo Ludens*, 89.

[23] Guy Debord, *The Society of the Spectacle* (New York, Zone Books, 1994), 37.

[24] Internationale Situationniste #1, *Definitions*. Translated by Ken Knabb.

[25] Taken from the prologue to the Spanish edition of *La sociedad del espectáculo* by José Luis Pardo (Valencia: Pre-Textos, 1999), 15.

[26] Guy Debord, "In girum imus nocte et consumimur igni." Accessed, April 11, 2018, at: *http://www.bopsecrets.org/SI/debord.films/ingirum.htm*

[27] Karl Marx, *Economic and Philosophic Manuscripts of 1844* (Moscow: Progress), 312.

[28] Marx, *Capital: A Critique of Political Economy*. Source: First English edition of 1887.

[29] Marx, *Capital: A Critique of Political Economy*. Source: First English edition of 1887.

[30] Agamben, *Stanzas: Word and Phantasm in Western Culture* (Minneapolis: University of Minnesota, 1993), 38.

[31] Debord, *The Society of the Spectacle*, 37.

[32] Agamben, *Stanzas*, 31.

[33] Agamben, *Stanzas*, 31-32.

[34] Agamben, *Stanzas*, 33.

[35] Agamben, *Stanzas*, 37.

[36] Agamben, *Stanzas*, 33.

[37] Agamben, *Stanzas*, 42.

[38] Agamben, *Stanzas*, 42.

[39] Agamben, *Stanzas*, 42.

[40] Agamben, *Stanzas*, 49.

[41] Jacobo Siruela, *Libros, secretos* (Vilaür: Ediciones Atalanta, 2015), 76. Author's translation.

[42] Ioan P. Culianu, *The Tree Of Gnosis: Gnostic Mythology from Early Christianity to Modern Nihilism* (San Francisco: Harper Collins, 1992), 261.

[43] Harold Bloom, *Genius: A Mosaic of One Hundred Exemplary Creative Minds* (Grand Central Publishing, 2003), xviii.

[44] Bloom, *Genius*, xviii.

[45] Comte de Lautréamont, *Les Chants de Maldoror* (New York: New Direction Books, 1943), 49-50. Translated by Guy Wernham

[46] Lautréamont, *Les Chants de Maldoror*, 55-56.

[47] Giorgio Agamben, *Means without End* (Minneapolis: University of Minnesota Press, 2000), 82.

[48] Agamben, *Means without End*, 82.

[49] Agamben, *Means without End*, 82. Aher (a word meaning "another person," "a vile thing"), whose historical name is Elisha Ben Abuyah (70 AD), is one of the main heretics of Rabbinic Judaism. His vision, according to the *Hekalot* mystical tradition (which focuses on the ascension to the heavenly palaces) maintains an interesting relation with Gnosticism that is intertwined with the history of Enoch, one of the most important figures of Hekalot and Merkabah (Chariot mysticism). Enoch, father of Methuselah and ancestor of Noah is, according to Judaism, one of the three patriarchs who ascended to heaven in life. According to a later tradition, by virtue of his purity, Yahweh converted Enoch into an angel named Metatron. When Elisha Ben Abuyah climbed to the celestial palaces, he found a figure of infinite purity sitting on a throne, which he confused with God since it could not be an angel, for, according to Jewish tradition, angels do not have joints and are unable to sit down. However, Ben Abuyah doubts his vision and becomes a heretic. The stories of Enoch-Metatron and Elisha Ben Abuyah meet at this point. When he became an angel, Metatron maintained a human characteristic that made him different from the rest of the celestial intelligences: he keeps his joints and is able to sit down. Actually, Ioan Culianu says, Ben Abuyah "has been deceived by Enoch-Metatron and becomes a ditheist, thinking: 'Perhaps—God forbid—there are two powers (in heaven)'." (Culianu, *Out of this World*, 117).

[50] Agamben, *Means without End*, 82.

[51] Agamben, *Means without End*, 83.

[52] Originally entitled *Guy Debord, l'atrabilaire*, the name of this book casually points to one of the essential features of Debord's character, his deeply melancholic disposition that led him to alcoholism and, ultimately, suicide. Before acquiring the meaning of "bad character" or "easily irritable," which apply perfectly to Debord, "atrabilarious" referred to the *atrabilis*, the Latin translation of the Greek *melaina cholos* or black bile, the Hippocratic humor that gives melancholy its name.

[53] Frédéric Schiffter, *Contra Debord* (España: Melusina, 2005), 39.

[54] Merrifield, *Guy Debord*, 57.

[55] Debord, *The Society of the Spectacle*, 12.

[56] Debord, *The Society of the Spectacle*, 12.

[57] Debord, *The Society of the Spectacle*, 12.

[58] Andy Merrifield, *Magical Marxism* (London: Pluto Press, 2011), 35-36.

[59] Debord, *The Society of the Spectacle*, 12.

[60] Debord, *The Society of the Spectacle*, 12.
[61] Debord, *The Society of the Spectacle*, 21.
[62] Debord, *The Society of the Spectacle*, 13.
[63] Debord, *The Society of the Spectacle*, 11.
[64] Merrifield, *Guy Debord*, 60.
[65] Debord, *The Society of the Spectacle*, 20.
[66] Debord, *The Society of the Spectacle*, 14.
[67] Debord, *The Society of the Spectacle*, 16.
[68] Debord, *The Society of the Spectacle*, 15.
[69] Debord, *The Society of the Spectacle*, 15.
[70] Debord, *The Society of the Spectacle*, 15.
[71] Debord, *The Society of the Spectacle*, 13-14.
[72] Debord, *The Society of the Spectacle*, 12.
[73] Debord, *The Society of the Spectacle*, 16.
[74] Debord, *The Society of the Spectacle*, 22.
[75] Debord, *The Society of the Spectacle*, 13.
[76] Debord, *The Society of the Spectacle*, 17.
[77] Debord, *The Society of the Spectacle*, 10. Note that this thesis is a *détournement* of Marx's passage according to which exchange value is the "*the fantastic form* of a relation between things"
[78] Debord, *The Society of the Spectacle*, 11.
[79] Debord, *The Society of the Spectacle*, 20.
[80] Debord, *The Society of the Spectacle*, 17.
[81] Debord, *The Society of the Spectacle*, 64.
[82] Debord, *The Society of the Spectacle*, 28.
[83] Debord, *The Society of the Spectacle*, 63.
[84] Debord, *The Society of the Spectacle*, 51.
[85] Debord, *The Society of the Spectacle*, 58.
[86] Debord, *The Society of the Spectacle*, 58.
[87] Debord, *The Society of the Spectacle*, 59.
[88] Debord, *The Society of the Spectacle*, 58.
[89] Giorgio Agamben, *Means without End* (Minneapolis: University of Minnesota Press, 2000), 124.
[90] Merrifield, *Guy Debord*, 57.
[91] Wilhelm Reich, *The Mass Psychology of Fascism* (New York: Farrar, Strauss and Giroux, 1980), xxvi.
[92] Debord, *The Society of the Spectacle*, 26.
[93] Debord, *The Society of the Spectacle*, 26.
[94] Debord, *The Society of the Spectacle*, 26.
[95] In *Stanzas*, Agamben draws a very interesting relationship between commodity metaphysics and the appearance of dandies such as George Bryan

"Beau" Brummell, who exerted a considerable influence on the European society of the first half of the nineteenth century.

[96] Debord, *The Society of the Spectacle*, 27.

[97] Debord, *The Society of the Spectacle*, 25.

[98] Debord, *The Society of the Spectacle*, 25.

[99] Guy Debord, *Comments on the Society of the Spectacle* (London: Verso, 1998), 9.

[100] Merrifield, *Guy Debord*, 72.

[101] Merrifield, *Guy Debord*, 72.

[102] John Gray, *The Soul of the Marionette: A Short Inquiry into Human Freedom* (New York: Farrar, Straus and Giroux and), 117.

[103] John Gray, *The Soul of the Marionette*, 119.

Part III The Gaping Jaws of Unreality.

Twentieth to Twenty-First Century

Mephistopheles: It's already done!
Now dark Cousins, hurry from the scene
To the mountain lake! Greet the Undines,
And beg from them their gleaming flood.
Their female arts, those difficult of knowning
Can divorce appearances from being,
And all still swear its being that they are seeing
Goethe, *Faust*, Second Part (1832)

The zone is a very complicated system of traps, and they are all deadly, I don't know what's going on here in the absence of people, but the moment someone shows up everything comes into motion. Old traps disappear and new ones emerge. Safe spots become unpassable. Now your path is easy, now it's hopelessly involved. That's the Zone. It may even seem capricious. But it is what we have made it with our condition. It happened that people had to stop halfway and go back. Some of them even died on the very threshold of the room. But everything that's going on here depends not on the Zone, but on us!
Stalker (1979)

7. Communalism, Cybernetics and the Digital Economy

>   Now i'm a citysick sailor
>   On a ship of noise
>   I got my maps all backwards
>   And my instincts poisoned
>   In a truth blown gutter
>   Full of wasted years
>   Like blown-out speakers
>   Ringing in my ears
>   Oh it's nausea, oh nausea
>   And we're gone
>
>   Now i'm a straight-line walker
>   In a black-out room
>   I push a shopping cart over
>   In an aztec ruin
>   With my minion fingers
>   Working for some god
>   Who could see his own reflection
>   In a parking lot
>   **Beck,** *Nausea (2006)*

Between 1965 and 1971 about 750,000 North Americans left their homes in cities and suburbs and settled in more than 10,000 communes in rural areas across the US. This figure, impressive in itself, is even more overwhelming if one takes into account that in the two previous centuries only about 500 to 700 such communities existed in the United States. The libertarian ideals that transcendentalists like Ralph Waldo Emerson and Henry David Thoureau had aspired to a little more than a century ago seemed to have spread to a considerable portion of the youth of the fifties and sixties who, disenchanted with politics and their prospects of life in a world on the brink of dehumanization, decided to take the road back to nature. This new generation, however, had to solve a problem that Emerson and Thoreau—sublime individualists—never confronted: how to found, on a massive scale, a new type of human society in harmony with the natural world. With this end in mind the communalist project combined the anti-authoritarianism of the transcendentalists with the idea of a human mass as an entity or a system endowed with a "collective soul" we already found in Gustave Le Bon: "a provisional being formed of heterogeneous elements, which for a moment are combined, exactly as the cells which constitute a living body form by their reunion a new being which displays characteristics very different from those possessed by each of the cells singly."[1]

The communalists believed that the creation of a self-regulating social system was possible and turned to ecology and biology in search for the conceptual framework for their project. The reason for the communalist's positive connotation of the psychological mass, in contrast to Le Bon's, is one of the themes developed by documentary filmmaker Adam Curtis: namely, that they imagined they were modelling their social organism in the structure of nature itself, when in reality they based it on an idea that originated in cybernetics. As we saw in the Intermezzo, the idea of nature as a self-sustaining system— an entirely religious notion intimately linked to the concept of *anima mundi*—is inseparable from the myth of the machine since Nicholas Oresme speculated that "God might have started off the universe as a kind of clock and left it to run by itself."[2]

This last part will be devoted to a historical account of the social, political and economic conditions of the transformation of the hunter of souls into institutions such as the think tank, the consulting firm and the market research group, which—as the world became considerably more complex and uncertain during the Cold War—assumed the tasks that were traditionally carried out by the political leader and the public relations officer. In the first chapter we will study the ways in which communalism acted as the middle link between the magical *weltanschauung* and its digital version, a theme we already addressed to some extent in the Intermezzo. The link between these two worlds, the magical and the cybernetic, is the metaphor of a self-regulated system that underlies both the magical idea of the *anima mundi* and the ideal of self-government present in both communes and cybernetic systems. This metaphor will help us find the intersection between the ideals of the counterculture and the technocratic establishment and determine how their joint influence gave rise to a new variety of market economy, the so-called digital economy, which is nothing but an evolution of the debordian spectacle.

In this third part I will use portions of the narrative presented by Curtis in his documentaries *All Watched Over by Machines of Loving Grace* and *HyperNormalisation*. However, I will reinterpret and complement some of these themes in the light of our research on erotic magic. If, for Curtis, the pseudo-reality we live in today is the product of the increasing complexity of the world that demanded imposing a simplistic version of reality on society in order to manipulate it, I will set out to complement his thesis and show that our current demiurgic bubble is part of a much longer historical process and that, in fact, it is the result of the magical processes I have been examining in this study.

Like Henry David Thoreau, the communalists believed that "government is best which governs not at all"[3] and with this end in mind they left the cities looking for a life according to this ideal of self-determination and independence. This was a generation that grew up during the height of the Cold War, trained in nuclear evacuation school drills and terrorized with the prospect of mutual assured destruction with the Soviet Union. In his book *Young Radicals: Notes on Committed Youth*, psychologist Kenneth Keniston traces the attitudes of many young activists of the sixties to the nuclear dialectic of the Cold War. One of the interviewees described to Keniston "the day an encyclopedia salesman sold her mother volume A of the *Encyclopedia Brittanica*: 'I remember reading it and seeing a picture of an atomic bomb and a tank going over some rubble. And I think I became hysterical. I screamed and screamed and screamed'."[4] In most cases the conflict had to do with a particular theme: how could one lead a normal adult life, a middle-class life, in a world where the possibility of a nuclear confrontation was highly probable? This generation carried "a deep anxiety, a ferocious sense of their own 'weightlessness' in the face of world events, and a 'deadening alienation' from the culture within which they were about to become adults."[5]

Many rebels of the time stopped believing that politics offered real options for changing the world, a matter succinctly expressed by an anonymous poem published in the San Francisco magazine *Seed* in 1967:

> We know the system doesn't work because we are living in its ruins. We know that leaders don't work out because they have all led us only to the present, the good leaders equally with the bad... what the system calls organization—linear organization—is a systematic cage, arbitrarily limiting the possible. It's never worked before. It always produced the present.[6]

A brief look at the environment of the time allows us to find the root of such feelings of anxiety and alienation. "The end of World War II and the arrival of the atomic era," says historian Fred Turner, "unleashed a wave of quietism and fear across American society. Gender boundaries stiffened, racial tensions slipped from public discussion, and leaders and citizens alike came to dread a vague but seemingly pervasive Communist menace."[7] Cold War paranoia turned postwar USA into a cluster of closed communities which, in the case of an armed conflict, could easily be characterized as "closed informational systems for purposes of military command and control."[8] As the army, politicians and urban planners designed a distrustful and self-contained society, a *suburbanized* society, "men and women sought to constrain their emotions, maintain their marriages, and build safe, secure and independent homes. Like the airforce soldiers who scanned America's borders for incoming Soviet bombers, many Americans took to monitoring the boundaries of their own lives."[9] In this fragment we can recognize the fundamental marks of psychological and urban armoring denounced by Reich and Debord: as the borders of the country and its cities became rigid and impermeable, the borders of its inhabitants followed suit. The beatniks and hippies, the rebels of the fifties and sixties were that portion of the population who refused to armor themselves and, in the process, decided to break the psychological chains that imprisoned their society.

The communalists, one of the many branches of the counterculture—which by then included the Civil Rights movement, the New Left, the anti-war movement and the hippies—took R. Buckminster Fuller, a prolific architect, designer and systems theorist, as one of their main influences. "Bucky" Fuller, who was already in his seventies by the mid 1960s, had been born into a unitary family in Massachusetts. His great-aunt had been Margaret Fuller, a prominent transcendentalist who, along with Ralph Waldo Emerson, had founded the literary journal *Dial*, where Henry David Thoreau's first essays were published. Such distinguished ancestry became a model for Fuller, who saw both his great-aunt and Emerson as his intellectual heroes.

In his essay *Nature*, Emerson evokes the Platonic sentiment of a world imbued with soul that we already found in the work of Bruno and Ficino.

> The granite is differenced in its laws only by the more of less of heat, from the river that wears it away. The river, as if flows, resembles the air that flows over it; the air resembles the light which transverses it with more subtle currents; the light resembles the heat which rides it through Space. Each creature is only a modification of the other; the likeness in them is more than the difference, and their radical law is one and the same. A rule of one art, or a rule of one organization, hold true throughout nature. So intimate is this Unity, that, it is easily seen, it lies under the undermost garment of nature, and betrays its source in Universal Spirit. For it pervades Thought also.[10]

The rule that Emerson refers to in his passage is the Great Chain of Being, the Universal Spirit that underlies nature is nothing other than the idea of *anima mundi* that the transcendentalists inherited from the English and German Romantics and that these in turn had taken from mystics like Jacob Boehme and Emanuel Swedenborg. Like Emerson, Buckminster Fuller also imagined the material world as "the reflexion of an otherwise intangible system of rules. But unlike Emerson and the Transcendentalists, [he] linked that system of rules not only to the natural world, but also to the world of industry."[11] In the same vein as many scientists and researchers of his time, Fuller understood the world as a gigantic information system, an idea he traced, on the one hand, to his transcendental lineage and, on the other, to his time as a naval officer, during which he learned to see the environment of US Navy ships as closed systems governed by information patterns.

An individual particularly aware of humanity's fate, Buckminster Fuller was convinced that the only real way to solve the problems facing our species to any extent was, in the words of his great-aunt Margaret, "to start in the universe and work down to the parts," that is, to acquire a type of holistic knowledge that would allow a person to contemplate a given problem in its entirety. Fuller was known for having invented the geodesic dome—an architectural framework capable of distributing structural stress along its surface—which had been put to use by the US army in the late 1940s to house its early warning system in the Arctic. He had designed these domes taking into account what he though was "the underlying system of order in nature,"[12] so that the network that made up the structure behaved like an ecosystem in which "each tiny strut was weak, but when thousands were joined together to form a giant interconnecting web, they became strong and stable."[13]

The purpose of Fuller's research was finding the fundamental principles of nature and with this end in mind he was to become a *comprehensive designer*, a "synthesis of artist, inventor, engineer, economist and evolutionary strategist,"[14] which would allow him to achieve what the bureaucrat, the man divided in his psyche and compartmentalized at work, clearly couldn't: seeing the full picture. "To do this work, the Designer would need to have access to all the information generated by America's burgeoning technocracy while at the same time remaining outside it."[15] The figure of the Comprehensive Designer presents two simultaneous facets that will develop in the establishment and the counterculture respectively: on the one hand he is the Brunian hunter —Culianu's "integral magician"—turned into a technological wizard (a postwar heir to the Wizard of Oz); a venator that by being outside of the whole could understand it and manipulate it at will.[16] On the other, he is an institutionalized version of the situationist who manages to see the environment as a whole, a "dealienated" type of human that the communalists saw as their goal of individual development.

While in Europe the latter attitude was the result of a radical response to the establishment, in the United States it was the demands of WWII and the Cold War that contributed to the formation of this line of thought in Fuller and many other researchers of the time. "As numerous historians of technology have pointed out," says Turner, "World War II triggered a transformation in american science. Before the war, science and scientists seemed to stand outside politics. University based researchers generally drew their funding from their universities or from industry. By and large, they maintained clear distinctions between science and engineering and between military and civilian research... When Germany invaded Poland, however, these relatively independent specialists found themselves thrown into new interdisciplinary and interinstitutional collaborations."[17] The situation required that the people in charge of the defense of the country should be able to solve problems of extreme complexity which spanned throughout various disciplines; the price of failure was a catastrophic change in the balance of power and the very likely destruction of their way of life.

Although somewhat "elevated," Fuller's idea of Comprehensive Designer is a "one-person condensation" of the need of coordination of thousands of mathematicians, physicists and engineers that needed to collaborate in order to design and implement new attack and defense systems. These efforts began right before the United States entered the second war when Vannevar Bush, then professor of electrical engineering at MIT, convinced President Roosevelt to create the Office of Scientific Research and Development (OSRD), an organization that channeled nearly half a million of dollars to dozens of universities and laboratories with the express purpose of developing new technologies for the military. One of the main laboratories that arose from this collaboration between academia, industry and the army, was MIT's Radiation Laboratory. Founded in 1940 for the purpose of designing better detection systems to bring down the Nazi bombers that besieged England at the time, the Rad Lab was characterized by a highly collaborative and flexible work ethic "and a distinctly nonhierarchical management style."[18] Among its employees, says Turner,

> entrepreneurship and collaboration were the norm and independence of mind was strongly encouraged. Formerly specialized scientists were urged to become generalists in their research, able not only to theorize but also to design and build new technologies... neither scientists nor administrators could stay walled off from one another in the offices or laboratories; throughout the Rad Lab... the pressures to produce new technologies to fight the war drove formerly specialized scientists and engineers to cross professional boundaries, to routinely mix work with pleasure, and to form new, interdisciplinary networks within which to work and live.[19]

Historian of science Peter Gallison refers to the Rad Lab as a "trade zone" —a term borrowed from anthropology—and its disciplinary divisions as tribes that "developed 'contact languages' with which to exchange ideas and techniques toward the common goal of producing weapon systems. These languages ranged from the most function-specific jargons through semiespecific pidgins, to full-fledged creoles; they also included nonverbal elements, such as shared tools, which could be used to demonstrate concepts across disciplinary boundaries or serve as sites for collaborative work."[20]

It was in this multidisciplinary environment that Norbert Wiener—who by then had already been researching disciplines as varied as mathematics, engineering, biology and computer science—set the foundations of cybernetics. In effect, this new discipline was the most complete and effective *lingua franca* that emerged from MIT's Radiation Laboratory. The ability of cybernetics to facilitate interdisciplinary collaboration arose from the fact that its analytical terms brought together "multiple, if formerly segregated, scientific communities. Wiener borrowed the word *homeostasis* from the field of physiology and applied it to social systems; he picked up the word *feedback* from control engineering; and from the study of human behaviour he drew the concepts of *learning*, *memory*, *flexibility* and *purpose*."[21]

The advantages of the cybernetic rhetoric were enormous: it allowed the material world to be understood under a single framework, as a self-regulated system that tended to a dynamic type equilibrium, to homeostasis, as any other living organism. And not only this, according to Turner "embedded in Wiener's theory of society as an information system was a deep longing for and even a model of an egalitarian, democratic social order."[22] The cyberneticist became a new variety of *venator* who, like the brunian hunter-magician, could foresee the general movements of the bonds within a system and correct them to return it, if necessary, to a state of homeostasis and self-regulation. A sort of *benevolent venator* whose mission is to maintain balance, either in a nuclear dynamic or in a natural ecosystem. However, such ability to encompass and give coherence to multiple fields of research, from biology to sociology and politics, came with a price that can be easily appreciated in one of the projects that Wiener developed together with the engineer Julian Bigelow: a "predictor" that could anticipate the position and trajectory of an enemy aircraft and shoot it down. In Wiener's words:

> in order to obtain as complete a mathematical treatment as possible of the overall control problem, it is necessary to assimilate the different parts of the system to a single basis,

either human or mechanical. Since our understanding of the mechanical elements of gun pointing appeared to us to be far ahead of our psychological understanding, we chose to find a mechanical analogue of the gun pointer and the airplane pilot.[23]

Thus, the cybernetic account required to conceptualize the human factor of the equation (the artilleryman and pilot) as another mechanical component of the system. In short, *understanding the world in cybernetic terms necessarily implied dehumanizing it*. No wonder, many activists and revolutionaries during the sixties were against such a conception and considered it essentially hostile to a humane understanding of the world. Many symptomatic acts, such as the marches at UC Berkeley or the throwing of tomatoes at the president of the French Cybernetic Society were aimed at making their stance against the industrial-military complex and the cybernetic rhetoric known. What they were not aware of was that their own vision, the communal alternative they thought they were offering society, had by then already been compromised by the cybernetic narrative.

The main foci of propagation of the cybernetic account took place in the field of contemporary art and in the social ideals of communalism. The vectors were, on one hand, Bucky Fuller, and on the other Steward Brand, one of the key figures of the counterculture, creator of the magazine *The Whole Earth Catalog* and co-founder of the consulting firm *Global Business Network*. Brand, who like many other kids of his generation grew up fearing an eventual nuclear holocaust, was afraid of growing up to become "a member of a gray, uninspired, orwellian mass,"[24] an automaton lacking emotions and individuality. These concerns were recorded in one of his 1957 journals, where he wrote:

> If there's a fight, I'll fight. I will not fight for America, nor for home, nor for President Eisenhower, nor for capitalism, nor even for democracy. I will fight for individualism and personal liberty. If I must be a fool, I want to be my own particular brand of fool—utterly unlike other fools. I will fight to avoid becoming a number—to others and to myself.[25]

When the time came to choose a profession Brand decided to study ecology at Stanford, where he attended Paul R. Ehrlich's biology class, who introduced him to the worldview of cybernetics and systems theory. Ehrlich's vision of ecology was specially stimulating for Brand, who began to understand the natural world in informational terms, no longer composed of Linnaean hierarchies of species, genera, family, etc., but by a "complex energy-matter nexus." In this network of biological relationships, the individual organism is a system that reflects in its own constitution the system to which it belongs and reacts spontaneously to any changes in it. True to the cybernetic *ethos*, this biological scheme could also be applied to human society, so that each individual was understood as a whole, an essential piece for the regulation of the system. Brand found in the systemic approach to cybernetics an "intellectual alternative to the cold war dualisms with which he had been struggling. If hierarchical leaders such as those in the Kremlin ruled by applying force from above, and so squeezed the individuality out of their subjects, biological systems as Ehrlich described maintained order by means of evolutionary forces at work in the life of every individual."[26] Of course, in their enthusiasm, Brand, Ehrlich and many others overlooked that the abstractions of cybernetics and ecology implied, from their very roots, the mechanization of the elements of the system and therefore were a source of regimentation and massification.

After graduating from Stanford, Brand spent two years in the Army where he underwent Ranger training, a somewhat strange choice, if not inexplicable, in the light of his struggle for individuality (and only understandable through tremendous restlessness and misplaced patriotism). Disenchanted with the regimentation of military life, he left the army and decided to move to New York in the early sixties. There he found a flourishing art scene influenced by the experiments initiated in the early fifties by artists such as John Cage and Robert Rauschenberg. These experiments undermined the romantic idea of the artist as an inspired being whose work was a symbolic act of creation. Rauschenberg denied the idea that a painting was an expression of his personality, in his concept, art rather than a conscious manipulation of materials, the classical artistic process that goes from conception to execution, was a *collaboration with the materials*. For Cage, who practiced Zen Buddhism since the 1940s, instead of simply representing the world art should be a means to integrate the viewer into the artistic process and thus "heighten the audience member's sensitivity to experiences of all kinds."[27] In 1952 Cage put together a piece called Theater Piece No. 1, a real-time "artistic system" that combined, in one space, paintings by Rauschenberg, improvised dance by Merce Cunningham, poetry by Mary Caroline Richard, piano by David Tudor, and Cage himself giving a lecture. The spirit of this installation, formally akin to that of the letterists and situationists, sought to blur the boundaries between art and life by creating theatrical environments where ordinary people could interact with artists and performers.

This artistic expression, later called *happening*, offered Brand "a picture of the world where hierarchies had dissolved, where each moment might be as wonderful as the last, and where every person could turn their life into art."[28] Intrigued by New York art scene, he contacted USCO (The US Company), an artistic community dedicated to multimedia happenings and offered his services as a photographer and technician. This "artistic tribe" led by poet Gerd Stern, proposed that the transformation of human consciousness, an ideal clearly influenced by philosophies such as Buddhism and Taoism, could be effected with the help of modern technology. Stern, a European Jew who had fled World War II, knew the work of Norbert Wiener and shared his cybernetic view of the world. Therefore, USCO's performances made use of various electronic devices such as strobe lights, cassette players, stereo speakers and slide projectors, "the products of technocratic industry served as handy tools for transforming their viewer's mind-set."[29] What for Wiener were exchanges of information between the elements of a cybernetic system, for Stern were a "mystical energy," *pneuma* that manifested itself as light, electricity, images and music (see the pneumatic circle in the Intermezzo). More than a collective or an artistic community, USCO "was a social system in itself."[30] This identification of the Renaissance *pneuma* with electricity and digital information is essential to understand the transformation of the pneumatic web of bonds into our current digital networks.

By then Brand and other characters like Allen Ginsberg were travelling constantly between the East and West coasts connecting both artistic scenes. Brand in particular acted as a bridge between art collectives like USCO and their counterparts in Northern California; his style of entrepreneurship, which brought together the worlds of art, academia and industry, was to become one of the staples of the networking economy that eventually rose out of the counterculture. In California he met Ken Kesey, who had just published his novel *Someone Flew Over The Cuckoo's Nest*, and was about to become one of the points of origin of the San Francisco's psychedelic scene and the communal movement. In 1962, inspired by the beatniks, Kesey began to host parties in his house near the Stanford campus that were frequented by figures like Jerry Garcia of The Grateful Dead and psychologist Richard Alpert, who would later be known as Ram Dass. Soon a gang formed around Kesey, the Merry Pranksters, whose aim was to create, with the help of LSD, "a new consciousness and a new form of social organization."[31] A few months later Kesey and the Pranksters bought a school bus they adapted with microphones and speakers and drove east, stopping in towns and cities to offer acid to its inhabitants and transform their consciousness. Like USCO, Kesey and the Pranksters had no problem with using technologies originally developed by the industry and the army for their own purposes, and even if they were not aware of Norbert Wiener's theory of cybernetics and Buckminster Fuller's ideas, Turner says, "their technological performances suggest a deep sympathy with both."[32]

In the case of Pranksters, technologies like LSD opened the door to a holistic and cybernetic way of seeing the world which, like many oriental philosophies, puts the whole over the parts of a system. In *The Electric Koolaid Acid Test*, his chronicle of the time he spent with Kesey's gang, Tom Wolfe describes a scene that makes this attitude plain:

> One night Kesey took about 1500 micrograms and several other Pranksters took lesser doses and they got down on the floor and started the Humanoid Radio. They started babbling, going into echolalia, ululation, all manner of nonverbal expression, talking in Tongues, as it were. The idea was to try to hit that beam and that mode that would enable you to communicate with beings on other planets, other galaxies...[33]

The humanoid radio is a self-regulated social system that can be described entirely in cybernetic terms. It is also a mass configuration in which the *pneuma* of each individual is synchronized with the pneuma of the other members of the system, producing Le Bon's provisional being. In fact, the communal formations that emerged from the psychedelic scene can be explained coherently through the pneumatic circle. Whether it is a Grateful Dead concert or an ashram in India, the mechanism is identical to the one I have described in this study: the libidinal energy, the pneuma of each of the individuals in the mass, flows freely through the system producing an erotic connection between its members.

In his biography of Kesey, Stephen L. Tanner highlights the influence that transcendentalists like Emerson and Thoreau had, via the beatniks and Walt Whitman, on the leader of the Pranksters. This influence is particularly evident in Kesey's indifference towards politics, an attitude that came to light in a brief speech he gave during a Berkeley demonstration against the Vietnam war: "you know, you are not going to stop this war with this rally, by marching... that's what *they* do,"[34] after which he took out his harmonica and started singing a folk song. Kesey's interests were in the direct experience and connection with nature and the cosmos, everything else was accessory. Like Thoreau, Kesey was a mystical individualist for whom all forms of government were coercive and therefore detrimental to individual freedom. Seen like this, it is not surprising that Thoreau's concept of civil disobedience lent itself to a "depoliticization" of society. Now, in the absence of politics, the vacuum must be filled by some alternative form of control, which in the case of communalism was the notion of a self-regulating social system—*homeostatic* in cybernetic terms—which could be inferred from Thoreau's writings and figured openly in Buckminster Fuller's thought and in cybernetics.

Making use of ecology, the communalists adapted the idea of a self-regulated system to their social project. Multitudes of young people moved to the deserts and rural areas of the country where they built geodesic domes and adapted them for housing. Since these domes were structures that supposedly reproduced the very order of nature, the ecosystem, they became the movement's symbol. Unfortunately, the neuroses and hierarchies of civilized life and patriarchy accompanied the inhabitants of the communes in their new lives. From the beginning, as in cities and suburbs, men took to the heavier jobs such as construction, while women took care of the children and tended to the homestead. The new notion of community was reinforced in group sessions where transpersonal integration exercises were carried out, influenced by some of the techniques developed by gestalt therapy, psychodrama and the human potential movement, whose origin can be traced back to the work of Wilhelm Reich. It is worth highlighting a series of mirroring exercises in which two members of the community imitate their gestures mutually in an attempt to establish an intimate emotional contact; these exercises can be explained in pneumatic terms as attempts to reach *rapport*.[35]

This feedback technique seemed to have some measure of success in giving stability and creating a group consciousness. Molly Hollenbach, a former member of the *The Family* commune, comments that the group came to have the feeling of "the organism of many who act as one. It would be like a dance where we're creating a new kind of society, freeing each person to be fully themselves in the group, but we're all affecting each other at all times."[36] However, the vision of a human society without hierarchies, where everyone could relate under equal conditions never came to fruition. The Pranksters, although they refused to admit it (and made all sorts of efforts to hide it), saw Kesey as their leader, they looked up to him and did what he suggested. Jerry Garcia was the *de facto* leader of The Grateful Dead. The same thing happened in the communes, the strongest and most active personalities dominated social interactions but, says Adam Curtis, "the rules of the self-organizing system refused to allow any organized opposition to this oppression."[37] That which was supposed to free the human from the oppression of hierarchies ended up oppressing them in an almost identical way. Without stopping to contemplate its roots or its veracity, the communalists used a theory about the functioning of the natural world that, at first glance, seemed sufficiently convincing. This oversight opened the doors of the communes to a genuine Trojan Horse; instead of an *anima mundi* what penetrated was an *anima machinalis*, the mechanized soul, that had begun to develop four centuries prior and had already penetrated fields such as cybernetics and ecology. Most communes did not last more than two or three years, some dissolved within the first six months.

Thus, we have that the emphasis on individuality and self-regulation present in transcendentalism—which was influenced by romanticism and neoplatonism—reappears in the collaborative practices of the Cold War laboratories that led to cybernetics, and through it, to communalism. The appearance of the self-regulation metaphor in both the establishment and the counterculture allows us to see its two facets: when applied to the natural world in a cosmic framework of thought and action, as in the case of transcendentalism and psychedelia, it becomes *anima mundi*, a community of beings that interact through a natural law of attraction and sympathy: eros. On the other hand, if it is applied in a material way, whether in an economic, industrial or military setting, as in the case of cybernetics, it becomes a closed system, an *anima machinalis*, with two essential objectives: equilibrium and control. Either modality coexists latently in the other. The result depends largely on the mode of application, but both trends are inseparable. This allows us to deduce that the self-regulated system is far from being neutral in political terms and that it can and, in fact has been used, as an efficient tool for control and manipulation.

Steward Brand, who had friends in the communal movement, understood the immense difficulty of the endeavor and founded a catalog to promote tools that would facilitate life in the communes. *The Whole Earth Catalog* began as a modest publication sold in a truck parked outside the Stanford campus. Divided into categories like "understanding whole systems," "shelter and land use," "communications," "community," etc., the catalog offered reviews of a variety of commodities, *tools* in Brand's jargon, that could be used by the new communities. Books by Buckminster Fuller and Norbert Wiener were reviewed next to Hewlett-Packard calculators, an aerial photography book and a chronicle about life in a Kibbutz. Texts by prominent figures of the second generation of cyberneticians like Gregory Bateson also appeared in the Catalog. On many occasions, the reviews came from readers themselves who had already used these tools and wanted to share their experience with a larger audience. This participative structure made the Catalog the first interactive forum of its kind and the analog predecessor of the digital forums on the internet which, incidentally, would also be sponsored by Brand in the eighties.

But there is something off with The Whole Earth Catalog. Many of its readers were communalists who wanted to abandon civilization to create a new type of society and still, encouraged by the Catalog, they became consumers of the tools reviewed in their pages. In the same way as USCO and the Pranksters, who had no problem using devices and technologies designed and manufactured industrially for their own purposes, communalists believed they could leave civilization without having to give up its commodities and amenities. The generation that gave rise to the counterculture had grown up with a "vision in which young people who had been raised on rock and roll, television, and the associated pleasures of consumption, need not give those pleasures up even if they rejected the adult society that had created them."[38] They were, in few words, sons and daughters of the spectacle. The system had created a counterculture of consumers who never had a real chance to propose an alternative to it and, even less, defeat it. The hippies and communalists were actually a generation of consumers just as their parents, the difference was their *style of consumption*, a matter we will examine in the next chapter.

Another instance that shows the ease with which commercial culture invaded the counterculture is the *Trips Festival*. By 1966, Ken Kesey was determined to make the psychedelic scene known to the country. To this end he contacted Brand, electronic music composer Ramón Sender Barayón and Michael Callahan of USCO with the idea of organizing a multimedia festival that included the already popular acid tests, a massive light show, and music by The Grateful Dead, Jefferson Airplane and other psychedelic bands. Longshoreman's Hall, the theater where the festival took place, received more than 10,000 people during the three nights of the event and raised $12,500. The success was such that

> two weeks later, Bill Graham [a musical impresario] could be found staging a trips festival every weekend at the Fillmore. Within a year, teenagers from across America would be streaming into Haight-Ashbury, looking for the sort of bohemian utopia Graham was marketing. Reporters for *Time* and *Life* were not far behind. Almost immediately, San Francisco became Oz to a generation that had feared it would grow up in a black-and-white Kansas of a world…[39]

After the foretold death of the counterculture in the early seventies, many communalists returned to the cities and took refuge in the New Age and the Human Potential Movement, which by then were already established movements in Northern California. Musicians and artists, seeing that social change was no longer an option, put activism aside and chose to take refuge in aesthetics; psychedelia was left behind as new musical genres such as funk and punk began to take the scene. The brutal police repression of the Nixon era had begun and many others, disenchanted with the failure of their comunal projects, allied themselves with groups of technologists who were taking the first steps in the field of personal computing. As early as 1972, says Turner, "Brand had suggested that computers might become a new LSD, a new small technology that could be used to open minds and reform society."[40] Apparently without having learned from the counterculture's mistakes, a sector of entrepreneurs insisted on a recurrent idea: using technologies and tools designed by the industry and the military to to try to subvert the *status quo*. Once again, they set out to use the same metaphor of self-regulation that had blatantly failed them in the case of the communes, now in the form of the new digital networks that were then being implemented by the military, the defense department and the technologists in universities like Stanford and MIT. These institutions' interest in the cybernetic account remained unchanged: it offered them a way to achieve a decentralized network of computers that was not as vulnerable as a centralized one in the case of a nuclear attack.

This amalgamation of counterculture and establishment may seem appalling in certain places that have not been thoroughly commodified, or where there is still memory of another type of life. In any case, it comes down to this: if one believes that the "natural environment" of the human being is the free market—as in the case of most North Americans whose existence has been thoroughly commoditized—this transition from counterculture to cyberculture is not only legitimate, it is perfectly natural. If, on the contrary, one understands that the dynamics of the market have developed in detriment of the human, the commodification of countercultural ideals and practices is a clear corruption of the methods that were previously believed to be able to effect a real change in the world. The only reason it is not a sell-out, is because the counterculture's generation had already been invaded by consumerism and cybernetics. However, we can call it a *self-cooptation*, which amounts to a treason of sorts. In any case, this assimilation of the counterculture by the establishment, which finds its definitive form in cyberspace, annihilated any real possibility of revolution, or even dissent, to this day.

Despite this irrational fixation with cybernetics, if anyone took advantage of his experience in the counterculture it was Brand, whose style of networking laid the foundations for the construction of a new type of economy. By the early eighties Brand had made a large number of contacts in the counterculture, the academia, and the industrial and corporate sector and realized that the model of a self-sustainable defense network that had been built in the army laboratories could be adapted to a new form of social and economic interaction. By then many communalists had ridded themselves of the idea of founding physical communes and saw in the new computer technologies a utopian "digital frontier" that would allow them to accomplish their frustrated collective aspirations. Larry Brilliant, a technologist and philanthropist who had spent years at the Majarishi ashram in the Himalayas, approached Brand with the idea of taking the Whole Earth Catalog online. Seeing the potential of the idea, Brand refused to publish already existing material and proposed instead that users of the forum could create their own content and save it according to pre-established categories. This was the origin of The WELL (The Whole Earth 'Lectronic Link), one of the first virtual communities to offer remote access via modem.

With The WELL the pneumatic dynamics that characterized psychedelia and communalism entered the virtual world for the first time. What USCO's Gerd Stern saw as a "mystical energy"—the pneuma that circulated through the social system of his collective in the form of light and electricity—was physically joined with the new digital substrate. This operation is not at all strange if we bear in mind that the psychological *phantasmata* had already found a home in the commodity and the market, an operation that intensified its level of operation in the material world. However, the transmutation of pneuma into information has an overtly religious dimension: the arrival of the pneuma to the digital realm implies a sort of *incarnation of the spirit* that justified the utopian-communalist ethics of The WELL. This metaphor has two faces and the opposite idea, namely, that the virtual world is a sort of dematerialization of the body is exposed by John Perry Barlow, Grateful Dead lyricist and recurring user of the forum:

> As a result of [the opening of cyberspace], humanity is undergoing the most profound transformation of its history. Coming into the virtual world, we inhabit information. Indeed, we become information. Thought is embodied and the flesh is made word.[41]

What looks like a virtualization from the point of view of the flesh is an incarnation from the point of view of the spirit. In accordance with H.C. Binswanger's alchemical interpretation of market economy, this operation corresponds to the first stage of the Great Work, *nigredo*, which consisted "in giving a body to the incorporeal and rendering the corporeal incorporeal."[42] Economy as a form of alchemy starts from the transmutation of matter into phantasm and viceversa. This process of virtualization, both in economy and psychology, is nothing other than the Western drive towards the sublimation of the material world—most likely an unconscious reaction to resolve the multiple dualisms that underlie it—and which will eventually lead to the foundation of a global unreality.

Such a virtualization, as I already mentioned in the fourth chapter, ends up becoming an unyielding quest to appropriate the unreal and negative, the fetish and its phantasms, in order to nourish the real and positive. This fact is particularly visible in the general movement of branding and corporate culture during the 1990s. In her classic *No Logo*, Naomi Klein comments how,

> after establishing the 'soul' of their corporations, the superbrand companies have gone on to rid themselves of their cumbersome bodies, and there is nothing that seems more cumbersome, more loathsomely corporeal, than the factories that produce their products.[43]

This process represents a later stage of the Debordian spectacle in which a brand's exchange value sublimates itself definitively, and which could be defined as a corporate variety of antisomatism, its shedding of the material and subsequent emphasis on the "spiritual" and phantasmatic. It is worth clarifying that the fact that the corporation tends increasingly towards unreality does not mean that it will "disappear" or "vanish into thin air," but that its inclination is to cultivate those aspects of corporate culture, such as branding and public relations, that identify it more clearly with the fetish and the phantasm. The implicit dematerialization of the digital age has offered the corporation the perfect environment for its 'unrealization.' "It is online that the purest brands are being built," argues Klein, "liberated from the real world burdens of stores and product manufacturing, these brands are free to soar, less as the disseminators of goods and services than as collective hallucinations."[44]

Now, if the psychological *phantasmata* penetrated the commercial culture and took on a life of their own in the market, their arrival into the digital world is equivalent to the foundation of a realm of their own, a non-place compatible with traits such as immateriality and the capacity to circulate freely according to the basic pattern of the pneumatic circle; a veritable *anima machinalis*. From the point of view of the medieval and Renaissance theory of the phantasm, cyberspace would be the concretion and externalization of the unconscious by technological means; a machine-like unconscious in which phantasms and archetypes are transmuted into advertising and celebrities. Psyche become spectacle.

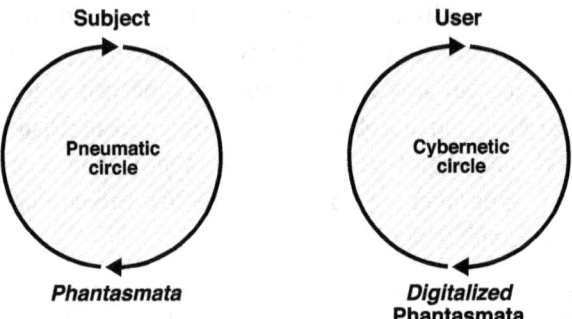

But let us go back to The WELL. This virtual community was built on the same cybernetic principles as a physical commune. In the words of *Wired* founder Kevin Kelly, the forum was meant to be a self-designed and self-governing experiment, whose use of the system co-evolved with the system as it was built.[45] This virtual forum brought many of the collaborative practices of communalism to the virtual and real lives of its members, who joined the community with "the comforting sense that that they had not betrayed the their youthful ambitions for alternative community."[46] On the other hand, the democratization of technology through personal computing created new business opportunities that reinforced the style of networking favored by Brand: the new way of working consisted in creating non-local networks that distributed information about possible contacts and jobs; a live version of LinkedIn.

As in the case of the Whole Earth Catalog, whose content came from contributions and reviews written by the readers themselves, the users of The WELL offered information free of charge to the virtual community, that is, they exchanged "potentially valuable information without expectation of immediate reward."[47] This dynamic established an economy based on "the gift," to use Marcel Mauss' term, which simultaneously contributed to strengthen the sense of community and the social status of the user within it. By the early nineties, the widespread application of this informal type of networked interaction—both online as well as offline—gave rise to a new set of economic practices that were based on decentralized forms of production, employment and global outsourcing that contributed to the change from an economy based on industrial production to an economy centered on the offering of services and the construction of the so-called *super-brands*. This change of emphasis, which substitutes the manufacture of commodities with the creation of images, consolidates the status of the phantasm in the commercial and corporate culture of late capitalism. It is important to bear in mind that this "new economy" is quite simply a variation of free market economy and, as such, it is based on the idea of a self-regulating system that can dispense with politics or any other form of intervention because of its supposed capacity to automatically adjust to the changes with in its system. It is nothing but the realization of the communal and cybernetic dream in the economic sphere.

This new variety of economic interaction entailed an evolution of the pneumatic aspect of market economy which, having seized the technological means, penetrated the virtual sphere without much effort. To understand this argument it is necessary to see a virtual community like The WELL as a miniature marketplace. The commodities that circulate through this community market are an "informational gift." Its use value is the same as the use value of a service or a physical commodity, it must be useful for someone or something, be it a job contact, a key piece of information or a specific skill. Like any other commodity, this informational gift also has an exchange value, but it is not immediate or described in quantitative terms, it is, rather, a future investment in the strengthening of the community, which we will call accordingly *community value*. This community value includes the *social value* of each user which, as in any other market, is configured as a set of pneumatic relationships between the users of the system. Thus, in a virtual community the social and community value, along with the use value of the "informational gift," is inseparable from a series of pneumatic interactions whose main function is to maintain the balance of the system.

What market economy achieved through commodity metaphysics, that is, encouraging constant consumption to keep the wheels of the economy turning, digital economy achieves through a *network ethic*, whose nodes (*us* in Facebook, Instagram or Twitter) participate actively to maintain a stable and self-regulated system. It should be noted the traditional economy's reliance on commodity fetishism continues and both schemes, metaphysical and networked, operate in tandem and reinforce each other. Consequently, we now not only consume to keep the system going, we also work for free for this digital economy, we give away our participation for the benefit of belonging to an exclusive club that includes everyone. Social networks are nothing other than the twenty-first century's maquila, as matter of fact, a gigantic middle class sweatshop. Needless to say, the abusive quality of this business model breeds injustice and inequality on a global scale. In the words of Jaron Lanier, it is a model in which the party with the most robust network gets to "gather data... often without having to pay for it. The data is analyzed using the most powerful available computers, run by the very best available technical people. The results of the analysis are kept secret, but are used to manipulate the rest of the world to advantage." [48] This economic model will eventually backfire, says Lanier, simply "because the rest of the world cannot indefinitely absorb the increased risk, cost, and waste dispersed"[49] by its operation.

But its not only injustice and inequality what should concern us about the advancement of these technologies, there is an even deeper problem. According to Jamie Bartlett, author and director of the Centre for the Analysis of Social Media at the British think tank Demos, the interest of big tech and democracy are incompatible. "They are products of completely different eras and run according to different rules and principles.

> The machinery of democracy was built during a time of nation-states, hierarchies, deference and industrialised economies. The fundamental features of digital tech are at odds with this model: non-geographical, decentralised, data-driven, subject to network effects and exponential growth. Put simply: democracy wasn't designed for this.[50]

It is important to make plain that Bartlett's argument leads to the following conclusion: applying the notion of the self-regulating system of cybernetics to politics leads, paradoxically, to a government (*cyber*) without a governor. As unhinged as this sounds, there have already been proposals to put an artificial intelligence in charge of a country.

Added to this, we must bear in mind that any economic or social application of cybernetic principles leads to two main faculties: control and manipulation. While the users of The WELL believed that "computer networks would return isolated, postindustrial workers to a state of pre-industrial communion, members of the corporate sector thought such networks might bring isolated, postindustrial consumers into a state of postmodern economic communion."⁵¹ Which of the two sides got away with it is more than evident. Today most of the population of the planet lives in this sordid state of "economic communion" that actually amounts to a communion with the *phantasmata* that circulate through cyberspace.

Now, if the appearance of the first virtual communities implies the arrival of the pneuma into the virtual realm, it also implies the entry of the hunter of souls into the digital world. The evolution of the *animarum venator* follows a very specific trajectory that reflects the general movement of the modern manipulative impulse: during the postwar period the brunian *venator* became a set of interdisciplinary military research and development practices that gave rise to cybernetics and led to the development of the first digital networks. This impulse was subsequently consolidated in the appearance of a new form of economy that optimized the pneumatic dynamics of our tradition and brought an increase in control and manipulation techniques. In the next chapter we will see how the *venator* assumes the form of the consulting firm and think tank and, in an even more advanced version, of the *intelligent agent*, an autonomous type of software capable of learning, finding patterns, solving problems and adapting in real time.

---

[1] Gustave Le Bon, *The Crowd* (Batoche Books, 2001), 15.
[2] Herbert Butterfield, *The Origins of Modern Science* (New York: G. Bell & Sons, 1957), 20
[3] Henry David Thoreau, *Civil Disobedience* (New York: Broadview Press, 2016), 1.
[4] Quoted by Fred Turner in *From Counterculture to Cyberculture: Steward Brand, the Whole Earth Network, and the Rise of Digital Utopianism* (Chicago: The University of Chicago Press, 2006), 31.
[5] Turner, *From Counterculture to Cyberculture*, 34.
[6] Quoted by Turner in *From Counterculture to Cyberculture*, 36.
[7] Turner, *From Counterculture to Cyberculture*, 17.
[8] Turner, *From Counterculture to Cyberculture*, 17.
[9] Turner, *From Counterculture to Cyberculture*, 30.
[10] Ralph Waldo Emerson, *Nature,* which appears in *The complete Works of Ralph Waldo Emerson, Volume 2* (London: Bell & Daily, 1866), 158
[11] Turner, *From Counterculture to Cyberculture*, 56.
[12] Adam Curtis, *All watched over by machines of loving grace*, part 2.
[13] Adam Curtis, *All watched over by machines of loving grace*, part 2.

[14] Buckminster Fuller, *Ideas and Integrities*. Quoted by Turner en *From Counterculture to Cyberculture*, 56

[15] Turner, *From Counterculture to Cyberculture*, 56.

[16] Note that being able to contemplate the whole objectively involves "alienating the alienation," that is, accessing a higher level in order to be able to contemplate the whole of the previous level.

[17] Turner, *From Counterculture to Cyberculture*, 17.

[18] Turner, *From Counterculture to Cyberculture*, 19.

[19] Turner, *From Counterculture to Cyberculture*, 19.

[20] Turner, *From Counterculture to Cyberculture*, 19.

[21] Turner, *From Counterculture to Cyberculture*, 25.

[22] Turner, *From Counterculture to Cyberculture*, 24.

[23] Wiener, *I am a Mathematician*, quoted by Turner in *From Counterculture to Cyberculture*, 20.

[24] Turner, *From Counterculture to Cyberculture*, 42.

[25] Turner, *From Counterculture to Cyberculture*, 42.

[26] Turner, *From Counterculture to Cyberculture*, 44.

[27] Turner, *From Counterculture to Cyberculture*, 47.

[28] Turner, *From Counterculture to Cyberculture*, 48.

[29] Turner, *From Counterculture to Cyberculture*, 49.

[30] Turner, *From Counterculture to Cyberculture*, 49.

[31] Turner, *From Counterculture to Cyberculture*, 63.

[32] Turner, *From Counterculture to Cyberculture*, 63.

[33] Tom Wolfe, *The Electric Kool-Aid Acid Test* (New York: Picador, 2008),

[34] Turner, *From Counterculture to Cyberculture*, 64.

[35] Curtis, *All Watched Over by Machines of Loving Grace*, part 2.

[36] Curtis, *All Watched Over by Machines of Loving Grace*, part 2.

[37] Curtis, *All Watched Over by Machines of Loving Grace*, part 2.

[38] Turner, *From Counterculture to Cyberculture*, 54.

[39] Turner, *From Counterculture to Cyberculture*, 66-67.

[40] Turner, *From Counterculture to Cyberculture*, 139.

[41] Turner, *From Counterculture to Cyberculture*, 174.

[42] Agamben, *Stanzas*, 26

[43] Naomi Klein, *No Logo*, (New York: Picador, 209) 196.

[44] Klein, *No Logo*, 22.

[45] Turner, *From Counterculture to Cyberculture*, 143.

[46] Turner, *From Counterculture to Cyberculture*, 159.

[47] Turner, *From Counterculture to Cyberculture*, 157.

[48] Jaron Lanier, *Who Owns the Future* (New York: Simon & Schuster, 2013), 55.

[49] Lanier, *Who Owns the Future*, 55.

[50] Jamie Bartlett, *The people Vs Tech* (London: Ebury Press, 2018), 4.

[51] Turner, *From Counterculture to Cyberculture*, 161.

8. Marketing, War and Demiurgy

> I'm all lost in the supermarket
> I can no longer shop happily
> I came in here for that special offer
> A guaranteed personality
> And it's not here
> It disappear
> **The Clash, *Lost in the Supermarket (1979)***

> And you may ask yourself
> How do I work this?
> And you may ask yourself
> Where is that large automobile?
> And you may tell yourself
> This is not my beautiful house!
> And you may tell yourself
> This is not my beautiful wife!
> **Talking Heads, *Once in a Lifetime (1980)***

The nuclear dynamic inaugurated by the Cold War definitively changed the way in which the world powers thought and made war. "Atomic weapons inaugurated a colossal shift in authority," says historian Sharon Ghamari-Tabrizi, "they swallowed up the personal wisdom of senior officers rooted in combat experience in favor of institutions arising from repeated trials of laboratory-staged simulations of future war."[1] The complexity of the situation faced by the US military in its confrontation with the Soviet Union was no longer something that could be encompassed by a general or even by the Joint Chiefs of Staff, the prediction of the various scenarios that could arise from a nuclear attack needed the joint work of a huge body of analysts armed with analog computers exclusively dedicated to the task. Hunters of possible futures. To this end, the Office of Scientific Research and Development (OSRD)—which had already financed a large number of the wartime laboratories—created a number of specialized centers for military planning focused on research and development. One of the most successful think tanks of this era was the RAND Corporation, whose chief strategist, Herman Kahn, is remembered today as one of the inspirations of Stanley Kubrik's character Dr. Strangelove.

Kahn, an eccentric individual who seemed to enjoy describing different nightmarish nuclear scenarios, resembled Dr. Strangelove in ways that go well beyond the circumstantial. His bestselling book *On Thermonuclear War* describes some of the ideas and circumstances portrayed in Kubrick's film, or perhaps it is more fair to say the opposite: *Dr. Strangelove, or how I learned to stop worrying and love the bomb*, takes many of its arguments and ideas from the contexts outlined by the chief strategist of RAND Corporation. Even the outrageous humor of the film (Gentlemen, you can't fight in here, this is the war room!) seem taken out of Kahn's life: "when officers objected that Kahn was ill-equipped to speak on military affairs, he'd shoot back 'how many thermonuclear wars have *you* fought recently?'"[2] All joking aside, his contribution to the discipline of futurology was lasting and influential on many fronts. Khan was one of the pioneers of *scenario planning*, a strategic thinking technique in which known facts about the future (demographic, geographic, political, industrial, etc.) are combined into games that yield simulations of the future. These are presented in the form of "scenarios," persuasive narrations about possible futures that offer clues on how to act in the present or, even, how to build a certain future. In his colorful language, Kahn once told a journalist: "We assume God's view. The president's view. Big. Aerial. Global. Galactic. Ethereal. Spatial. Overall. Megalomania is the standard occupational risk."[3] This is the megalomania of Bruno's universal master, his narrations are so compelling because instead of numbers and statistics they work by means of *phantasmata*.

By the seventies, scenario planning began to be used by companies such as Royal Dutch Shell to predict economic trends that could affect their business. In 1971, Pierre Wack, head of the Shell Group Planning Office, began to use Kahn's techniques, which he considered superior to the exclusively quantitative methods used by the company so far. But Wack did not use scenario planning as practiced by Kahn. "In his college days, during World War II"

> Wack had attended weekly salons at the Paris home of the mystic philosopher Georges Ivanovich Gurdjieff. During his time there, Wack began to develop a deep preoccupation with

"seeing"—that is, with perceiving the hidden order of events and the inner nature of individuals.[4]

Wack was a very peculiar executive: he spent several weeks a year meditating in India and an incense stick always burned in his office. To explain his prediction process Wack used an anecdote he had been through with a Japanese gardener: "The gardener pointed to a smooth bamboo trunk as thick as a person's arm. He explained that if a small pebble was thrown at it and hit the trunk even slightly off-center, it would glance off, making hardly any sound. If, on the other hand, the pebble hit the trunk dead center, it would make a very distinctive 'clonk.' To be sure to hit the trunk in this way, said the gardener, it was necessary to 'hear' this distinctive sound already in one's mind and focus on it."[5] Thus, in Wack's concept, "seeing the future is about being in the right state of focus to put your finger unerringly on the key facts or insights that unlock or open understanding. Scenario-making is about acute perception, or better, about reperception—becoming free of old perceptions and prejudices at the same time."[6] As strange as it may seem, with his peculiar technique, Wack and his team predicted the rise in oil prices in the early 1970s and their narratives were convincing enough for the company to adjust its policies to the conditions that came with the 1973 crisis. "By the mid-seventies," says Turner, "his scenarios had welded the quantitative modeling of wartime operations and the fantastic futurism of cold war atomic forecasting to the experiential, insight oriented practices of the mystics and gurus favored by the hippies. Scenarios became a form of corporate performance art; in Wack's form of scenario planning, two traditions, corporate and countercultural, merged."[7]

But it is not only these two traditions that meet in Wack's prediction methods. In fact, the mystical and "countercultural" tradition of Gurdjieff belongs to the magical tradition that we studied in the first part of this book. According to Ioan Culianu—an authority, as well as an assiduous practitioner of several divinatory techniques—divination can be seen as a game, a closed system governed by certain logical rules, such as chess or go. A game, says Culianu, "fascinates the mind because the mind recognizes in it its own functioning."[8] In the same vein as Wack, Culianu understood divinatory arts as a set of techniques that allow one to contemplate the very processes of the mind, to listen to the sound of the pebble before it hits the bamboo. Culianu also asserted that rather than in a hidden and esoteric matter, divination can be carried out in "physical steps comparable to those of an analog computer, each [divinatory] art sought to create a transparent logic, perfectly mastered and followed through to the last consequence, that did not offer predictions so much as permutations. Each [art] was a self-enclosed system that worked by quantifying possible outcomes of any situation and then choosing the most likely."[9] From this point of view, the scenario planning technique, in which each presented scenario is a permutation of a total system of variables, would be a modern form of divination similar in essence to pre-modern techniques such as tarot and I Ching, an oracle of probabilities. Thus, Cold War think tanks and, later on, the planning groups of various corporations, not only assumed the role of a *venator* capable of visualizing the network of bonds that form a system in its entirety, but also made use of magical techniques to predict and control an increasingly complex and uncertain world.

While the corporate sector was doing its best to predict and adjust its policies to an increasingly unstable global economy, North American commercial culture was faced with a new challenge: by the mid-seventies the ideals and aspirations of the young people of the country seemed to have changed radically. Among the first sectors to notice the change were insurance companies, which noticed that fewer students fresh out of college bought life insurance. When they looked into it, they found that one of the distinctive features of the new generation was that they were not as interested in the future as in living in the present, therefore those forms of consumption that did not encourage a way of life based on experience did not call their attention. In conclusion, young people were still consumers—that they had never stopped being—but their interests and priorities had shifted out of focus. Instead of looking for the typical products of the American consumer culture, they wanted products that represented them as individuals, that *allowed them to express themselves*. The couple of decades in which the counterculture had proposed different ways of satisfying their "inner being" had opened the mind of an entire generation to the idea that the most important thing was that they were individuals, and as such their highest duty was their own self-realization. However, this new ideal of individuality was not really positive and was intimately related to the overwhelming defeat of the New Left at the hands of the police. By the time the National Guard killed four students at Kent

State University in Ohio in May 1970, the counterculture understood that there was no way to change the establishment through politics; if they had not been able to change the world, all they had left was to change themselves. Therein lied the origin of this sudden explosion of individuality.

Faced with this unexpected situation, Jay Ogilvy, a personal friend of Steward Brand and director of the Stanford Research Institute (SRI), undertook the task of mapping and categorizing the consumption patterns of the new generation. In 1978, Ogilvy and his team designed a method to measure the motivations, values and desires they though had been overlooked until then. The project, called the Values and Lifestyles Program (VALS), designed a questionnaire to investigate the way young people saw themselves and detect the values that impelled their behavior.

The first thing that SRI researchers realized was that the vast majority of persons who received the questionnaire seemed to enjoy answering the questions, these were people who liked to talk about themselves and the way they saw the world. When they analyzed the data they found "a new way to categorize society, not by social class but by different psychological desires and drives,"[10] a method that constitutes a refinement of the regimentation that Edward Bernays began to apply in his work on public relations. Like Pierre Wack's variety of scenario planning, SRI was steeped in magic. In fact, says Jaron Lanier, VALS "classified consumers and customers into a system that was reminiscent of Gurdjieff's 'enneagrams',"[11] a group of geometric figures that were to be understood as *living symbols* and which apparently master Shaykh Abdullah of the Sufi Naqshbandi order in Dagestan had transmitted to Gurdjieff prior to World War I.

The VALS system predicted the presence of a group of individuals that cut across all social classes, which was "not defined by their place in society but by the choices they made themselves [...] these are people for whom personal satisfaction is more important than status or money. They tend to be self-expressive, complex and individualistic."[12] This group, was deemed *inner directed* and divided in three subgroups: the I-am-me's, people that break "away from traditions and invent their own standards";[13] the *experientials*, who "seek inner growth through direct experience [...] this is the try-anything-once crowd";[14] and the *societally conscious*, who focus their energy on social or environmental causes. Looked at closely, these three categories of inner directed people still work out to describe certain fundamental aspects of the most recent generations. In fact, one could argue that *the hipster*—the lifestyle consumer par excellence—condenses traits of these three groups in one individual.

It is hardly surprising to find that the sudden explosion of interiority and individualism that took place in the wake of the 1960s counterculture was suppressed in the same way as the explosion that occurred during the Renaissance of the twelfth century. In both cases the threat was dealt with through police repression: nine centuries ago with the creation of the inquisition and the brutal repression of the Cathars in Southern France, and fifty years ago with the intervention of modern police forces, themselves descendants of the manipulation system emerged from the inquisition, and the National Guard in the case of the United States, a reserve military force whose history can be traced back to the Spanish and English militias of North America. Once the threat was eliminated, literally annihilated in the case of the Cathars, and demoralized and thrashed by the end of the sixties, some of its characteristics were coopted to guarantee the establishment's continuity. While the Catholic Church turned the phantasm of the beloved, *the lady of thoughts*, into the Mother of God under the invocation of the Immaculate Conception, consumer culture, far more versed in "desire management," went a step further and used the same interiority and individualization that emerged from the counterculture against the interests of its members. Marketing began to foster the idea that the individual must define him or herself through consumption, thus, the desire to become an individual became the main enemy of individuality. *Difference in uniformity* is what Orwell would say. This moment marks a new level for the modern manipulative impulse: *the possibility of manipulating a mass not as a mass, but as individuals.*

Aware of this sorry state of affairs, Culianu wrote in 1987: "[...] the state that wants to subsist [...] must seek to produce its own counterculture whose ideological components must be organized in such a way as to hinder the cohesion of the marginalized as well as the increase of their power."

> The simplest and most effective method, but also the most immoral, consists in letting the market of all kinds of

destructive and self-destructive phantasms prosper, while at the same time fostering the idea that there are alternative sources of power, among which the most important would be "mental power." The effects of violence turn against the aggressors, the self-destruction annuls another part of the marginalized, and, meanwhile, the remaining third is occupied pondering ecstatically the unknown, but always inoffensive possibilities of the human psyche. Although, in certain cases, some violent rituals are associated with mental practices, it is unlikely that they will really manage to attack the state's culture. The advantage of these subtle operations lies in not having to resort to direct repression so that the idea of freedom remains unharmed, a tactic whose importance should not be underestimated. On the other hand, alternative fashions also represent a considerable source of prestige and wealth for its creators; and this ensures the proper functioning of all the industries that are related to them: image, disco, apparel fashion.[15]

This is one of the most painfully honest descriptions of the cultural appropriation that took place in the United States and good part of Europe during the sixties and seventies.

But let us go back to the VALS hunting method. Here it is important to mention that the network of bonds imagined by Bruno doesn't even come close to the immense complexity of the statistical matrix of VALS or, case in point, to any modern database. The conditions of the modern world make it impossible for the soul hunter to remain a single person, it must become a market research group, a think tank or a consulting firm. With this transformation the *animarum venator* becomes an entity or organization capable not only of forecasting the general movements in the desire of its preys, it must also be able to note and adjust its projections in order to perceive the most subtle fluctuations in the consumption habits of both individuals and masses.

Regarding the complexity of the hunter's task Bruno comments: "That which is bound is so barely sensible in its depths, that it is possible to examine them only fleetingly and superficially."

> They change from moment to moment and are related to the bonding agent like Thetis fleeing from the embraces of Peleus. It is necessary to study the sequence of the changes and how the power of a subsequent form is influenced by its predecessor, for although matter is indeterminate in relation to innumerable

forms, still its present form is not equally distant from all the others.[16]

This is precisely what a marketing group or a think tank does in varying degrees of success, identifying the changes in the desire of a given population to predict its behavior and influence it. In his role as research director at SRI, Jay Ogilvy emphasized to his clients the need to segment and individuate potential consumers in increasingly specific groups in order to offer products and services specially designed for these target populations. The relationship of this scheme with Bruno's pneumatic network of bonds is rather evident. Like Bruno and Bernays, VALS researchers understood that there was not a single bond that could bind all individuals, but they also understood that all these bonds were subordinated to a primordial bond: desire. As long as people's values and lifestyles were understood, their desires could be deduced, produced and sold back to them. In the *De Vinculis in Genere* Bruno established the basic criteria for this kind of operation:

> The bonding agent is said to be predisposed to bonding in three ways: by its order; by its measure; and by its type. The order is the interrelation of its parts; the measure is its quantity; and its type is designated by its shapes, its outlines and its colours.[17]

This precept, of course, is intended to a human hunter and the example that Bruno offers is that of a sonorous bond, in which "the order consists of a rising and falling through high, low and intermediate notes; the measure is the use of thirds, fourths, fifths, sixths, etc., and the progression of tones and semitones; the type is the harmony, softness and clarity."[18] A human hunter, as well as a *venator-commodity*, must combine these three criteria in their proper proportions to achieve an effective set of bonds.

In the case of a *venator*-research group the process is the inverse. By understanding that "all things are predisposed to bonding," instead of going out hunting with a direct approach, this type of hunter puts all its effort in deducing the susceptibility of a certain group of individuals to this or that type of bond, which may be interests, hobbies, aspirations, etc. After identifying the operating bonds through questionnaires, surveys and other data collection methods, the group is divided into the criteria dictated by Bruno, which, in broad strokes, coincide with what we would now call quality (order), quantity (measure) and appearance (type). This yields a qualitative definition of the relationships established within a group (for example, within the inner directed group); a quantitative definition that determines its proportions (percentages inside and outside the group); and a formal definition that defines its characteristic aspects and differences from other groups and subgroups. Once there is a complete scenario of a certain group, you can proceed to elaborate "commercial bonds" that allow you to bind its members through products or services specially designed for them. Thus, a market research group is an analog machine for the analysis and processing of magical bonds that identifies sectors of the population according to the Brunian criteria of order, measure and appearance. The bonds, instead of being cast in the direction of the prey, are carefully studied, analyzed and optimized until their operational essence is attained. Only then they are converted into external bonds, transmuted into phantasms and sold as commodities, whether it be a service, an ideal or a product.

Something stands out of this whole process: the commitment and passion that the hunter felt as he developed the desires he wanted to impose on his prey are absent in this new type of *venator*. The market research group feels nothing when unveiling the bonds that tie different sectors of the population. The Brunian goal according to which "the perfect hunter will be the one who can project and stimulate desire in others without really feeling it" finds its realization in the impersonal systems of post-war research and development. Lacking a genuine form of consciousness, the think tank or research group is free of phantasms that could be called its own. Therefore, it is not in danger of succumbing to Bruno's warning: "be careful not to change yourself from manipulator into the tool of phantasms." On the other hand, having no identity and lacking self-love (*philautia*), the *venator*-institution is not tied down by any bond and this position allows it to "bind or unbind in any way." Ultimately, the perfect *venator* was always a possibility that lay beyond the human.

There are two ways to achieve this inhumanity. The first, as we have just seen, was the result of the dehumanization inherent in bureaucracy and technocracy; the second lies in the work of the artistic avant-garde. The avant-garde project, as we saw in the previous chapter, focused on the conversion of the artistic object into an absolute commodity, so that the artist, like his work, had to transmute itself into an object, "a creature essentially non-human or antihuman."[19] This is why, according to Agamben, Apollinaire wrote in *Les Peintres Cubistes*, "above all, artists are men who wish to become inhuman."[20] Once dehumanized, the artist acquired the capacity to create situations and happenings, to create an "unreality" free of the fetishistic alienation that lies hidden within the reality imposed by the commodity. Thus, the modern artist became one of the guardians and administrators of this new unreality which manifested itself mainly in performance arts such as Bertolt Brecht's avant-garde theater with is distancing effect technique (*Verfremdungseffekt*). In the last chapter we'll see how this techniques are currently being used in post-Soviet Russia.

Back to our main storyline, the accuracy of the bonds devised by the SRI marketing group was such that they managed to predict the triumph of Ronald Reagan in the 1980 presidential election. As the former governor of California, Reagan was in a privileged position: he could observe the attitudes of the new electorate in his own state which, incidentally, was the epicenter of the counterculture and the main focus of propagation of the group of *inner directeds* identified by the program of Values and Lifestyles. His campaign was aimed at the generation of Baby Boomers who, by then, were attaining true spending power and whose main motivation was their individual realization. Reagan closed one of his campaign speeches with this remark:

> I would like to think that the kind of leadership that I would exercise in Washington, is not the kind of leadership that I would pretend that I can solve all the problems I've been discussing here, but that together, you and I can... I would like to take the lead in taking government off the backs of the american people and turning you loose to do what I know you can do.[21]

Never before had a presidential candidate suggested reducing the role of politics in the lives of US citizens. The most conservative members of his party called it a professional suicide and his competitor, Jimmy Carter, deemed it ridiculous. But Reagan, a former Hollywood actor, knew how to please his audience. By appealing to this individualist sentiment, he achieved something completely unexpected: breaking with the conception that elections depended exclusively on external social factors, such as belonging to a party or being loyal to traditional political ideals.

By speaking to his voters as "individuals"—whose whole individuality lay on their consumption habits—he managed to overcome the political barriers that held traditional parties together and steal a large number of votes from the Democrats. Reagan scored 50.7% against 41% for then President Carter, and a difference of more than eight million popular votes. Under his administration, inflation was countered with unbridled consumption. The eighties were an orgy of luxury and consumerism brilliantly portrayed by writers like Tom Wolfe and Bret Easton-Ellis, a decade in which a good portion of the American public sank into the unreality promoted by free market economy.

Soon enough, this new level of efficiency for mass manipulation would be deployed not only to sell desire but to refresh the greatest allies of the *pax americana*: fear and paranoia. With the Perestroika still far from the horizon and after a decade of realpolitik at the hands of Secretary of State Henry Kissinger, by the early eighties the United States had cultivated a series of new enemies in the Middle East that threatened to alter irrevocably its geopolitical plans. Thanks to Kissinger's Machiavellian manipulations, the Ayatollah Khomeini, Hezbollah and Syrian President Hafez Al-Assad, formed an unlikely and vague alliance that managed to expel the United States from the Middle East after bombing the American embassy and blowing up the headquarters of the Marine Corps in Lebanon. Humiliated and baffled with the situation, the United States decided to save face in the media on two simultaneous fronts: first, creating a smoke screen to cover their retreat by invading the Caribbean Island of Grenada, a military operation against the smallest independent country in the western hemisphere that was harshly criticized by allies such as Canada; and second, by laying the blame not on the complex alliance that had chased them out of the region, but on the weakest link in the chain of Arab extremists: Libyan leader Muammar Gaddafi. As in Guatemala, the United States argued that Gaddafi was a puppet of the Soviet Union (when in fact the Soviets looked at him with caution and considered him unpredictable), and raised him to the rank of international terrorism mastermind. Against all evidence, they accused him of a series of terrorist attacks in Europe that Gaddafi, always thirsty for publicity for his cause, accepted as his own. This spiral of unreality, in which the United States created a quasi-imaginary villain to justify its actions, included the presumption that Libya was close to reaching nuclear capacity and had missiles that could reach Southern Europe. This postmodern farce about good and evil had its apex in two events of international relevance: the fall of Romanian dictator Nicolae Ceaușescu and the Persian Gulf War.

On December 16, 1989, after a quarter of a century of communist dictatorship in Romania, a Hungarian minority initiated a protest in the city of Timişoara in response to the government's attempt to expel pastor László Tőkés from the country. The protests quickly spread to other cities and the Romanian Revolution took an openly mediatic character. The next day it was revealed that, in its attempt to suppress the revolts, the Ceaușescu regime had killed more than four thousand people in Timişoara. At the time very few people noticed a rather telling detail: the advanced state of decomposition of the supposed victims of the massacre. The new regime, says Giorgio Agamben, "succeeded in doing something that Nazism had not even dared to imagine: to bring Auschwitz and the Reichstag fire together in one monstrous event."

> For the first time in the history of humankind, corpses that had just been buried or lined up on the morgue's tables were hastily exhumed and tortured in order to simulate, in front of the video cameras, the genocide that legitimized the new regime. What the entire world was watching live on television, thinking it was the real truth, was in reality the absolute non-truth; and, although the falsification appeared to be sometimes quite obvious, it was nevertheless legitimized as true by the media's world system, so that it would be clear that the true was, by now, nothing more than a moment within the necessary movement of the false.[22]

Ceaușescu was tried for genocide and executed with his wife Elena on December 25 of the same year. Edited recordings of the trial and execution were transmitted that same night in Romania and sent to different international media outlets. Ioan Culianu, who was living in the United States at the time and had become a tireless critic of the lies and ruses of his country's politics, soon reported that "what began as a genuine popular uprising in the city of Timişoara was soon co-opted by factions within the Securitate, the Army and the party that had long been planning to topple the Ceaușescu regime."[23] Two years later he became yet another victim of his country's violence.

An avid practitioner of various magical and divinatory techniques, Culianu used his skills as a political tool against the communist regime in his native Romania. In 1986 he published a political farce entitled *L'interventionzione degli Zorabi in Jormania* (The intervention of the Zorabis in Jormania) in which he predicted, to the letter, a sequence of events that took place three years later during the fall of Nicolae Ceaușescu's regime. Such 'coincidences' attracted the attention of members of the *Securitate*, the Romanian intelligence agency, and the fact that Culianu had continued to write scathing fictions and political commentaries in various international publications, before and after Ceaușescu's fall, may have contributed to form a conspiracy against him. For Culianu, all the events his country was going through "were a repetition of some archetypes embedded in our religious history."[24] He saw, according to Ted Anton, "events following a pattern—but at a deeper level than the players knew."[25] In his writings Culianu always gave the impression of knowing more than what could actually be known—although here "knowing" understood in strictly rational terms becomes irrelevant—and refusing to take heed of the constant threats of his enemies he continued to flood the international press with articles against the new regime that had taken hold of his country. He was murdered with a shot to the back of the head in a bathroom stall of the University of Chicago's Divinity School on May 21, 1991. His crime was never solved.

In another of his "fictions" Culianu escapes his tragic destiny. *The Language of Creation*, a short story written with his fiancée Hillary Wiesner, tells the story of a professor who works in a "grey" midwestern university who is clearly based on himself. During a trip to the Netherlands this professor buys a mysterious music box in an auction of articles of the Romanian extreme right and concludes that the box has the key to decipher "the language spoken by God: the language of Creation. Yet, the three former owners of the box each met with murder."[26] Although he tries to break the divine code by all possible means, he can't seem to solve the enigma. Some exceptional occurrences, based on the experiences of Culianu himself, make the protagonist of the story feel simultaneously fascinated and threatened by the presence of the box in his life. The teacher acquires the ability to foresee minor events or to enchant and make some of his female students fall in love with him, events he calls by the name *charismata*.

"After a certain moment," says Culianu, "my conviction of an occult connection between the charismata and the box had become so solid that I was tempted to make a test of its powers against a distasteful political regime [...] The hypothesis that I might immediately resume the fate of [the former owners] came to haunt me."[27] After a long deliberation the teacher decides to leave the music box at a yard sale "and escapes to freedom from what had become an intellectual prison posed by its secret."[28] As his alter ego, Culianu could have steered clear from danger at any moment, but led by a peculiar mix of intellectual vanity and political commitment, he continued on the path that led to his death. It could be said that when composing his articles and fictions, Culianu ignored Bruno's great warning: be careful not to change yourself from manipulator into the tool of phantasms.

Culianu's murder did not receive considerable coverage in the press and the atrocities of the Romanian Revolution and the new regime were soon overshadowed by the media display of the Gulf War, which focused on an eternal loop made up of a few images: oil wells burning in the desert; guided missiles blowing strategic targets with breathtaking precision; Nighthawks spraying Baghdad with smart bombs; over and over again. The war machine and the media machine joined together in a perfect combination. In a series of articles published in the French newspaper *Libération*, Jean Baudrillard argued that the Gulf War had not really happened. Of course, Baudrillard did not deny that an armed confrontation had taken place because of Iraq's invasion of Kuwait, but that this war was the first to happen entirely in the hyperreal territory of the media. In the first of his three articles, Baudrillard posited that the West had developed an obsessive fear of any event or enjoyment that was too real, one further step in the armoring implicit in Reich's pleasure anxiety, an *armoring from reality*. Decades of nuclear uncertainty that were dealt with the scenario planning method bred a political uncertainty that was dealt with exactly the same tool, simulacra. To counter this new uncertainty we "created a gigantic apparatus of simulation which allows us to pass to the act 'in vitro' [...] we prefer the exile of the virtual, of which television is the universal mirror, to the catastrophe of the real." War, says Baudrillard,

> has not escaped this virtualisation which is like a surgical operation, the aim of which is to present a face-lifted war, the

cosmetically treated spectre of its death, and its even more deceptive televisual subterfuge (as we saw in Timisoara).²⁹

The reasons why the United States withdrew from the Persian Gulf and left Saddam Hussein in relative peace after achieving its goal of expelling him from Kuwait seem manifold. For one, the UN Security Council never gave its authorization for the Coalition to invade Iraq, and Hussein's regime continued after its defeat. Twelve years later, George W. Bush would finish his father's work by invading and completely destroying the country under the "undeniable" evidence of a vast assortment of weapons of mass destruction that never surfaced. The post-truth label was late by several decades.

In fact, in his 1988 book *Comments on The Society of The Spectacle*, Guy Debord offers a straight description of this phenomenon when he talks of "unanswerable lies" as one of the distinguishing features of the integrated spectacle:

> The simple fact of being unanswerable has given what is false an entirely new quality. At a stroke it is truth which has almost everywhere ceased to exist or, at best, has been reduced to the status of pure hypothesis. Unanswerable lies have succeeded in eliminating public opinion, which first lost the ability to make itself heard and then very quickly dissolved altogether. This evidently has significant consequences for politics, the applied sciences, the legal system and the arts.³⁰

What post-truth ultimately means is that truth is not only obfuscated but that it genuinely disappeared as a relevant category with which we can grasp reality.

In *HyperNormalisation*, Adam Curtis narrates how one of the sources that supposedly had direct access to Saddam Hussein's weapons program confirmed that Iraq was producing "vast quantities of VX and Sarin nerve agents. The nerve agents were being loaded into linked hollow glass spheres. But then someone in MI6 noticed that the detail the source was describing was identical to scenes in the 1996 movie *The Rock* starring Sean Connery and Nicholas Cage." Despite this "detail," the US and the UK went on with the invasion. If by the early sixties Stanley Kubrick had used Herman Khan as an inspiration for *Dr. Strangelove*, by the early twenty-first century government agencies were using Hollywood movies as an excuse to invade other countries. Where does fiction end and reality begin? The film about Prince Harry of Wales and Meghan Markle's romance premiered on May 13, 2018, seven days before their real-life wedding took place. Spectacular time begins to gain on real time, the first won't allow the latter a *dénouement*; the demiurgic circle is closing up for good. Two versions of Harry and Meghan will coexist for a brief moment in time. Which of the two will we remember in a few years, the "real sugar-coated-by-the-media people," or their "fake" sugar-coated TV movie versions? Unreality is quickly devouring reality.

Regarding the lack of evidence that Iraq was providing weapons of mass destruction to terrorist organizations, Secretary of Defense Donald Rumsfeld gave a statement that acquired a reputation that was not at all unwarranted:

> Reports that say that something hasn't happened are always interesting to me, because as we know, there are known knowns; there are things we know we know. We also know there are known unknowns; that is to say we know there are some things we do not know. But there are also unknown unknowns –the ones we don't know we don't know. And if one looks throughout the history of our country and other free countries, it is the latter category that tend to be the difficult ones.[31]

Unsurprisingly, the unknown unknown is a term with a long tradition in the field of strategic planning that grew out of the Cold War. A few months later, Slavoj Žižek published an article in *In These Times* in which he added a fourth permutation to Rumsfeld's epistemology: the "unknown knowns," that is, those things we don't know we know, "the disavowed beliefs, suppositions and obscene practices we pretend not to know about, even though they form the background of our public values."[32] For Žižek, this type of knowledge corresponds to the Freudian unconscious and is an integral part of the political life of the West; Abu Ghraib and Guantánamo come to mind. But going further, the unknown known also exemplifies the twilight that lies between our reality and Baudrillard's hyperreality, the gray area in which the pneumatic circle is drawn and all magical operations begin. A place known to the hunter, to some extent and certainly not as magic, but completely unknown to the prey.

The virtualization of war—a journey to this *terra incognita* that began in Guatemala and was perfected in the Persian Gulf—is one of the most aggressive instances of demiurgy, a magic spell that devours emotional energy in exchange of falsehood and injustice on a global scale. This aesthetic of death, the lifted face of war, becomes the new countenance of the world/goddess, unique and indisputable, and assumes its original *cosmetic* functions. But while the original countenance, the *psyche kosmou*, ordered and harmonized by putting the whole together, the new face of the world, the face of the magic spells of the media, does exactly the opposite, it creates differences in uniformity which then proceeds to unite in separation. The result is a mosaic of phantasmagoria: a man standing in the way of a Chinese army tank; O.J. Simpson's Bronco in hot pursuit on an LA highway; Princess Diana's Mercedes-Benz crashed against the pillars of a Paris' tunnel; the Twin Towers falling again and again on televisions all over the planet; two gigantic Buddha statues blown to bits; the pieces are endless and ever shifting. But this is a reality that, in the terms of the Kabbala, has "sucked the milk of evil," it has separated from the minds of its creators and taken on a life of its own. It has already absorbed our entire mental space, it has our undivided attention, what else could it steal from us?

The absurdity of the unreality which we all inhabit is perfectly represented in a conversation in Barry Levinson's comedy film *Wag the Dog*. In it a spin doctor played by Robert De Niro and a Hollywood producer played by Dustin Hoffman are hired to create the "appearance of a war" with Albania to draw away the attention from accusations of sexual abuse on the part of the president (any resemblance to reality is a coincidence, the movie was released a month before the Lewinsky scandal). Once their assignment is completed and a "peace agreement" is achieved, the characters talk about whether they should start a campaign to nominate the president for the Nobel Peace Prize:

>—Well, if Kissinger can win the Peace Prize, I wouldn't be surprised to wake up and find out I'd won the Preakness.
>—Well, yes, but our guy did bring peace.
>—Yeah, but there wasn't a war.
>—All the greater accomplishment.

If our greatest accomplishment, as the conversation suggests, is to aspire to act upon this fictitious reality, we are condemned to live in Žižek's "unknown known," constantly confronted, like the fetishist, to the presence of an absence, a shadow, a negative in the twilight of our consciousness that we can sense but we can never really apprehend. This is what the human condition has been reduced to.

Behold, our dogs are already here.

---

[1] Sharon Ghamari-Tabrizi, *The Worlds of Herman Kahn: the intuitive science of thermonuclear war* (Massachussets: Harvard University Press, 2005), 48.
[2] Ghamari-Tabrizi, *The Worlds of Herman Kahn*, 49.
[3] Turner, *From Counterculture to Cyberculture*, 186.
[4] Turner, *From Counterculture to Cyberculture*, 187.
[5] Hardin Tibbs, "Pierre Wack: a Remarkable Source of Insight" in *Netview, Global Business Network News, Volumen 9 No. 1*. Accessed, May 18, 2018, at: https://www.researchgate.net/publication/287493967_Pierre_Wack_a_Remarkable_Source_of_Insight
[6] Hardin Tibbs, "Pierre Wack: a Remarkable Source of Insight"
[7] Turner, *From Counterculture to Cyberculture*, 187.
[8] Ioan P. Culianu, *The Tree of Gnosis: Gnostic Mythology from Early Christianity to Modern Nihilism* (San Francisco: Harper Collins, 1992), 247.
[9] Ted Anton, *Eros, Magic and the Murder of Professor Culianu* (Evanston: Northwestern University Press, 1996), 176.
[10] Adam Curtis, *The Century of the Self*, Third part.
[11] Jaron Lanier, *Who Owns the Future* (New York: Simon & Schuster, 2013), 215.
[12] Taken from an SRI promotional video. Curtis, *The Century of the Self*
[13] Taken from an SRI promotional video. Curtis, *The Century of the Self*
[14] Taken from an SRI promotional video. Curtis, *The Century of the Self*
[15] This fragment does not appear in the English version of Culianu's *Eros and Magic in the Renaissance* and was translated from the Spanish version: *Eros y magia en el renacimiento, 1484* (Madrid: Ediciones Siruela, 1999), 150-151.
[16] Bruno, *A General Account of Bonding*, 154.
[17] Bruno, *A General Account of Bonding*, 151.
[18] Bruno, *A General Account of Bonding*, 151.
[19] Giorgio Agamben, *Stanzas, Word and Phantasms in Western Culture* (Minneapolis: University of Minnesota Press, 1993), 50.
[20] Agamben, *Stanzas*, 50.
[21] Adam Curtis, *Hypernormalisation*.
[22] Giorgio Agamben, *Means without End* (Minneapolis: University of Minnesota Press, 2000), 80.
[23] Ted Anton, "The Killing of Professor Culianu." Accessed, May 18, 2018, at:
http://linguafranca.mirror.theinfo.org/9209/culianu.html
[24] Ted Anton, *Eros, Magic and the Murder of Professor Culianu* (Evanston: Northwestern University Press, 1996), 191.
[25] Anton, *Eros, Magic and the Murder of Professor Culianu*, 197.
[26] Anton, *Eros, Magic, and the Murder of Professor Culianu*, 13.
[27] Culianu, quoted by Anton in *Eros, Magic, and the Murder of Professor Culianu*, 13.
[28] Anton, *Eros, Magic, and the Murder of Professor Culianu*, 14.

[29] Jean Baudrillard, *The Gulf War did not Take Place* (Bloomington: Indiana University Press, 1995), 25.
[30] Guy Debord, *Comments on the Society of the Spectacle* (London: Verso, 1990), 12-13.
[31] "DOD News Briefing – Secretary Rumsfeld and Ge. Myers." Accessed, May 28, 2018, at: *http://archive.defense.gov/Transcripts/Transcript.aspx? Transcript ID=2636*
[32] Slavoj Žižek, "What Rumsfeld Doesn't Know That he Knows About Abu Ghraib." Accessed, May 10, 2018, at: *http://inthesetimes.com/article/747/what _rumsfeld_doesn_know_that_he_knows_about_abu_ghraib/*

9. The Digital Tide.
From real to virtual pneuma

You are a true believer. Blessing of the state, blessings of the masses.
Thou art a subject of the divine, created in the image of man,
by the masses, for the masses. Let us be thankful we have commerce.
Buy more. Buy more now. Buy and be happy
THX 1138 (1971)

Underneath the sky where the cold winds cross
There is an ocean where data flows
One man in a boat out on the sea
A sea of little bits of you and me
Peter Gabriel — The Veil (2016)

By the mid-eighties John Perry Barlow's ranch in Wyoming was headed towards serious economic trouble. Shortly before, the Grateful Dead lyricist had bought a computer with a word processor to write some television scripts that were never produced. Instead of getting into his writing project, Barlow was increasingly intrigued with the machine itself. In an interview with Fred Turner, he admitted wanting to hide away inside the computer. He wanted to flee from the fact that his family's ranch had ceased being a good business and sooner than later he would have to sell it. In his peculiar and playful style, he described his situation in this way: "I was as culturally doomed as the Tasaday of New Guinea... yanked from the 19th century, I found myself... tossed unceremoniously onto the doorstep of the 21st."[1]

Barlow turned to his friends in San Francisco and in 1986 he joined The WELL. Thanks to his gift for concise and colorful writing and his great charisma, in a few months he was one of the most outstanding personalities of the forum. His fusion of libertarian ideals with an optimistic interest in the new digital technologies made him the ideal spokesman for the virtual world that was beginning to shape up in dozens of servers around the world. A few years later Barlow co-founded the Electronic Frontier Foundation, the first organization in the world to safeguard civil rights on the internet and provide legal assistance. However, his optimistic vision of cyberspace where everyone would have a voice and there would be no hierarchies—largely drawn from the communalist ethos of The WELL—was far from being unanimous. There were other groups of digital enthusiasts and technologists for whom Barlow's vision was extremely naive.

The clash between idealists such as Barlow, Steward Brand and Kevin Kelly, and a group of hard-core realists from the East Coast took place in an online conference proposed by Harper's Bazaar and hosted by The WELL in December 1989. During the first session, entitled "*is computer hacking a crime?*" the participants tried to determine the principles of a hacker ethic, but two young hackers from New York who called themselves *Acid Phreak* and *Phiber Optik* expressed their disagreement in no uncertain terms:

> ACID PHREAK [Day 1, 6:34 P.M.]: There is no one hacker ethic. Everyone has his own. To say that we all think the same way is preposterous. The hacker of old sought to find what the computer itself could do. There was nothing illegal about that. Today, hackers and phreaks are drawn to specific often corporate, systems. It's no wonder everyone on the other side is getting mad. We're always one step ahead. We were back then, and we are now.[2]

The hackers of old referred to by Acid Phreak were the direct ancestors of his own lineage, electrical and electronic engineers born of the academic dynamic that emerged from the Cold War who experimented with the possibilities of the computerized systems that were being built during the fifties and sixties. With the emergence of the first digital networks there appeared a new generation that acquired a taste for deciphering how to break into these and into the existing telephone networks. It is worth noting that hackers, crackers (criminal hackers) and phreakers (hackers expert in breaking into telephone networks), come from a distinguished lineage that goes back to the abbot and magician Trithemius von Würzburg, one of the most outstanding cryptographers of the fifteenth century and mentor of Cornelius Agrippa. Cryptography, which consists of the art of hiding written messages by means of secret codes, Culianu reminds us, was considered as a branch of magic during the sixteenth century. Of course, the art of producing secret forms of writing is inseparable from the art of knowing how to decipher them. *The Legion of Doom*, a group of hackers of which Phiber Optik was a member, used the maxim of English occultist and magician Aleister Crowley "do what thou wilt shall be the whole of the law." Many hackers shared an attitude that was simultaneously quasi-esoteric, libertarian and pro-free speech.[3]

But let us return to the controversy between the cyber-libertarians of The WELL and the East Coast hackers. As the conversation developed, Barlow, faithful to his communalist vision of the virtual world, described it as an open place, a sort of global village whose integrity depended precisely on this condition. Barlow resented that hackers such as Acid Phreak and Phiber Optik wanted to break into computer systems for the simple pleasure of doing so, although one might ask the following question: if the digital world was an essentially open place why were there hackers that had to break into its systems? As the discussion heated up, Barlow argued that everyone in the virtual world should leave their doors open and voluntarily offered his Wyoming ranch address as a show of openness. Irritated by the gesture (and a couple of dismissive comments from Barlow) Phiber Optik decided to break into the TRW system, one of the largest credit centers at the time, extract Barlow's credit info and post it in the forum.

> ACID [Day 11, 1:37 P.M.]: For thirty-five dollars a year anyone can have access to TRW and see his or her own credit history. Optik did it for free. What's wrong with that? And why does TRW keep files on what color and religion we are? If you didn't know that they kept such files, who would have found out if it wasn't for a hacker? Barlow should be grateful that Optik has offered his services to update him on his personal credit file.[4]

Hackers like Phiber Optik and Acid Phreak knew first hand that for years large corporations had begun storing all kinds of information about the general public; the virtual world had never been the cluster of open communities that Barlow imagined and such a vision prevented taking action against this reality; forums like The WELL were an exception, an island in an ocean of secrets. Seen in this light, it is practically impossible that what had begun as a decentralized system of military communication designed to survive a nuclear attack, could ever become a decentralized structure designed to nullify the hierarchies of modern life and create an electronic utopia. The WELL's communalist ideology shaped many of the collaborative practices that led to the new economy, but the spirit of our current internet is that described by Phiber Optik and Acid Phreak.

Not long after the conference was over, *Harper's Bazaar* organized a dinner in Manhattan to ingratiate Barlow, Acid and Optik. Like the good-natured gentleman hippie he was, Barlow befriended the two hackers who were then in their early twenties. By mid 1990, Barlow was visited by the FBI to inquire about illegal activities that might be going on from his computer; the *Harper's Bazaar* article had led them there. In January of the same year Phiber Optik and Acid Phreak had been raided by the Secret Service in relation to the crash of AT&T's network—later on the company admitted that the crash was the result of faulty software and not of intrusion. Barlow wrote an essay about these experiences titled "Crime and Puzzlement" which he posted on The WELL, where he questioned the nature of cybernetic crime and defended Optik and Phreak from the attacks of the FBI and the Secret Service. And yet, besieged by the powers that be and against all evidence to the contrary, Barlow continued insisting on the innate openness of the virtual world. In his famous essay "Declaration of Independence of Cyberspace," which he presented at the Davos forum in 1996, Barlow begins:

> Governments of the Industrial World, you weary giants of flesh and steel, I come from Cyberspace, the new home of Mind. On behalf of the future, I ask you of the past to leave us alone. You are not welcome among us. You have no sovereignty where we gather.
>
> We have no elected government, nor are we likely to have one, so I address you with no greater authority than that with which liberty itself always speaks. I declare the global social space we are building to be naturally independent of the tyrannies you seek to impose on us. You have no moral right to rule us nor do you possess any methods of enforcement we have true reason to fear.
>
> Governments derive their just powers from the consent of the governed. You have neither solicited nor received ours. We did not invite you. You do not know us, nor do you know our world. Cyberspace does not lie within your borders. Do not think that you can build it, as though it were a public construction project.

You cannot. It is an act of nature and it grows itself through our collective actions.[5]

Someone had to say it, and Barlow did so in a concise and elegant manner, but even then it was too late. The internet may have seemed to shut its doors to government interests but certainly not to corporate ones. By the mid-nineties large corporations such as America Online, Time Warner and Microsoft had already begun to take possession of the virtual world and their actions, even if they were meant to keep the world governments at bay, brought with them the same dynamic of cooptation and profit that converted the counterculture into an appalling mosaic of lifestyles.

The net had begun to close in on itself but cyberlibertarians like Brand and Barlow kept insisting on its openness, on the intrinsic possibility of self-determination of the digital realm. Here it is important to note that digital technology is not essentially open or closed and the fact that it can be used both for military (ARPANET) or civil (Internet) purposes does not mean that it is *neutral*. However, taking this vague notion of neutrality as a starting point,

> there arose the equally diffuse idea that digital networks tend naturally to non-hierarchical and decentralized structures that facilitate collaboration and teamwork. With this idea, fueled by certain currents of the sixties counterculture, came the promise of new forms of interaction that would turn the internet into a paradise of freedom of expression in which individuals could regain their voice in an increasingly impersonal world, where free participation and privacy would be ratified as the ideals par excellence of post-industrial societies.[6]

As I argued elsewhere, rather than neutral, technology "is 'specular,' anything that we feed it, that is precisely what we get in return, a circumstance perfectly expressed in the old computer maxim *garbage in, garbage out*. This specularity, in combination with the automatic and programmable nature of the digital, is the reason why our devices and networks perfectly *reflect our unconscious tendencies and limitations.*"[7] In this sense, modern technology, and in particular digital networks, are part of Žižek's unknowns knowns, of everything that we do not know we know but that still has an effect in our lives. We may not know that we constantly feed technology because we do so unconsciously, although we could sense it by looking at the results. The communalists believed that they would obtain a certain result by applying cybernetics to their social project, but they were unaware that the "unconscious" of cybernetics' was the *anima machinalis*. We all know where the failed hopes and promises of the counterculture have led us, we live *in* them. We are no more free now than fifty years ago and, in fact, we have become a new breed of happy and entertained slaves who do not recognize themselves as such. In the last two decades, digital technology has become a gigantic mirror and, truth be told, there is nothing we like more than our own reflection. This may not be news now that we live immersed in social networks and surrounded by selfies, but it was an unpleasant discovery in the mid-sixties, when Joseph Weizenbaum, a pioneer in the field of artificial intelligence, caught a glimpse of this tendency.

In 1966 Weizenbaum, then a professor at MIT, designed a computer program capable of conversing in an apparently coherent way with a human through a keyboard. Weizenbaum christened his creation ELIZA in honor of Eliza Doolittle, the cockney flower girl of George Bernard Shaw's play *Pygmalion*. Like his literary counterpart, who learned to speak English with an upper class accent, the more it was exposed to human interlocutors, ELIZA started to become more fluid in conversation. Because of its structure, the program could use the patterns it encountered in its conversations but could not create new patterns or understand the context of the alluded events; its programming was limited to asking non-directional questions depending on the input of the human users, as if it were a particularly vague and distracted psychotherapist. And yet, people loved it. Everyone who came into contact with ELIZA seemed to believe that it was a conscious being. Many forgot that they were talking to a computer and, on one occasion, Weizenbaum's secretary asked him to leave the room to give her privacy in her conversation with the machine. "I had not realized," wrote Weizenbaum, "that extremely short exposures to a relatively simple computer program could induce powerful delusional thinking in quite normal people."[8] Soon enough, ELIZA caught the attention of psychotherapists and science fiction writers who saw in the program a possible future for therapy. In *THX 1138*, George Lucas and Walter Murch incorporated a computer which operated in a way similar to ELIZA, to which the characters in the film could turn to in case of needing psychological assistance. OMM 0000, the name of the machine, was a confessional deity that more than consoling indoctrinated in an automatic fashion.

Appalled by the gullibility and thoughtlessness of his fellow humans, Weizenbaum went from technology enthusiast to one of its staunchest critics. No matter how much he stressed that ELIZA wasn't aware and didn't have any real thoughts or feelings—in the absence of which there could not be a true "interaction"—most people did not understand the implications of the experiment: ELIZA offered a parody of human communication. The apparent interiority of the computer program was, in fact, the users' interiority reflected back at them. The program acted as a mirror and that was what was so reassuring and rewarding about talking to her (sorry, "it"). When we are in trouble, us humans tend to talk to ourselves to try and sort things out in our heads, to assess what's the best course of action and convince ourselves that we are right and the decision we have taken is correct. ELIZA allowed people to act out that impulse in the real world, and it felt amazing; it was like having a friend that always tells you that you can't be wrong, that everything is going to be ok. Interacting with ELIZA was like being immersed in your own mind; the moment just before Narcissus hits the water.

Instead of offering true openness, the most basic forms of AI and the primitive digital networks gave us back a reflection of ourselves and entrapped us in a closed cybernetic system; a system which, as I will explain briefly, can be characterized as the most recent version of the pneumatic circle. The essential trait of our current form of social reality is that *it appears as an ever expanding openness that nonetheless conceals a proportional enclosure.* How closed this brave new world is was one of the revelations that came with the classified information exposed by WikiLeaks and Edward Snowden, although, to be honest, we had plenty of chances to catch up with this trend long before that. However, most people dismissed it as mere conspiracy theory. After 9/11 the so-called democratic states became surveillance states right under our noses. In their role as technological wizards—cryptographers in the tradition of Trithemius and Cornelius Agrippa—Assange and Snowden tried to break the spell of the establishment by revealing some of its most sordid secrets; both ended up living in exile. In the opening lines of his book *Cypherpunks*, Assange declares:

> The world is not sliding, but galloping into a new transnational dystopia. This development has not been properly recognized outside of national security circles. It has been hidden by secrecy, complexity and scale. The Internet, our greatest tool for emancipation, has been transformed into the most dangerous facilitator of totalitarianism we have ever seen.[9]

Even if it only had the potential but never got to be the tool of emancipation many expected, Assange is absolutely right in the second part of his argument, there has never been such an effective tool for the control and manipulation of the masses as digital networks; *rete* in Marsilio Ficino's language. And have we fallen into them. As it turns out, Jeremy Bentham's dream of a panopticon would not yield its most perfect version in architecture but in the digital world. The digital panopticon, an idea that I outlined in the introduction to this study by way of new media theorist Lev Manovich, is a reality in its own right. But it is not just a social structure that blinds the majority of the population to the interests and manipulations of its leaders, "our modern panopticon," says theorist Jamie Bartlett, "doesn't have just one watchman: everyone is both watching and being watched. This kind of permanent visibility and monitoring, is a way to enforce conformity and docility. Being always under surveillance and knowing that the things you say are collected creates a soft but constant self-censorship,"[10] a situation that should remind us of the environment produced by the Gestapo or, case in point, by the secret police in any totalitarian regime.

In the first chapter of Part III we saw that during the postwar period the pneuma began to be characterized as information circulating within closed cybernetic systems and that its arrival in the digital realm implies a sort of *incarnation of the spirit* in a material substrate. Far from an arbitrary assertion, this matter has been noted by scholars like Leon Marvell who argue that the idea of a subtle essence (pneuma), was not cast out by the scientific establishment, it was integrated to its system in another disguise:

> Contra the opinion that both applauds and hypostatizes the notion of a disjunctive scientific/materialistic break with the animistic past, I regard the imagery of the pneumatic economy as fundamental to a project that would reexamine the bases of contemporary natural science. In this reexamination the pneumatic economy would no longer be predicated on the

interactions of a 'subtle' material medium; rather it would be predicated on what it so closely resembles: the communicative/cybernetic notion of a world constituted by information exchange.[11]

Now, if the pneuma actually transmuted into information we should be able to identify its characteristic movement in the "movements" of digital networks, it should be possible to make out the pneumatic circle in the operation of the most widespread type of network today: the social network. As in the case of Bruno's pneumatic hunting, I will describe this process in the individual and then proceed to find it in the masses.

First of all we must determine the closed nature of social networks, something we can achieve through one of its most characteristic manifestations: the selfie. In pneumatic terms, a selfie is a closed pneumatic circle that, unlike the basic circle of erotic magic, revolves not around the subject and the phantasms of the beloved, but between the subject and his own phantasms.

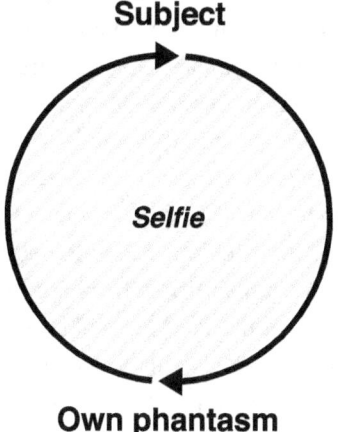

This configuration has been described countless times as narcissistic. However, it is important to clarify that the narcissism implicit in a selfie adjusts not only to the psychological sense with which we currently use the term but also to the original mythological sense. Narcissus was not in love with himself, as inferred from the Freudian interpretation of the myth, he was in love with an image he thought was a real creature. The question here is: how real are the creatures we see reflected in our mobile devices? This aspect, which we tend to overlook in favor of a psychoanalytic reading, is clear in Ovid's *Metamorphoses*, in which Narcissus, finding a unsullied pond, approaches it to quench his thirst. However, the young man found

> another thirst, for while he drinks he sees a beautiful face and falls in love with a bodiless fantasy, and takes for a body what is no more than a shadow.[12]

Ovid tells Narcissus with heartfelt urgency:

> Gullible boy, grasping at passing images! What you seek is nowhere. If you look away you loose what you love. What you see is a shadow, a reflected image, and has nothing of its own. It comes with you and it stays with you, and it will go with you, if you are able to go.[13]

Only after some some time, when it's already too late, the young hunter realizes that what he is facing is his own image. "So great is the confusion in which this lover wanders, lost!"[14] he says, dismayed. If I may adapt Ovid's verse, in the case of a selfie "so great is the confusion in which this lover of his own image wanders, lost!," so great as to shut himself in his own phantasm. That the love of one's image implies a true *philautia*, instead of love for a phantasm, is an unjustified presumption and it may well mean the opposite, low self-esteem and crippling self-doubt. The selfie can even be seen as an attenuated form of surveillance on the self, an auto-monitoring with which the subject verifies that his image remains static, intact within the pneumatic circle. What this love, malnourished in its autism, cries out for is the satisfaction and certainty that can only be obtained from a mirror, from a program like ELIZA or, in its most recent version, from the feed of a social network.

Narcissus' water mirror, which became the Fountain of Love during the Middle Ages, reappears in multiple forms in the modern world, its dynamic has a clear echo in the totality of the system. With the appearance of consumer culture, the watery surface where the phantasms of the beloved are reflected transforms into display windows, TV sets and cinema screens and, more recently, into smart phones, tablets and laptops. The mechanism is identical: whether we talk about the commodities in a window display or the feed of a social network, the surface, like the fountain in the garden of delights of the *Roman de la Rose*, reflects the totality of the wishes and aspirations of those who look at them. But whereas a display window reflects generic commodities designed for everyone, a live feed is nourished by all the information the users feed into the system which is then reflected back to them in the form of customized goods, services and options for their tastes and aspirations. Thus, the world becomes smaller for each individual, who can only contemplate their own desires and opinions constantly reflected in his or her devices.

The downside to this situation is rather evident and has been addressed by many commentators: you will never see anything beyond your own nose. Once again, people thought technology was offering them open-ended tools with which they could exercise their individuality and self-determination freely, when in reality it was offering them an ever closing world in which, sooner or later, they would not be able to exercise anything beyond what they already knew or thought; anything beyond the known knowns. Here's important to bear in mind that anyone operating exclusively in this epistemological category is inherently manipulable as it is unaware of the hidden motivations (unknown unknowns and unknown knowns) that drive his or other people's behaviors. This also means that in such a situation we are not only at the mercy of the willing manipulations of our hunters but also of their unconscious desires.

This closing down of points of view and opinions takes two main forms in the media: the echo chamber and the filter bubble. The echo chamber, a term derived from acoustic chambers in which a sound reverberates in a space specially designed for this purpose, is a concept with a long history in traditional media. In this context, an echo chamber refers to the fact that a group of individuals, composed sometimes of hundreds of thousands or even millions of people, only have access to certain types of information, which is being disseminated with a specific bias and through a usual channel, usually with dulling repetition. The information ricochets on the "walls" of the system rendering any alternative source invisible. The coverage of O.J. Simpson's trial and Fox News' rush to declare George W. Bush as president elect are prototypical examples of echo chambers. The 24-hour news cycle doesn't help the situation. Sheer repetition has always done the trick with the masses.

Here it is worth noting the mythical roots of the echo chamber in the context of Narcissus' myth: Echo is a nymph that falls in love with beautiful Narcissus, but her love is unrequited and she languishes in the forest. Seeing this, Nemesis, the goddess of retributive justice (revenge), decides to punish the conceit of the young hunter by spellbinding him so that he falls in love with his own image. Thus, Narcissus' fate is such due to his lack of empathy for Echo's suffering; like Echo, whom by a curse of Hera can only repeat the last words directed at her, Narcissus is trapped in a similar prison, but one made not of sound but image. The destinies of Echo and Narcissus seem intertwined from their mythical origins to their contemporary media manifestations. Digital narcissism is always preceded, and why not contained, by an Echo chamber.

The second manifestation of the closing down of the media, the filter bubble, is a variety of echo chamber exclusive to the digital world. The filter bubble, a term coined by Internet activist Eli Pariser, occurs when a search algorithm stars to determine what information a specific user would like to see based on factors such as location, search patterns and browser history. For example, Google's personalized search, introduced in 2004, extracts information through the browser's cookies and presents its results based not on the relevance of each webpage, but on the user's history and previous searches. For its part, Facebook announced in 2013 a revamped news-stream capable of filtering more than two thousand posts each time the application is opened, based on metrics that take into account the number of clicks, reactions and reading time of similar posts by the user and his or her friends, among other factors. The result of these algorithmic operations is an information bubble, a personal echo chamber (in fact "personalized"), that encloses the subject preventing access to information from sources with different points of view. As in the myth of Echo and Narcissus, nowadays most people live in the personal filter bubbles presented by their social media which are contained by the echo chambers of traditional media. "A world constructed from the familiar," says Pariser, "is a world in which there's nothing to learn." As far as communication goes such a world amounts to a form of "invisible autopropaganda, indoctrinating us with our own ideas."[15]

What opinions will we hold and who will we try to inform? I asked a few years ago in another essay, and even more important, why, if ultimately there will be no one else to include and inform? This topic is masterfully treated by Dave Eggers in his novel, very appropriately titled *The Circle*, which was later adapted into a movie starring Emma Watson and Tom Hanks. The uncertainty of the modern world overcompensated into a huge demiurgic bubble, a pneumatic circle of certainty and control where everyone sees only what they, unconsciously, want to see. With the echo chamber and the filter bubble, the unreality promoted by the media reaches a new level of penetration in human life. Not only are we subject to the constant meddling of our mental space at the hands of the traditional media's tactics of disinformation, but now we have also been imposed a personalized layer, and as such substantially more efficient, which we inadvertently maintain and update with each one of our online actions. Our hunters no longer need to operate on each of us, now we do most of the work for them. In fact, if we fulfil some conditions *we can even become a version of them*.

In the previous chapter we saw how in any consumer society the abundance of commodities and its phantoms coalesces into a number of pneumatic figures that fulfill the same function as the figure of the dictator in totalitarian states, a fact that leads to the appearance of a new variety of hunter of souls: the celebrity. According to this dynamic, the entry of consumer culture into the virtual world brings with it a new transformation of this type of *venator*. With the democratization of technology that characterizes the "digital era" the possibility arises for the celebrity status to spread throughout the population and take on a new form, that of the *influencer*: a consumer/commodity "famous" for its ability to collect likes and views in social networks and thus move digital masses toward the most diverse products, services or ideologies. As the psyche is aestheticized people become brands in an enormous market of phantasms. *Tiny softened lifestyle dictators.*

"It is in these conditions that a parodic end of the division of labor suddenly appears," says Guy Debord,

> with carnivalesque gaiety, all the more welcome because it coincides with the generalized disappearance of all true competence. A financier can be a singer, a lawyer a police spy, a baker can parade his literary tastes, an actor can be president, a chef can philosophize on the movements of baking as if they were landmarks in universal history. Each can join the spectacle, in order to publicly adopt, or sometimes secretly practice, an entirely different activity from whatever specialty first made their name. Where the possession of "mediatic status" has acquired infinitely more importance than the value of anything one might actually be capable of doing, it is normal for this status to be easily transferable and to confer the right to shine in the same fashion to anyone anywhere.[16]

Everyone's fifteen minutes of fame are finally here. But their price is high: the democratization of desire and technology *opened the possibility to the democratization of pneumatic manipulation.* The *phantasmata* of old become selfies, videos and digital marketing campaigns, they go viral in the form of hashtags. Everyone's life becomes a human-scale spectacle, a personal commercial filled with digital editing effects to make it more alluring for everyone else. Publicity becomes ubiquitous and invisible, it intertwines with everyday life.

And even if we can express ourselves incessantly about everything and everyone, never before, says Debord,

> has censorship been so perfect. Never before have those who are still led to believe, in a few countries, that they remain free citizens, been less entitled to make their opinions heard, wherever it is a matter of choices affecting their real lives. Never before has it been possible to lie to them so brazenly. The spectator is simply supposed to know nothing, and deserve nothing. Those who are always watching to see what happens next will never act: such must be the spectator's condition.[17]

That such is the situation in any of the so-called new media is so evident that it does not need further verification. Suffice it to say that as opinion spaces, blogs and social networks have centered themselves on the diffusion of memes and other spectacular techniques that, rather than clarifying our situation, obscure it solely through their sheer volume. Even those opinion media such as blogs on politics, religion, ecology, science and feminism have resorted to a variety of pop ideology and language that bows its head to the spectacular mentality; these attempts, instead of helping their respective causes, end up appealing to a wider audience by banalizing them. Instead of calling to action, most of the time they engender a peculiar mixture of indignation and paralysis. Zeynep Tufekci, the leading sociologist researching the social implications of technology, argues that social networks help "small groups to mobilise quickly and easily—but often at the cost of enabling them to make a real-world impact."[18]

So far we have seen that the functioning of an individual within a social network can be described coherently by means of the pneumatic circle, but we have not characterized the functioning of the network itself. The pneumatic circle of a social network is a concentric superstructure that contains within itself the pneumatic circles (filter bubbles) of each one of its members, an immense water mirror where millions of people can observe themselves daily. Its exceptional power to spellbind rests on the way in which it processes and emits its bonds, which is essentially an automation of the processing tasks of the *venator*-market research group I described in the previous chapter; a digital machine for the analysis and processing of magical bonds.

Social Network

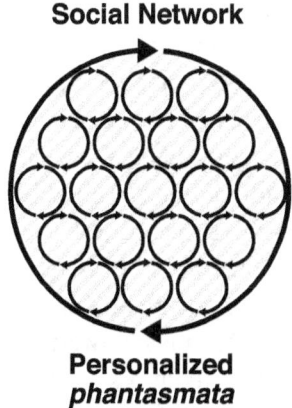

Personalized *phantasmata*

The main virtue of this machine lies on its ability to decipher the unknown knowns of each of its members (the patterns and habits of consumption that not even we know about) and then turn them into known knowns, thus confining the users to a realm of predictable and perpetually reproducible desires. Always a little bit more of the same, lest the user itself becomes an unknown. Thus, a social network is a digital machine whose processing transforms unknown unknowns and unknown knowns into known knowledge. *Venator* and predictor at the same time. The logical end of this tendency, says Bartlett, "is for each of us to be reduced to a unique, predictable and targetable data point."[19] Apart from the disgusting dehumanization intrinsic to this situation, we must also bear in mind that the pneumatic circles of technological firms such as Google, Facebook, Uber or Airbnb reproduce themselves at an exponential rate. The more users a network has, the more users it can attract at a given moment; according to Bartlett, the biggest problem for these companies is not to capture their user base—which in reality are unpaid workforces—but that in a finite world like ours the user base is quickly running out.

In this context the hunter of souls continues its process of dehumanization and becomes a *software agent*, a type of program commonly known as a bot, whose function is to explore and analyze enormous amounts of information (data mining) to extract relevant patterns for consumption trends, investments and online behavior, among many other tasks. With this development, the modern manipulative impulse is attenuated and subtilized to the point of dissolving into proprietary algorithms, while simultaneously it extends its influence and recruits those it used to manipulate to manipulate (and manipulate themselves) in its name. Cyber-cooptation of the masses.

The intrinsic problems of echo chambers and filter bubbles have been the subject of intense debate in the media and the academy following the triumph of Donald Trump in the 2016 US presidential election; those of us who saw it happen "live" can attest to the surreal quality of the moment. But is it so surprising that this "wretched, ignorant, dangerous, part-time clown and full-time sociopath," as Michael Moore has called him, has become President of the most powerful country in the world? No, not really. For Morris Berman, Trump's election is a logical result of the path American politics took many decades ago, the "spectacular" road so to speak:

> For those of us who were around at the time, it seemed beyond belief that Richard Nixon, little more than a two-bit hood and a red-baiter, could actually become president of the United States. And the damage he did to the country was immense: Kent State, Chile, Southeast Asia, Watergate, and so on. With Nixon, we became a different country, and hardly a better one.
>
> And then there was Reagan. Who could have imagined that this knucklehead, as Philip Roth has called him, this B-movie actor, could accede to the presidency? But there he was, with a simplistic economic theory that dramatically widened the gap between rich and poor, and a budget that tripled the national debt and poured wasted billions into the military. As in the case of Nixon, he was another downturn from which we have never really recovered. His destructive legacy is with us to this day.[20]

It is more than worrying that Trump—as others of his ilk, like media mogul Silvio Berlusconi or even Arnold "the *governator*" Schwarzenegger—have reached the highest instances of political power, but it is even more worrying that most of us didn't hear the thumps of a large animal. What if Facebook and Twitter's filter bubbles were just the tip of the iceberg, the symptom of a much wider malaise that prevents us from seeing macro trends that ought to be evident? What if it actually has a lot more to do with the fact that we have lived for almost a century in a falsified reality, a spectacular bubble (Debord) or a hyperreality (Baudrillard), fostered by the magical operations of the market and the media? In our present state such a conclusion is neither improbable nor far-fetched.

As the exceptional hunter he is, Trump shrewdly used the bonds at his disposal, a task at which Hillary Clinton, with an intellectual discourse directed at elites the of both coasts, failed miserably. Apart from this, Trump understood and applied post-truth's basic tenet: coherence in political discourse is a thing of the past, each sector of the population, each group of prey, must be addressed on their own terms, regardless of whether these openly contradict the terms of other groups. And although Clinton won the popular vote with a margin of almost three million, it is undeniable that she never came close to producing the kind of irrational fervor which Trump managed to whip up in the masses. The reason, in Brunian terms, is as follows:

> Whoever wishes to bind must take note of the fact that some of the things that can be bound are affected more by nature, others more by judgement or prudence, and still others more by practice and habit. As a result, the skilful person obliges and binds the first type of things with bonds provided by natural things, the second type by reasons and proofs, by symbols and arguments, and the third type by what is at hand and is compelling.[21]

It is no mystery that articulating complex arguments is much more difficult than exposing "facts" in a dogmatic and simplistic manner, hence, the second category is particularly inefficient when it comes to swaying, or simply, making a mass doubt itself. "Affirmation pure and simple," Le Bon reminds us, "kept free of all reasoning and all proof, is one of the surest means of making an idea enter the mind of crowds. The conciser an affirmation is, the more destitute of every appearance of proof and demonstration, the more weight it carries."[22] On the other hand, the first and third categories, as any public speaker knows, can be manipulated with overwhelming results. Natural things, such as fear of a known or unknown enemy, or customs, such as xenophobia, can be manipulated with impressive efficiency and ease. This, it should be noted, is only possible for a person who is already in possession of these bonds.

Of course, there is no *venator* that has access to all bonds, and

> rather, the one who is found to be fortunate and skilful in more ways and at more levels will bind more things, will rule in more ways and will win out over more people of their own species.[23]

Trump constantly appealed to the individuals of his own species with carefully tailored speeches to rouse them to fear, anger and greed. As we know, this technique worked wonders for him. But rhetorics aside, what about digital media? How did Trump manage to sway an online electorate that was highly skeptic about some of his most outrageous proposals, like massive deportations or walls adjoining neighbouring countries? The online division of Trump's campaign, called Project Alamo, got in touch with Cambridge Analytica, a British company founded by Trump strategist Steve Bannon and early artificial intelligence researcher Robert Mercer, which declared insolvency in early may 2018 after a scandal regarding its use of the personal data of millions of Facebook users. Unsurprisingly, Cambridge Analytica emerged as the politics research division of a company called Strategic Communication Laboratories which, according to Jamie Bartlett, "had extensive experience in branding and influencing public opinion, specialising in military and intelligence psychological operations, or 'psy-ops'."[24] In fewer words, a propaganda and disinformation machine.

Cambridge Analytica's role in the Trump campaign consisted in using the data of 230 million american citizens (inherited from Ted Cruz's presidential campaign and the RNC database) to build target groups they called "universes," which comprised detailed sectors of the population such as: "American mums who hadn't voted before and were worried about childcare; pro-gun males living in the midwest; Hispanics who were worried about national security; and so on."[25] All these universes were arranged in terms of how persuadable they were and—according to brunian rules of manipulation—were exposed through their social networks to thousands of permutations of specially tailored political propaganda (bonds) in order to find out which kind of add gave the best results. Their research revealed that key portions of the population in swing states could be swayed to the Trump ticket; by key I mean thousands of voters (and not tens of thousands or millions) that were just enough to steal states from Hillary Clinton. At first sight, these techniques may seem a legitimate extension of the electoral process (after all you are not "forcing" anyone to vote for this or that candidate), but there is in fact a hidden depth to them. All this micro-targeting and ultra-personalization, says Jamie Bartlett, represents a considerable threat to democracy: in a world where we all receive personalized political messages, how can we debate publicly (and coherently) about them?

It is worth mentioning that Cambridge Analytica's data analysis methodology is based on the research of Michal Kosinski, a Polish social scientist and psychologist who designed an algorithm capable of determining, only from the likes of a Facebook profile, "the sexual orientation, ethnicity, religious and political views, personality traits, intelligence, happiness, use of addictive substances, parental separation, age and gender,"[26] with breathtaking accuracy. So far it has not been possible to determine if Project Alamo made use of this particular tool. And even if it's not easy to determine the extent of Facebook's help to Trump's campaign, it is not difficult to see that the collaboration between social networks and political campaigns has ushered a host of new uses for our personal data, most of them clearly immoral and illegal.

A few days before declaring insolvency, Cambridge Analytica executives boasted about the company's role influencing "more than 200 elections across the world, including Nigeria, Kenya, the Czech Republic, India and Argentina."[27] Needless to say, the ease with which social networks can be manipulated for political purposes has led to a pandemic of ignorance and unaccountability on the part of the electorate, in which any person with a Facebook or Twitter account can become—in most cases against their own knowledge and will—a dupe for a cause that he or she doesn't really endorse, a repeater antenna for a disinformation tsunami that has dropped us at the gates of the authoritarianism and fascism which, let it be said, lurk on both sides of the political spectrum.

As we have seen, it turns out that manipulating the public consent via social networks is an already firmly defined process. It takes money, good intelligence, technical savvy and, depending on the level of interference, quite a lot of people. But judging by how this techniques have spread far and wide in the last decade, it is a form of manipulation with a rather "democratic" potential. The US 2016 presidential election showed us—and it remains to be determined if we learned anything—that the pneumatic circles (filter bubbles) that make up a social network can be intervened in an quasi-automatic manner (if you have a considerable amount of money, as a presidential campaign does, you can even get personalized help from said social network's employees). This in turn demonstrated that not everything depends on the specific algorithms of each network and that it is perfectly possible to introduce disinformation into gigantic clusters of pneumatic circles to influence the voting intention of hundreds of thousands of people at a time.

In September 2017, Facebook admitted to having identified more than 3,000 ads—propaganda in the strictest sense of the word—that circulated in its network between June 2015 and May 2017 and for which it was paid close to 100,000 dollars. These ads, which did not refer to a particular US presidential candidate but focused on controversial issues such as race, immigration, arms control and gay rights, "were linked to some 470 fake accounts and pages the company said it had shut down."[28] According to Facebook, the fake accounts were created and financed by a St. Petersburg based company called Internet Research Agency (IRA), a *troll farm* with close ties to the Russian intelligence community that works with the Kremlin on its online media warfare operations. About a quarter of the ads were targeted to specific geographic areas in the United States, which suggests a possible collaboration from US agents. According to Vitaly Bespalov, who worked at the IRA for three and a half months, this company's troll army is divided on four independent floors, the first of which houses the "media Department; the second, the social networks; the third, the bloggers, and in the last, in addition to the dining room, groups that upload information on networks such as Facebook, Vkontakte (the Russian version), Twitter and YouTube."[29]

And then there are the shocking revelations about the intervention of Russian Military Intelligence (GRU) and a hacker ring presumably associated with the Kremlin to damage Hillary Clinton's presidential campaign and benefit Trump's. According to Reuters, Vladimir Putin considered that the latter "would be much friendlier to Russia, especially on the matter of economic sanctions"[30] and hinted that the cyber-attacks to the DNC servers might be the work of "patriotically minded hackers" that, nonetheless, were *not* acting on behalf of the Russian government. This maddening ambiguity, as we will see in the next chapter, is one of the marks of putinian politics. *Russiagate*, as the scandal has been called in the media, should mark an inflection point in our beliefs about democracy. Although, if we were more thorough, and our media less biased, we would have noticed that the same type of cybernetic intervention took place, at the hands of the same power, in the 2014 Ukraine presidential election. In any case, by the end of 2017, British Primer Minister Theresa May pointed in the direction of Russia in reference to the cyber-attacks to the Danish Defense Ministry and the German Parliament, and indicated the participation of the Kremlin in a huge disinformation campaign prior to Brexit and the Catalonia Independence Referendum. The objective of these attacks is most likely the destabilization of the European Union. Latin America is far from being on the sidelines of this trend: the revelations of Colombian hacker Andrés Sepulveda about his participation in disinformation campaigns in Mexico, Guatemala, Nicaragua, Colombia and Costa Rica show that both means and motivation exist in the region.

But at times the purpose of these cyber-attacks is not clear at all. At the end of May 2016, RT and Sputnik, Russia's main state-sponsored english speaking news outlets, broke the news that the Turkish armed forces were surrounding the United States Air Force base of Incirlik in the city of Adana, Turkey, only 34 miles from the Mediterranean and very close to the Syrian border. In fact, the Incirlik base is a strategic military location not only for the USAF but also for the RAF and the Spanish army; the news seemed to suggest a possible coup against turkish president Recep Tayyip Erdogan. Within minutes the content aggregators posted the news online, comments began to pop up and more Twitter accounts began to spread panic over the nuclear arsenal housed in the facility:

> # Incirlik There r 25 underground vaults, each holds up to 4 bombs. The estimated total is 50 B61 thermonuclear bombs—1/4 of B61 stockpile.
>
> Why is USA MSM failing to report on events in Turkey surrounding Incirlik AFB and Erdogan's accusation that USA orchestrated the coup?
>
> Nothing on #msm, no #potus, no #dem or #gop speaking out! Nuclear warheads, up to 90 at stake!

The reason traditional media did not report the news was that it was fake. There was no plot to overthrow Erdogan (that would come in July of the same year, although it is still not clear if it was a false flag operation) nor were the US nuclear warheads in any danger. According to analysts Clint Watts and Andrew Weisburd, one of the first English tweets came from the account of one Marcel Sardo, a troll who deems himself a "pro-Russian media sniper," known for spreading online campaigns in favor of Putin. Once the hashtags began to go round in the platform, "the evolving pattern of retweets" say Watts and Weisburg, "reveal a close-knit network and circular information flow where key amplifiers re-broadcast the base #Incirlik story adding commentary and fomenting fears."[31] Unsurprisingly, many of the tweeters who commented and reproduced the news were trump fanatics, most of them unwitting trolls (one hopes!) for who knows what agenda. And here is the point: the agenda behind this manipulations is an *unknown unknown* and, if I am right, it is so even for its own demiurges. Of course, these hunters expect to get a result out of their actions but it is not something fixed in advance, it is constantly flowing and shifting. On the other hand, what purpose could this sort of actions have but falsifying an already turbid environment? That confusion breeds paralysis is something known by every *venator*, but the sort of obfuscation we are living in is completely unprecedented.

This new game is an evolution of the disinformation program undertaken by the Soviet Union during the Cold War—that is, the *first* Cold War—under the name of *active measures*. In essence, these measures sought to use "slogans, arguments, disinformation and selected true information to influence the attitudes and actions of foreign publics and governments."[32] According to Watts and Weisburd, during the postwar period the application of these techniques, particularly in foreign countries, was especially difficult since it involved the set up of an expensive and conspicuous dissemination apparatus; nowadays all you need is a Facebook or a Twitter account. As difficult as the task may have been, according to Stanislav Lunev, the highest ranking Soviet officer to defect to the United States, GRU invested a billion dollars financing practically all the anti-war movements during the sixties and seventies; an invisible but appalling defeat for both the US government and the country's counterculture. This ideological infestation continues to afflict the most diverse social movements inside and outside Russia to this very day.

The fact that we have moved the whole of our existence—both social and psychological—to a demiurgic bubble is tacit knowledge since the term *post-truth* entered our lexicon; the most glaring proof is that it has already penetrated pop-culture. Two relevant examples: *House of Cards*, promoted as the first television series engineered from Big Data, a fancy name for data mining, has done a good job at predicting certain trends in American politics; its depiction of the twists and turns of 2016 election is disturbingly accurate. Is "TV reality" mimicking "real reality" or the other way around? Even further, do both belong to the same demiurgic bubble and therefore complement each other? The second example: in the last episode of the first season of hacker drama *Mr. Robot*, right in the middle of the main character's nervous breakdown, we find the following monologue:

> Is any of it real? I mean, look at this. Look at it! A world built on fantasy. Synthetic emotions in the form of pills. Psychological warfare in the form of advertising. Mind-altering chemicals in the form of... food! Brainwashing seminars in the form of media. Controlled isolated bubbles in the form of social networks. Real? You want to talk about reality? We haven't lived in anything remotely close to it since the turn of the century. We turned it off, took out the batteries, snacked on a bag of GMOs while we tossed the remnants in the ever-expanding dumpster of the human condition. We live in branded houses trademarked by corporations built on bipolar numbers jumping up and down on digital displays, hypnotizing us into the biggest slumber mankind has ever seen. You have to dig pretty deep, kiddo, before you can find anything real.

This is the Gnostic's terror, the revelation that there is nothing in the outside world that we can call truly "real," that practically all of our existence has already been intervened and falsified. However, as in many Gnostic myths, the Demiurge is not in control of his creation, which constantly surpasses and surprises him. Could this be enough comfort in such trying times, in the era of *unrealpolitik*?

---

[1] Quoted by Turner en *From Counterculture to Cyberculture*, 166.
[2] "Is Computer Hacking a Crime." Accessed, April 15, 2018, at: *http://www.textfiles.com/news/hackers.txt*
[3] Would it be too much to speculate that the letter "k" in the names of Phiber Optik and Acid Phreak refers to Aleister Crowley's magic system, who used the

k, an archaic Elizabethan diction, to distinguish stage magic, called simply *magic*, from the true magic that works through the will of the operator, *magick*?

[4] "Is Computer Hacking a Crime."

[5] John Perry Barlow, "A Declaration of Independence of Cyberspace." Accessed, May 28, 2018, at:
https://www.eff.org/cyberspace-independence

[6] Taken from my essay "El espejo oscuro: la opacidad hiperrealista y los medios digitales," 5. Available at: https://independentresearcher.academia.edu/MauricioLoza. Author's translation.

[7] Loza, *El espejo oscuro*, 5. Author's translation.

[8] Joseph Weizenbaum, *Computer Power and Human Reason: From Judgement to Calculation* (New York: W.H. Freeman and Company, 1976), 7.

[9] Julian Assange, *Cypherpunks, Freedom and the Future of the Internet* (New York: OR Books, 2012), 1.

[10] Jamie Bartlett, *The people Vs Tech* (London: Ebury Press, 2018), 27.

[11] Leon Marvel, *The Physics of Transfigured Light: The imaginal realm and the hermetic foundations of science*, (Rochester: Inner Traditions, 2016), 108.

[12] Ovid, *Metamorphoses* Translated by Stanley Lombardo (Indianapolis: Hackett Publishing Company, 2010), 78.

[13] Ovid, *Metamorphoses*. 78.

[14] Ovid, *Metamorphoses* Translated by Charles Martin (New York: W.W. Norton & Company, 2004), 108.

[15] "Invisible Sieve." Accessed, May 28, 2018, at: https://www.economist.com/node/18894910

[16] "Comments on the Society of the Spectacle." Accessed, May 28, 2018, at: http://www.notbored.org/commentaires.html

[17] Debord, *Comments on the Society of the Spectacle*, 22.

[18] Quoted by Bartlett in *The People Vs. Tech*, 151. In this regard, in *Ten Arguments for Deleting Your Social Media Accounts*, Jaron Lanier argues that there is a distinct pattern through which social causes end up being betrayed by social media and gives the example of the Black Lives Matter movement that arose after two black unarmed US citizens were killed at the hands of the police 2014. The first phase of this pattern is a honeymoon, in which the movement seems to advance and gain new ground. However, as soon as the movement becomes visible enough to the social network's system, says Lanier, "Black activists and sympathizers were carefully catalogued and studied. What wording got them excited? What annoyed them? What little things, stories, videos, anything, kept them glued to [whatever network]. What would snowflake-ify them enough to isolate them, bit by bit from the rest of society. What made them shift to be more targetable by behavior modification messages over time? The purpose was not to repress the movement but to earn money. The process was automatic, routine, sterile, and ruthless." (*Ten Arguments*, 124). After saturation of the original target group via carefully crafted bonds has taken place, "automatically, black activism was tested for its ability to preoccupy, annoy, even transfix other populations, who themselves were then automatically cataloged, prodded, and studied. A slice of latent White supremacists and racist who had previously not been well identified, connected, or empowered was blindly,

mechanically discovered and cultivated, initially only for automatic, unknowing commercial gain—but that would have been impossible without first cultivating a slice of [...] black activism and algorithmically figuring out how to frame it as provocation." (*Ten Arguments*, 124). Everyone knows that angry people click more and, as a result, says Lanier, "Black Lives Matter became more prominent as a provocation and object of ridicule than as a cry for help... Meanwhile, racism became organized over [social networks] to a degree it had not been in generations." (*Ten Arguments*, 125). In sum, if the trade-off of advancing a cause online not only strengthens the grip social networks have on reality, but also generates more resistance in the short term, is this exchange really worth it?

[19] Bartlett, *The people Vs Tech*, 23.

[20] "The Final Act" from Morris Berman's personal blog. Accessed, May 20, 2018, at: *http://morrisberman.blogspot.ca/2017_01_08_archive.html*

[21] Giordano Bruno, *A General Account of Bonding* (Cambridge: Cambridge University Press, 2004), 158.

[22] Le Bon, *The Crowd*, 72.

[23] Bruno, *A General Account of Bonding*, 149. In Richard J. Blackwell's translation the latin word *felix* appears as "happy," which I changed to "fortunate," which I believe better expresses the meaning of the sentence.

[24] Bartlett, *The people Vs Tech*, 73.

[25] Bartlett, *The people Vs Tech*, 74-75.

[26] Bartlett, *The people Vs Tech*, 21.

[27] "Cambridge Analytica says it worked for Uhuru Kenyatta." Accessed, July 6, 2018, at: *https://www.nation.co.ke/news/politics/How-Cambridge-Analytica-influenced-Kenyan-poll/1064-4349034-le7xbuz/index.html*

[28] Scott Shane, Vindu Goel, "Fake Russian Facebook Accounts Bought $100.000 in Political Ads." Accessed, May 30, 2018, at: *https://www.nytimes.com/2017/09/06/technology/facebook-russian-political-ads* .html

[29] Susana Gaviña, "La granja de trolls rusos que trabaja las 24 horas del día." Accessed, June 2, 2018, at: *https://www.abc.es/internacional/abci-granja-trolls-trabaja-24-horas-201711192233_noticia.html*. Author's translation.

[30] "Putin turned Russia election hacks in Trump's favor: U.S. officials." Accessed, May 28, 2018, at: *https://www.reuters.com/article/us-usa-trump-cyber-idUSKBN1441RS*

[31] Andrew Weisburd, Clint Watts, "How Russia Dominates your Twitter Feed to Promote Lies (And Trump Too)." Accessed, May 28, 2018, at: *https:// www. thedailybeast.com / how - russia-dominates-your-twitter-feed- to -promote-lies-and-trump-too*

[32] Sophia Porotsky, "Analysing Russian Information Warfare and Influence Operations." Accessed, December 20, 2018, at: *https://globalsecurityreview .com/cold-war-2-0-russian-information-warfare/*

10. The Polymorphous Demon.
Magic in the post-soviet era

I too, my lady, am the Bright Star of the Morning. I was before John spoke, because there is a Patmos before Patmos, and mysteries prior to all mysteries. I smile when they think (I think) that I am Venus in another scheme of symbols. But what does it matter? All this universe, with its God and with its Devil, with its men and the things they see, is a hieroglyphic still to be deciphered. I am, of course, Master of Magic: yet, I know not what it is.
Fernando Pessoa, *The Devil's Hour*

Do I need? / Destiny
Do I need? / Schedule life
Do I need? / Working trends
Do I need? / Recess lines
Lucky and unhappy
Vote for a freestyle life
Lucky and unhappy
Driving on the freeway flash line
Do I feel? / Helium dreams
Do I feel? / Fresh impacts
Do I feel? / Endless nights
Do I feel? / Venus joy
Air, *Lucky and Unhappy (2001)*

The first part of this chapter will be devoted to a brief genealogy of the unreality that I have attempted to describe in this study. In the previous part I described its emergence through what Debord called the society of the spectacle. However, our unreality is a *terra incognita* with other entry points. Two of these points are inscribed in the main epigraphs of Part III of this book, which correspond to two distinct phases of the demiurgic war in which we have been involved for just over a century.

The first, from the second part of Goethe's Faust, represents media war as we have known it since the Nineteenth Century, through the First World War, Guatemala and up until the two Persian Gulf wars. This is a psychological disinformation war whose purpose is the manipulation of public opinion; its objective is divorcing "appearances from being," so that we constantly confuse one for the other. The second epigraph, from Andrei Tarkovsky's *Stalker*, represents a new phase of the Western manipulative impulse which, apart from seeking to confuse appearance and reality, aims to paralize the population by constantly casting doubt on the system's own veracity.[1] The world presented to us in this new phase is a maze as disconcerting as the Zone in *Stalker*, a place where "old traps disappear and new ones emerge. Safe spots become unpassable. Now your path is easy, now it's hopelessly involved."

These epigraphs present us with two paths, two phases and two facets through which we can inquire about unreality. The epigraph from the second part of Faust comes from a rich esoteric and alchemical tradition whose underground current led to the *avant-garde* of the twentieth century, and which I will call the esoteric tradition of unreality.[2] Regarding this fragment, it is not at all gratuitous that it is Mephistopheles the one who pronounces himself on appearance and reality. Since ancient times the power of the devil has been to tempt us through images and illusions, his kingdom are our dreams and nightmares. However, Goethe's devil belongs to another era of manipulation and, consequently, has lost its effectiveness; this is not the polymorphous demon that gives this chapter its name.

Unlike Mephistopheles, Pessoa's devil—who complains of the mistreatment of his image at the hands Milton and Goethe—is another type of demon, a Gnostic devil who claims his place as the god of imagination "who creates without creating, whose voice is smoke, and whose soul is an error."[3] This devil, as this chapter's epigraph suggests, is Venus in another symbol scheme, the hidden face of the world for which dream "is an action turned into an idea, which therefore retains the strength of the world and repudiates matter, which is being in space."[4] By rejecting the reality of matter and space, Pessoa's devil becomes the master of unreality, of the twilight from whence the *phantasmata* that form the basis of any kind of manipulation arise. This particular conception makes this devil the "absolute master of the interstice and the intermediate, of that in life which is not life. Since night is my kingdom, dream is my domain. What has no weight or measure, that is mine."[5] Pessoa's devil is a demiurge and supreme magician who, by operating from the twilight of the world, is capable of manipulating its appearances. As the trickster archetype—

which we already examined in the fourth chapter in reference to the Wizard of Oz and Edward Bernays—this kind of devil is fluid and ambivalent, he is a master of boundaries and transitions because he inhabits them. His magic is *maya*, understood in its original sense of a great power or a divine will. Let's recall here that in some dualistic religions, the trickster fulfills the function of a demiurge that produces a counter-creation inferior to that of the original god.

Regarding the second epigraph, the ever-uncertain and shifting reality of the Zone in *Stalker* allows us to realize that when reality is constantly challenged—as it happens daily in a thoroughly mediated world such as ours—it becomes apparent that it can't be anything but a deception, a massive delusion. This new world, "braver" then any literary dystopia, is the product of the fusion of the two main varieties of the western manipulative impulse, the officialist (inquisition/secret police/concentrated spectacle) and the magical/heretical (Renaissance magic/public relations/marketing/diffuse spectacle) which merge into a new and powerful strain of unreality that Debord called *integrated spectacle*.

This type of demiurgic creation can be characterized in two ways: as a theater or war scenario, or as a very particular type of game with very intriguing tactical possibilities. As a performance art, war becomes a spectacle that is witnessed in the distance, a play which is familiar only to those who live it directly, that is, for civilian victims or troops. For the high commanders, or for those who witness a military scenario from the distance, war appears as a strategy game. These two characterizations are actually two sides of the same coin: every game based on rules *is* a form of war. This double characterization, game or war scenario, gives rise to a warlike tradition of unreality.

Understood as a game, the first phase of the manipulative impulse, let's call it "goethian," resembles chess; the current phase, however, resembles the Chinese game of *wei-chi*, better known in the West by its Japanese name *Go*. In 1969 North American mathematician Scott Boorman published an analysis entitled *The Protracted Game: A Wei-Chi Interpretation of Maoist Revolutionary Strategy*, in which he argued that "Mao Zedong was able to defeat the Kuomintang because he was using a Go (*Wei-chi* in Chinese) strategy, while the Kuomintang sought, à la chess, to stake out and occupy—that is, striate—territory."[6] The contrast between chess and Go was taken up by Gilles Deleuze and Felix Guattari in

Nomadology: The War Machine, in which they characterized the first as a state game (*polis*) and the second as one pertaining to nomadism (of *nomos*, grass). Deleuze and Guattari explain that chess pieces are coded and respond to interior characteristics that define their movements, so that "a knight remains a knight, a pawn a pawn, a bishop a bishop." On the contrary,

> Go pieces, in contrast, are pellets, disks, simple arithmetic units, and have only an anonymous, collective, or third-person function. "It" makes a move. "It" could be a man, a woman, a louse, an elephant. Go pieces are elements of a nonsubjectified machine assemblage with no intrinsic properties, only situational ones. Thus the relations are very different in the two cases. Within their milieu of interiority, chess pieces entertain biunivocal relations with one another, and with the adversary's pieces: their functioning is structural. On the other hand, a Go piece has only a milieu of exteriority, or extrinsic relations with nebulas or constellations, according to which it fulfills functions of insertion or situation, such as bordering, encircling, shattering. All by itself, a Go piece can destroy an entire constellation synchronically; a chess piece cannot (or can do so diachronically only). Chess is indeed a war, but an institutionalized, regulated, coded war, with a front, a rear, battles. But what is proper to Go is war without battle lines, with neither confrontation nor retreat, without battles even: pure strategy, whereas chess is a semiology.[7]

The main difference between these two forms of warfare is in their idea of space. "In chess, it is a question of arranging a closed space for oneself, thus of going from one point to another, of occupying the maximum number of squares with the minimum number of pieces. In Go, it is a question of arraying oneself in an open space, of holding space, of maintaining the possibility of springing up at any point: the movement is not from one point to another, but becomes perpetual, without aim or destination, without departure or arrival. The "smooth" space of Go, as against the "striated" space of chess."[8] The similarity of the type of space presented by Go with *Stalker's* Zone is remarkable. The smooth space in which the Go pieces move has no real borders—unlike the squares of a chess board—and, in fact, it is an undefined space that can be understood as a border in itself, a "no-place" where the categories and norms of known space become undone; the perfect *topos* for magic and illusion. Go, in

Deleuze and Guattari's terminology, deterritorializes (and territorializes) space constantly creating a fluid strategy that lends itself to constant improvisation. If chess is diachronic, that is, linear, Go works in a synchronic and non-linear way; a movement can have simultaneous repercussions on what is perceived, from the point of view of chess, as several "fronts." In a similar manner, the Zone is thoroughly unpredictable because it has been deterritorialized, one could say that it is playing a game of Go with someone who is unaware of the game's rules. It is a form of war that is not only non-linear but, in most cases, also asymmetric. In this new stage of the manipulative impulse the demiurgic bubble becomes unpredictable.

This new type of liminal space, analogous to the one inhabited by Pessoa's devil, consists of four main attributes: 1. it lacks a fixed or single frame of reference; 2. it does not work from predefined purposes; 3. its strategies are synchronic and non-linear; 4. it constantly deterritorializes and reterritorializes space. These characteristics point to a radical change in armed and media warfare tactics that move away from the scenario planning techniques (with its permutations of variables) that characterized Cold War, and approach other types of strategies that, as we will see in this chapter, have their origin in the *avant-garde*, the performance arts and literature; strategies that form the core of the so-called Second Cold War. The form of demiurgic magic that results from this liminal space (Zone/ Go) is an evolution of Western militarization and compartmentalization techniques, its passage from a linear, vertical and categorial scheme to non-linear, horizontal and fluid contexts, which allow for subtler forms of manipulation based on the situation of the prey within the game and not in the category to which they belong. It is undoubtedly the most direct and fluid form of manipulation of the brunian network of bonds, its emphasis is on the process itself and not on its specific bonds.

The predominant form of this new type of manipulation is the social space that emerged from the media apparatus of the New Russia. As in all previous phases of the manipulative impulse the demiurge devil lies hidden behind his illusion. However, if one looks closely enough, it is possible to see how this new layer of unreality came into existence.

In 1974 the son of an NKVD policeman (the People's Commissariat of Internal Affairs) and a munition factory worker, was exiled and arrived in New York City. Eduard Savenko, who from his time in the bohemian circles of the city of Kharkov in Ukraine, called himself Limonov (a reference to his acid and belligerent humor, *limon* translates lemon and *limonka*, hand grenade),[9] quickly found employment in the immigrant newspaper *Novoe Russkoe Slovo* for which he wrote twenty articles in a year, before stirring up a scandal with a piece called "Disillusionment" in which he expressed his disenchantment with both the Soviet system and capitalism. In his spare time, Limonov established relations with the Socialist Workers Party, an American Trotskyist group, and joined the punk scene that thrived in the city by the mid-seventies. In it he befriended Richard Hell of Television and the Voidoids, Patti Smith and the Ramones. It was during his time in the NYC underground, while he lived in near destitution, that he realized something nobody wanted to mention: "that the West was in many ways just a more sophisticated version of the Soviet Union, with more sophisticated propaganda—plus a similar intolerance of real dissent."[10] Something that other immigrants, like Wilhelm Reich, had found out the hard way.

Back in the USSR, the new generation felt just like Limonov. They were deeply disillusioned with the system and had given up believing that there was any kind of political solution to their situation. In a desperate search to give their lives meaning, they turned to radical forms of art, some local and others imported from the West, which formed the basis of an artistic underground that began to flourish in Moscow and Leningrad. During the late seventies and eighties there emerged bands like Popular Mechanics of composer and pianist Sergey Kuryokhin and Grazhdanskaya Oborona (Civil Defense) led by Yegor Letov, a radical singer and poet from the city of Omsk in Siberia, who is widely considered one of the most important voices of his generation. In his song *Everything is Going According to Plan*, Letov sings in a crude and angry voice:

> And under communism everything will be fucked,
> It will come soon, you just have to wait,
> Everything will be free there, everything will be fun,
> There probably you just won't have to die,
> I woke up in the middle of the night and realized that
> Everything goes according to plan...
> Everything goes according to plan...[11]

All these artists shared a deep distrust towards the soviet establishment and the idea that politics, in its current form, could offer no solution to the existential putrefaction that afflicted their country. Unsurprisingly, *It's Me, Eddy*, a novel Eduard Limonov published in Paris in 1979, in which he recounted his experience as an exile and exposed his disenchantment with Soviet and American politics, became an overnight cult success. When it was first published in Russia in 1991, it sold by the hundreds of thousands.

The fall of the Soviet Union came with an avalanche of criticism that the system had repressed for decades. Soon after the dam blew up in pieces, Sergey Kuryokhin appeared in a cultural TV program arguing that the October Revolution had been the product of "people who had been hallucinating on mushrooms for years, and in the long run, mushrooms had replaced their personalities turning them into mushrooms. So, I just want to say that *Lenin was a mushroom*."[12] Such surreal comedy was, according to his wife, a way to express that anything, regardless of how absurd it seemed, could 'pass as true' on live television. After decades of constant disenchantment and disappointment, the people of the former Soviet Union had stopped believing that it was possible to believe in something. "Soviet stagnation led to Perestroika, which led to the collapse of the Soviet Union, liberal euphoria, economic disaster, oligarchy, and the mafia state. How can you believe in anything when everything around you is changing so fast?"[13] With his skit, Kuryokhin was alluding to one of the foundations of Soviet propaganda that the New Russia would resume as quickly as a bad habit, namely, that "in a society where no one believed in anything the media could be used *to make anything real*."[14] As a subject of the soviet system Kuryokhin knew perfectly well what he was talking about. In the words of historian Martin Malia:

> socialism leads not to an assault on the specific abuses of 'capitalism' but to an assault on reality *tout court*. It becomes, in effect, an effort to suppress the real world, and this is something that cannot succeed in the long run. But for a protracted period this effort *can* succeed in creating a surreal world, one defined by the paradox that inefficiency, poverty, and brutality can be officially presented as the *summum bonum* of society.[15]

An even if a demiurgic bubble cannot last forever, as Malia argues, it can last long enough to cause untold damage to millions of people. Suffice it to say that all post-soviet attempts to tap this demiurgic potential are directly influenced by communism's repressive capacity to alter the whole of human reality, now combined and reinforced with the demiurgic capacity inherent to free market fetishism.

By 1994, after a brief incursion in the Yugoslav wars where he fought on the serbian side, Eduard Limonov had settled back in his country and watched aghast at the implementation of some of Boris Yeltsin's economic measures. After the fall of the Soviet bloc and a brief period of liberal optimism, which quickly degenerated into economic and political instability, President Yeltsin announced that he planned to modernize the country by imposing a full-fledged free market capitalism. His privatization plan, commonly known as the 'loans for shares' auctions, has been called the heist of the twentieth century. In broad strokes, the Russian government proposed to the largest banking groups of the country that they lend money to the government to salvage their debts in exchange for shares in state industries, which would serve as collateral. Of course, "everyone knew the government would never repay the loans, which meant that the enterprises would become the property of the creditor banks."[16] But in this scheme, brainchild of the first Deputy Minister Vladimir Potanin and minister Anatoly Chubais, banks would only serve as intermediaries in a series of pre-arranged auctions in which entrepreneurs who had already made money during the Perestroika were able to acquire the oil, natural gas and telecommunications companies at a fraction of their real price; their trick was in arbitraging the great difference between the prices for such industries in Russian and international markets. Small entrepreneurs such as Boris Berezovsky, Mikhail Khodorkovsky, Mikhail Fridman and Potanin himself, went from being the privileged few to billionaires. In a matter of days, a whole new social class was born: the Oligarchs.

His exile in the United States and France had polarized Limonov against free market economy and, outraged by Yeltsin's "democratic" takeover, he decided to make opposition and formed a political organization under the name of National Bolshevik Party. Among its earliest members were Sergey Kuryokhin, Yegor Letov and Alexandr Dugin, a Russian ultra-nationalist and promoter of Eurasian ideals. With National-Bolshevism, Limonov set out to create a "revolutionary party of a new style" that would attract a large portion of the young population "frustrated by the hardships of reforms and embittered at the West."[17] But *Nazbol*, as the party was known, was far from being a youth movement. According to Ilya Ponamarev, leader of the Young Left Front, in reality it was

> a postmodernist aesthetic project of intellectual provocateurs (in the positive meaning of the word)… It was an effort, and, a quite successful one, to mobilize the most passionate and intellectually dissatisfied sector of society (in contrast to the Communist Party, which utilized the social and economic protests of the leftist electorate). For this mobilization, the NBP used a bizarre mixture of totalitarian and fascist symbols, geopolitical dogma, leftist ideas, and national-patriotic demagoguery.[18]

In fact, the postmodern exercise of appropriation of symbols and ideologies—so common to Western advertising—was taken to a new level by *Nazbol*.[19] To honor its disconcerting name, the National-Bolshevik flag incorporated the Soviet hammer and sickle with the red background and the white circle of the Nazi swastika. A master aesthete, Limonov put together, in a single symbol, something that Walter Benjamin had identified decades ago: the aestheticizing of the politics of all forms of fascism and the politicizing of art of communism. This move revealed the raw and essential power of symbols: mere instruments of psychological manipulation that Limonov stripped of their original content and meaning and repurposed for an aesthetically driven revolution. This may be difficult to understand from a Western point of view, but *Nazbol* has been the only counterculture that the new Russia has known, the only organization capable of gathering under a single banner a small portion of a disenchanted, proud and avid population that wished to act, to take the reins of a devastated country and reinvent it once again.

In line with the Agambenian interpretation of fetishism, *Nazbol's* flag is a perfect fetish: it simultaneously deals with the presence of an absence (the swastika eclipsed by the hammer and sickle and vice versa) and the absence of a presence (the denial of both symbols at the hands of the other). With this symbol the National Bolsheviks achieved something unusual: they evinced the intersection between the extreme left and the extreme right, while proposing a radical alternative to the modernization of Russia, an authentic 'brown-red' politics. In its political program, nationalism was put against communist internationalism and globalization; Eurasianism against the hegemony of the North Atlantic powers (NATO); pure Leninism and fascism (admittedly, the NBP made a series of rather complicated alliances with some racist, xenophobic or anti-Semitic parties and organizations) against free market economics and Putinism; every option put against all others, in an absurd struggle between left and right that reveals the futility of agonistic politics and falls right in the 'center' of the spectrum; whatever the word is taken to mean in this context. Suffice it to say that in a country where the establishment has passed through the brutality of Stalinism to the psychological stupor of the Brezhnev era, neoliberal globalization is not met with soft center-left positions but with the staunchest forms of nationalism; ultra-right against ultra-right. In Russia the political spectrum stops being a linear structure that confronts two opposites and becomes a Möbius strip, unwittingly elegant and unorientable; Stalker's Zone made political arena. Also, since *Nazbol* acted as the counterculture to the Russian establishment, we may be witnessing the historical moment when both 'political poles'—as in the case of counterculture and cyberculture—collapse as distinct entities and unite in a single structure.

This social and political relativism has enormous and paradoxical repercussions. Not believing in anything opens the door to believe in everything—and nothing—at once. Except Limonov did believe this was a viable way to "break through the fake ideas of Western democracy to show how the new bourgeois elites were greedily destroying the Russian state."[20] As hard as it is to believe, the National Bolshevik Party was far from a passing fad and it remained active until 2010 (*sans* the Eurasian ideals that characterized it during the 1990s), when it was disolved and changed its name to The Other Russia, perhaps the only opposition movement to Vladimir Putin's government. However, the idea of opposition in Russia, as we will see later on, is quite ambiguous and fraught with complexities. As unorientability would have it, Limonov's particular brand of brown-red politics turned out to be not so distant from Putin's. Since 2014, with the Ukraine revolution, Limonov changed sides and now supports his old political enemy: "he is an authoritarian leader," he says of Putin, "but not an evil one. It is that we could be much worse,"[21] he declared to a media outlet often criticized for being pro-Kremlin.

A few decades earlier, while the Soviet Union had begun to crumble under the economic reforms of the Perestroika, a young man of half-Russian and half-Chechen descent finished his military service in Hungary and settled in Moscow. Little is known about Vladislav Surkov, other than he was born in September 1964 in the Lipetsk region as Aslambek Dudayev. His father, a Chechen teacher, abandoned the family so his mother changed his name to Vladislav and his surname to her own. According to journalist Soya Svetova, Surkov "was considered good-looking, he was constantly pursued by female admirers. He enjoyed music, listened to Pink Floyd and Deep Purple, tried to look good and fashionable, wore velvet jeans, and wrote a lot of poems and stories. Literature teacher Vera Petrovna Rozh recalls that he was reserved in his manner and looked more grown-up than the others."[22] From early on Surkov had a rather black sense of humor: regarding the great poet Vladimir Mayakovsky he wrote that after the communist revolution he claimed that life was good and it was good to be alive, "however, this did not stop [...] from shooting himself several years later." Surkov graduated from high school with A-grades in almost all subjects.

Upon his arrival to the capital, Surkov entered the Institute of Steel and Alloys but not being technically minded he dropped out claiming difficult family circumstances. Upon being discharged he went to the army to fulfill his military service, from 1983 to 1985. When he returned to Moscow in '86, he entered a theater direction program at the Institute of Culture from which he was expelled after a year because of a fight with a fellow student who was opposed to compulsory military service. Apparently, the police had to intervene. The case was so unusual that the faculty decided to expel him. In the next couple of years Surkov lingered around the late soviet counterculture until a friend of his introduced him to an unarmed combat trainer who worked for oligarch Mikhail Khodorkovsky and began working as his bodyguard. Soon the millionaire realized that he was wasting Surkov's talent on his security detail and promoted him to the PR department, which by then was beginning to be practiced in Russia. Surkov was in charge of Bank Menatep's first advertising campaign, which featured Khodorkovsky "in checked jacket, moustache, and a massive grin... holding out bundles of cash: 'Join my bank if you want some easy money,' was the message. 'I've made it; so can you!'" Surkov had finally found his trade.

Once given the chance, he quickly made it to the top of the food chain. In less than a decade he managed to ascend to the bank's board of directors, but seeing that his colleagues would not agree to make him a partner, he decided to go it alone. After a bitter falling out with Khodorkovsky he landed a job heading the PR department at Alfa Bank, owned by oligarch Mikhail Fridman, and later on at Channel One, the first TV station to broadcast to the entire Russian Federation. From there Surkov made the leap to the political arena by first advising Boris Yeltsin and then Vladimir Putin who, as prime minister, inherited the presidency when Yeltsin resigned in late 1999. Still, Putin had to win the May 2000 election to stay in office. Surkov was his campaign manager in what has been called the "dirtiest election campaign in Russian history." By the end of the same year, Putin made a rather strange decision (although not surprising at all if seen with almost twenty years of hindsight): dusting off the old Soviet anthem—albeit with new lyrics—arguing that since some of his government's economic reforms were going to hurt the population, pensioners in particular, it was better to give them something to rejoice in; a token of times gone by. One of his most famous quotes goes: "whoever does not miss the Soviet Union has no heart. Whoever wants it back has no brain." True to this dictum Putin built, with Surkov's help, a style of autocracy hitherto unknown.

It is with good reason that Vladislav Surkov has been called the "Kremlin demiurge." An accomplished aesthete and man of letters—he has published several short stories and two novels under a pseudonym—he keeps in his Kremlin office portraits of Tupac Shakur, Che Guevara, John Lennon, Joseph Brodsky, Barack Obama and Jorge Luis Borges next to that of his president. It is quite interesting to learn that one of Vladimir Putin's closest advisers is a modern art and pop culture connoisseur, known for citing postmodernist texts by Lyotard and Baudrillard, reciting Allen Ginsberg's "Sunflower Sutra" (in English and by heart) and writing lyrics for *Agatha Christie*, one of the most popular Russian punk bands of the second half of the nineties. One of his novels, translated into English as *Almost Zero*, deals with the adventures of Yegor, a PR man and gangster who works selling the poems of marginal writers to politicians and businessmen who want to pose as artists. In the novel's world everything and everyone has a price, the literary mafia to which the protagonist belongs to, the blackbookers, engages in homicidal fights with rival gangs for the rights of writers like Nabokov or Pushkin. According to Peter Pomerantsev, an English journalist of Russian origin who has worked with various media of the Putin era, Surkov's novel is "the key confession of the era, the closest we might ever come to seeing inside the mind of the system."[23]

Surkov talks of his role in Putin's administration in these terms: "I am the author, or one of the authors, of the new Russian system. My portfolio in the Kremlin and in government has included ideology, media, political parties, religion, modernization, innovation, foreign relations and... modern art."[24] But if his resume is impressive, the guiding idea of his political project is even more so: "if the West once undermined and helped to ultimately defeat the USSR by uniting free-market economics, cool culture, and democratic politics into one package... Surkov's genius has been to tear those associations apart, to marry authoritarianism and modern art, to use the language of rights and representation to validate tyranny, to recut and paste democratic capitalism until it means the reverse of its original purpose."[25] Vladislav Surkov is considered almost unanimously as one of the founders "of the modern pro-Kremlin state propaganda machine, which involves the Kremlin's direct control of most online and offline media outlets and the state-sanctioned trolling."[26]

In the same vein of thought initiated by Hobbes and developed by Freud and Bernays, the cornerstone of Surkov's thought is that

> there is no real freedom in the world, and that all democracies are managed democracies, so the key to success is to influence people, to give them the illusion that they are free, whereas in fact they are managed. In his view, the only freedom is "artistic freedom"[27]

When he proclaims himself as the author of the new Russia, Surkov is far from boasting. After Putin's first term, when the pro-Russian candidate to the Ukraine presidency lost the 2005 elections on account of a robust popular opposition movement, it was him who devised a new concept that ended up being essential to the Kremlin's idea of government: *sovereign democracy*. According to this political ideology, beyond having to "manage" democracy, Russia must be able to protect its sovereignty against the external enemies who are constantly planning to undermine it. In order to facilitate this situation, Surkov readjusted the country's electoral system through "a sharp reduction in the number of parties and a tightening of the registration rules, essentially allowing only puppet parties approved by the presidential administration to participate in the election."[28] This move, together with the abolition of governor elections for each region, which now were "handpicked by the president and rubber-stamped by the regional parliaments,"[29] produced a form of government completely malleable to Putin's interests, *a soft form of authoritarianism.*

Now, if in Surkov's system of thought the only possible form of freedom is artistic freedom, this idea implies the freedom to practice politics as a purely aesthetic exercise.[30] The fear that an opposition movement such as the Ukrainian could arise in Russian territory, offered Surkov the perfect opportunity to apply his aesthetic vocation to politics. His response to this threat was to create a youth political party known as *Nashi*, "ours," which has acted as an urban counterrevolutionary front. To this end Surkov studied the forces that contributed to the revolution in Kiev—such as the youth political party *Pora!* ("it's time") and the participation of Ukrainian musicians in the revolution—which he proceeded to co-opt and invert to suit his own purposes. Surkov, says journalist Mikhail Zygar, "acted as if he were preparing a revolution. He selected the most active and enterprising young people and the loaded them with ideology—the idea of uprising and rebellion against external enemies, which in this case were the United States and the global conspiracy against Russia."[31] In the same vein as Limonov, Surkov took an assortment of fascist, nationalist and pop culture influences to give shape to the ideological core of the party. Unlike the National Bolsheviks Surkov was successful, in the mainstream sense of the word, at articulating everything around a Putin cult of personality. Nashi and the Nazbols have had multiple clashes over the years and, unsurprisingly, Limonov and Surkov detest each other. Although it would be more accurate to compare *Nashi* to an updated version of the Komsomol—the youth league of the Soviet Communist Party—some foreign commentators have equated it to the *Hitlerjugend*, a Putin youth of sorts trained in urban combat tactics and quick to intimidate or bash political opponents and journalists or burn books by unpatriotic authors in the Red Square. Ironically enough, Surkov's novel is exactly the kind of book that *Nashi* would burn in a public square.

It is essential to notice that the surkovian exercise of aestheticization of politics requires a psychological flexibility that few individuals possess and which seems to occur frequently in the more recent Russian generations which, used to living in a world that is constantly changing, are able to adjust themselves to the most drastic of shifts, regardless of whether in politics, music or art. Peter Pomerantsev condenses the *ethos* (and *pathos*) of this generation briefly:

> over the last twenty years we've lived through a communism we never believed in, democracy and defaults and mafia state and oligarchy, and we've realized they are illusions, that everything is PR.[32]

Forced by extremely demanding political, economic and social conditions, the new Russian generations have attained a deeply ingrained cultural cynicism that still eludes the majority of us Westerners: the realization that we live submerged in a world of advertising spells and propaganda. But knowing this amounts to little and neither the Russians nor we have been able to do anything to change this state of affairs.

The most recent and accomplished artistic expression of this type of psychological hyperelasticity is the film *Hardcore Henry* by Illya Naishuller, in which a quadriplegic scientist, played by Sharlto Copley, creates a series of modified copies of his body with different personalities (a bum, a geek, a cocaine addicted party animal, a pot-smoking hippie biker, a camouflaged sniper, a punk, a dandy gentleman and a WWI British soldier) he can control from his wheelchair. Like any of these avatars, Surkov is able to switch disguises according to the political needs of the moment. "Unlike the old USSR or present-day North Korea," says Pomerantsev, in Surkov's Russia,

> the stage is constantly changing: the country is a dictatorship in the morning, a democracy at lunch, an oligarchy by suppertime, while, backstage, oil companies are expropriated, journalists killed, billions siphoned away.[33]

Let's recall here that in Giordano Bruno's system the psychological compartmentalization is one of the requirements for magical manipulation. The post-Soviet version of this psychological phenomenon is a multimodal variety of the binary compartmentalization of the Brunian venator that allows it to be "intoxicated with love and totally indifferent to all passion, continent as well as debauche."[34] In *Hardcore Henry* this psychological tension is particularly evident in the character of the hippie biker, whose psyche operates simultaneously on two contradictory levels of reality: the ego, embodied in his gun, and the higher-self, represented by a joint of weed. This disintegration and hyper-facetization of personality is nothing other than a reflection of the disintegration and hyper-facetization of post-soviet reality.[35]

Regarding politics as a form of aesthetics, Surkov made use of concepts devised by philosophers such as Jean Baudrillard, Jean-François Lyotard and Gilles Deleuze, who began to be translated into Russian by the end of the nineties. The social and economic environment of the country after the fall of the Soviet Union—an unsurprising and at the same time completely unforeseen event[36]—was fertile ground for postmodern concepts such as Lyotard's *collapse of metanarratives*, which refers to the disintegration of all sorts of totalizing narrative schemes that organize and bring coherence to human experience. Unlike the West, in which the collapse took place in slow motion during the postwar period, in the Soviet bloc it was sudden and extremely turbulent and painful. In the new Russia, the disintegration of the great socioeconomic narrative of communism was accompanied by an almost immediate regression to the totalitarian tradition whose most recent incarnation had been the Soviet state. After all, Russia has never lived by the rules of democracy: before the communists there were the Romanovs and before them a long list of tsars, emperors and kings that reaches down to the ninth century. In post-soviet Russia the word democracy is just that, a word, and its associated concepts are what Lyotard calls *language games*.

Lyotard's motivation for using the concept of game in his theory of postmodernity is mainly political, since it reveals the close link between knowledge, play and power. Like Debord, Lyotard was fully aware of the ludic quality of political power. Now, it is important to note that the rules of the games described by Lyotard, "do not carry within themselves their own legitimation, but are subject to a 'contract' between 'players',"[37] that is, they are based on the relations generated by the game itself. An example: a language game such as the idea of "democratization" has certain rules that must be fulfilled to be legitimized; hence, the transition from the former Soviet Union to a democratic state, according to Pomerantsev, was carried out through the compliance with "objectively verifiable indicators of democratization;" requirements (rules) that were crossed out when fulfilled, even if this fulfilment, and its subsequent legitimization, were true within the bounds of the game but entirely cosmetic in reality:

> Elections? Check
> Freedom of expression? Check
> Private Property? Check[38]

But it was not just postmodern thought that informed Surkov's hunting method. In addition to these ideas we also find a great affinity with Russian formalism and avant-garde theater, to the point that Eduard Limonov argues that, in his role as Kremlin's main political strategist, Surkov "turned Russia into a wonderful postmodernist theater, where he experiments with old and new political models."[39] It is very likely that Surkov studied formalism during his time in the theater direction program at the Moscow Institute of Culture. I should note his application of the concept of "defamiliarization" (*ostranenie*), which according to Viktor Shklovsky—the great theorist of Russian formalism—is at the core of every art form. *Ostranenie* is a technique that consists in making "objects 'unfamiliar'… to increase the difficulty and length of perception because the process of perception is an aesthetic end in itself and must be prolonged,"[40] so that our our idea of the familiar is irrevocably altered. A masterpiece of defamiliarization in cinema is Tarkovsky's *Stalker*, in which the Zone, despite looking like an ordinary industrial landscape, is actually "a minefield of perceptual illusions, booby traps, and shifting geography, making each step a potentially life-threatening danger."[41] An indeterminate and unpredictable world in which truth has lost all meaning and we can only live according to the relationships raised at a given moment.

It is worth mentioning that this technique was taken up by Bertolt Brecht, who learned it from Sergei Tretyakov, playwright and personal friend of Shklovsky. Brecht renamed the formalist technique *Verfremdungseffekt* (distancing effect) and made it one of the hallmarks of his epic theater movement, in which the public was not encouraged to simply suspend their disbelief but were forced to think consciously about the content of the work, thus producing an estrangement that allowed them to witness and question the play from a point of view completely unrelated to the action. It is precisely to this theatrical technique that Surkov's political strategy adheres to. When Limonov asserts that he transformed Russia into a postmodern theater he is being completely literal, the social space of the new Russia is a place where constant defamiliarization reigns, a Go board in which the relationships between the pieces change from one moment to the next so that it is impossible to know what is true and what isn't.

The method Surkov uses to achieve this distancing effect is a fluid and incessant cooptation which, in the words of Pomerantsev, consists of owning "all forms of political discourse, to not let any independent movements develop outside [the Kremlin's] walls."[42] But the real trick is this: everyone knows that all social and political movements are being financed by the government—and so they get distanced from their own political lives, confined to seeing themselves from the outside. In such a situation it is impossible to know which movements are "genuine" and which aren't. Are they all genuine or are they all false? If it's impossible to tell, does it even matter? "The brilliance of this new type of authoritarianism," says Pomerantsev,

> is that instead of simply oppressing opposition, as has been the case with the twentieth-century strains, it climbs inside all ideologies and movements, exploiting and rendering them absurd. One moment Surkov would fund civic forums and human rights NGOs, the next he would quietly support nationalist movements that accuse the NGOs of being tools of the West. With a flourish he sponsored lavish arts festivals for the most provocative modern artists in Moscow, then supported Orthodox fundamentalists, dressed all in black and carrying crosses, who in turn attacked the modern art exhibitions.[43]

The effect of this form of manipulation is completely unusual. It is a *negative spell* that instead of directly stimulating the desire of its prey, it exploits the fact that they know they are being manipulated; a spell that instead of deriving its force from an esoteric formulation, has been rendered exoteric, and even more, almost public. It is the art of *self-delegitimization as camouflage*. The extraordinary thing is that, regardless of whether the manipulation is carried out openly, the illusion (or disillusion) produced by the demiurgic bubble remains intact; it continues working *qua* magic. The parallel between Pessoa's devil and Vladislav Surkov is evident: since both function from a liminal and defamiliarized form of space—an altered space that acts as an enormous *phantasmata* theater—they operate as demiurges of the imagination capable of creating whole sectors of reality.

This technique goes one step further than the "art of contradiction" that Hitler and Goebbels perfected with the German masses, which was aimed at nullifying the possibility of choosing a real position toward the world's problems. Surkovian manipulation aims at *generating the impossibility of establishing a truth*, whatever this concept may mean in this context. It is at this point that Musil's epigraph with which I opened this book, "whoever seizes the greatest unreality will shape the greatest reality," acquires its full relevance. Surkov's negative spell is the most efficient way to grab hold of unreality and transmute it into reality, since it approaches it not from the positive, from "real reality," but directly from a constant negation that seeps into the territory of the unknown unknowns, as a lie that no matter how many times is told will never manage to rise to consciousness and become truth. The negative spell turns the world into a very particular type of fetish, its operation implies not a *post-truth* but having to live in the face of *the presence of an absence of truth*.

One of the most outstanding instances of this matter is the hybrid war with which Russia has faced the threat of Ukrainian dissension. Since the collapse of the Soviet Union Russia has maintained a strained relationship with neighboring Ukraine, which in 1991 declared itself as an independent country. In short, the problem lies in the fact that Surkov's and Putin's sovereign democracy is a continuation of the so-called Brezhnev doctrine of "limited sovereignty," according to which "the sovereignty of Ukraine [...] can not be significantly wider than that of the members of Warsaw Pact prior to the collapse of 'the socialist camp'."[44] This means that even now, Ukraine's sovereignty, or that of any other country within the post-Soviet space, is not as important as Russia's interest in establishing itself as the alpha geopolitical force in Eurasia. The fact that Ukraine has shown interest since 1994 in joining NATO is considered by Russia as a threat to its national security and its plans for geopolitical hegemony.

Since then the situation has only worsened, to the point that in 2014, after a new revolution ousted Ukrainian (pro-Kremlin) President Viktor Yanukovych, Russia decided to take the Crimean peninsula from Ukraine, annex it to the Russian Federation and send troops to occupy a swath of territory to the south of the country with the aim of cutting off its access to the Black Sea and, in passing, gain control of most Ukrainian industries. This wide strip of territory was called Novorossiya or "New

Russia," a name with somewhat alarming historical implications. Novorossiya is an archaism that dates back to the eighteenth century and was used to designate the Ottoman territory that Catherine the Great conquered during the Russo-Turkish War (1787-1792). Putin's use of this term can be interpreted as an admission to the Kremlin's imperialist aspirations. For a moment, the name seemed to resonate with thousands of pro-russian protesters in the Ukrainian cities of Donetsk, Luhansk and Kharkov, who shouted the tsarist term in the streets while waving Russian flags. Soon, as if by magic, reports appeared in the Russian media about the geography of the new Novorossiya, and pro-kremlin authorities began to write textbooks on the history of the territory that should be ready before the start of the next school year. This immense Black PR operation, closely supervised by Surkov, included the creation of a flag for the New Russia as well as a news agency in Russian and English.

Beyond creating a revolution—or, rather, the appearance of a revolution, as in the case of Bernays and the CIA in Guatemala—or manipulating the electoral system through puppet political parties, Surkov raised the stakes by creating, out of nowhere, a new country. This move, some commentators have noticed, bears a curious resemblance to Jorge Luis Borges' story *Tlön, Uqbar, Orbis Tertius*, in which a benevolent secret society, to which alchemist and theologian Johannes Valentinus Andreae and immaterialist philosopher George Berkeley supposedly belonged, invents a country through an elaborate encyclopaedia which, after centuries of laborious efforts by its creators, ends up becoming a complete reality that enshrouds ours. The product of deep gnostic and esoteric erudition, this short story is perhaps the most elegant and accomplished account of demiurgy in modern literature; no wonder it was one of Ioan Culianu's favorite literary pieces. In Borges' story, the mystery of Tlön and Uqbar is solved through a letter found between the pages of a book by British writer and mathematician Charles Howard Hinton, known for the mathematical description of the concept of fourth dimension. According to the letter, Uqbar and Tlön are in fact the work of the imagination of a secret society called *Orbis Tertius* and its extensive encyclopaedia. Despite their imaginary character, the inhabitants of Uqbar speculated that Tlön—which, in fact, was a fantastic region invented by them—could be "the scripture produced by a subordinate god in order to communicate with a demon."[45] Borges' short-story is, in essence, a matrioska of demiurges and their respective creations.

It is important to note that the work of Charles Howard Hinton exercised a deep and lasting influence on Borges' literature. Ioan Culianu says that one of the books of the British mathematician entitled *A New Era of Thought* (1888), was sold "with a set of eighty-one colored cubes that would enable one to think four-dimensionally. Borges (who was born in 1899) played with them as a child in his uncle's house."[46] That Borges chose a book by Hinton as the vehicle to reveal the fictional nature of Uqbar and Tlön is of great importance for our study, since it suggests that the Argentinian author probably considered that the fourth dimension described by Hinton was related to another reality (or another level of reality) that can not be accessed directly. Thus, Uqbar would be a kind of fourth dimension for the inhabitants of earth, in the same way that Tlön would be a fourth dimension for the inhabitants of Uqbar. According to this borgesian logic, Novorossiya—the work of the Kremlin demiurge—would be a fourth dimension of sorts from the point of view of our reality; an idea that, as curious as it may seem, will make sense in a moment.

Unlike Tlön, the demiurgic bubble that Surkov wove around southeastern Ukraine lasted only a few months and, in its place, appeared two very real pseudo-states by the name of the People's Republic of Donetsk and the People's Republic of Luhansk that up to now lack diplomatic recognition and are considered terrorist organizations. It is speculated that at least one of these pseudo-republics was involved in the downing of Malaysia Airlines flight 17 on July 17, 2014. Untangling the reasons for the failure of the Novorossiya project is a complex matter. One of them has to do with the fact that Surkov's Internet propaganda dissemination technique was inadequate since most digital media in Ukraine supported the opposition's mass protests. Meanwhile, another Russian politician named Vyacheslav Volodin—who succeeded Surkov as the deputy head of the presidential administration—began to implement a strategy to manipulate public opinion through social media. Its success was such that it led to the founding of the Internet Research Agency (IRA), the troll farm involved in the scandal of the US 2016 presidential elections.

In March 2014, a few days before the Russian annexation of Crimea, Surkov published a story in the *Russky Pioneer* magazine, titled "Without Sky" under the pseudonym Natan Dubovitski (the same he used for his novel Almost Zero), which sparked a debate among several political analysts for it seemed to contain some "key insights to the political and ideological strategy of the Kremlin."[47] In his story, Surkov presents World War V, which he describes as the first "non-linear war." In this war, where there are no infantry or armadas, only air forces, four coalitions face off in the clear skies over the main character's town, a six-year-old boy. "In the primitive wars of the nineteenth, twentieth, and other middle centuries," says Surkov, "the fight was usually between two sides: two nations or two temporary alliances. But now, four coalitions collided, and it wasn't two against two, or three against one. It was all against all."[48] This was a non-linear war in the sense that the objectives of the coalitions that entered the confrontation were not as simple as achieving victory and avoiding defeat:

> The simple-hearted commanders of the past strove for victory. Now they did not act so stupidly. That is, some, of course, still clung to the old habits and tried to exhume from the archives old slogans of the type: victory will be ours. It worked in some places, but basically, war was now understood as a process, more exactly, part of a process, its acute phase, but maybe not the most important.
>
> Some peoples joined the war specifically to be defeated. They were inspired by the flowering of Germany and France after being routed in the second World War. It turned out that to achieve such a defeat was no simpler than achieving victory. Determination, sacrifice, and the extraordinary exertion of all forces were required, and, in addition, flexibility, cold-bloodedness, and the ability to profitably administer one's own cowardice and dullness.

The different coalitions had different types of technology for their airplanes and drones. Those of the North Coalition were completely silent and made of ultralight materials, so that they made no noise in the air and very little damage when they fell to the ground. Others, like those of the Southeastern League, were relatively silent but heavy. Surkov does not go into detail about which countries belong to which coalition, but these differences in technology lend themselves to assuming that the Northern Coalition could refer to NATO and that of the Southeast to China. These possible associations aroused the interest of analysts such as Peter Pomerantsev and Mira Milosevich-Juaristi, who argue that Surkov could be disguising the Russian ideological agenda under an "artistic package." In a country like Russia, where literature is an essential part of the culture, this is a long way from a far-fetched assertion. Indeed, the nature of the coalitions portrayed in "Without Sky" reflects some of the characteristics of the Novorossiya project. Just as the cities of Donetsk and Lugansk, which officially belong to Ukraine, decided to align themselves with the fictitious Novorossiya,

> It was a rare state that entered the coalition intact. What happened was some provinces took one side, some took the other, and some individual city, or generation, or sex, or professional society of the same state - took a third side. And then they could switch places, cross into any camp you like, sometimes during battle.
>
> The goals of those in conflict were quite varied. Each had his own, so to speak: the seizing of disputed pieces of territory; the forced establishment of a new religion; higher ratings or rates; the testing of new military rays and airships; the final ban on separating people into male and female, since sexual differentiation undermines the unity of the nation; and so forth.

The volatility that characterizes the objectives of non-linear war resembles the practice of *wei chi*. Let's recall here how according to Deleuze and Guattari a Go piece "has only a milieu of exteriority, or extrinsic relations with nebulas or constellations, according to which it fulfills functions of insertion or situation, such as bordering, encircling, shattering." Like this game, Surkov's non-linear war breaks up the single frame of reference—that is, the linear axis composed of the victory-defeat poles—and does away with the possibility of a campaign having pre-defined purposes, a matter noticed by former US National Intelligence Director James Clapper who recently said of Putin: "what his long term plan is, I'm not sure he has one. I think he is kind of winging this day to day."[49] This attitude is seen from a Western point of view as impulsive and opportunistic, terms that clearly don't do justice to the subtlety and sophistication of Surkovian manipulation.

This non-linear tendency to improvisation lends itself to constant obfuscation and confusion as the battlefield seems to shift; non-linear war, like *wei chi*, deterritorializes and reterritorializes it along with its short-term objectives. More than a war scenario in the traditional sense of the term, the Russian occupation of Ukraine and its subsequent entry into the conflict in Syria, have taken place in a rarefied environment that looks more like a sequence out of *Stalker* than a military campaign in the traditional sense of the term. Putin's *mise-en-scène* is packed with disinformation and ambiguities, such as deploying thousands of troops in Syria and then declaring before the General Assembly of the United Nations that, "we should finally acknowledge that no one but President Assad's Armed Forces and Kurd militia are truly fighting the Islamic State." [50] Maybe the key to this declaration lies on how literal we take the word "truly" to be, for Russia's participation in the conflict lies not so much in lending troops or weapons to Bashar Al-Assad's regime but in gaining control of the region through dependence on its patronage.

But let us go back to Surkov's short story. The main character of "Without Sky" tells us that once World War V began the inhabitants of a nearby city refused to let the people of his village take refuge with them. Faced with this situation the father decided to dig into the frozen sand and make a small cave for his family, with such bad luck that one of the heavy planes of the Southeast League fell on them during the night. Both parents die and when the boy wakes up he realizes that the third dimension, height, has evaporated from his consciousness:

> When they dug me out in the morning, chilled to the bone because my parents had quickly grown cold and become like the sand, I saw a two-dimensional world, endless in length and width, but without height. Without sky. Where is it, I asked? It's right there, they answered. I don't see it, don't see it! I became frightened.
>
> They gave me treatment, but didn't cure me. This kind of contusion, severe, can't be cured. The tail of the attack fighter crushed my consciousness into a pancake. It became flat and simple. What do I see in place of the sky above our village? Nothing. What does it look like? What does it resemble? It looks like nothing, resembles nothing. It's not that this is incommunicable, inexpressible. There's nothing of that. There's just nothing.

The protagonist and fifty other children suffer from this alteration of perception. Books and treatises are written about their condition, they are taken to symposiums and television shows, charities are opened in their name until, finally, they go out of fashion and are left behind. But perhaps the most outstanding feature of these children is not that they could not perceive the third dimension and therefore the sky, but that their thoughts lost their "verticality" and were subordinated to the plane, to the X and Y axes.

> We became two-dimensional. We understood only "yes" and "no," only "black" and "white." There was no ambiguity, no half-tones, no saving graces. We did not know how to lie.
>
> We understood everything literally, and that meant we were absolutely unsuited for life, helpless. We required constant care, but they abandoned us. They wouldn't let us work. They wouldn't pay us a disability pension. Many of us deteriorated, fell and perished. The rest of us organized ourselves to stay afloat, to save ourselves together or perish together.

As usual with Surkov, there is yet another layer to his yarns. To my knowledge, no analyst has noticed that the protagonist's two-dimensional perception is reminiscent of the novel *Flatland: A Romance of Many Dimensions* by Victorian professor, theologian and critic Edwin Abbott, who anticipated by a few years the ideas on the nature of spatial dimensions that Charles Howard Hinton developed mathematically. Abbott's novel tells of the encounter of a square from Flatland with a sphere from Spaceland and the revelations that come from it. As in Surkov's story, the perceptions of the less dimensioned beings of Flatland are severely constrained and disadvantaged in comparison to that of Spaceland folk who, like us, can perceive three-dimensionally. Later on, Hinton took on Abbott's metaphor and developed his own version of Flatland, called Astria, with which he intended to show that if we can "imagine the response of an Astrian citizen to our three-dimensional space, then we can begin to picture our own bafflement before geometries of four or even more dimensions."[51] As I already mentioned, it was through Hinton that Jorge Luis Borges developed a lifelong interest in the theme of the fourth dimension, which figures in many of his stories and which Surkov has apparently inherited.

But let us go back to Flatland. It is rather telling that upon being elevated to the third dimension from where he is able to contemplate Flatland from on high, Abbott's square exclaims:

> "Behold, I am become as a God. For the wise men in our country say that to see all things, or as they express it, OMNIVIDENCE, is the attribute of God alone."[52]

Confronted with the third dimension the square becomes aware of the limitations of his ordinary perception and he is, in a sense, enlightened. The process Surkov portrays in his story is exactly the opposite. After the accident the boys' perception becomes flattened and looses those abilities that seem common to most people in the story: that of telling literal from metaphorical, of discerning the ambiguities and nuances in a situation or discourse. In other words, they have been demoted from Spaceland to Flatland. The boys become like "the simple-hearted commanders" of old, they turn into throwbacks of another age who deal in absolutes and can only address everything head on. They grow up marginalized and after years of frustration and suffering

> decide to prepare a revolt of the simple, two-dimensionals against the complex and sly, against those who do not answer "yes" or "no," who do not say "white" or "black," who know some third word, many, many third words, empty, deceptive, confusing the way, obscuring the truth. In these shadows and spider webs, in these false complexities, hide and multiply all the villainies of the world. They are the House of Satan. That's where they make bombs and money, saying: "Here's money for the good of the honest; here are bombs for the defense of love."

> We will come tomorrow. We will conquer or perish. There is no third way.

And perish they will, as any disadvantaged group confronted with more "dimensioned" enemies. At heart, their situation is determined by the fact that they cannot glimpse a third way, devise a third plan. Confined in a two-dimensional world, they are unable to penetrate into the twilight, where the truth is obscured and "all the evils of the world hide and multiply." They are unable to see the place where the spells are produced and, therefore, to understand them. To them, confronting a demiurgic bubble like Novorossiya would be like facing the third dimension, they would be unable to figure it out. Meeting face to face with the political Möbius strip of contemporary Russia would leave them completely baffled.

Ultimately, the question posed by Surkov's story is this: who is he attempting to portray with these bi-dimensional kids? My interpretation:

us. Novorossiya is for us three-dimensional beings a place stemming, so to speak, from the fourth-dimensional shadows. A non-place that surrounds and enshrouds us but that we can only perceive through signs and objects that are as material as they are uncertain, through fetishes: an ersatz flag flying on top of a public building, a textbook describing a falsified geography. Even if it failed, Surkov's Novorossiya is a feat that shows the immense creative (and destructive) capacity of post-Soviet magic spells.

One might wonder if this demiurgic capacity, both in Russia and the West, is sustainable in the long run or if, taken to the extreme, it would begin to degenerate and wither. Ioan Culianu poses a similar question in *Eros and magic in the Renaissance* when he asks if today the state is "a true magician, or is it a sorcerer's apprentice who sets in motion dark and uncontrollable forces?"[53] His answer is far from simple and does not take into account the development of the integrated spectacle that took place along with the fall of the soviet communism. And yet, it reaches the heart of the matter:

> ... the magician State—unless it involves vulgar conjurers—is vastly preferable to the police State, to the State which, in order to defend its own out-of-date "culture," does not hesitate to repress all liberties and the illusion of liberties, changing itself into a prison where all hope is lost. Too much subtlety and too much flexibility are the main faults of the magician state, which can degenerate and change into a sorcerer-state; a total lack of subtlety and of flexibility are the main defects of the police state, which has abased itself to the status of jailer State. But the essential difference between the two, the one which works altogether in favor of the first, is that magic is a science of metamorphoses with the capacity to change, to adapt to all circumstances, to improve...[54]

Given that since the arrival of the integrated spectacle there is no substantial difference between liberal democracies and totalitarianisms, it is worth asking: has the new system fallen prey to the subtlety of its own spells? That is, have both Russia and the West become sorcerer-states that might end up devoured by their own dogs? Without a doubt. Their ability to "develop new possibilities and new tactics"[55] of manipulation is unquestionable. Moreover, we could say that they are "devil-states," which in their obsession with separation (*diabolos*) and hyper-facetization, have created unitary societies. But their flexibility might be their undoing, for how long could a state stretch its demiurgic capacities—not to say reality itself—until it snaps to its original state and disintegrates taking the state with it. The more a state invests in these magical operations the more it is at risk. Its only a matter of time until the backlash of unreality hits us with its full force.[56]

Until then we must put all our effort in bringing to light the damage inflicted by our hounds, in exposing their demiurgic bubbles, the disinformation and the echo chambers and, of course, we must make every effort to not propagate them. Only then, free from phantasms and illusions, like Actaeon redeemed from his destiny, can we begin to see the world anew and build a reality in which a true form of participation—personal and political—becomes possible.

❉

If, by Hermetic law, that which is above is like that which is below, what is at the beginning should also be at the end, and this book should end with Empedocles.

According to one interpretation we are told that "in the cosmology of Empedocles there is no place for the House of Hades: the true realm of death is this existence on earth."[57] This assertion, undoubtedly platonizing and certainly incorrect, is explained by the dualistic lens with which Plato interpreted the sage of Agrigento, and which he then proceded to project in his myth of the cave. But I ask: is it not like the platonic cavern having to live surrounded by shadows and phantasms, with our backs to the real world? If so, we are walking in a Hades of our own making, dead in life until we manage to break free from our shackles.

This claim may seem extreme and, nevertheless, by acting as demiurges and bringing our phantasms to the real world, we have invited the twilight and have sown it, in the words of Lucretius, on "the shores of light." By bringing our phantasms to the light of day we have ended up becoming them. Like them we do not live here, in the real world, nor there, in the secondary reality we have concocted as bored gods. If not a Hades, at least we could say that we inhabit a purgatory.

In his *Ecclesiastical History of the English People*, Bede the Venerable tells of one Drythelm of Cunningham who went through a near-death experience in which he was shown the realms of the afterlife. He saw hell as a deep and burning pit from which the souls of the condemned leaped like sparks; paradise was a beautiful field where the blessed dwelled peacefully. In limbo, those whose faults were not so terrible to send them straight to the flames of hell jumped from one side to the other of a narrow valley in which one of the slopes was covered with ice and the other with burning embers. This alternating between fire and ice was meant to purify the soul as the prerequisite to entering paradise.

Our situation shares its ambiguity with Cunningham's purgatory but lies far from its purpose, for what sin could we be atoning by alternating between the ice of reality and the embers of its negative? Our fault, if there's any, is having forgotten the richness of real life, the endless possibilities it offers for our growth and our understanding of the world. Remaining in this exile, tied down in our phantom cave, depends entirely on our will.

But talking about the will to regain freedom means nothing, or close to nothing, if we can't transform it into action. The question then is how? A proposal outlined by Colin Wilson in *The Outsider*:

> Freedom posits free-will; that is self-evident. But will can only operate when there is first a motive. No motive, no willing. But motive is a matter of *belief*; you would not want to do anything unless you believed it possible and meaningful. And belief must be belief in the *existence* of something; that is to say, it concerns what is *real*. So ultimately, freedom depends upon the real.[58]

According to Wilson regaining our freedom implies holding fast to what is real, however tenuous it might be. Thus, a more pertinent question would be, what is our motivation to return to reality?

---

[1] I owe this metaphor to Adam Curtis who uses *Stalker* to characterize the New Russia in *HiperNormalisation*.

[2] Regarding the inks between esotericism, occultism and surrealism the reader may refer to *Surrealism and the Occult* by Tessel M. Bauduin.

[3] Fernando Pessoa, *La hora del diablo* (Barcelona: Acantilado, 2003), 32. Author's translation.

[4] Pessoa, *La hora del diablo*, 16.

[5] Pessoa, *La hora del diablo*, 33-34.

[6] Morris Berman, *The Twilight of American Culture* (New York: W.W. Norton and Company, 2000), 137.

[7] Gilles Deleuze and Félix Guattari, *Nomadology: The War Machine* (Seattle: Wormwood Distribution, 2010) 5.
[8] Deleuze and Guattari, *Nomadology*, 5.
[9] Emmanuel Carrère, *Limónov* (Barcelona: Anagrama, 2013), 70. Author's translation
[10] Adam Curtis, "The Years of Stagnation and the Poodles of Power." Accessed, June 18, 2018, at: *http://www.bbc.co.uk/blogs/adamcurtis/2012/01/the_years_of_stagnation_and_th.html*
[11] Accessed, June 18, 2018, at: *https://www.youtube.com/watch?v=DD* CDs KHCE8s
[12] Accessed, June 18, 2018, at: *https://www.youtube.com/watch?v=ExX* Dxp BFFR0
[13] Peter Pomerantsev, *Nothing is True and Everything is Possible* (New York: Public Affairs, 2014), 71.
[14] Curtis, "The Years of Stagnation and the Poodles of Power."
[15] Emmanuel Carrère, *Limonov: The Outrageous Adventures of the Radical Soviet Poet Who Became a Bum in New York, a Sensation in France, and a Political Antihero in Russia* (New York: Farrar, Straus and Giraux), 54.
[16] Mikhail Zygar, *All the Kremlin's men: Inside the Court of Vladimir Putin* (New York: Public Affairs, 2016), 54.
[17] Victor Yassman, "Russia: National Bolsheviks, The Party Of 'Direct Action'." Accessed, June 18, 2018, at: *https://www.rferl.org/a/1058689.html*
[18] Victor Yassman, "Russia: National Bolsheviks, The Party Of 'Direct Action'."
[19] Here it is important to note that the contradiction implicit in National Bolshevism lay within the Nazi (Nationalsozialismus) ideology, all Limonov did was take it to it logical extreme, a tendency he calls "Russian maximalism."
[20] Curtis, "The Years of Stagnation and the Poodles of Power."
[21] Svetlana Kyrzhaly, "Famous Kremlin Critic Changes Course, Says Putin Not a Monster (Limonov)." Accessed, June 18, 2018, at: *https://russia-insider.com/en /politics/ famous-kremlin-critic-changes-course-says-putin-not-monster-limonov/ri10433*
[22] Zoya Svetova, Yegor Mostovshchikov, "Spin Doctor of all Russia. Valdislav Surkov." Accessed, June 18, 2018, at: *https://www.facebook.com/notes / the-school-of-russian-and - asian-studies /* spin-doctor - of - all-russia-vladislav-surkov/10150125425664601/
[23] Pomerantsev, *Nothing is True and Everything is Possible*, 70.
[24] Pomerantsev, *Nothing is True and Everything is Possible*, 65.
[25] Peter Pomerantsev, "The Hidden Author of Putinism: How Vladislav Surkov Invented the New Russia." Accessed, July 22, 2019, at: *https://www.theatlantic.com/international / archive / 2014 / 11/hidden-author-putinism-russia-vladislav-surkov/382489/*

[26] "Despite rumors of resignation, Putin's gray cardinal Surkov keeps job." Accessed, July 22, 2019, at: *http://euromaidanpress.com/2018/06/14/despite-rumors-of-resignation-putins-gray-cardinal-surkov-keeps-job/*

[27] Richard Sakwa, "Surkov: Dark prince of the Kremlin." Accessed, July 22, 2019, at: *https://www.opendemocracy.net/od-russia/richard-sakwa/surkov-dark-prince-of-kremlin*

[28] Zygar, *All the Kremlin's men*, 114.

[29] Zygar, *All the Kremlin's men*, 80.

[30] Ned Resnikoff, "Phantasmagoria." Accessed, July 26, 2018, at: *https://medium.com /@resnikoff/phantasmagoria-3beac7fe516d*

[31] Zygar, *All the Kremlin's Men*, 100.

[32] Pomerantsev, *Nothing is True and Everything is Possible*, 73.

[33] Peter Pomerantsev, "Putin's Rasputin." Accessed, July 22, 2019, at: *https://www.lrb.co.uk/v33/n20/peter-pomerantsev/putins-rasputin*

[34] Culianu, *Eros and Magic in the Renaissance*, 102.

[35] Andrei Illiaronov, Putin's presidential adviser during his first term, comments how on the occasion of the arrest and imprisonment of Mikhail Khodorkovsky, the oligarch who helped Surkov kickstart his career in PR, he asked him: "Slava [Vladislav], what do we do now! What are *you* going to do?" To which Surkov replied with a smile on his face, "Andryusha [Andrei], there are no limits to human flexibility." (Zygar, *All the Kremlin's Men*, 61). And apparently there aren't. While the psychological integrity of many politicians prevented them from continuing their careers, this did not seem to be an impediment for Surkov.

[36] Brandon Harris, "Adam Curtis's Essential Counterhistories." Accessed, July 22, 2019, at: *https://www.newyorker.com/culture/culture-desk/adam-curtiss-essential-counterhistories*

[37] Internet Encyclopedia of Philosophy, entry: Jean- François Lyotard. Accessed, July 22, 2019, at: *https://www.iep.utm.edu/lyotard/*

[38] Pomerantsev, *Nothing is True and Everything is Possible*, 37.

[39] Peter Pomerantsev, "Putin's Rasputin."

[40] Viktor Shklovsky, *El arte como artificio*. Accessed, July 22, 2019, at: *http://www.catedramelon.com.ar / wp-content/uploads / 2013 / 08/El-Arte-como-Artificio.pdf*

[41] Zoë Heyn-Jones, "Temporal Defamiliatization and Mise-en-escène in Tarkovsky's Stalker." Accessed, July 22, 2019, at:
http://offscreen.com/view/temporal_defamiliarization

[42] Pomerantsev, *Nothing is True and Everything is Possible*, 67.

[43] Pomerantsev, *Nothing is True and Everything is Possible*, 67. Although the effort to achieve this disconcerting effect is considerable, Surkov already had quite the fertile ground. By the beginning of the twentieth century, G.K. Chesterton had already noticed this tendency, which he makes plain in *Orthodoxy*:

"the new rebel is a Sceptic, and will not entirely trust anything. He has no loyalty; therefore he can never be really a revolutionist. And the fact that he doubts everything really gets in his way when he wants to denounce anything. For all denunciation implies a moral doctrine of some kind; and the modern revolutionist doubts not only the institution he denounces, but the doctrine by which he denounces it. Thus he writes one book complaining that imperial oppression insults the purity of women, and then he writes another book (about the sex problem) in which he insults it himself. He curses the Sultan because Christian girls lose their virginity, and then curses Mrs. Grundy because they keep it. As a politician, he will cry out that war is a waste of life, and then, as a philosopher, that all life is waste of time. A Russian pessimist will denounce a policeman for killing a peasant, and then prove by the highest philosophical principles that the peasant ought to have killed himself. A man denounces marriage as a lie, and then denounces aristocratic profligates for treating it as a lie. He calls a flag a bauble, and then blames the oppressors of Poland or Ireland because they take away that bauble. The man of this school goes first to a political meeting, where he complains that savages are treated as if they were beasts; then he takes his hat and umbrella and goes on to a scientific meeting, where he proves that they practically are beasts. In short, the modern revolutionist, being an infinite sceptic, is always engaged in undermining his own mines. In his book on politics he attacks men for trampling on morality; in his book on ethics he attacks morality for trampling on men. Therefore the modern man in revolt has become practically useless for all purposes of revolt. By rebelling against everything he has lost his right to rebel against anything." (G.K. Chesterton, *Orthodoxy*, 293-94)

[44] Ilioan Chifu, Oazu Nantoi, Oleksandr Shusko, *The Russian Georgian WarA trilateral cognitive institutional approach of thecrisis decision-making process* (Bucharest: Editura Curtea Veche, 2009), 181. Accessed, July 22, 2019, at: *http://www.cpc-ew.ro/pdfs/the_russian_georgian_war.pdf*

[45] Jorge Luis Borges, *Labyrinths: Selected Stories & Other Writings* (New York: New Directions, 1964), 10. It is worth mentioning that in his novel *Almost Zero* Surkov depicts Sveta, the ex-wife of the main character, as an expert in the civilizations of Tlensky and Ukbarsky recently discovered in Patagonia, a clear nod to Borges' short-story.

[46] Ioan Culianu, *Out of this World* (Boston: Shambhala Press, 1991), 16.

[47] Mira, Milosevich-Juaristi, "La guerra no-lineal rusa." Accessed, July 22, 2019, at: *https://www.files.ethz.ch/isn/188633/Comentario-MilosevichJuaristi-la-guerra-no-lineal-rusa.pdf*

[48] Natan Dubovitski (Valdislav Surkov), "Without Sky." Accessed, June 3, 2018, at: *http:// www.bewilderingstories.com / issue582 / without_sky.html*. Translated to English by Bill Bowler. All subsequent quotes come from the same translation.

⁴⁹ John R. Haines, "A Method to Madness: The Logic of Russia's Syrian Couterinsurgency Strategy." Accessed, December 23 2018, at: *https://www.fpri.org/ article/ 2016 / 01/method -madness-logic-russias-syrian-counterinsurgency-strategy/*

⁵⁰ John R. Haines, "A Method to Madness: The Logic of Russia's Syrian Couterinsurgency Strategy."

⁵¹ Robert Barry, "These Digital Artworks Depict the Impossible-to-Visualize Hypercube." Accessed, July 22, 2019, at: *https://motherboard.vice.com/en_us /article/ xygdbk/manfred-mohr -these-digital-artworks-depict-the-impossible-to-visualize-hypercube*

⁵² Edwin Abbott, *Flatland: A Romance of Many Dimensions* (http://gutenberg.org), 81.

⁵³ Culianu, *Eros and Magic in the Renaissance*, 105.

⁵⁴ Culianu, *Eros and Magic in the Renaissance*, 105.

⁵⁵ Culianu, *Eros and Magic in the Renaissance*, 105.

⁵⁶ As I'm writing this note on May 5, 2020, prior to the publication of the English version of this study, this backlash has already happened in the form of the COVID-19 pandemic. As has become apparent in the last few weeks, China's delayed reaction to the contagion was due partly by the government's intent on carefully selecting the information that was filtered to the international press in an attempt to control its "narrative" (read demiurgic bubble), a disastrous attitude that, according to Ai Wei Wei, provided a "chance for the virus to spread." (cnn.com, "Dissident artist Ai Weiwei says virus has only strengthened China's 'police state'"). As for the United States, by early March Trump—notorious for his tendency to twist facts, lie about the distortions and then, brazenly, deny his previous lies—tried to downplay the gravity of the situation, which by then was already wreaking havoc in Europe, until it was far too late to deploy a feasible containment plan. Political commentator and consultant David Axelrod described the president's attitude succinctly: "The problem is that we have a reality show president who has run headlong into a grim reality for which he was ill-equipped and unprepared. You can't spin a pandemic, Mr. President. And the numbers that matter aren't your TV ratings." (cnn.com. "Donald Trump stunning flip-flops").

⁵⁷ Peter Kingsley, *Filosofía antigua, misterios y magia* (Vilaür: Atalanta, 2008), 69. Author's translation

⁵⁸ Colin Wilson, *The Outsider* (New York: Tarcher/Penguin, 1982), 39.

Epilogue

Hounds of hunt, hounds of hell

We talked of the universe, of its creation and of its future destruction; of the leading ideas of the century—that is to say, of progress and perfectibility—and, in general, of all kinds of human infatuations… She complained in no way of the evil reputation under which she lived, indeed, all over the world, and she assured me that she herself was of all living beings the most interested in the destruction of Superstition, and she avowed to me that she had been afraid, relatively as to her proper power, once only, and that was on the day when she had heard a preacher, more subtle than the rest of the human herd, cry in his pulpit: "My dear brethren, do not ever forget, when you hear the progress of lights praised, that the loveliest trick of the Devil is to persuade you that he does not exist!"

Charles Baudelaire, *The Generous Gambler*

As a tribute to Ioan Culianu, I would like to tie some of the topics Covered in this study with one of his favorite myths: Faust. Near the end of *Eros and magic in the Renaissance* Culianu makes a brief summary of the historical development of the Faust Legend, from its Gnostic origins in the story of Simon Magus—an enigmatic figure known in Rome as *Faustus*, the favored one—through the legend of Cyprian of Antioch, the *Volksbuch* compiled by Andreas Frei, and the interpretations of Marlowe, Calderón de la Barca and Goethe. In most of these versions we find Helen of Troy, an essential figure in the legend of Simon Magus, who married a prostitute that went by that name that, in his mind, embodied the divine wisdom or *ennoia,* the divine intellect that had detached itself from the true god and became imprisoned in our world, condemned to reincarnate for all eternity. Here is one Gnostic version of the theme of divine wisdom and beauty embodied in a female figure.

Throughout the centuries the tone of Faust's legend changed to accommodate the morals of the time. If by the time of Cyprian and Justina (3rd century AD), victims of the Diocletianic persecution, the story celebrates the triumph of Christianity over pagan antiquity, by the seventeenth century, in the midst of the Counter-Reformation, Calderón de la Barca's treatment of the story, entitled *El mágico prodigioso* (The Mighty Magician), presents the devil with the mannerisms and language of a Renaissance magician, putting the legend against its original Gnostic heritage. And even though the devil changes "sides" depending on the historical moment, in the most recent versions the figure of Faust becomes more and more independent until, with Marlowe and Goethe, he becomes the archetype of the modern magician, and through it, of the natural philosopher and the modern "man of science." It is in this archetype where we find the root of the motivations of the lineage of magicians to which men like Giordano Bruno and John Dee belong. The Brunian idea of the magician as a hunter of souls and universal master ended up influencing, albeit surreptitiously, some of the great figures of the Scientific Revolution, such as Francis Bacon, René Descartes and Isaac Newton who, unlike the other two, cultivated his magical inheritance through alchemy.

It is not at all surprising to find out that the life of Ioan Culianu was an expression of this Faustian archetype. His personal and professional life was marked by a tenacious impulse to overcome the possibilities marked for an individual. His political integrity and his meteoric rise from being an academic from a communist country to becoming the protégé of Mircea Eliade and his successor at the University of Chicago— where he died at the age of forty-one—speak eloquently of the strength with which the Faustian imperative governed his life. Like a worthy Faust, always confident in the favors of his devil, Culianu risked his own life to expose the Ceaușescu and Iliescu's regimes in a brave and sometimes reckless manner. His integrity was met with a brutal and cowardly display of power.

When secularized and applied to a social scale, the faustian imperative focuses on the acquisition of power and the satisfaction of desire through progress, an impulse that governs all the activities that characterize the modern human. And while it is true that through the pact with our contemporary demons, humans have acquired enormous powers over our environment and our peers, this type of dominance—derived in most cases of magic reified into technology—is still sadly immature and insufficient. Modern man,

> is only the master of those traits of nature he has discovered in order to pursue his own ends. This is so because man asks only how the elements and their relationships can be explained and

how they function. The questions, what the things are and what their essence is, are neglected, because they do not contribute to men's control.[1]

In this sense the modern human is very similar to the *zauberlehrling*, the sorcerer's apprentice of Goethe's ballad of the same name, who knows how things work but does not know why and therefore "is able to make the broom carry the water into the bath, but he is unable to stop it again."[2] Both Faust and the sorcerer's apprentice desire vigorously but never stop to wonder where their appetites and whims could take them. It is in these Goethian legends that we find a particularly clear portrait of the intersection between the libidinal and the utilitarian that defines the limits of the modern world.

There is yet another layer that binds the legend of Faust with the themes I presented on this study. The image of Actaeon devoured by his own dogs is, on another level, the image of a human tortured by its intellect and ambitions. Thus, with another twist to this myth's spiral we find that the dogs of the young hunter are the demons of our ingenuity that torture us once we have begun to pay them attention. Past a certain a point we can only sell them our souls or, at least, pay them constant tribute. Now, unlike Actaeon, Faust is not a victim of his circumstances, he is not a man who has seen beyond his due and has been punished for this transgression, he is a man willing to be deceived to get what he wants, and who better at deceiving than the demons of our longings and ambitions? The fact that every demon is perfectly charming and irresistible—like certain ideas and flaws we always return to—is what makes the transition from the hunting dogs to the hounds of hell surprisingly natural. We cannot stop paying attention to our obsessions just as we cannot stop trying to make them come true. It is desire, over reason or moderation, what presides over them.

This dark and lacerating charm that brings us closer to our inner demons and impels us to put them at the service of progress is one of the main traits of the devil for the romantic and symbolist poets, a figure that in Baudelaire occasionally manifests itself in a fascinating feminine form:

> The Demon is always moving about at my side;
> He floats about me like an impalpable air;
> I swallow him, I feel him burn my lungs
> And fill them with an eternal, sinful desire.
>
> Sometimes, knowing my deep love for Art, he assumes

> The form of a most seductive woman,
> And, with pretexts specious and hypocritical,
> Accustoms my lips to infamous philtres.
>
> He leads me thus, far from the sight of God,
> Panting and broken with fatigue, into the midst
> Of the plains of Ennui, endless and deserted,
>
> And thrusts before my eyes full of bewilderment,
> Dirty filthy garments and open, gaping wounds,
> And all the bloody instruments of Destruction![3]

In this sonnet we see how the poet's love of art, for delighting in beauty, is his greatest weakness before the devil, how nature becomes a diabolical and evil place if we contemplate it with the eagerness of a hungry heart, allowing our passions to devour us. The beautiful woman in which the devil presents itself shows us the negative face of the goddess of desire, the image of the feminine as the supreme vehicle of seduction, an irresistible figure that uses tedium as an excuse to take us to its endless and deserted plains, where we can appreciate the mechanisms of destruction, which, like hellhounds, devour us mercilessly.

In Baudelaire's time, "the bloody instruments of Destruction" were already taking on their modern form and were spreading like a huge mechanical and impersonal web of desire that would cover the planet in a matter of a century. Magic turned into machine and media enshrouds the world in electrical, telegraphic and digital networks, and with this change human perception is modified and enclosed by technique and aesthetics. The media apparatus is the culmination of the nineteenth-century idea of *l'art pour l'art*, of the extreme aestheticization that circumscribes our possibilities to the realm of desire and war. Walter Benjamin, who anticipated Debord, stands out for his lucidity in a particularly bleak period:

> Humanity, which once, in Homer, was an object of contemplation for the Olympian gods, has now become one for itself. Its self-alienation has reached the point where it can experience its own annihilation as a supreme aesthetic pleasure. *Such is the aestheticizing of politics, as practiced by fascism. Communism replies by politicizing art.*[4]

Beauty, like any other quality, in the absence of a complement or a counterpart can only be perverse, compatible with the most horrific and inhuman totalitarianisms. If once this quality could have been considered the very sensibility of the cosmos, in the modern era the world consumes itself in a huge and fatuous spectacle presided over by the goddess of love and desire. Seen in this light it is remarkable that the demon of the fragment of *The Generous Gambler* with which I opened this epilogue is a she, a demon who fears that her spell, her supreme form of *maya*, is made plain for all to see.

My intention, of course, is not to literally "demonize" media, since doing so would entail demonizing those who make up the establishment as well as those who use it, including myself. If we can say that the media is a "devil" it is because we have made a pact with it, an agreement with which we hope to obtain something in return: no longer the love and desire of a young maiden, as in the Faust legend, but control over the desire of others. My purpose with this metaphor is to outline the nature of our "pact" and to take stock of what we might lose. For this we must become aware of the hazardous situation in which we find ourselves and re-evaluate our dependence and affinity with the media. We must not lose sight of the fact that this media "devil," like Marlowe's or Goethe's devil, is very human and, in many respects, is our best and most committed ally, the source of some of our greatest recent cultural achievements.

As Baudelaire's epigraph suggests, the most clever of the devil's tricks is to persuade us that it doesn't really exist. In the same way, the most astute ruse of modern media is that we do not notice them or the nature of its operations, that we take them for granted and yield to their spells without doubts or strange superstitions or, in its post-Soviet version, that we feed its power by taking them as "über-superstitions," like a devil that exists with every imaginable face. Here I wish I could say that just as it is only through superstition that the devil can be made out—and for this reason he wants to destroy it—it is only through magic that we can understand the network of desire that the media has weaved around us; but I would not be telling the whole truth. Post-communist Russia has shown that achieving a negative spell is perfectly possible, that the overexposure and hyper-facetization of the hounds of hell can achieve the same, if not better results, than their concealment.

Now that we have entrusted ourselves to this brilliant and splendid demon to inform us, assist us and entertain us in our leisure and spectacle, now that we have entrusted it with the enormous power to influence, to charm and enchant, for good and evil, other people and even entire continents, we must bear in mind that the devil will always know more about us than we do about him, he will always make amazing propositions and take them away as soon as we turn our backs to him. Hopefully we will never be seized by the feeling that overwhelms the main character of *The Generous Gambler* at the end of the poem. After leaving the den where he talked with the devil and in disbelief of such happiness, at bedtime he prayed in his slumber: "my God, my Lord, my God! Do let the Devil keep his word with me!"

Lest the fog lifts from our eyes and we wake up in this nightmare!

---

[1] H.C. Binswanger, M. Farber, R. Manstetten, *Economics, Environment and the Faustian Imperative*, que aparece en *The Evolution of Economic Systems: Essays in honor of Ota Sik*, 55.

[2] Ibid.

[3] Baudelaire, *Destruction*, translated by William Aggeler.

[4] Walter Benjamin, *The Work of Art in the Age of its Technological Reproducibility*, featured in *Selected Writings Volume 4, 1938-1940* (Cambridge: The Belknap Press of Harvard University Press, 2003), 269.

Bibliography

Agamben, Giorgio. *Stanzas, Word and Phantasm in Western Culture.* Minneapolis: University of Minnesota Press, 1995.

—, *Means Without End, Notes on Politics.* Minneapolis: University of Minnesota Press, 2001.

Anton, Ted. *Eros, Magic and the Murder of Professor Culianu.* Evanston: Northwestern University Press, 1996.

Assange, Julian. *Cypherpunks, Freedom and the Future of the Internet.* New York: OR Books, 2012.

Barfield, Owen. *History, Guilt and Habit.* Oxford: Barfield Press, 2015.

Bartlett, Jamie. *The people Vs Tech.* London: Ebury Press, 2018.

Baudelaire, Charles. *The Flowers of Evil.* Translated by William Aggeler. 1954.

Baudrillard, Jean. *The Gulf War Did not Take Place.* Indianapolis: Indiana University Press, 1995.

Beniger, James. *The Control Revolution,* Cambridge: Harvard University Press, 1986.

Benjamin, Walter. *Selected Writings Volume 4, 1938-1940.* Cambridge: The Belknap Press of Harvard University Press, 2003

—, *The Arcades Project.* Cambridge: The Belknap Press of Harvard University Press, 1999.

Bloom, Harold. *Genius: A Mosaic of One Hundred Exemplary Creative Minds*, London: Fourth State, 2002.

Berman, Morris. *Coming to Our Senses: Body and Spirit in the Hidden History of the West.* Vermont: Echo Point Books and Media, 1989.

—, *The Reenchantment of the World.* Ithaca: Cornell University Press, 1981.

—, *The Twilight of American Culture.* New York: W.W. Norton & Company, 2000.

Bernays, Edward. *Propaganda.* New York: Ig Publishing, 2005.

Binswanger, Hans Christoph. *Money and Magic: The Modern Economy as an Alchemical Process.* London: Quantum Publishers, 2016.

Borch-Jacobsen, Mikkel. *Sigmund Freud, la hipnosis, textos (1886-1893).* Bogotá: Arial, 2017.

Borges, Jorge Luis. *Labyrinths: Selected Stories & Other Writings.* Translated by James E. Irby. New York: New Directions, 1964.

Bruno, Giordano. *Cause, Principle and Unity*. Cambridge: Cambridge University Press, 2004.

Butterfield, Herbert. *The Origins of Modern Science*. New York: G. Bell & Sons, 1957.

Camillo, Giulio. *La idea del teatro*. Madrid: Siruela, 2006.

Campbell, Joseph. *The Mythic Image*. Princeton: Princeton University Press, 1974.

Carrère, Emmanuel. *Limonov*. Translated by John Lambert. New York: Farrar, Straus and Giroux, 2014.

Cirlot, Victoria. *Figuras del destino. Mitos y símbolos de Europa medieval*. Madrid: Siruela, 2005.

Culianu, Ioan P. *Eros and magic in the Renaissance*. Chicago: The University of Chicago Press, 1987.

—, *The Tree Of Gnosis: Gnostic Mythology from Early Christianity to Modern Nihilism*. New York: Harper Collins, 1992.

—, *Out of this world: other-worldly journeys from Gilgamesh to Albert Einstein*. Boulder: Shambhala, 1991.

Curtis, Adam:

All Watched Over by Machines of Loving Grace. Directed by Adam Curtis. 2011. London, UK: BBC Two, 23 May 2011.

The Century of the Self. Directed by Adam Curtis. 2002. London, UK: BBC Two, 17 March 2002.

HyperNormalisation, Directed by Adam Curtis. 2016. London, UK: BBC iPlayer, 16 October 2016.

Daniélou, Alain. *The Myths and Gods of India: The Classic Work on Hindu Polytheism*. Rochester: Inner Traditions International, 1985.

Debord, Guy. *The Society of the Spectacle*. New York: Zone Books, 1994.

—, *Comments on the Society of the Spectacle*. London: Verso, 1990.

Deleuze, Gilles, and Guattari, Félix,. *Nomadology: The War Machine*. Translated by Brian Massumi. Seattle: Wormwood Distribution, 2010.

de Lautréamont, Comte. *Maldoror*. Translated by Guy Wernham. New York: New Directions, 1965.

de Lorris, Guillaume, and de Meun, Jean. *The Romance of the Rose*. New York: E.P. Dutton & Co, 1962.

de Rougemont, Denis. *Love in the Western World*. Princeton: Princeton University Press, 1956.

Drury, Nevill. *Wisdom Seekers: The Rise of the New Spirituality*. Winchester: O Books, 2011.

Edwards, Paul N. *The Closed World: Computers and the Politics of Discourse in Cold War America*. Cambridge: MIT Press, 1996.

Emerson, Ralph Waldo. *The Complete Works of Ralph Waldo Emerson, Volume* 2. Cambridge: Bell & Daily, 1979.

Empedocles. *The Poem of Empedocles: a Text and Translation With and Introduction by Brad Inwood.* Toronto: University of Toronto Press, 2001.

Ficino, Marsilio. *Commentary on Plato's Symposium.* Columbia: University of Missouri, 1944.

Freud, Sigmund. *The Standard Edition of the Complete Psychological Works of Sigmund Freud.* New York: Vintage, 1999.

Gauld, Alan. *A History of Hypnotism.* Cambridge: Cambridge University Press, 1992.

García Márquez, Gabriel. *One Hundred Years of Solitude.* Translated by Gregory Rabassa. New York: Harper and Row, 1970.

Ghamari-Tabrizi, Sharon. *The Worlds of Herman Kahn: the intuitive science of thermonuclear war.* Cambridge: Harvard University Press, 2005.

Goodall, Jane. *Stage Presence.* New York: Routledge, 2008.

Gray, John. *Seven Types of Atheism.* London: Allen Lane, 2018.

—, *False Dawn, The Delusions of Global Capitalism.* New York: The New Press, 1998.

—, *The Soul of the Marionette: A Short Inquiry into Human Freedom.* London: Penguin, 2015.

Goodrick-Clarke, Nicholas. *The Western Esoteric Traditions: A Historical Introduction.* Oxford: Oxford University Press, 2008.

Harpur, Patrick. *The Philosophers' Secret Fire: A History of the Imagination.* Glen Waverley: Blue Angel Gallery, 2002.

Hillman, James. *The Essential James Hillman: A Blue Fire.* Hove: Routledge, 1989.

—, *A Terrible Love of War.* London: Penguin, 2004.

Huizinga, Johan. *Homo Ludens.* London: Routledge & Kegan Paul, 1949.

Immerman, Richard H. *The CIA in Guatemala: The Foreign Policy of Intervention.* Austin: University of Texas Press, 1982.

Jappe, Anselm. *Guy Debord.* Berkeley: University of California Press, 1993.

Kingsley, Peter. *Ancient Philosophy, Mystery, and Magic.* Oxford: Oxford University Press, 1995.

Klein, Naomi. *No Logo.* New York: Picador, 2000.

Laplanche, Jean, and Pontalis, Jean-Bertrand. *The Language of Psychoanalysis.* New York: Routledge, 1988.

Lanier, Jaron. *Who Owns the Future.* New York: Simon & Schuster, 2013.

Leach, William. *Land of Desire: merchants, power and the rise of a new American culture.* New York: Vintage Books, 1993.

Le Bon, Gustave. *The Crowd: A study of the Popular Mind.* Kitchener: Batoche Books, 2001.

Lee, Edwin. *Animal Magnetism and Magnetic Lucid Somnambulism: With Observations and Illustrative Instances of Analogous Phenomena Occurring Spontaneously.* London: Longmans, Green & Co., 1866.

Lippmann, Walter. *Public Opinion*. New Jersey: Transaction Publishers, 1991.

Mann, W. Edward. *Orgone, Reich and Eros*. New York: Simon and Schuster, 1973.

Manovich, Lev. *The Language of New Media*. Cambridge: The MIT Press, 2002.

Martín-Barbero, Jesús. *De los medios a las mediaciones: comunicación, cultura y hegemonía*. Ciudad de México: Anthropos, 2010.

Marvell, Leon. *The Physics of Transfigured Light: The imaginal realm and the hermetic foundations of science*. Rochester: Inner Traditions, 2016.

Marx, Karl. *Capital: A Critique of Political Economy*. London: Penguin, 1976.

Mazzarella, William. *The Mana of Mass Society*. Chicago: University of Chicago Press, 2017.

Merrifield, Andy. *Guy Debord*. London: Reaktion Books, 2005.

—, *Magical Marxism*. New York: Pluto Press, 2011.

Musil, Robert. *The Man Without Qualities*. New York: Picador, 1995.

Ovid. *Metamorphoses*. Translated by Stanley Lombardo. Indianapolis: Hackett Publishing Company, 2010.

Pessoa, Fernando. *La hora del diablo*. Barcelona: Acantilado, 2003.

Pomerantsev, Peter. *Nothing is True and Everything is Possible*. New York: Public Affairs, 2014.

Reich, Wilhelm. *The Function of the Orgasm*. New York: Farrar, Straus and Giroux, 1973.

Richter, Horst-Eberhard. *All Mighty: a Study of the God Complex in Western Man*. Claremont: Hunter House, 1984.

Sala Rose, Rosa. *Diccionario crítico de mitos y símbolos del nazismo*. Barcelona: Acantilado, 2003.

Schiftter, Frédéric. *Contra Debord*. Tenerife: Melusina, 2005.

Sharaf, Myron. *Fury on Earth: A Biography of Wilhelm Reich*. Boston: Da Capo Press, 1994.

Siruela, Jacobo. *Libros, secretos*. Vilaür: Atalanta, 2015.

Spring, Joel. *Educating the Consumer-citizen: A History of the Marriage of Schools, Advertising and Media*. New Jersey: Lawrence Erlbaum Associates. 2003.

Strayer, Joseph. *The Albigesian Crusades*. Ann Arbor: The University of Michigan Press, 1992.

Tasca, Cecilia, and Rapetti, Mariangela, and Carta, Mauro Giovanni and Fadda, Bianca. "Women and Hysteria in the History of Mental Health," Clinical Practice & Epidemiology in Mental Health Journal, (August 2012): 110-119

Thoreau, Henry David. *On the Duty of Civil Disobedience*. New York: Broadview Press, 2016.

Trotter, Wilfred. *Instincts of the Herd in Peace and War*. London: T. Fisher Unwin Ltd., 1921.

Turner, Fred. *From Counterculture to Cyberculture*. Chicago: The University of Chicago Press, 2006.

Tye, Larry. *The Father of Spin: Edward L. Bernays and the Birth of Public Relations*. New York: Henry Holt and Company, 1998.

Yates, Frances. *The Art of Memory*. London: The Bodley Head, 2014.

Waller, John. "Dancing Plagues and Mass Hysteria," *The British Psychological Society Journal*, Vol. 22 (July 2009): 644-647.

Weizenbaum, Joseph. *Computer Power and Human Reason: From Judgement to Calculation*. W.H. Freeman and Company, 1976.

Zajonc, Arthur. *Catching the Light*. Oxford: Oxford University Press. 1993.

Zweig, Stefan. *Mental Healers: Mesmer, Eddy, Freud*. London: Pushkin Press, 2012.

Zygar, Mikhail. *All the Kremlin's men: Inside the Court of Vladimir Putin*. New York: Public Affairs, 2016.

Index

A

Abbé Faria (José Custodio de Faria), 84, 85.
Abbott, Edwin, 389, 397n52.
Actaeon, Myth of, 11-16, 35, 42, 45, 57, 132-33, 149, 174, 210, 268, 284, 392, 401.
Agamben, Giorgio, 28, 29, 34, 35, 60n11, 60n19 62n49, 120, 136n59, 152, 258, 261-64, 268, 281, 291n95, 297, 318, 328, 330, 373.
Albigesian crusade, 10n10, 36, 232.
Alchemy, 13, 67, 68-69, 95n1, 133n1, 140-42, 157n5, 202n26, 312, 400; Alchemical, 69, 140-42, 202 *n* 26, 276, 312, 366.
Alienation (marxist theory), 172, 207, 228, 254, 261, 265, 269, 273-74, 277, 286, 328.
Alientation (psychology), 269, 274, 277, 286, 303, 298, 402.
Amor hereos, 32, 39-40, 42, 63n60, 87.
Anima machinalis, 146, 151, 272, 308, 313, 344.
Anima mundi, 6, 8, 45, 68, 69, 79, 81, 95, 109, 139, 144-45, 147, 148, 151, 154, 176, 242, 296, 299, 308; as *psyche kosmou* 13, 335. *See* Soul of the world.
Animal magnetism, 67, 71-73, 75, 77-83, 91, 92, 95, 100, 103, 127, 134n12, 155, 164, 220-21, 240, 241; as animal gravity, 70, 71, 144.
Animal spirits, 28, 41, 67.

Animarum venator, 54, 56-57, 104, 170, 231, 317, 325. *See also* Hunter of souls.
Antinomianism, 36, 232-33.
Anton, Ted, 8n1, 336-37.
Apollo, 15.
Árbenz Guzmán, Juan Jacobo, 192, 194-95, 197-98, 206n84.
Aristotle, 17, 25, 32, 46, 60n11, 60n17, 62n49, 82, 123.
Aroux, Eugene, 4.
Assange, Julian, 345-46.
Automatic (*Automatos*), 143.
Avant-garde, 252, 258-59, 263-65, 270, 327-28, 366, 369, 381.
Avicenna, 28-29, 31, 37, 39.
Avril, Jane, 90, 100.

B

Bacon, Francis, 400.
Baker Eddy, Mary, 164.
Banana Massacre, 191, 199.
Barfield, Owen, 25, 41, 59, 60n22.
Barlow, John Perry, 312, 339-40, 341-43, 362.
Bartlett, Jamie, 316, 318n50, 346, 353, 356-57, 362n18,
Barton, Bruce, 177.
Baudelaire, Charles, 137n74, 200n2, 204n54, 250-52, 263-64, 399, 401-03, 404n3.
Baum, L. Frank, 165-68, 170-72, 201n24.
Barberin, Chevalier de, 79, Barberinist school, 80.
Bateson, Gregory, 157n16, 309.

Baudrillard, Jean, 332, 334, 337n29, 355, 376, 380.
Bede the Venerable, 392.
Bellona, 152.
Beniger, James, 147, 158n20, 175, 203n35.
Benjamin, Walter, 151-52, 174, 200n2, 202n30, 204n54, 253, 264, 373, 402.
Bentham, Jeremy, 254, 346.
Berkeley, George, 144, 163, 384.
Bertrand, Alexandre, 84, 103.
Binet, Alfred, 261.
Black Friday, 115, 276.
Blavatsky, Helena Petrovna (Madame Blavatsky), 165.
Bloom, Harold, 266, 289n43, 289n44.
Bellum omnium contra omnes, 59, 129, 182; as war of all against all, 59, 132, 181, 224.
Berman, Morris, 4, 10n11, 34, 58, 96n1, 175, 215, 216, 354.
Bernays, Edward, 49, 59, 131, 161, 177-90, 193-98, 204n54, 205n70, 228, 246n44, 254, 261, 323, 326, 367, 377, 384.
Bernheim, Hyppolyte, 92-95, 118.
Binswanger, Hans Christoph, 58, 140-41, 202n26, 276, 312,
Bion (Wilhelm Reich), 237-39, 242-43.
Boehme, Jakob, 80, 299.
Bonaparte, Napoleon, 112, 135n42.
Bonds, 48-57, 115-16, 156, 174, 176, 182, 184, 185-87, 189, 196, 204n54, 222, 231, 254, 276, 302, 305, 322, 325-28, 353, 355-56, 362n18, 369; as libidinal bonds, 121-22 125, 126, 184; bonding 49-51, 55, 57, 111, 116, 325, 326; as network of bonds, 174, 182, 187, 254, 276, 322, 326, 369; as *vincula*, 49.

Borges, Jorge Luis, 376, 384-85, 389, 396n45.
Braid, James, 85-86, 88-89.
Brand, Steward, 303-05, 309-12, 314, 323, 340; The Whole Earth Catalog, 303, 309, 312, 314.
Breuer, Josef, 94-95, 118-19.
Brecht, Bertold, 328, 381.
Brill, A.A., 189-90,
Brodsky, Joseph, 376.
Browning, Robert, 99, 104.
Bruno, Giordano, 1, 2, 5, 13-17, 19n20, 45, 47-54, 56-58, 68, 81, 93, 95, 111, 115, 120, 126, 131-32, 174, 182-85, 187, 189, 204n55, 222, 231, 236, 254, 269, 277, 287, 299, 320, 325, 326, 327, 332, 347, 379, 400; Brunian, 48-49, 54, 58, 94, 147, 170, 188, 189, 275, 300, 302, 317, 327, 355-56, 369, 379, 400.
Bunyan, John, 167.

C

Calderón de la Barca, Pedro, 399.
Cambridge Analytica, 356-57.
Camillo, Giulio, 47.
Campbell, Joseph, 34.
Capellanus, Andreas, 36.
Character armor, (characterological armor) 207, 213-14, 216-18, 220-21, 234-35, 252.
Cathar heresy, 4, 5, 10n10, 32, 36, 222, 231-32; as Catharism, 35-36, 54, 223, 231-33, 267.
Catholic, 9 n 10, 36; as anti-catholic, 4, 232; Catholic Church, 4, 9n10, 36, 197, 324.
Ceaușescu, Nicolae, 330-31, 400.
Charcot, Jean-Martin, 71, 87-91, 93, 100-01, 104, 118-19, 218, 220, 254n20, 261.
Chateaubriand, René de, 84, 135 n 42.
Chesterton, G.K., 395n43.

Christian Science, 163-65.
Chomsky, Noam, 1, 132.
Choreomania, 90, 100-01, 104, 109, 223, 233; as St. Vitus Dance, 90, 100-01, 105, 218, 276.
Chrysippus of Soli, 26.
Cirlot, Victoria, 13.
Clairvoux, Bernard de, 36.
Communalism, 295-96, 303, 307-08, 312, 314; as communes, 250, 295-96, 307-09, 311.
Comprehensive designer, 300-01.
Consolamentum (Cathar ritual), 44.
Copernicus, 48.
Cosmetic, 12-13, 152-53, 333, 335.
Cosmos, 13, 15-16, 24, 32, 37, 39, 44-47, 74, 144-45, 182, 236, 241-42, 307, 403; as human-cosmos ecosystem, 147.
Counter-representation, 119, 212.
Courtly love, 9n9, 32-33, 35-36, 38, 44, 122, 127, 128, 134n15, 149, 208, 221-23, 233, 262.
Culianu, Ioan P., 1, 3, 5, 6, 8, 14, 17, 19n20, 26, 42, 48, 55-56, 58, 124-26, 265, 290n49, 300, 321, 324, 330-32, 340, 384-85, 391, 399, 400; *Eros and Magic in the Renaissance*, 1, 391, 399.
Curtis, Adam, 296-97, 308, 333.
Cybernetics, 3, 6, 139, 146-49, 154, 156, 157n16, 176, 272, 295-96, 302-04, 306-08, 311, 316-17, 344.

D

Dadaism, 250-51.
Daniélou, Alain, 46, 62n49, 64n64.
Dante Alighieri, 4, 34, 37-41, 50, 62n41, 72, 81,
Death instict (Freud), 128, 136n57, 212-13, 222.
Debord, Guy, 156, 250-259, 261, 265-80, 282-83, 285-87, 290n52, 298, 313, 333, 351-52, 355, 365; as debordian, 297.
Delboeuf, Joseph, 94.
Deleuze, Gilles, and Guattari, Félix, 367-69, 380, 387.
Deleuze, Joseph Philippe François, 103.
Demiurgy, 161, 172, 187, 199, 261, 269, 319, 335, 384; as Demiurgic bubble, 6, 200, 287, 297, 360, 361, 369, 372, 382, 385, 390, 392; as Demiurge Satan, 42, 44.
Determinism, 139, 140, 142, 143.
Détournement, 252, 253, 286, 291n77.
Desire, 12, 14-18, 24, 40-41, 47, 50-52, 55-57, 61, 63, 64n73, 65n97, 66n98, 78, 90, 95, 102, 103-05, 111-12, 115, 121-22, 127-28, 131, 149, 154, 161-65, 171-75, 177, 179-80, 183, 184, 187, 189, 198, 200n2, 210, 212, 220, 222-23, 225-26, 229, 231, 233, 242, 261-63, 266, 268, 271, 276-78, 279, 284, 232-25, 326-27, 329, 349, 352-53, 382, 400-03; Democratization of 162, 271, 352; Economy of, 202 *n* 26; as *Desidia*, 162; *Desidia Americana*, 187-88, 271.
Diana (Goddess), 11-166, 18, 45, 121, 152, 268, 335.
Dichter, Ernest, 211n70.
Diocletianic persecution, 100, 399.
Disraeli, Benjamin, 131-32.
Doomsday clock, 158n42.
Dolce stil novo, 35, 122; *Stilnovisti*, 56, 72.

E

Echo chamber, 133, 349, 350, 354, 392.
Ecology, 3, 6, 139, 145-46, 272, 296, 303-04, 307-08, 352.
Einstein, Albert, 144, 241.

Eggers, Dave, 350.
Ego ideal, 121-27, 233; as *ichideal*, 121, 124.
ELIZA (computer program), 344-45, 348.
Ellul, Jacques, 137n89.
Emerson, Ralph Waldo, 295, 299, 307.
Empedocles, 17, 18, 23-26, 33, 60n11, 104, 134n14, 155, 392.
Encratism, 35, 232.
Enlightenment, 2, 131, 139.
Epilepsy, 74, 86-87, 92, 100. See *also* Epileptiform histeria.
Eros 1, 12, 16, 18, 19n20, 23, 31, 51-52, 91, 99, 121, 126,-28, 134n15, 136n59, 145, 147, 149, 151-52, 154, 223, 234, 236, 241, 308; eroticism, 12, 23, 39, 78, 103; erotic magic, 5, 6, 19n20, 48, 95, 118, 120, 123, 147, 155, 231, 233, 297, 347.
Esoteric marxism, 141, 250, 259.

F

Feedback, 116, 146-48, 175-76, 302; as Feedback control, 148; negative feedback, 149; feedback loop, 146, 154; feedback technique, 308.
Fetishism, 35, 259, 261-63, 270, 313, 373; as commodity fetishism, 259, 261, 264, 270-71, 315;
as free market fetishism, 372.
Ficino, Marsilio, 11, 15, 16-17, 19 *n* 20, 27, 30, 42-44, 48, 63n53, 68, 78, 85, 118, 120, 123-24, 136n69, 145, 174, 269, 299, 346.
Filter bubble, 349-50, 353-55, 358.
French Revolution, 105, 109, 110, 134n15.
Freud, Sigmund, 2, 49, 59, 90-91, 94, 99, 107-32, 177-81, 189, 205n70, 207-14, 216, 220, 222-24, 228, 235-36, 261-63, 377.

Fukuyama, Francis, 140.
Fuller, Buckminster R., 298-301, 303, 306, 307, 309.

G

Galen of Pergamum, 37.
Galvani, Luigi, 82, 97n39; galvanism, 80.
Ganglion system (nervous system), 83, 86.
Gauld, Alan, 72, 84.
García Márquez, Gabriel, 191, 199.
German Romanticism, 33, 63n60, 145.
Ghamari-Tabrizi, Sharon, 319.
Ginsberg, Allen, 305, 376.
Go (game), 368-69, 387. See *wei-chi*.
Goodrick-Clarke, Nicholas, 233.
Gordon, Bernard de, 39.
Goebbels, Joseph, 195, 230, 383.
Goethe, Johann Wolfgang von, 63n60, 140, 145, 202n26, 239, 264, 365-66, 399, 400-01, 403.
Guevara, Che, 376.
Gnosticism, 7, 34, 170-71, 265-67, 290n49; Gnostic, 6, 32, 38, 46, 79, 157n16, 165, 223, 250, 265-267, 269, 290n49, 361, 366, 384, 399, 400.
Grande hypnotisme, 89.
Grande hystérie, 89.
Gravity, 67-69, 96n4, 144.
Gray, John, 2, 66n98, 139, 287.
Great Chain of Being, 46, 70, 299.
Gurdjieff, George Ivanovich, 265, 320-21, 323.

H

Harpur, Patrick, 68.
Hegemonikon, 26-27, 41, 82, 123.
Hehl, Maximilian, 71-72.
Hermeticism, 7.
Hicks, Bill, 281,
Hildegard of Bingen, 30, 32.
Hillman, James, 12, 15.

Hinton, Charles Howard, 384-85, 389.
Hippocrates, 29-32.
Hitler, Adolf, 9n6, 112, 127, 152, 229, 230-34, 247n57, 247n58, 383; as *hitlerjugend*, 378.
Hobbes, Thomas, 59, 66n98, 129, 132, 181-82, 224, 377. See also *bellum omnium contra omnes*
Homer, 16, 25, 143, 402.
Hooke, Robert, 208.
Horney, Karen, 205n67.
Huizinga, Johan, 256-57.
Humboldt, Alexander von, 82, 97n39, 144.
Hunter of souls, 48, 52, 54, 55-56, 109, 112, 116, 184, 187, 210, 231, 233, 254, 261, 296, 317, 351, 354, 400. See also *animarum venator*.
Hypnosis, 67, 84-95, 99-100, 106, 118-19, 125-27 155, 212, 245n20; Deep hypnotic state, 119.
Hysteria, 29-32, 61n28, 71, 84, 87-91, 99-100, 102-03, 105, 108, 112, 118-19, 127-28, 133n1, 218, 220-21, 230, 245n23, 284; as epileptiform hysteria, 71, 89-90, 218, 220, 233; as mitigated collective histeria, 276.

I

Ibsen, Henrik, 212.
Iatromancer, 17, 24, 69, 104, 207.
Inquisition, 1, 4, 5, 10n10, 36, 102, 223, 324, 367.
Irritability, 72, 88, 220.
Isou, Isidore, 251-52.

J

James, William, 163.
Jappe, Anselm, 141, 252-53.
Jefferson, Thomas, 139, 186.
Jones, Ernest, 178.

Jung, Carl Gustav, 34, 61n32, 90, 125.
Jung-Stilling, Johan Heinrich, 80-81.

K

Kāma, 47, 51, 64n73.
Kesey, Ken, 305-08, 310; Merry Pranksters; 306.
Keynes, John Maynard, 95n1.
Khan, Herman, 320, 333.
Khodorkovsky, Mikhail, 372, 375-76, 395n35.
Klein, Naomi, 176, 313.
Kluge, Carl Alexander Ferdinand, 83.
Kuryokhin, Sergey, 370-72.

L

Laertius, Diogenes, 23.
Laissez faire, 156n1.
La Mettrie, Julien Offray de, 88.
Lanier, Jaron, 316, 323, 362n18.
Lasswell, Harold, 132.
Lautréamont, Comte de (Isidore Lucien Ducasse), 250, 252, 266-67.
Leach, William, 161, 163, 166-67, 169-71, 173, 182.
Le Bon, Gustave, 107-16, 121-22, 125-26, 130-31, 177, 181, 183, 200n3, 228, 296, 306,
Le Corbusier (Charles-Édouard Jeanneret), 254, 288n17.
Lennon, John, 376.
Letov, Yegor, 370, 372.
Libido, 34, 99, 118, 120-21, 126, 128, 151, 153, 162, 184, 208, 220-22, 224, 227-28, 234-36, 246n46, 276; theory of, 2, 120, 236; libidinal bonds, 121-22, 125-26, 184; libidinal energy, 127, 152, 187, 306.
Liébeault, Ambroise-Auguste, 91-95, 118.

Lieben, Anna von (Baroness Von Todesco), 118-120.
Lieberman, Philip, 157n13.
Limonov, Eduard (Eduard Savenko), 370-74, 378, 381.
Lippmann, Walter, 181, 183.
Locus Amoenus (pleasant place), 173.
Lorris, Guillaume de, 33, 50.
Lyotard, Jean-François, 376, 380.

M

Machiavelli, Niccolò, 1, 49; Machiavellian, 188, 329.
Macondo, 199-200.
Magnetic fluid, 71-72, 74, 76, 78-80, 82-86, 88, 91, 95, 105, 127, 217, 219, 220, 242.
Magnetic sommnabulism, 81, 86, 87, 100. See Animal magnetism.
Magnus, Albertus, 36, 40.
Maimonides, 31.
Malia, Martin, 371-72.
Malinowski, Bronislaw, 9n6, 224, 238.
Manovich, Lev, 3, 346.
Marinetti, Filippo, 153.
Martín-Barbero, Jesús, 106.
Martinism, 97n29.
Marvell, Leon, 8, 58, 96n4, 197n16, 346.
Marx, Karl, 139, 141-42, 252, 259, 260-61, 263, 266, 270, 272-73, 276, 278, 282, 291n77.
Marxism, 141, 259, 265; Marxist Theory, 172. *See also* Esoteric marxism.
Mass (congregation of people), 1, 2, 6, 49, 52-55, 95, 99, 104-09, 111-18, 120, 122, 125-26, 128, 130-32, 133n1, 137n74, 137n76, 152-54, 170, 175-77, 180-85, 188-89, 208, 225, 229-31, 233, 278, 282-85, 296, 303, 306, 324-25, 339, 347, 349, 351, 354-55, 383, 385; mass behavior, 100; mass control, 5, 48; mass manipulation, 5, 135n42, 222, 246n44, 254, 287, 329, 346; mass media, 65, 110, 148, 156; mass production, 177, 279; mass psychology, 86, 155; mass psychosis, 74; mass relations, 122, 127; weapons of mass destruction, 333-34.
Mass psychogenic illness, 90, 99, 218.
Mauss, Marcel, 8n6, 255, 324.
Maya (Hinduist concept), 16-18, 367, 403. *Maya/Venus*, 51, 57, 127.
Mayakovsky, Vladimir, 375.
Mazzarella, William, 8n6, 65n82.
Media, 1, 3, 6, 7, 44, 56, 58, 132, 148, 152, 154, 182, 250, 282, 287, 329-30, 332, 334-35, 349-52, 354-55, 358-59, 360-61, 371, 374, 377, 384, 402-03; media war, 191, 195-96, 358, 365, 369; new media, 3, 156, 346, 352; mass media, 65n82, 110, 133, 148, 156; social media, 316, 350, 362n18, 385.
Melancholy, 29-30, 32, 35, 40, 168, 288n17, 290n52; *cholos melaina*, 29; melancholic, 29-30, 33, 35, 63n60, 123-24, 262-63, 266, 290n52; melancholic introjection, 123.
Mesmer, Franz Friedrich Anton, 69-75, 78, 80, 84, 88-90, 101, 144, 207-08, 217, 219-20, 236, 239, 241, 245n27; mesmerism, 80, 83, 85.
Merrifield, Andy, 254, 270, 273.
Metamorphoses (Ovid), 11, 347.
Milgram, Stanley, 205n63.
Miller, Mark Crispin, 182, 204n51.
Milosevich-Juaristi, Mira, 386.
Mind-cure, 156, 163-69.
Möbius, Karl August, 145.
Modern Manipulative Impulse, 3, 176, 284, 317, 324, 354.

Monier-Williams, Monier, 17.
Montravel, Tardy de, 77, 81-82.
Moore, Michael, 354.
Musil, Robert, 16, 23, 111, 383.

N

Narcissism, 34, 43-44, 65n97, 118, 120-21, 123, 125, 127-28, 134n15, 136n69, 173, 347, 350; Narcissus, 39, 34, 173, 345, 347-50; Narcissus myth, 34, 173, 347-350; narcissistic view, 33; narcissistic identification, 121-22, 127.
Nazbol (National Bolshevik Party), 373-74, 378.
Nazism, 2, 229, 230-34, 244; Nazi Germany, 5, 127.
Neikos, 18.
Neill, A.S., 238.
Nelli, René, 4.
Neoplatonism, 7, 308; islamic neoplatonism, 32.
Newton, Isaac, 67-70, 95n1, 96n4, 144, 208, 242, 400.
New Thought (religion), 163-65.
Nigredo, 13, 312.

O

Obama, Barack, 376.
Occitane, 4, 36; occitan trobadours, 37-38, 203n33; occitan poetry, 32, 233.
Odum, Eugene and Howard, 146.
Ogilvy, Jay, 323, 326. See VALS.
Oresme, Nicholas, 143, 145, 296.
Orgasm reflex (Wilhelm Reich), 219-20.
Orgastic impotence (Wilhelm Reich), 221, 246n46,
Orgone (Wilhelm Reich), 217, 220, 234, 239-43, 247n76.
Ostranenie, (performing arts) 381.
Ovid, 11, 347-48. See *Metamorphoses*.

P

Parrish, Maxfield, 174.
Plato, 7, 15-17, 25, 31, 43, 52, 60n11, 61n28, 62n43, 121, 155, 185, 392; platonic, 47, 61n28, 299
Pleasure anxiety, 213, 222-23, 230-31, 234, 332.
Pessoa, Fernando, 365-66, 369, 382.
Petrarch, Francesco, 4, 34, 37.
Pico della Mirandola, Giovanni, 17, 44, 68.
Pied Piper of Hamelin, 99, 104-05, 112, 134n14.
Philotes, 18, 127. 348.
Pneuma, 25-28, 30, 33, 40-42, 46-47, 57, 60n17, 67, 72, 76, 81, 83, 90-91, 94, 100, 103-04, 109-10, 112-14, 115-16, 123, 125-27, 147, 184, 207, 217, 221, 240, 276, 305-07, 312, 317, 339, 346-47; pneumatic apparatus, 26, 37, 39, 41-42, 44, 53-54, 57, 60n19, 77, 82-83, 233; pneumatic currents, 26-27, 42, 72, 74, 78, 101, 102; pneumatic circle, 39, 43, 53, 110, 112, 173-74, 190, 222, 257-58, 262, 274-75, 280-81, 313, 334, 345, 347-48, 350, 353, 358; pneumatic economy, 23; pneumatic manipulation, 277, 352; pneumatic network, 174, 176, 260-61, 263, 276, 326; pneumatological system, 29.
Phantasm, 26-30, 33-35, 37, 39, 40-42, 53-54, 56-58, 59n4, 60n9, 61n22, 62n49, 65n82, 76-77, 82, 94, 105, 109-10, 118, 123-25, 136n59, 174, 176, 210, 221-23, 233, 260, 263, 267, 269, 271-73, 275-76, 279, 281-83, 312-15, 324-25, 327, 332, 347-48, 351, 392; *phantasmata*, 27, 37, 39, 40-42, 58, 82, 94, 109, 110, 119-20,

174, 177, 183, 203n33, 221, 261-62, 271, 275-77, 282, 312-13, 317, 320, 352, 366, 382; phantasmagoria, 263, 274, 278, 284, 335; *phantasmic*, 8, 30, 56, 124.
Philautia, 57, 327.
Pomerantsev, Peter, 377, 379-80, 382, 386.
Post-Soviet Russia, 3, 229, 285, 328, 380.
Post-truth, 333, 355, 361, 383.
Prana, 72, 240.
Proton Organon, 25-26, 46, 82, 95, 123.
Public Relations, 3, 49, 131-32, 156, 177, 180-81, 186, 193-94, 196, 198, 296, 313, 323; as PR, 58, 195.
Putin, Vladimir, 358, 360, 374, 376-78, 383-84, 387-88.
Puységur, Marquis de, 74-78, 80, 84, 88-89, 95, 164, 207, 217, 220, 236.

Q

Qi, 72, 240.

R

Rapport, 77, 78, 92, 95, 114, 164, 256, 307.
Reality principle (Freud), 128-29, 224.
Reich, Wilhelm, 2, 73, 144, 150, 156, 207-30, 233-44, 246n46, 254, 269, 274-76, 282, 298, 307, 332, 370; *reichian*, 250, 252, 263.
Renaissance, 1, 5-6, 8, 16, 23, 47, 58, 60n11, 67-68, 72, 74, 79, 81, 109, 184, 217, 221, 264, 305, 313, ; Islamic Renaissance; 38; Renaissance magic, 2, 18, 19n20, 46, 48, 58, 77, 81, 95, 118, 120, 131, 155, 174, 176, 208, 231, 233, 367, ; of the twelfth century, 37, 324.
Rendich, Franco, 17.
Rete (net), 16, 346.
Richter, Horst-Eberhard, 32-33, 37.
Riefenstahl, Leni, 152, 239.
Roman de la Rose, 33, 49, 173, 348.
Rosicrucians, 73, 80.
Rossetti, Gabriele, 4.
Rougemont, Denis de, 4, 9n10, 37, 44, 62n41, 63n59, 134n15, 137n76, 149, 150-53.
Rousseau, Jean-Jacques, 269.
Rumsfeld, Donald, 334.

S

Sala Rose, Rosa, 230, 232, 247n58.
Salpêtrière (hospital), 87, 89-93, 100, 103, 118, 261.
Sambursky, Samuel, 81.
Scientific Revolution, 2, 8, 58, 142, 400.
Schiffter, Frédéric, 258, 269.
Sensus interior, 26, 29, 83, 95.
Shakespeare, 45, 63n59.
Sharaf, Myron, 212, 229, 238-39.
Shaw, George Bernard, 334.
Shklovsky, Viktor, 381.
Sidis, Boris, 105-06, 114,
Silva (Forest, Selva), 13.
Siruela, Jacobo, 265.
Situationist, 250, 265, 269, 273, 286-87, 300, 305.
Snowden, Edward, 345.
Solutio et coagulatio, 140
Soranus of Ephesus, 31.
Soros, George, 141.
Soul of the world, 13, 45-46, 68-69, 79, 144-46, 242; See *anima mundi*.
Soviet Union, 5, 282, 297, 319, 329, 360, 370-71, 375-76, 380, 383.
Spirit, 24-28, 40-41, 44-45, 47, 57, 60n19, 67, 69, 72, 78, 80-81, 93, 97n39, 102, 119, 134n10,

136n56, 144, 164, 224, 228, 230-32, 242, 247n76, 263-64, 267, 270, 276, 305, 312, 342, 346; *spiritus*, 123; *spirare*, 72, 247; universal spirit, 21, 68, 145, 299.
Spiritism, 80, 84, 164.
Stalker, 293, 366-68, 374, 381, 388, 393n1.
Stomach vision (magnetic somnambulism), 76, 83, 84.
Strayer, Joseph, 5.
SRI (Stanford Research Institute), 323, 326, 328. See VALS.
Surrealism, 250-52, 265, 393n2.
Surkov, Vladislav, 375-91, 396n45.
Sympathy (*sympathetic magic*), 122, 127, 308.
Swedenborg, Emanuel, 80, 264, 299.

T

Tansillo, Luigi, 128.
Tansley, Sir Arthur George, 145-46.
Tarkovsky, Andrei, 366, 381.
Tarde, Gabriel, 110.
Teleology, 140, 143, 148; *telos,* 68, 140, 143, 149; *teleological behavior*, 148-49.
Tesla, Nikola, 241.
Theosophy, 163-65.
Thomas Aquinas, 32.
Thoreau, Henry David, 295, 297, 299, 307.
Tiresias, 12, 16, 45, 210.
Transcendentalism, 163, 308.
Transference, 39, 126-27, 147, 184, 213, 221-22.
Tretyakov, Sergei, 381.
Trickster (archetype), 169-72, 182, 201n24, 366, 367.
Trobriand Culture, 9n6, 224-25.
Trota of Salerno, 32.
Trotter, Wilfred, 99, 113-18, 136n53, 181, 183.
Troyes, Chrétien de, 38, 40.
Tufekci, Zeynep, 352.

Trump, Donald, 354-58, 360.
Turner, Fred, 298, 300-02, 306, 310, 321, 339.
Tye, Larry, 19-93.

U

Universal Master, 49, 320, 400.
Unreality, 29, 187, 199-200, 265, 271, 277-79, 293, 313, 328-29, 334-35, 350, 366-67, 369, 383, 392.
USCO (The US Company art collective), 305-06, 309-10, 312.

V

VALS (Values and Lifestyles Program), 323, 325-26.
Vegetative system, 88, 109, 215, 217-18, 220, 226, 235, 242.
Venator. 14, 16, 50, 63n59, 109, 116, 126, 132, 147, 149, 184, 272, 300, 302, 317, 322, 326, 327, 351, 352, 356, 360, 379. See also *animarum venator* and hunter of souls.
Venatus, 14, 16, 50, 53, 63n59, 116, 126, 132, 147, 149.
Venus (Goddess, Aphrodite), 14-16, 18, 50, 63n59, 115, 121, 152, 268, 365, 366; as Venus/Maya, 51, 57, 127.
Verfremdungseffekt, 328, 381.
Villanova, Arnaldo de, 40.
Vital spirit, 28.
Volta, Alessandro, 97n39.
Voltaire, 96n4, 259.
Voluptas (*volo*), 50, 78, 162.

W

Wack, Pierre, 320-21, 323.
Wanamaker, John, 171, 173, 200n3, 260.
Wei-Chi (game), 367, 387. See *Go*.
WELL, the, 340-42.
Weizenbaum, Joseph, 344-45. *See* ELIZA.

Wiener, Norbert, 148, 302, 305-06, 309.
Wilson, Colin, 393.
Wolfe, Tom, 306, 329.

Y

Yates, Frances, 8, 58.
Yeltsin, Boris, 372, 376.

Z

Zajonc, Arthur, 25.
Žižek, Slavoj, 334-35, 343.
Zweig, Stefan, 73-74, 105, 121.
Zygar, Mikhail, 378.

www.ingramcontent.com/pod-product-compliance
Lightning Source LLC
Chambersburg PA
CBHW051828230426
43671CB00008B/876